Logics o

T&T Clark Enquiries in Theological Ethics

Series editors
Brian Brock
Susan F. Parsons

Logics of War

The Use of Force and the Problem of Mediation

Therese Feiler

LONDON • NEW YORK • OXFORD • NEW DELHI • SYDNEY

T&T CLARK
Bloomsbury Publishing Plc
50 Bedford Square, London, WC1B 3DP, UK
1385 Broadway, New York, NY 10018, USA

BLOOMSBURY, T&T CLARK and the T&T Clark logo are
trademarks of Bloomsbury Publishing Plc

First published in Great Britain 2020
Paperback edition first published 2021

Copyright © Therese Feiler, 2020

Cover design: Terry Woodley

A catalogue record for this book is available from the British Library.

Library of Congress Control Number:2019949290

ISBN: HB: 978-0-5676-7828-7
PB: 978-0-5676-9893-3
ePDF: 978-0-5676-7829-4
eBook: 978-0-5676-7830-0

Typeset by Newgen KnowledgeWorks Pvt. Ltd., Chennai, India

To find out more about our authors and books visit
www.bloomsbury.com and sign up for our newsletters.

Meinen Eltern

Contents

Acknowledgements

This book is based on my doctoral thesis, written at Oxford University between 2008 and 2013, for which I was grateful to receive a doctoral award from the Arts and Humanities Research Council.

Politically, much has changed since I began the thesis. The Western occupation of Iraq formally ended, but the rise of the so-called Islamic State, the wars in Syria and Libya and the spread of Islamist terrorism into Western cities have moved the battlefields. Economic crises and the European migration crisis have not only exacerbated previously existing tensions but also created new fault lines. While these developments have shifted the accents in my appreciation of the traditions discussed here, my theological interpretation remains largely unchanged. I have, I suppose, become at once more open-minded and unyielding, and quite in this sense I continue to learn from those I have studied.

No book is the result of the author's toils alone, so I would like to express my heartfelt gratitude to those who have supported me over the years. My first thanks go to Nigel Biggar, my DPhil supervisor at Oxford, for his patience, his open-mindedness and wisdom. Many thanks to Joel Rasmussen, Bernd Wannenwetsch, William Wood as well as my examiners John Perry and Esther D. Reed for their thoughtful, constructive comments at various stages. I thank the participants of the Christian Ethics Postgraduate Research Seminar at Christ Church for many memorable debates and insights. I will always remain greatly indebted to John-Paul McCarthy, without whom the thesis would not have held together.

Since 2015, I have been fortunate to work with Joshua Hordern, whose strategic planning gave me the time to revise this book and who encouraged me to pursue various new strands of research. For that, and much more, I thank him and Andrew Papanikitas. I could not have wished for better colleagues.

My heartfelt thanks also go to this series' editors Brian Brock and Susan F. Parsons for their faith in this project – to Susan in particular also in her role as editor of *Studies in Christian Ethics*, where portions of this book were initially published and where two anonymous reviewers gave much valued criticism. Many thanks to Anna Turton and Sarah Blake at Bloomsbury for seeing the manuscript through to publication. My particular thanks to Frederice Stasik for her assistance with compiling the index.

For their friendship, humour and the various ways in which they have inspired me, I am forever grateful to Mahima Mitra, Christopher V. Jones, Alex Lambeth, Mandy Izadi, Cosima Gillhammer and Stephen Pax Leonard, Anselm Oelze, Michael Mayo and Natalia Klimina-Schultz. My family, especially Sabine, Peter and Ava, and my love Alexander are true anchors and teachers. The greatest source of strength over the last five years, however, have been my parents Dietmar and Ina. Their support, faith and enthusiasm kept me going. This book is dedicated to them with my deepest gratitude and love.

T. F.

Munich, August 2019

Introduction

War is regarded as one of the great evils in human history, yet the pursuit of justice cannot rely upon non-violent means alone. This tension has prompted political philosophers throughout the ages to formulate the moral conditions for, and restrictions on, the use of violent force as well as the sanctions for excessive bloodshed.[1] With roots going back as far as Cicero, Augustine and Aquinas, the Western *bellum iustum* thus developed as a set of criteria to determine when military interventions are justified. That includes questions on the justice of a cause, on the right political authority and their intention. It requires force to be used proportionately to the wrong to be righted. The tradition also includes the discrimination between the innocent and the guilty or, in modern versions, between combatants and civilians. However, if just war thinking is merely taken as a self-contained 'just war theory' or a set of self-explanatory criteria, their application becomes a form of opinion or, worse, prejudice masquerading as deliberation. In fact, the precise meanings of these criteria depend on ramified philosophical and, in the last instance, theological presuppositions. Moreover, there are several disciplines in which these are formed. Besides IR and international law with its early modern and medieval precedents, analytical moral philosophers, theorists in the continental traditions as well as theologians, political theorists and historians shape the moral discourse on war.[2]

The present project seeks to bring voices from these different fields into a critical comparative conversation. For this conversation to be constructive, it will be examined how the logics of war suggested by different ethicists are the result of explicit or implicit theological assumptions. More specifically, it will be shown how they depend on arguments about the nature of God and his relationship to humanity, in particular the mediation between the two. Who or what, in the last instance, mediates between

---

[1]   See M. Tullius Cicero, *De re publica*, 2, 17, 31 and 3, 23, 35; *De officiis*, 1, 36–9 and 3, 46–8; Andrea Keller, *Cicero und der gerechte Krieg: Eine ethisch-staatsphilosophische Untersuchung* (Stuttgart: Kohlhammer Verlag, 2012); Augustine of Hippo, *Letter to Boniface* (No. 189); cf. John Mark Mattox, *Saint Augustine and the Theory of Just War* (London; New York: Continuum, 2006); Thomas Aquinas, ST IIaeIIae, Qu.40. NB: Just war in the following is used as a shorthand for 'the justified use of violent force', which may escalate into war.

[2]   Mark Evans (ed.), *Just War Theory: A Reappraisal* (Edinburgh: Edinburgh University Press, 2005); Daniel R. Brunstetter and Cian O'Driscoll (eds), *Just War Thinkers: From Cicero to the 21st Century*, (London: Routledge, 2017).

the (violent) world and the divine? And how is this mediation taking place? These questions function as both an analytical and a critical hermeneutic for the political concepts at work. It casts light on the nature of political authority, assumptions about the nature of 'reality' as well as moral-political action.[3] War's underlying theo-logic of mediation, it will be suggested, permeates its ethical and, subsequently, its historical logic. It not only fuels the machines of war but also determines the nature of just war thinking as such. In other words, whether just war is a 'theory', a 'doctrine' or a 'proposal' (as I prefer with Oliver O'Donovan) or whether it is any kind of *bellum iustum* at all depends on the *Sitz im Leben*.[4]

The systematic focus on mediation is not a random choice. Mediation is a central thought and movement of thought underlying ethics. Just war thinking begins by taking seriously harm and existential *separation*, a violent duality and opposition between human beings – and so the experience, human beings and God.[5] It seeks to grasp and formulate a response to unjust violence that leads to horrendous, frequently large-scale, long-term suffering and damage. Whether theologically or philosophically, ethicists of war conceptualize and respond to this abyss, this theodicy. They do so in order to identify a mediation, that is, a response, a reconciliation – part of which is, for example, punishment. Without *presuming* it, this tradition seeks peace, however tenuous or eschatological that may be. The question is then how effective and coherent that response to theodicy is: whether a benevolent empire grounded in defence and a 'realistic' sense about the *conditio humana* is not, after all, an idealism par excellence. Or whether the underbelly of legal cosmopolitanism is not, after all, a cataclysmic antagonism. Similarly, nuclear warfare or drone warfare may seek to pacifically oppress violence (which is conceived as bad per se). But they rely on it in its most extensive, deadly, non-reciprocal form. In other words, where seeking mediation, we may after all encounter an oscillation between two negatives. Indeed, it is a characteristically modern oscillation that obfuscates the possibility to discern the right and good even within the 'bad life' (Theodor Adorno).

---

[3] I take this triadic structure from Oliver O'Donovan in *Resurrection and Moral Order* (see Chapter 5), reiterated e.g. in 'The Trinity and the Moral Life', in *A Transforming Vision: Knowing and Loving the Triune God*, ed. George Westhaver (London: SCM Press, 2018), pp. 218–27, p. 219: 'Moral reason needs to be understood … as having a threefold reference: to the agent self; to the world that comprises an order of values; and to the horizon of emerging time before which we deliberate on action. The impasse into which modern moral reason has run, frequently diagnosed by philosophers in the last generation, springs from a tendency to be monothematic, and so unable to reconcile these points of reference, a horizon of constituted obligation, a horizon of future possibility and an imperative of action, each apparently absolute. This leaves modern man with the intolerable alternative of stagnation, on the one hand, and unrooted spasmodic exertion on the other, with no imagination of how we may be *ourselves* when we act, taking new steps in faithful reflection of the good we have seen and loved.'

[4] Cf. Howard Williams, *Kant and the End of War: A Critique of Just War Theory* (London: Palgrave Macmillan, 2012).

[5] Richard Faber, *Political Demonology: On Modern Marcionism* (Eugene, OR: Wipf & Stock, 2018), pp. 105–16, esp. p. 109, citing Hans Blumenberg's *Work on Myth*: 'Metaphysical dualism is not the threat that arises from the reduction of polytheism; rather, it results from the self-splitting of a monotheism that cannot cope with the problem of justifying its God in defense against the accusation of a world that is inadequate to the concept of him.' On theodicy, see also Claudia Welz, *Love's Transcendence and the Problem of Theodicy* (Tübingen: Mohr Siebeck, 2008), esp. pp. 70–82 on Hegel and history as theodicy.

On the following pages, I will further sketch out how the notion of mediation sets the stage for the book's enquiry and how it shapes the structure of each chapter. Before I give a brief overview over the argument developed throughout the book, I will clarify how secularization theory helps understand a decisive shift in human–divine mediation.

Logics of war: Sovereign realisms and cosmopolitan idealisms

The first part of each chapter will turn to practical ethics, introducing each author's concrete 'just war theory' or 'proposal'.[6] At this point of departure, we encounter the first moment of mediation. Beyond responding to unjustified violence and suffering – that is, conceptualizing a preliminary, practical response to it – the ethics of war are already an attempt to steer between two 'extreme' positions. Neither amoral, potentially merely technocratic facticity (of evil, of the political) nor a pacifist acquiescence is seen as an acceptable moral response.[7]

But even leaving out these 'extremes', just war thinkers can still be located between the poles of political realism and idealism. Just war realists initially cast their lot in the sphere of the Is, of politics 'as they are'. What matters primarily is the factual, political situation, though not only that: a 'realistic' approach takes into account the human capacity to do evil. In the tradition of Hobbes and Machiavelli, potentially invoking the liberalisms of Locke or Fichte, realism prioritizes the essential and natural right to individual or national self-defence within and against a violent 'state of nature'. The catchphrases of realists, one might say, are 'politics', 'defence' and 'necessity'. Just war idealism, by contrast, takes a Kantian or quasi-Kantian route of moral reason. It prioritizes the universal, inviolable value of each individual above and beyond their political settings. But it also appeals to the human capacity to be and do good. The moral 'Ought' is decisive for ethics. It is frequently framed as a progressive current that flows in the direction of the full recognition of a universal, if not peaceful, then at least regulated and thus pacified system of global justice. Although appealing to universal human rights, idealism may also draw on the theological theme of God's equal love for each individual, finding precedents in Aquinas and Dante.

These distinctions are not quite clear-cut and remain general, even sterile. In fact, modern realism may well appeal to universal human rights, whereas idealism

---

[6] I will be using the almost tautologous 'violent force' analogously to the German *Gewalt*. It comprises 'force' as justified, legitimate, public, even surgical, but it retains the disturbing, harmful and ultimately unjustified aspect indicated by 'violence'. For a conceptual analysis of 'violence', see also C. A. J. Coady, *Morality and Political Violence* (New York; Cambridge: Cambridge University Press, 2008), pp. 21–43.

[7] Michael Walzer, *Just and Unjust Wars* (New York: Basic, 1977), pp. 3–16; Roland Bainton's classical distinction is between pacifism, crusading and just war. R. John Elford, 'Christianity and War', in *Cambridge Companion to Christian Ethics*, ed. Robin Gill (Cambridge: Cambridge University Press, 2000), pp. 171–82.

may argue that a cosmopolitan vision is altogether realistic.[8] Again, each just war proposal represents an attempt to *mediate* and reconcile these positions to suggest its own 'realistic utopia'. Thinking about the morality of war is never a singular or straightforward 'third way'. The challenge is therefore to figure out how exactly the two directions of thought are related and depend on each other.

In the chapters that follow, five authors from now quite disparate strands of just war ethics will be played off against each other: a sovereign realist (Jean Bethke Elshtain) and a cosmopolitan idealist (David Rodin); a realist individualist (Uwe Steinhoff) and a Christian ethicist moving from pacifist idealism to political realism throughout a career spanning a lifetime (Paul Ramsey). An evangelical ethic is finally introduced, mediating and integrating elements from sovereign-realist and cosmopolitan-idealist thinking (Oliver O'Donovan). To an extent this will then be called into question again in the final chapter, in which I argue for what one might call a transitional, confrontative realism.

The theo-logics of mediation: Political reality, authority and action

The second section of each chapter will locate and make explicit the theological and 'theo-logical' context and assumptions at work in the ethics of war. Theo-logic may be understood as an intrinsic permeance between theology and logic, between the universal biblical (hi)story and the logic and truth of categories, even history itself, unfolding in its wake. Investigating the logic of mediation within the ethics of war means investigating the relationship between the human and the divine, between Is and Ought, between the finite and the infinite. This relationship holds together any ethical account of war, whether explicitly or implicitly. It relates the political and the church, morality and law, reactive defence and compassionate love. Whether conceived as Being, Event or Process, the predicates of mediation problematize and negotiate the relationship between these dimensions. Does the relationship consist in a separation or continuity/identity of the divine and the human? Are the dimensions to be conceived analogously, separate to the point of dualism, or do they collapse into each other, resulting in an imposed continuity, sheer violence? And, secondarily, how do these logical constellations relate to each other? These questions draw attention to predicates, to verbs and categories of relation and distance.

With the focus on the theo-logic and problem of mediation, the present project sits on the borderline between ethics, the philosophy of religion and systematic theology, since what could appear to be a trip to 'the icy seas of abstraction' (Adorno) is in fact an inherently Christological quest: mediation on its grandest, exemplary scale is that between humans and the divine. Already a problem for Plato, for Christianity the single and unique mediator between God and humankind becomes Jesus Christ (1 Tim. 2.5).

---

[8]　Lisa Sowle Cahill, *Global Justice, Christology and Christian Ethics* (Cambridge: Cambridge University Press, 2013). Although a theological realist, I would count Sowle Cahill's work into this category, due to the parallelisms explained in Chapter 2.

Nicolaus of Cues calls Christ the *coincidentia oppositorum*, the *medium absolutum*. And Vladimir Solovyev writes, 'The mystery of God's humanity revealed in Christ – the personal unification of the perfect divinity with the perfect humanity – is not only the greatest theological and philosophical truth; it is the nodal point of world history.'[9] For all the differences between these thinkers, mediation for them is the pivotal point that condenses and ignites the logic of ethico-political form, action and critique.

As an analytical horizon, the Christian notion of mediation puts into context any alternative claims to facilitate or embody an identity of Is and Ought or what Augustine explicitly called 'false mediators'.[10] In political thought, such an identity can be claimed for historical, perhaps revolutionary, moments and events. It can be claimed by mythologized sovereign states, a theocracy or an existing international order.[11] A Christological analysis is therefore not merely a negligible aspect of political ethics. Understanding the relationship particularly between the two natures of Christ is a constitutive exercise. These metaphysical relationships ground the relationship between the political and the spiritual and therefore illuminate how the political and the moral cohere or clash. Notably, in most cases, this is not presented as a basic framework: frequently, ethicists of war leave what is regarded here as foundational to a small section or polemical aside. Hence, an important element in the analysis is to explore how (anti-)theological premises impact on the entire ethical proposal.

In modernity, the notions of 'mediation' and dialectics are inextricably linked to the work of G. W. F. Hegel. And it is perhaps no coincidence that Hegel is a frequent, if only brief and critical, reference point for contemporary just war thinkers. Hegel's work marks a transition from traditional Christology to modern immanent mediation and dialectics.[12] This interpretation has recently been extended by Graham Ward, with reference to Michael Wendte and Nicholas Adams.[13] Revisiting Hegel's early works already in 2013, Ward emphasized the specific connection between the logic of mediation and Christology. Hegel, he writes,

> is interested in Jesus Christ as an historical event in which the divine is made human. He is interested in the *theo-logic* that such an event manifests and

---

[9] Cited in Wilhelm Blum, *Wirklichkeit des Lebens: Vom Wesen der dialektischen Vermittlung in Politik und Religion* (Rheinfelden: Schäuble, 1985), p. 133.

[10] Conf. x, xliii.

[11] This is how I read Oliver O'Donovan's work (see Chapter 5), but it is arguably also a guiding hermeneutic for his historical work, e.g. *From Irenaeus to Grotius: A Sourcebook in Christian Political Thought 100–1625*, ed. Oliver O'Donovan and Joan Lockwood (Grand Rapids, MI; Cambridge: William B. Eerdmans, 1999). On institutional mediation see e.g. Régis Debray, *God: An Itinerary*, trans. Jeffrey Mehlman (London: Verso, 2004), 'The Mediating Body', pp. 131–56.

[12] Blum, *Wirklichkeit des Lebens*, p. 134.

[13] Graham Ward, *How the Light Gets In: Ethical Life I* (Oxford: Oxford University Press, 2016); Martin Wendte, *Gottmenschliche Einheit bei Hegel: Eine logische und theologische Untersuchung* (Berlin; New York: Walter de Gruyter, 2007), pp. 4–10; Nicholas Adams, *The Eclipse of Grace: Divine and Human Action in Hegel* (Chichester: Wiley-Blackwell, 2013); Andrew Shanks' works on Hegel would require greater appreciation than possible here, especially *Theodicy Beyond the Death of 'God': The Persisting Problem of Evil* (London: Routledge, 2018) and *A Neo-Hegelian Theology: The God of Greatest Hospitality* (London: Routledge, 2016).

inaugurates – the logic of incarnation whereby god and human beings both share a nature and yet remain fundamentally distinct.[14]

In fact, the 'Incarnation of the Logos itself' becomes '*the* model for the logic of all mediation'.[15] Ward underlines that in his mature *Lectures on the Philosophy of History* Hegel continues to describe Jesus Christ as the 'axis on which the History of the World turns'.[16] But there is a specific shift in Hegel's thought: 'the philosophical project of modernity, the advance of human reasoning, was only possible if the sacred – if Jesus as the revealed Logos of God – established the position from which to speak philosophically'.[17] *Pace* George Lukács and Hegel's non-religious interpreters, Ward argues, 'Hegel's [early] Christological investigations are investigations into that which makes dialectic possible at all'; and 'the later dialectic is a working out of a Christological and philosophical principle'.[18] There is an intrinsic connection between Christo-logic and immanent logic. Both are thought and lived, permeating natural, social and political processes, albeit upholding – residually – a transcendence of the Logos.[19]

In the present project, the Christo-logic of mediation sets the horizon for the analysis of each just war thinker's conceptual ethical architecture. Hegel may not be the answer to modern Christian theology's questions. But certainly he is one way to *ask* them. So in the second part of each chapter, it is examined how the conception (or rejection) of the Christ mediator coheres with potential problems in terms of war and conflict. A dialectic or logic of separation, identity and continuity between the real and the ideal takes hold.[20] States, wars or realities may be idealized but kept separate from a transcendent 'utopia'. Conversely, ideals may require realization or institutional instantiation over against realistic forms of politics. Both approaches share the logic of the excluded Other which returns in an unmediated confrontation. In this sense, we will frequently encounter an oscillation on this level as well: between a human–divine duality and immediacy and between individualism and collectivism, to name just two.

Structurally, the analysis will focus on three pivotal, formal but irreducible points of morality. First, I will explore the understanding of political reality. How is it 'realistic' and how is that theologically or philosophically sustained? Where is the locus of a moral ideal or a moral Ought? Second, from these premises emerges the conception of the moral agent in war. What is the scope of the 'realistic' agent, what its 'idealist' counterpoint, and how is this theologically maintained, whether explicitly or implicitly? Here the notion of the sovereign state, the individual with defensive rights, or a global state will come into focus. Third, I will analyse the mediatory potential of moral-political action. What is a realist/idealist conception of moral action? More

---

[14] Graham Ward, 'How Hegel Became a Philosopher: Logos and the Economy of Logic', *Critical Research on Religion*, 1 (2013), 270–92, p. 271.

[15] Ibid., p. 271.

[16] Ibid., p. 273.

[17] Ward at times uses theo-logic interchangeably with 'systematic theology'.

[18] Ward, 'How Hegel Became a Philosopher', p. 275. See also Ward, *How the Light Gets In*, pp. 298–303.

[19] Cf. e.g. the logic of developmental biology in Hegelian terms; Sönke Roterberg, *Hegels Begriffslogik und die Embryologie* (Würzburg: Königshausen & Neumann, 2015).

[20] See especially' Hegel, *Wissenschaft der Logik II* (Frankfurt: Suhrkamp, 1986), pp. 64–8.

specifically, how does the law and love cohere? All these questions are driven by one focus: the relation between the real and the ideal in the light of a possible or absent logic of mediation. It will be either connected to a divine Mediator as described by Augustine of Hippo and others or it may fall apart into a singular focus: Jesus as a mere historical occurrence may be irreconcilably opposed to a future or merely fictional Christ.

Mediation in a modern key

While Hegel's work presents a pivotal, transitional moment for modern theology, it also allows us to discern a fundamental, secularizing shift in Christological mediation.[21] Kant and the earlier Enlightenment push Christ the mediator behind the horizon of reason. As a result, the gaze eventually falls onto the human being as the locus of ultimate mediation. Theology is *summed up* or sublated into anthropology. If Augustine's theology had sublated Platonic philosophy, this is now reversed: anthropology-as-theology is the heart piece of political ethics; we live in the 'age of anthropology', as Wolfhart Pannenberg diagnosed it. Now, individuals are the *princes of peace*, ends in themselves and moral standards.[22] For Nietzsche, this anthropocentrism was the result of humans, at least since Copernicus, 'rolling out of the Centre into the x'. But then, Eberhard Jüngel asks, how could the human become the measure of all things? His answer is: *because* of that.[23] The critical question is whether this marks the success or failure of Christianity. For some philosophers, it marks a *success* of Christianity – quite against its own grain – in that the infinite value of the individual and the moral equality of all are now politically recognized. In this view, moral anthropocentrism means the necessary rectification of a premodern, illiberal decentring and subjection of the individual to political authorities, supposedly ruling, unquestionably, by divine right, with divine sanction. In the reading of many *Christian* ethicists, however, it marks a *failure* in that it represents a return to the Old Age of the law. What Nietzsche lauded as the Renaissance's 'modern' choice between sovereign state and supra-political, quasi-papal institution, the very death of Christianity returns as a serious possibility, albeit

---

[21] On Hegel as either attacking Christian theology *or* defending Christianity in the language of philosophy, cf. Karl Löwith, *Weltgeschehen und Heilsgeschehen: Die theologischen Voraussetzungen der Geschichtsphilosophie* (Stuttgart: J. B. Metzler, 2004), pp. 61–8, 224. Disagreement on the interpretation of Hegel underlies not least the contrary positions of John Milbank and Slavoj Žižek, *The Monstrosity of Christ: Paradox or Dialectic?* (Cambridge; London: MIT Press, 2009). While Milbank frequently thinks dialectically within his genealogies and a Catholic participatory ontology, Žižek takes from Hegel the irreversible self-exhaustion of divine essence in the Incarnation; on the cross, the death of God inaugurates the age and logic of the Spirit that infuses matter.

[22] Similarly on Nietzsche: Hans Blumenberg, *The Legitimacy of the Modern Age*, transl. Robert M. Wallace (Cambridge: MIT Press, 1985), pp. 105, 140. A more focused study similar to the present project is Milan Babík, *Statecraft and Salvation: Wilsonian Liberal Internationalism as Secularized Eschatology* (Waco, TX: Baylor University Press, 2013).

[23] Cited in Eberhard Jüngel, *Gott als Geheimnis der Welt: zur Begründung der Theologie des Gekreuzigten im Streit zwischen Theismus u. Atheismus*, 3rd ed. (Tübingen: Mohr, 1978), p. 17. 'Inwiefern kann man dann aber behaupten, daß der Mensch sich zum Maß aller Dinge mache und die Grundprobleme der Neuzeit allemal anthropologische Probleme seien? Die Antwort muß lauten: gerade deshalb.'

now anthropocentrically transformed.[24] Whether this death is complete or reversible depends on one's specific notion of God. Yet if the Christian God is as he is confessed since Nicaea, then the 'return' is reversible and never complete.

In this sense, the framework suggested here also relies on an interpretation of 'secularization', which requires some explication. Two key figures, Karl Löwith and Hans Blumenberg, represent the two different positions in what became known as the *Säkularisierungsstreit*: either secularization must be understood as a transformation of Judaeo-Christian forms or as a new self-foundation. Thus, Karl Löwith had observed in *The Meaning of History* (1949) that the modern 'faith in history' is the secularization of messianism in the terms of political economy.[25] While St Augustine had separated the Christian eschaton from temporal and contemporary political quarrels, world history and salvation history in modernity have 'merged into something strange – the faith *in* history itself – not in a "future world," but in the future of the world'.[26] Hans Blumenberg, in contrast, denied that one may discard modern forms of thought and life as 'merely' secularized Christian concepts. That would imply that there is a 'substance' that could be secularized (which, in line with Ward and Wendte would be a Christo-logic, no matter how heterodox). Instead, Blumenberg insists on the self-standing legitimacy of the modern age; the autonomous subject grounded in itself fills the vacancy left by the metaphysics of God and king.

In line with Blumenberg, analytical moral philosophy frequently thinks in terms of a radical severance with the theological past. The legitimacy of the contemporary human rights paradigm (usually taken for granted) is grounded in a self-mediation, the mediation of the *humanum* by human beings as an ultimate Ought.[27] However, the severance with the past comes at a price: the loss of concepts such as 'sacrifice', the 'nation' or 'national defence' means that basic moral-political intuitions are increasingly difficult to explain. Hence, the constructive task that lies ahead is to recover essential, theologically rich concepts without falling back behind and below a level of reflection previously achieved. This requires some continuity with Löwith's interpretation, even if Löwith for his part moved into a post-Christian direction.[28] Historical repetitions, consonances and recurrences are central not only to locate and critique present-day ethics of war but also to identify conceptual analogies. At the same time, ethicists of

---

[24] See Friedrich Nietzsche, *Ecce Homo*, ed. Giorgio Colli and Mazzino Montinari (Berlin: de Gruyter, 1988), p. 359, 'Der Fall Wagner': 'Luther, dies Verhängnis von Mönch, hat die Kirche, und, was tausend Mal schlimmer ist, das Christentum wiederhergestellt, im Augenblicke, wo es unterlag.'

[25] Karl Löwith, *Meaning in History: The Theological Implications of the Philosophy of History* (Chicago, IL: University of Chicago Press, 1957).

[26] Jean-Claude Monod, 'Heaven on Earth? The Löwith-Blumenberg Debate', in *Radical Secularization? An Inquiry into the Religious Roots of Secular Culture*, ed. by Stijn Latré, Walter Van Herck, and Guido Vanheeswijck (London: Bloomsbury Academic, 2014), pp. 7–16.

[27] The debate on whether 'rights' or 'Right' are the more fundamental moral order feeds into this. For another 'just war theory' grounded in rights, see Kai Draper, *War and Individual Rights: The Foundations of Just War Theory* (Oxford, New York: Oxford University Press, 2015). Cp. also Hans Joas, *Die Sakralität der Person: Eine neue Genealogie der Menschenrechte* (Berlin: Suhrkamp, 2011).

[28] For his part, Löwith was sceptical of the philosophy of history's modern hubris. While exiled in Japan during the 1930s he became deeply interested particularly in Japanese culture and Zen Buddhism, looking for a post-Christian culture 'without faith in the future'. Löwith's view was then taken up by postmodern figures such as Foucault and Lyotard. Monod, 'Heaven on Earth?', p. 10.

war frequently refer to the Christian tradition (Grotius, Vitoria, Suárez, including also Kant). In that sense, they are always already dependent on theological groundwork. To say it with Karl Barth (who echoes Luther), 'There is no philosophy that is not to some extent also theology.'[29] The present project may thus well be seen to (re-)theologize the just war debate, opening it up to further enquiries into subtle theological nuances shaping denominational differences and their political expressions in the present. The Reformation, it turns out, is a much more consequential shift than the Enlightenment.[30]

Summary of chapters

With these preliminary methodological considerations in place, we now move to an overview over the argument developed throughout the book. Part One analyses the two dominant approaches to war today, often oversimplified as the idealism–realism debate but in fact deeply engrained in the political history of the 'Occident': the 'just war' of the sovereign state versus the war authorized by a supra-political, legal and moral authority. Through the work of the neoconservative Christian Jean Bethke Elsthain, Chapter 1 explores sovereign realism as a form of modern Marcionite dualism. Elshtain fervently argued in favour of the Bush government's invasion of Afghanistan and Iraq. Here I will show how her 'liberal Augustinianism' actually posits the state as Christ-like mediator between a world of violence and a God who remains de facto absent. This, I argue, results in a dialectic or oscillation between defensive, apocalyptic empire and moral-political utopia. Elshtain's just war thinking could be read as moral edification or – in more hostile terms – a form of propaganda.

International law presents itself as the more credible counterposition to sovereign realism, a promising Enlightened alternative to imperial mythology. Chapter 2 shows that, nonetheless, it is subject to the same problematic theo-logic and effects. As an immanent mediator rivalling sovereign states, international law as presently proposed extends and deepens the scope of war. I will discuss this through David Rodin's work, a major contribution of contemporary so-called revisionist just war theory. Rodin has argued influentially that a legal right to national defence cannot be constructed as an analogy to the right to self-defence; and that human rights can only be consistently defended within a universal state. I argue that Rodin's universal state as a cosmopolis emerges from the universalization of the moral–legal individual, reintroducing a transformed medieval *ekklesia*. As Christ's representative and mediator, it claimed the highest sovereignty; it held the central political, though simultaneously non-political *plenitudo potestatis*. However, despite the fact that Rodin represents a significant

---

[29] Cf. Karl Barth, *Evangelical Theology: An Introduction* (London: Collins, 1965), pp. 9–10; notably, Barth himself loathed 'heretics' hats', but his argument in the second *Römerbrief* that there should be agreement between his critics before they put one on his head hardly convinces.

[30] See also e.g. Mario Biagioni, *The Radical Reformation and the Making of Modern Europe: A Lasting Heritage* (Leiden: Brill, 2017); John Milbank, 'Nothing Is Ever Over until the End: On Religion, Power and Order', Opening Lecture of the academic year 2016–17, 2 September 2016, Protestantse Theologische Universiteit Utrecht, https://www.pthu.nl/actueel/nieuws/Nieuwspdf/oajtekstrede.pdf (accessed 4 March 2019).

challenge to sovereign realist thinking, on the grounds of shared version of post-Enlightenment dualism, the logics of these ethical programs actually mirror and even depend on each other, conceptually and often in concrete conflicts. As each imagines the other as the (undesirable) exceptional case, they collapse into their respective opposite: legal cosmopolitanism into sovereign decisionism, sovereign decisionism into a hegemonic legal globalism.

Both Elshtain's and Rodin's logics of war are a symptom of returning post-Enlightenment and pre-Reformation Investiture constellations, though now they imply an increased potential of violence. Nonetheless, both positions need to be partially appreciated – if only in hindsight – for defending both the possibility of 'the political' and the protective residue of international law. As practical 'ethics' they remain problematic, implying irony or tragedy as the answers to the theodicy posed by war.

This leads to the question of whether there is something like a 'Protestant' alternative to the 'Catholic–Marcionite' pair Rodin–Elshtain. Part Two introduces Uwe Steinhoff and Paul Ramsey, who represent two very different kinds of radical scepticisms towards the sovereign-cosmopolitan paradigm. Chapter 3 delves into the work of Uwe Steinhoff, who has been profoundly critical of cosmopolitanism. From this point he has taken Enlightened, rationalist liberalism into a different, all-round critical direction and at the same time pushes it to its consequence: for him, self-defensive torture and terrorism are permitted in extreme cases. Steinhoff draws on John Locke and J. S. Mill and notes the essentially liberal character of postmodern ethics. His scientific approach echoes several alternative, heterodox theo-political constellations that posit a distinction between human and divine to the point of rejecting the latter altogether. Nonetheless, Steinhoff's critical work – unmasking moralistic pretentions, busting false myths and attacking logical inconsistencies –certainly bears a contemporary prophetic character.[31]

A sceptic too, but in quite a different way, was Paul Ramsey, the focus of Chapter 4. The career of this (sometimes) neglected Christian ethicist spanned over fifty years, well into the 1980s, and since then has been hugely influential on Anglo-American Protestant ethics of war. Over the course of his career, Ramsey underwent a movement: from idealist pacifism, via transformism, to realism. My chapter will focus on his early Christological-ethical oscillation between human–divine duality on

---

[31] A brief note on my use of 'heresy' is in order here. Beyond the cynical view that heresy is merely 'an opinion held by a minority of men which the majority declares unacceptable and is powerful enough to punish' (David Christie-Murray, *A History of Heresy* (Oxford: Oxford University Press, 1976), p. 1), it is used here with a view to three divisive historical periods: the patristic era, particularly its struggles with Marcionite and Gnostic dualisms; the Reformation, particularly its spiritualist and unitarian strands; and finally, the post-Hegelian period, in so far as it loses its epistemological moorings in Christianity and prepares the way for 'religion' as, among others, an indistinct 'spirituality' or fuzzy 'dimension' entirely independent of dogmatic-theological or institutional mediations. Nonetheless, as Mark J. Edwards has pointed out, several church fathers now deemed orthodox frequently held views later deemed heterodox. At the same time, the heterodox may preserve and even initiate vital impulses for existing orthodoxies, provided the difference between the two has not dissolved into oblivious indifference. Cf. Christie-Murray, *A History of Heresy*; Milbank and Žižek, *Monstrosity of Christ*, pp. 27–8; Mark J. Edwards, *Catholicity and Heresy in the Early Church* (Farnham, Surrey; Burlington, VT: Ashgate, 2009).

the one hand and continuity (or identity) on the other and in particular on how it is biblically grounded. I argue that, in order to overcome the impractical or unsavoury implications of agapism, Ramsey then developed his own version of Christian 'transformism'. At this point a practical, political logic of mediation became a brief, though *theologically* unarticulated, possibility.

Even though both Steinhoff and Ramsey successfully target some difficulties posed by it, Elshtain's or Rodin's logics of war reappear in new guises and at unexpected points. Nonetheless, both authors preserve necessary prophetic impulses: Steinhoff exercises merciless conceptual critique, while Ramsey pushes for the (messianic) option of kenotic neighbour love. Thus, their theo-logics of *breaking* –human reason breaking out of the theocratic or the divine breaking into the world –negatively affirm both the sovereign-cosmopolitan paradigm and the possibility of theological-political mediation in Christ. In Ramsey's work this appears as the political act, presenting the possibility of a systematically reflected mediating praxis between conflicting ends and values.

The third and final part of the book will investigate how a practical just war ethic may be sustained by a theo-logic of mediation. I will first look at Oliver O'Donovan's explicitly theological ethics, based on the belief that Christ has mediated all antagonisms (Chapter 5). O'Donovan's Christology, so my argument, re-sublates philosophical-idealist dialectics of mediation into biblical specificity. As he relocates Hegel's question of mediation (and the sceptical oscillation he sought to overcome) within exegesis, he incorporates the Ramseyan-Hegelian mediating logic like a *fetus in fetu*. Precisely in that way O'Donovan walks through the door to the *totaliter aliter* opened by Ramsey/ Nietzsche and gives extensive biblical-theological content to Ramsey's political act. For O'Donovan, mediation means the final unity of political and spiritual, political and moral or Is and Ought in Christ which, before the end of the *saeculum*, persist in a residual duality. This theo-logic is crystallized in the tension-filled narrative of Israel's politics before and after the Christ event. However, I argue that O'Donovan's systematic-ethical comprehensiveness is partly won at the cost of political advocacy and the ability to speak to those beyond the community of faith. If O'Donovan gives theological content to Ramsey's mediating political act, and if Ramsey risked the embarrassment of (political) advocacy, then in order to preserve both advocacy and theological comprehensiveness, we require a continuous *transition* between the views of Ramsey and O'Donovan.

Chapter 6 will reflect on this transition as something that connects the ethics of war to discourses which are frequently theologically illiterate. How can this transition be theologically conceptualized? Here, I will attempt to recast it as closely related to *grace*. Arguably grace allows and encourages those who take on or hold political responsibility to risk the embarrassment of political engagement. But this means the connection between the ethics of war and a theology/philosophy of history cannot be dismissed. And it raises another question of the nature of practical engagement: *combat*. How can confrontation be thought of as having anything to do with mediation? As we live in a supposedly post-heroic age, remote-controlled warfare might appear to make war less bloody and destructive, allowing militaries to 'remove' threats, while reducing the need for their own forces to risk injury or death. However, the inner logic of these weapons is troubling. Precisely *because* they remove confrontation and battle, they replace mediation with an amalgamation of 'humanism' and war that entirely eradicates the enemy. It replaces the very possibility of victory and subsequent reconciliation with a symmetrical, faceless *stasis* of war between terrorists and (increasingly ineffective) counterterrorists.

With this, the enquiry comes full circle. The concluding remarks will draw out particularly the logics of political authority that have emerged throughout the course of the chapters and indicate further theological paths ahead. Finally, it will highlight the need for a political ethics grounded in mediation for the conflicts to come.

Part One

A modern investiture: National sovereignty versus international law

1

Sovereign demonology: The state of exception(alism)

Introduction

In 2003, the political theorist and religious thinker Jean Bethke Elshtain (1941–2013) entered an already feverish debate on the so-called War on Terror. Her sweeping public defence of the Bush administration's invasion of Afghanistan and Iraq, *Just War against Terror: The Burden of American Power in a Violent World,* sounded a voice of feminist toughness and common sense. As a Christian neoconservative (a word she never used), Elshtain pushed all the buttons of archetypal do-gooders in the United States and beyond. Appended to the book was 'What We're Fighting For: A Letter from America',[1] a public philosophical pledge signed by several public intellectuals supporting the Bush government.[2]

It will not be the primary task here to discuss whether these wars were 'just' but to examine what kind of political theology sustains Elshtain's just war arguments. Who or what is the ultimate mediator in Elshtain's proposal? What is the (theo-)logic of the politically real and the morally ideal that results in Elshtain's practical justifications? Even though she claims that the realist-idealist divide 'serves no useful heuristic or even polemical purpose', she puts forward an 'Augustinian realism' that persistently polemicizes against moral 'idealism'.[3] Elshtain's work in fact represents a major theo-political option centred on political realism, the nation-state and empire.[4] Through Elshtain's work we are able to explore sovereign realism as a potential form of modern Marcionite dualism. We will see how the liberal Augustinian Elshtain posits the state as Christ-like mediator between a world of violence and a God who remains de facto absent, even unknown. This

---

[1] *What We're Fighting For: A Letter from America,* February 2002, Institute for American Values, http://www.americanvalues.org/search/item.php?id=858 (accessed 1 August 2017).

[2] As a historical parallel comes to mind the 1914 'Manifest of the 93', an open letter by signed by ninety-three German public intellectuals defending the German emperor Wilhelm II's preparations for war.

[3] Jean Bethke Elshtain, 'On Never Reaching the Coast of Utopia', *International Relations,* 22 (2008), 147–72.

[4] See also Nicholas Rengger, 'Jean Bethke Elshtain (1941—2013)', in *Just War Thinkers: From Cicero to the 21st Century,* ed. by Daniel R. Brunstetter and Cian O'Driscoll (London; New York: Routledge, 2017), pp. 216–26.

results in a problematic dialectic of defensive, apocalyptic empire and moral-political utopia. But first, a short recapitulation of Elshtain's just war arguments.

Just War in a neoconservative key – Jean Bethke Elshtain's *Just War against Terror*

Facing the reality of the situation

In light of the severity of the events of 9/11, Elshtain's 'civic primer' *Just War against Terror*[5] begins with a polemic against 'humanists'. Humanists, Elshtain argues with Albert Camus, are always inclined to close their eyes before evil. They are 'dominated by their own internal preferences rather than the concrete realities of the situation' (*JWT*, 1). However, 'politics is not the nursery', she quotes Hannah Arendt. But we need to heed the actual 'reality of the situation'. In that case, 'What happened on September 11?' For Elshtain, one could not describe the attacks other than as the work of terrorists, religious fanatics who wanted to kill as many Americans as possible and attack 'who we are'. Elshtain's emphasizing 'right description' was also a repeat attack on a postmodern, historicist pragmatism such as Richard Rorty's.[6] Rorty had suggested that the 'truthful' description of a situation is contingent upon people's moral agenda, embedded within historically grown values. As a result, there were no neutral facts. The ironic redescription of any situation may even be a particular liberal virtue.[7] Against this, Elshtain upholds that there is a moral and metaphysical truth to which events do or do not correspond.[8] 'Misdescription' or '[resisting] calling things by their right names' is done 'in the interest of furthering an ideology', with 'corrosive effects'.[9] This nervousness about irony, its ability to discover a potential *lie* that subverts unironic 'truth', locates Elshtain's reaction not least firmly within a *modern* epistemological and therefore theological set of problems we will return to later.

Terrorism

Elshtain then puts forth a 'Just War theory' in the form of frequently revisited 'criteria'. First, she clarifies the nature of terrorism. Alluding to *total war*, she understands it as the

---

5　Jean Bethke Elshtain, *Just War against Terror: The Burden of American Power in a Violent World* (New York: Basic, 2004), hereafter JWT.

6　Cf. Elshtain, 'Don't Be Cruel: Reflections on Rortyian Liberalism', in *Richard Rorty*, ed. Charles B. Guignon and David R. Hiley (Cambridge: Cambridge University Press, 2003), pp. 139–57.

7　Convincingly critical on Elshtain's 'common-sense' attacks on Rorty's ironism: William Curtis, *Defending Rorty: Pragmatism and Liberal Virtue* (Cambridge: Cambridge University Press, 2015), pp. 135, 156–60.

8　This is not without problems, as she similarly elides fact and description: 'Any description of an evil act as good is *false to the facts*.' Noteworthy, David Kim refers to Elshtain as 'postmodern' in 'City of God', in *Christian Body Politic: 21st Century Reformed Perspectives on Church and State*, ed. Christian Kim (Philadelphia, PA: Hermit Kingdom Press, 2004), pp. 125–52, p. 127.

9　By ideology Elshtain means 'a totalizing and closed system that discounts or dismisses whatever does not "fit" within it' and 'has very little use for accurate descriptions of what is going on' (JWT, 16).

killing directed against all ideological enemies indiscriminately and outside the context of a war between combatants. According to the logic of terrorism, enemies can legitimately be killed no matter what they are doing, where they are, or how old they are. (*JWT*, 18)

With Michael Walzer, terrorism 'is the random murder of innocent people', by which are meant non-combatants (a term, some have pointed out, already invoking a state of war) (*JWT*, 18). Either way, terrorism is not a military strategy. Consequently, terrorists have no status as political or military subjects: 'They have taken leave of politics. ... No political solution is possible ... when the terrorism is aimed at the destruction of innocent civilians – when that itself is the goal' (*JWT*, 18). Whereas war is the (Clausewitzian) 'continuation of politics by other means', terrorism is 'the destruction of politics by all possible means' (*JWT*, 152). Developing a 'political arm' may be possible for terrorists, Elshtain admits, but their actions are 'most often in the service of wild and utopian goals that make no sense at all in the usual political ways' (*JWT*, 18). Since terrorists are murderers, she continues, 'using terms like "fighter" or "soldier" or "noble warrior" is not only beside the point but pernicious'. 'Such language' – here she points at postmodern rhetoricism as well as Islamism – 'collapses the distance between those who plant bombs in cafés or fly civilian aircraft into office buildings and those who fight other combatants, taking the risks attendant upon military forms of fighting' (*JWT*, 19). Despite this restriction of combat to military fighters, Elshtain at several points refers to the attempted Hitler assassination of 1944. This was an admirable 'exceptional case' and later in her argument will play an important role in justifying governmental powers.

Problematically, while terrorists are murderers 'with a nihilistic edge', their actions nevertheless count as 'acts of war under international law'. Hence, they trigger national defence (*JWT*, 20, 59). Elshtain needs the definition of terrorists as both nihilist murderers and combatants in order to distinguish terrorism from 'resistance' but simultaneously to justify war. Hence, she refuses to call the murderers (as she calls terrorists earlier) perpetrators of murder explicitly on 11 September 2001. Terrorists thus are neither criminals nor military fighters, yet at the same time they commit murders that amount to military attacks – which justify national defence.

As it turned out, outside the Geneva Conventions and domestic jurisdiction, 'the War on Terror' created the category of 'unlawful combatants'.[10] Giorgio Agamben critically described these kinds of humans as *homines sacri*, banned individuals, a juridical contradiction. As enemies they were deprived of a legal, and here it appears also of any moral, status, but they were still firmly incorporated subjects of the sovereign state.[11] As Elshtain explains it, terrorists have catapulted themselves into an anarchic 'no-man's land' through their own 'nihilistic' actions, their 'unlawful fighting'. The places of detainment such as Guantanamo and other semi-secret

---

[10] Jill Lepore, 'The Dark Ages. Guanatanamo and Legal History', *New Yorker*, 18 March 2013, pp. 28–33.
[11] See Giorgio Agamben, *Homo Sacer: Sovereign Power and Bare Life* (Stanford, CA: Stanford University Press, 1998), esp. 'The Camp as the "Nomos" of the Modern', pp. 166–81. See also Chapter 2, Paul Ramsey on the modern world as concentration camp.

prisons are also no man's land. With Michael Walzer, Elshtain thinks the prisons are 'neither zones of war nor zones of peace'.[12] She finds this 'tricky': 'What norms, rules, laws cover these zones, this no-man's land? Much remains to be sorted out.' Yet instead of 'sorting it out', she then sustains the category as part of the national emergency.[13] These politics of the 'state of exception', 'the no-man's-land' for Elshtain, also defines the 'tragedy' of the political world – an essential element of her 'realistic' understanding of politics.

Discrimination

While Elshtain abhors terrorists on the grounds of their indiscriminate tactics, she also sets herself apart from 'distinction-obliterators for whom, crudely, a dead body is a dead body and never mind how it got that way' (*JWT*, 20). This critique specifically targets contemporary human-rights pacifism, of which Diana Francis gives us a taste: '"Discrimination" on any grounds (in this case in favour of civilians) is contrary to the nature of human rights, whose ethical foundation is their unconditionality'.[14] In response, however, Elshtain praises the American military for its training in discriminate fighting according to 'strict rules of engagement' and advertises America's war to her readers (*JWT*, 20–3). She supports it with selected evidence, for example, the contrast between terrorist videos and American military training manuals.[15] Since the right intention of the United States is taken for granted, any destruction is 'tragic', like 'a flood roaring through a canyon' (*JWT*, 108).

Significantly, indiscriminate killing here triggers a kind of 'Responsibility to Protect' (R2P). Thus, Elshtain harnesses the internationalist concept to sovereign realism: 'To do nothing when people are slaughtered makes one complicit in injustice.' *Anyone* sufficiently powerful is responsible for stopping indiscriminate killing. And such responsibility cannot remain innocent: '"Responsible action" involves contamination – one cannot altogether avoid getting "dirty hands" when acting in the political world in a responsible way' (*JWT*, 25). Elshtain's 'dirty hands' argument later included a form of 'torture light' as a result of political 'necessity' and a government's 'responsibility' in the light of 'human wretchedness'.[16]

Government authority and civic peace

As opposed to idealists, humanists or (terrorist) utopians, Elshtain wants to develop a sense of political realism. In the chapter entitled 'What Is a Just War?' she explains,

---

[12] Jean Bethke Elshtain, 'Response to Tom Farer's "Un-Just War against Terrorism and the Struggle to Appropriate Human Rights"', *Human Rights Quarterly*, 30 (2008), 758–66, p. 764.

[13] Ibid.

[14] Diana Francis, *Rethinking War and Peace* (London: Pluto Press, 2004), pp. 88–9.

[15] On Elshtain's problematic use of 'tragedy', see also Maja Zehfuss, 'The Tragedy of Violent Justice: The Danger of Elshtain's Just War against Terror', *International Relations*, 21 (2007), 493–501.

[16] Elshtain, 'Reflection on the Problem of "Dirty Hands"', in *Torture: A Collection*, ed. Sanford Levinson (New York: Oxford University Press, 2004), pp. 77–89.

The primary responsibility of government is to provide basic security – ordinary civic peace. St. Augustine calls this form of earthly peace *tranquillitas ordinis*. This is not the perfect peace promised to believers in the Kingdom of God, the one in which the lion lies down with the lamb. (*JWT*, 46)

Civic peace or simply 'order' provides the formal, neutral ground for the 'goods that human beings cherish, including the free exercise of religion … [mothers] and fathers raising their children; men and women going to work; citizens of a great city making their way on streets and subways', and so on (*JWT*, 46).

The alternative is Hobbes' 'state of nature', that 'horrible circumstance' in which 'all persons have the strength to kill each other, "either by secret machination, or by confederacy with others" ' (*JWT*, 47, 166). Elshtain refers to Hobbes with some reluctance: he 'somewhat overstated his point' (*JWT*, 47). Either way, the result is a formal minimalism: 'When government becomes destructive of the most basic end for which it is instituted, *tranquillitas ordinis*, it abandons its minimal raison d'être and can no longer be said to be legitimate. This assumption is essential to political theory' (*JWT*, 48).

In a consequentialist mode, the task of government is 'to prevent the worst from happening'. And, 'Any government that fails to do what is within its rightful power and purview in these matters is guilty of dereliction of duty' (*JWT*, 49). If we found a government had failed to prevent a certain catastrophe or were the agent of destruction, 'we would rightly seek the restoration of basic, minimally decent civic peace and order' (*JWT*, 49). Here Elshtain seems to invoke the Rawlsian concept of 'decent peoples', who secure minimal human rights. At the same time, she disconnects government from any substantial account of justice. 'Earthly peace, as imperfect as it is, is better than the nightmare of Thomas Hobbes's war of all against all' (*JWT*, 52).

After a cursory foray into the just war tradition, including the remarkable emphasis that Tertullian and Origen are not 'Christian mainstream', Elshtain presents a *ius ad bellum* 'checklist':

First, a war must be openly declared or otherwise authorized by a legitimate authority, so as to forestall random, private, and unlimited violence. Second, a war must be a response to a specific instance of unjust aggression perpetrated against one's own people or an innocent third party, or fought for a just cause. Third, a war must begin with the right intentions. Fourth, a war must be a last resort after other possibilities for redress and defence of the values at stake have been explored. Another *ad bellum* criterion usually noted is the prudential one: Do not enter a conflict without reflecting on whether the cause has a reasonable chance of success. (*JWT*, 57–8)

Elshtain then directly reads St Paul's 'there is no authority except from God, and those that exist have been instituted by God' (Rom. 13.1) as a just war criterion: 'It is the *rightful authority* of earthly kings and kingdoms to punish wrongdoers' (*JWT*, 52). In this context, the United States has a divine warrant. A just cause is national defence. Indeed, in Elshtain's reading, 'justice' is identical with 'defence' (*JWT*, 150).

The 'War against Terror' – a 'just war'

Elshtain's demonstration of the 'War against Terror' as a 'just war' is then an effectively tautological exercise. Her sources are government speeches, sources close to the American establishment at the time, proclaimed principles of the military forces and her own experience of fear on 11 September 2001. The event provided the *casus belli*, a clear break between the peaceful, bucolic domesticity of American life and the national state of emergency.

Regarding the invasion of Afghanistan in 2001, Elshtain then declared national defence coextensive with a 'humanitarian' mission. It implies 'the love of our neighbour' or 'less theologically … equal regard for others based on human dignity and our common humanity' (*JWT*, 59). American forces are 'authorized' to act on the principle that 'vital human goods, such as healthy children and mothers, cannot be achieved without a minimal level of civic peace' (*JWT*, 60). Moreover, the principle of 'equal regard' underlies the Universal Declaration of Human Rights, 'just as it lies at the heart of our Declaration of Independence and Lincoln's matchless Gettysburg Address' (*JWT*, 168).

At the same time, she argues consequentially, more people would have died without the 'intervention'. The 'just cause' in Afghanistan was met, since Americans were there 'to punish wrongdoers and to prevent them from murdering civilians in the future' (*JWT*, 61). As 'right authority', she counts the self-authorization of the United States by both houses of Congress. The invasion was also the 'last resort', since all other options had been 'explored'. And 'in any event; because what [the terrorists] seek is our destruction, there is nothing to negotiate about'. The prospect of success as a 'prudential consideration' remains 'always tricky'. There is no certainty about the American global war being successful, but 'the entire world … will be better off if the effort is successful'. Elshtain then *assures* the reader that the United States has no genocidal, revenging or crusading intentions. Moreover, unlike Islamist terrorists, American military observe the *in bello* criteria of proportionality and discrimination. Here she hints at a doctrine of double effect: the United States takes the matter of 'collateral damage' 'very seriously' and 'is doing everything to minimize civilian death' (*JWT*, 69).

In subsequent chapters, Elshtain again polemicizes against those who disagree with her on intellectual ('leftist') or religious ('sectarian') grounds. Returning to the 'just war' in a section on the sovereign state, she invokes national unity in the face of an 'unprecedented crisis' (158). In the pivotal historical moment after 9/11, 'the time had come to put warmaking, peacekeeping, and justice together' (*JWT*, 158).

The nation-state and American empire

Elshtain's final chapters repeat two arguments about political authority. The first one is a realist argument, here in the sense of 'positivist', explicating existing power structures of the post-Westphalian nation-state system.[17] Elshtain insists on the plurality of

---

[17] Nicholas Rengger also notes the mixing of 'just war' theories from different contexts: 'Just a War against Terror? Jean Bethke Elshtain's Burden and American Power', *International Affairs*, 80 (2004), 107–16, p. 114.

sovereign states in the international sphere and juxtaposes them with unaccountable international bodies and positive legal restraints. International law, including the traditional laws of war, is affixed with a question mark: 'So what is to be applied when? Is the court to make up law as it goes along? Even the definition of a "war crime" is often not so clear' (*JWT*, 164). Hence,

> Moving in the direction of international criminal justice, international justice of a noncriminal nature, and the like and diminishing the power, responsibility, and legitimacy of states not only will prove ineffective, even disastrous in some cases, in the short run but will undermine the minimal or even major (depending on the states involved and the situation) pressure that the system of states can put on rogue actors among their own ranks over the long run. (*JWT*, 166)

Elshtain is equally suspicious of NGOs, 'professional bodies that often have deep pockets and the ability to move in and through the international system' (*JWT*, 162). She does not entirely disavow 'transgovernmental and international connections' and generally recognizes 'religious institutions and organizations that have been border-crossers for centuries' (*JWT*, 162). In terms of the authority to go to war, however, '[there] is nothing in the just war tradition that stipulates that a decision to go to war is legitimate only if it is made by a group of states in concert or by any other body than a *de jure* state itself' (*JWT*, 184). Thus, in so far as international law still embodies statism, it remains acceptable to her: the United Nations Charter 'presumes that its members are sovereign entities that have a right to defend themselves and this means, in turn, that they have the right to determine in what that defence consists' (*JWT*, 184).

Elshtain's second point about political authority is a version of Wilsonian idealism, the case for global, though non-utopian, humanitarian justice:

> But equal regard, as the American founders knew, as Lincoln understood, and as we are coming to understand, must sometimes be backed up by coercive force. This is an ideal of international justice whose time has come. Equal regard is a mixture of old norms given new urgency and new possibilities. ... But in our less-than-ideal world, the one candidate to guarantee this principle is the United States, for two reasons: Equal regard is the foundation of our own polity, and we are the only superpower. (*JWT*, 168)

With Michael Ignatieff, Elshtain imagines 'a sort of imperialism ... an image of the world's superpower taking on an enormous burden and doing so with a relatively, though not entirely, selfless intent' (*JWT*, 166).[18] The primary concerns of this empire are forestalling chaotic 'failed states' without minimum stability – 'a new version of deterrence'. Moreover, '[These] ethical considerations are themselves central to our

---

[18] For separate commentary on Ignatieff's work, see Derrick O'Keefe, *Michael Ignatieff – The Lesser Evil?* (London: Verso, 2011).

national interest, correctly understood. It is in our long-term national interest to foster and sustain an international society of equal regard. Strategic necessity and moral requirements here meet' (*JWT*, 170).

In the appended essay on Iraq, Elshtain once again finds her four *ius ad bellum* criteria met. However problematic the claim that Saddam Hussein had weapons of mass destruction, she thinks his previous crimes warranted the invasion of 2003: 'It is a striking, and saddening, commentary that the emphasis had to be placed on the danger of WMD since Saddam's well-documented mass murder of his own people did not rise to the level of a *casus belli* in and of itself' (*JWT*, 186).

In short, for Elshtain, American civic tranquillity was destroyed by a terrorist attack, which triggered the right to national defence. This right can be exercised only by a sovereign nation-state. In this sense, Elshtain embraces the 'realist', post-Westphalian notion of international order and international law.[19] Yet America, the superpower, plays a special role: not only is it essentially and constitutionally committed to equal regard and human rights, but its global commitment to these universal values is in fact their national interest. At the same time, the exceptional emergency state opens up legal and moral grey zones for 'unlawful combatants'.

Theo-political dualism: J. B. Elshtain, Schmitt and Marcion

Elshtain got much flak for her book. Stanley Hauerwas called it 'nothing more than an uncritical justification of the ideology of America as empire … whose argument should not convince anyone thoughtful'.[20] Nicholas Rengger concluded his review saying, 'To make the United States as a polity the permanent agent of the global common good … is to take up the ring of power. And the only beneficiary of that, as we know, would be Sauron.'[21] Many reviews also saw an incisive break with Elshtain's earlier more pacific writings. However – and this is our focus here – if one consults her *Augustine and the Limits of Politics*, her journal articles as well as her 2006 Gifford Lectures, *Sovereignty: God, State and Self*,[22] a continuous logic emerges, intrinsic to her liberal Augustinianism.[23] In the following, I will reconstruct this theo-logic by drawing on all of these sources, looking at three pivotal, formal points of morality. First, Elshtain's understanding of political reality: how is her realism theologically or philosophically sustained? Where is the possibility for a moral ideal or even 'idealism'? Second, from these premises emerges the conception of the moral-political agent in

---

[19] Notably, Elshtain was also taught by Kenneth Waltz, the founder of structural realism in International Relations. According to Waltz, the world has no central enforcer so that states are constrained in their choices by the pressures of anarchy.

[20] Stanley Hauerwas and Paul Griffiths, 'War, Peace & Jean Bethke Elshtain', *First Things*, October 2003, http://www.firstthings.com/article.php3?id_article=534 (accessed 24 November 2008).

[21] Rengger, 'Just a War against Terror?', p. 116.

[22] Elshtain, *Sovereignty: God, State and Self* (New York: Basic, 2008), hereafter, *S*.

[23] Elshtain, *Augustine and the Limits of Politics* (Notre Dame, IN: University of Notre Dame Press, 1995); hereafter, *ALP*.

war. What is the scope of the 'realistic' agent, what its 'idealist' counterpoint and how is this theologically maintained, if at all? Here the notion of the sovereign state having migrated from a particular notion of God will be central. Third, I will analyse Elshtain's view of moral-political action. How does 'realistic' action relate to faith and what is the object of that faith? Although Augustine is a frequent reference point, his relationship between 'making earthly peace' and the 'heavenly peace' will be discussed in contrast to Elshtain's. All these questions are driven by one focus: the relation between the real and the ideal in the light of a possible or absent theo-logic of mediation described by Augustine and others.[24]

A violent world and the dead man on the cross

The earthly city and its tragedies

Not only is politics 'not the nursery' but it also demands 'dirty hands'. For Elshtain, politics is inherently 'tragic' and consequentialism – 'preventing the worst from happening' – an intrinsic demand of political action. She has several sources for this notion of reality, which imposes its 'necessities' on the politician (*JWT*, 50, 102, 105).

A 'violent world' engenders a fundamental dynamic. There is the constant possibility of a Hobbesian war of all against all. This 'state of nature' thinking is hardly the result of a theo-political reflection on the reality of creation and redemption but early modern scepticism. It is derived from an anthropology that, with Hobbes, doesn't recognize a pre-political order.[25] Reminiscent of Hobbes and Carl Schmitt – though less Hellenophile than either of them – Elshtain draws on the Wild West, one of America's own mythological spaces.[26] The movie *The Man Who Shot Liberty Valance* depicts such a 'violent world'. Here, in the absence of a viable authority, that is, a steadfast sheriff who usually enforces the law, a robber roams the land. Only stout-hearted 'tragic hero' Tom Doniphon is courageous enough to kill and thus disarm the villain.[27] Elshtain's conclusion is that

> [law] exists. Who will enforce it? The film tells us that settled law and its routine enforcement are possible only when random violence and the fear it instills have been pushed back. … [It] is a parable on the use of force at the service of civic peace in the fog of an undeclared war in which the forces of violence are pitted

---

[24] Elshtain mentions Augustine's divine Mediator at least twice. ALP, 66; S, xiv.

[25] Also ALP, 25–6.

[26] Eric Hobsbawm, 'The Myth of The Cowboy', *The Guardian*, 20 March, 2013, http://www.guardian.co.uk/books/2013/mar/20/myth-of-the-cowboy (accessed 30 April 2018). In his scathing critique of American 'Sovereignty, Empire, Capital, And Terror', Milbank regards bin Laden, with his gun in the desert as the 'American anti-hero' and 'first cousin' to Joseph Smith; Harold Bloom (not least a connoisseur of Gnosis) regards Mormonism as the 'archetypical American sect'. John Milbank, *The Future of Love: Essays in Political Theology* (Eugene, OR: Cascade, 2009), p. 232.

[27] NB: Not Tom Doniphon, but the lawyer from town is the 'tragic hero' of the film. Doniphon obfuscates all attempts to bring law and executive together. Even when Doniphon is offered the official post of sheriff, acclaimed (and thus 'legitimized') by the community, he refuses and prefers executing robbers according to his own estimate.

against all those who want to settle, raise their families, and educate their children. (*JWT*, 55)

Hence, the political task of '[keeping] the forces of anarchy at bay' is different from the enforcement of law. This original act recalls Carl Schmitt's figure of the *nomos*: it is an *ordo ordinans* (order of ordering), rather than law, which is the 'enactment of acts in line with the *ought*'.[28] Although (potentially) criminal, the act of ordering is justified because it provides the possibility of regular law over against chaos and wilderness. Elshtain then groups her theological material around this Hobbesian (or Schmittian) 'katechontic' task.[29]

Yet she is careful not to walk straight into a political Gnosticism. Initially, 'the world' is a good place: 'For believers, the created order is fundamentally good: God saw it and said it was good. This order includes human beings' (*JWT*, 102).[30] In *Augustine and the Limits of Politics*, she points out that Augustine 'was in love with the world, a world he called a '"smiling place." ... Only someone caught up in a love affair with the world would describe so deliciously its many delectations and articulate so artfully its temptations' (*ALP*, 89). Here she even contrasts Augustine's 'presumption of the peace and its priority over war' with Hobbesian 'mythical beginnings that presume disorder' (*ALP*, 94). Nonetheless, effectively she turns away from this Augustinian 'ontology of peace': 'But the political *gravamen* seems to me to lie elsewhere' (*ALP*, 101).

For Elshtain, the earthly city is the *only* place where political gravamen lies. While one of her initial reference points, John Milbank, grounds a political ecclesiology in the Augustinian ontology of peace, Elshtain puts the reader on the track of a liberal social ontology. At times she equates it with the state, inadvertently repeating Robert Markus's reading of Augustine's earthly city as a neutral, separate realm: 'Within *each* earthly city, the saved and unsaved come together: that is a given. At the same time, one can distinguish between better and worse earthly cities (S, 9).[31] So politics are distinct from, if not opposed to, the 'religious'.

As it stands, Elshtain's good creator-God could equally be invoked by a transcendentalist or America's Deist founding fathers.[32] And it is with these that she travels, beginning with anthropology. She rarely uses the term 'liberalism', but for her,

---

[28] Carl Schmitt, *The Nomos of the Earth*, transl. Gary L. Ulmen (New York: Telos Press, 2003), p. 78; see also p. 73f. While Hobbes drew on Tacitus's descriptions of ancient Roman forces of disorder, his admirer Schmitt also invoked Pindar, whose hero Heracles brings law as an act of crime.

[29] Cf. Richard Faber, *Political Demonology: On Modern Marcionism*, translated and ed. Therese Feiler and Michael Mayo (Eugene, OR: Wipf & Stock, Cascade, 2018), pp. 96–8. On the state as the *katechon*, see below.

[30] NB: the constructivist or subjectivist tendency in 'for believers'.

[31] More explicitly in *Sovereignty*, pp. 59, 272n.5.

[32] Transcendentalism is not far-fetched here: Elshtain held the Ralph Waldo Emerson Award 1997–8, and this heritage undergirds also her Gifford Lectures; like the transcendentalists Orestes Brownson and Isaac Hecker, Elshtain eventually converted to Roman Catholicism. Already Adolf von Harnack notes a proximity between Marcion and Deism. This may be anachronistic, as Sebastian Moll complains, but nevertheless of conceptual value. Notably Harnack, also an admirer of Marcion (the subject of his first extensive study), also signed the 'Manifesto of the 93', at least a formal parallel to the letter 'What We're Fighting For'. Cf. Sebastian Moll, *The Arch-Heretic Marcion* (Tübingen: Mohr Siebeck, 2010), p. 3 n.11.

God created individuals: 'That a beginning was made, man was created – one singular human being. ... God did not begin with the human species but with singularity' (*ALP*, 101). Essential rather than contingent, human beings' fragile desirous bodies are then the basis for social community:

> Each child enters a world whose Creator declared it good. Each child enters a world as the heir of Adam's foundational sin. Each child, therefore, is in need of God's grace and forgiveness. All human beings are driven by hunger and desire and experience frustration at their inability to express themselves fully and decisively, in a way that prompts others to respond, to be at one's beck and call.[33]

As creatures, humans are marked by needful weaknesses. And these *construct* the earthly city: 'There is no ur-Founder, no great bringer of order. It begins in ties of fellowship, in households, clans, and tribes, in earthly love and its many discontents. And it begins in an ontology of peace, not war' (*ALP*, 97). In other words, Elshtain holds two rival versions of political reality: either we face 'random violence' without a state structure or there is after all a pre-constitutional nation, an 'earthly city' grounded in sinful sociality.[34] This tension is artfully glossed over: despite the goodness of its beginnings and sociality, Elshtain's earthly city can after all become a Hobbesian state of nature because of misguided desires.

In a problematic way, Elshtain ties the politics of minimal stability and containment to Augustine. He 'tethers [the need for coercion] to his repudiation of perfectionism: If one would do the least damage (stop "people from devouring one another like fish"), then one must be aware of the always-lurking possibility of widespread disintegration, the unravelling of social peace, and the spread of devastating fear' (*ALP*, 98). So behind Augustine, supposedly, stands Hobbes' chaos. In this view, violence is never possibly tied to natural ends but rather 'random' and 'meaningless' – unless politically 'authorized'. In other words, a natural law or a natural moral order in an objective sense is absent here. 'Natural law' is rather equated with the natural will to survival and procreation ('earthly loves'). It is then *the state* that mediates between 'misguided', 'random' desires and the possibility of rightly guided desires.

Crucially, this view is sustained by a misinterpretation of Augustine's *tranquillitas ordinis*. According to Augustine, the tranquillity of order is the peace of *all* things. It signifies the peace of body, ordered appetites, the rational soul's 'ordered agreement of knowledge and action' as well as domestic peace and peace between humans. Elshtain here leaves out the 'peace between mortals and God ... an ordered obedience in the faith under an everlasting law'. She omits 'the peace of the heavenly city ... [,] a perfectly ordered and fully concordant fellowship in the enjoyment of God and in mutual enjoyment by union with God'.[35] Augustine insists that this peace abides

---

33 Jean Bethke Elshtain, 'Augustine', in *The Blackwell Companion to Political Theology* (Oxford: Blackwell, 2004), pp. 35–47, p. 37.
34 Elshtain refers to social bonds of earthly love when talking about America and especially to morally justify moral right to national defence. When referring to states and societies to be saved by intervention, 'failed states', she uses the Hobbesian dichotomy.
35 Augustine, CD, XIX.13.

even through the most raucous political disorder, indeed that even the wretched are separated from the blessed by a law of order.[36] Since Elshtain extracts only the liberal domestic 'peace' of unharmed individuals from Augustine as politically commanding, she must consequently rely on the state, rather than God, to warrant a *tranquillitas ordinis*.[37]

This is secured by an ultimately dualist theology. Elshtain takes careful Christological and eschatological steps to neutralize the impact of the Christ event on 'the world of politics', which oscillates between wilful, terrorist anarchy and governmental control. Salvation history is disconnected from profane, secular history. The 'here and now' is 'historic time', not that of redemption (*JWT*, 30). The *saeculum* is entirely separate from the Kingdom of God, a 'beatific landscape … at the end of time' (*JWT*, 127). With this, an investigation of the implications of the reign of God here and now is obsolete. For someone who wants to 'use theological categories', as Elshtain does, this shifts the focus to a Jesuology. Jesus the man, indeed the most *atheist* of moments, validates an anthropology of weakness: 'the overwhelmingly central icon, symbol of the Christian faith is of a bleeding broken body on a cross.'[38] Christianity, she modifies, is about a 'bleeding broken man'. The cross demonstrates the essence of humanity as weakness and death. In effect, to use a phrase from Nietzsche's friend Franz Overbeck, Elshtain's Christians 'live with a corpse'.[39]

If Jesus could be seen as providing an 'ethic', then against any non-violent *imitatio-*Jesuologies Elshtain emphasizes that he 'preached an ethic for the end time'.[40] He urged his disciples to 'rely on grace and, in anticipation of the end time, [he] directed them away from temporal pursuits' (*JWT*, 99). A form of supererogation or superhuman 'church ethic', this ethic is 'unattainable in principle, save by the few saints among us'. In this context, Elshtain emphasizes God's essential unintelligibility, echoing the Lutheran *deus absconditus* inaccessible to philosophical reason.[41] Either way, political rationality cannot rely on Jesus:

> All nuance falls out of the pleas of those who seem to know *precisely* what Jesus would do in certain circumstances – forgetting that Jesus, for Christians, is God Incarnate and it is rather presumptuous to claim a direct pipeline to Him. … Most of us do not feel authorized to drag Jesus to our own side in a political dispute with such dogmatic certainty. (*JWT*, 229, n. 4)

[36] Ibid.: 'verum tamen quia merito iusteque sunt miseri, in ea quoque ipsa miseria sua praeter ordinem esse non possunt, non quidem coniuncti beatis, sed ab eis tamen ordinis lege seiuncti.'

[37] Elshtain takes this reading from George Weigel, *Tranquillitas Ordinis: The Present Failure and Future Promise of American Catholic Thought on War and Peace* (Oxford: Oxford University Press, 1987), p. 31.

[38] Jean Bethke Elshtain, Interview with Krista Tippett, http://www.onbeing.org/program/moral-man-and-immoral-society-rediscovering-reinhold-niebuhr/extra/complete-transcript-2 (accessed 4 July 2019).

[39] Franz Overbeck, *Christentum und Kultur*, cited in Friedrich W. Graf, *Der heilige Zeitgeist. Studien zur Ideengeschichte der protestantischen Theologie in der Weimarer Republik* (Tübingen: Mohr Siebeck, 2011), p. 125.

[40] Cf. Reinhold Niebuhr, *Faith and History: A Comparison of Christian and Modern Views of History* (New York: Charles Scribner's, 1949).

[41] Martin Luther, Psalmenvorlesung 1513/15 (Ps. 1–84), WA 3, 124.

Refusing an authorized 'dragging' of Jesus into politics, the crucifixion of the man, 'that moment where violence seems to have triumphed', provides the paradigm for political reality in 'historic time'. It is 'pervaded with conflict'. Book XIX of Augustine's *City of God*, Elshtain thinks (perhaps with Locke), is Augustine's conceptual starting point. He can then positively be referred to as assenting to modern power politics: 'Augustine appreciated that power is a *basic reality* of political life' (*JWT*, 49; italics added).

In short, beyond a general, good creator God of individuals, Elshtain clears 'the earthly city' of the impact of the Christ event. It remains a sphere oscillating between pure violence and 'tragic necessities' of dirty hands installing order to keep the 'forces of anarchy' at bay.[42]

The realm of utopia

The great, unmediated opposite of this vision is the realm and category of *utopia*, the fancy flights of 'intellectuals'.[43] This deep rift is in fact dualistic but remains the logic of an abiding world-historical nuisance: 'But utopias never go away, it seems. We never seem to know better – although that is a lesson a compelling realism should surely teach us.'[44]

So, who are the utopians? Elshtain fights on several fronts with those denying 'responsible' possibilities of action in the light of perceived present necessities.[45] 'Utopians' are ideologues of various stripes. Besides utopian terrorism, communism remained a key opponent for Elshtain.[46] Her anti-communism here is also a connective point with Albert Camus, who, for his part, may be read as a proponent of an *absurd* worldview rather than a champion of meaningful politics. Vulnerability and woundedness are the premises of politics here, a suffering that desires no consolation. The concomitant 'refusal to mourn' – and eventually heal – perpetuates a politics of fragmented negativity that is both postmodern and conservative.[47] Second, there are Kantian 'legalists' or 'liberal humanists' who insist on a positive international

---

[42] One could regard this as an inheritance of the Christian sense of redemption. Since God reconciled humanity to himself, everyone seems equidistant. Without a definition of the relationship between divine justice and human failure, this can quickly turn into an 'inexpensive levelling of victims and perpetrators'. Hans-Richard Reuter, 'Ethik und Politik der Versöhnung. Prinzipielles zu einem aktuellen Thema', in *Politik der Versöhnung*, ed. Gerhard Beestermöller and Hans-Richard Reuter (Stuttgart: Kohlhammer, 2002), pp. 15–36, p. 19.

[43] On Elshtain's problematic juxtaposition of Augustine and philosophy, see Eric Gregory, *Politics and the Order of Love. An Augustinian Ethic of Democratic Citizenship* (Chicago, IL: University of Chicago Press, 2008), p. 123, n. 89.

[44] Elshtain, 'On Never Reaching the Coast of Utopia', p. 149.

[45] Agamben points out the crucial difference between suspending the law out of 'necessity' in favour of the *salus hominum* and 'necessity' as 'the ultimate ground and very source of law' in modern states. Giorgio Agamben, *State of Exception* (Chicago, IL: University of Chicago Press: 2005), pp. 25–6.

[46] Elshtain frequently drew on, and admired, Václav Havel. More generally, the links between US (neo-)conservatives and the liberal democratic movements in Eastern Europe during the 1980s were strong, providing a continuous narrative undergirding security politics. Interestingly, it did not translate into popular support for the Iraq War in these countries.

[47] See Matthew H. Bowker, *Rethinking the Politics of Absurdity: Albert Camus, Postmodernity, and the Survival of Innocence* (New York: Routledge, 2014), esp. pp. 58–71, 78–84.

legal order to which every state is subject (*JWT*, 110). (We will analyse this view in Chapter 2.) Third, there is the 'biblically inspired vision in which the lion lies down with the lamb and the lamb does *not* have to be replaced frequently' (*JWT*, 126). This highly critical stance towards a 'sentimentalized Christianity' Elshtain takes from Reinhold Niebuhr and not least Nietzsche (*JWT*, 106–10).[48] These utopian visions have in common that they take responsibility not for restoring the *tranquillitas ordinis* but rather 'world peace' as a political project.

A central target for Elshtain's critique of modern utopias is Hegel, whom she seems to read together with the radical Reformation and above all as a precursor to Marx. '"Hegelianism"', she writes in *Sovereignty*, 'destroys any received notions of transcendence (derived from Jerusalem, one might say) in favour of dismantling that transcendence as its remainders are then folded into the logic of history's dialectic' (*S*, 143). For Elshtain, the absence of a transcendent horizon – Christian or otherwise naturally supernatural – becomes the cause and chronic symptom of utopianism. Against this, she holds up the *historical* facts of violence:

> The conflict and reconciliation of human wills that is politics no longer mars the beatific landscape. One way or another, the 'eschatological moment' of the Kingdom of God at the end of time is brought down to earth, secularized, placed within time, and embraced as a realizable goal – despite the fact that over the long course of humankind's bloody history nothing remotely approximating this vision has ever been attained. (*JWT*, 127)

As she interprets the early modern dichotomy between sceptical power politics and political utopia, as well as the nineteenth-century concept of ideology, as a feature of Augustine's theology, utopian proposals become the counterparts to his 'the earthly city':

> [Augustine] strenuously repudiates utopian possibilities and, from Plato's republic to Rousseau's polity, to Marx's classless society, to Mill's happy ordering of liberal choosers, we in the West have enshrined thinkers who promised to remove obstacles to the good life, or who assured us that such obstacles were, in principle, removable. (*ALP*, 90)

In contrast, Augustine 'displays the negative of ideology by articulating a canny and scrupulous attunement to the here and now with its very real limits'.[49]

Elshtain is well aware that 'it is useful to distinguish utopianism from moral norms and ideals *tout court*', especially since 'moral norms, utopian projects, and hard-headed political schemes are so intertwined one cannot separate them, as realists (at least in IR) insist'. However, since alternatives to the necessities and emergencies of the present

---

48 This dichotomy also appears in Werner Elert, against Nietzsche's reading of Christianity as purely but resentfully weak. Werner Elert, *Der Christ und der völkische Wehrwille* (Leipzig: A. Deichertsche Verlagsbuchhandlung, 1937).

49 A comparable project of 're-educating Augustine' is Gregory's, *Politics and the Order of Love*.

moment are unthinkable, a conceptual distinction between (morally attainable) 'ideals' and 'utopia' cannot be made. This is then the point at which Elshtain's realism reverts into a political idealism.

The historical opportunity – the coincidence of reality and ideal

Elshtain remains keen to retain transcendence, even if it remains without fundamentally transformative effects on the 'earthly city'. Her notion of it rather echoes, amplifies and re-enforces earthly loves, bonds and 'limits'. Yet with various forms of utopianism rejected, the reality of politics itself is now transcendentalized and has moral implications in itself.

As Gierke pointed out, the modern theory of human society and the state 'was a theory of the ideal or natural Law of human society, and of the ideal or natural Rights of man'.[50] So for Elshtain a 'natural law', effectively a set of *affects*, finds an ally in a Christian notion of creation in a transcendentalist key:

> Emerging from 'one' creates a fragile bond of peace, or relative peacefulness. Bonds of affection tied human beings from the start. Bonds of kinship and affection bound them further. The more these relationships are dispersed ... the more difficult it is to repair to this fundamental kinship or sociality in order to strike a blow for a decent civic order and against anarchy and random violence.[51]

On the back of this, she is less interested in *Christian* ethics than in a 'naturalistic morality written on the hearts of sentient creatures' (*ALP*, 25). It translates into an earthly civic morality: 'Augustine creates a complex moral map that offers space for loyalty and love and care, as well as for a chastened form of civic virtue' (*ALP*, 91). The *imago Dei* also provides the ground for liberal 'individual dignity'. Elshtain gives it her own terminology: 'human beings *qua* human beings deserve equal moral regard. Equal regard means one possesses an inalienable dignity that is not given by governments and cannot be revoked arbitrarily by governments or other political bodies or actors.'[52] So from a created 'is' Elshtain draws the 'ought' of equal regard. This, she argues, is then congruent with the human rights ideal:

> The post-World War II universalization of human rights deepens and enhances the importance and reach of the just war perspective rather than running counter to it. Just war argument and universal human rights are not only not incompatible, they should, instead, be placed within the same frame.[53]

---

[50] Otto Gierke, *Natural Law and the Theory of Society*, 2 vols., transl. Ernest Barker (Cambridge: Cambridge University Press, 1934), vol. 1, p. xi.

[51] Elshtain, 'The Just War Tradition and Natural Law', *Fordham International Law Journal*, 28 (2004), 742–55, pp. 748–9.

[52] Elshtain, 'International Justice as Equal Regard and the Use of Force', *Ethics and International Affairs*, 2 (2003), 63–75, p. 66.

[53] Ibid., p. 64.

This is a moral and, more importantly, a judicial and political concept of a claim right. Acts of aggression, which qualify as injustice, 'trigger a justice claim'.[54] As a result, in Elshtain's concrete just war proposal the defensive necessities of a 'violent world', the 'discontents' of the earthly city understood as a global polity, now merge with a globally 'expanded ideal' warranted by creation. The seemingly fixed duality is unstable and dialectically reverses its poles. In other words, no mediation between political realism and idealism takes place; rather, they oscillate in contradictory simultaneity.

For Elshtain, in this unique historical moment after 9/11 the violent realities of the situation and the real presence of a moral ideal became identical. It became a progressivist, immanent-apocalyptic moment that could catalyze American supremacy. Since many neoconservatives were former Trotskyists, it echoed familiar *revolutionary* moments.[55] For either of them, crisis is *the* mediating event, a *skandalon* rivalling the incarnational event. And if the violent confrontation with the terrorist-utopian Other brought the mythic space of bucolic American domesticity to collapse, it was simultaneously restored as utopian empire. Simultaneously, the opportunity of this-worldly political fulfilment could still claim to be 'minimal', since it merely demands 'stability'.

Notably, the collapse of the reality of politics into an ideal order – America's exercised 'enlightened self-interest' – to an extent explains Elshtain's and Walzer's indecision about the status of 'unlawful combatants'. Because of its total comprehensiveness, the *actual* externality of Elshtain's realist–mythic–utopian whole has to remain undefined. As we heard, it is the reality of extralegal detention. These camps functioned as 'grey zones' of pending moral and juridical indecision.[56] Significantly, this no man's land of reigning and reined-in fear is not just an 'included exclusion' of enemy fighters, as Agamben puts it, or an ongoing 'state of emergency'. It is also a historical *motor* that sustains the collapsed dichotomy of violent reality and ideal human rights order in the American War on Terror.[57] In terms of Elshtain's theo-logic, not entirely in line with Schmitt and Hobbes, this is effectively a locus of the messianic. It is an 'alien' like Adolf von Harnack's Marcionite Christ—albeit an apocalyptic, *demonic* one to be fought.

In short, the basic pattern of Elshtain's political reality is a collapse of the real into the ideal in the (American) 'earthly here and now', supported by a neutral notion of God or supernatural transcendence. This is then starkly opposed to philosophical or theological 'utopias'. Yet the poles of this constellation dialectically reverse – the

---

54 Ibid.
55 Tony Judt, 'Bush's Useful Idiots', *London Review of Books*, 28.18 (2006), 3–5. The Neoconservative Project for a New American Century had hoped for a 'new Pearl Harbor' to trigger the project of global American supremacy, so 9/11 was greeted as a moment of opportunity. Elshtain never explicitly aligns herself with neoconservatism, but her arguments are almost identical to theirs. Christopher Hitchens was the most prominent former Trotskyist 'convert' to neoconservatism around 2003.
56 Agamben points out that the concentration camps under the Nazi regime were a spatial arrangement of the state of exception, an essential indeterminacy, where juridical rule did not apply but where law and fact became a curious hybrid. Hence, Rudolf Diels, head of the Gestapo, could say the camps 'were not instituted; they were simply there one day'. It partly explains why as late as 1941 the Jews could still be seen as a 'question' that needed a 'Final Solution'. In this sphere of paradoxical state of exception, as Hannah Arendt observed, 'everything is possible'. *Homo Sacer*, pp. 169–173.
57 Ibid., p. 174.

realist becomes a utopian. This logic becomes nowhere more visible than in Elshtain's understanding of the political agent and authority. Here, via Carl Schmitt, Elshtain's specifically Marcionite dualism comes once again into focus.[58]

The Leviathan as a city upon a hill

The 'rebel' government

How does Elshtain construct the moral-political agent? Initially, she declares that the United States as a sovereign state 'has a fundamental right to defend itself' (*JWT*, 78). Sovereignty comes with a 'right to integrity' and consists in 'the right to determine what self-defence consists in'. Sovereign states are 'accountable, organized entities' with which to diplomatically engage.[59] On a normative level, the United States is the bearer of universal values and human rights. So as with political reality, in Elshtain's notion of the state the 'realistic', factual and 'ideal' bases merge: the Leviathan and the universal values of human rights.

As mentioned, states initially arise from a *negative* task in a 'violent world'. Their *raison d'être* is maintaining civic stability. For Elshtain, justice *is* stability: 'States themselves … may become disturbers of civic peace, hence agents of injustice.' And, 'An ossified, dictatorial order also qualifies as a violator of minimal civic peace given the instability human beings suffer in situations in which fear reigns supreme.'[60]

Effectively, ordering might makes right for Elshtain. Somewhat uncomfortable with this implication, Elshtain seeks to evade it: '…might may sometimes, on balance, serve right'.[61] Hence, America's 'superpower' authorizes it to enforce human rights everywhere; it is a 'burden', a term that consciously invokes nineteenth-century connotations of civilizing empire. Despite attempts to not 'divinize' the state, it after all takes on the traits of the 'mortal god'. The idea that the *katechontic* state protects the world from descending into chaos precisely *is* the marker of divinity.[62] Elshtain's splicing together of Augustine's divine *tranquillitas ordinis* with civic peace or 'stability' thus *is* a (quasi-)Hobbesian divinization of the state.

In America, Elshtain discerns a special confluence: the good is mediated in America, a metaphysical body of particular moral prominence. Here, the reality of power

---

[58] Authoritative on Marcion is still Adolf von Harnack, *Marcion, Der Moderne Gläubige des 2. Jahrhunderts, der erste Reformator: Die Dorpater Preisschrift (1870)*, edited by Friedemann Steck (Berlin: Walter de Gruyter, 2003) and the mature work *Marcion: Das Evangelium vom Fremden Gott: eine Monographie zur Geschichte der Grundlegung der katholischen Kirche* (Leipzig: J. C. Hinrichs, 1924).

[59] The insistence on states as 'right authorities' to go to war is general, not just confined to Elshtain's particular case of the United States. Cf. Elshtain, 'Against the New Utopianism', *Ethics and International Affairs*, 19. 2 (2006), 91–5, pp. 94–5.

[60] Elshtain, 'Equal regard and the Use of Force', p. 3.

[61] Elshtain, 'Just War and Humanitarian Intervention', *Ideas*, 8 (2001), 2–21, p. 5.

[62] NB: Here is also an important diversion from Bonhoeffer, according to whom human rights are 'warranted' by God. Dietrich Bonhoeffer, *Ethik*, ed. Ilse Tödt et al. (München: Kaiser, 1992), pp. 173–4; similarly, for Bonhoeffer in his reading of 2. Thess 2:7 on the *katechon* has to go hand in hand with an awakening of faith [*Glaubenserweckung*]; see Fritz W. Röcker, *Belial und Katechon: eine Untersuchung zu 2Thess 2,1-12 und 1Thess 4,13-5,11* (Tübingen: Mohr Siebeck, 2009), pp. 424–7.

and stability is justified by and *coincides with* the ideal of universal human dignity. To explain 'what is at stake' in the War on Terror, Elshtain appeals to the 'Christian imagination' that structures American political (self-)imagery:[63] 'Ideas about the dignity of the human person are central to American democracy because they flow directly from the religiously shaped commitments of Americans.'

American democracy provides the ground of this religious fabric. There is no secular society but a 'panoply and interplay' of different faiths and religions.[64] Its 'great movement toward equality' – following Alexis de Tocqueville – 'was unintelligible without the Christian insistence that all human beings are equal in the eyes of God' (*JWT*, 38). Moral equality is an American foundational principle, which 'was secured in revealed and natural theology and philosophy alike', intelligible today with or without Christianity (*JWT*, 27). In that sense, a modern self-mediation of the humanum lies at the heart of Elshtain's conception, quite despite her attempts to invoke 'theological categories'.

The open letter 'What We're Fighting For' touches again on the nation founders' deist references to universal moral truths or 'laws of Nature and of Nature's God' as the basis of 'transcendent human dignity' (*JWT*, 195). Yet this remains formal. Indeed, as Elshtain says in *JWT*, a common good should not be part of the state, since

> a politics of the common good, which always sounds good, may prompt its adherents to evade doing what is necessary to curb violence, domestic and international; they may indulge in naive advocacy and refuse to engage with the least pleasant realities of a world in conflict. (*JWT*, 108)

The *institutional* locus of the confluence of politics and morality is the American constitution. It is beyond the scope of this chapter to analyse American civil religion but suffice to say that the constitution is its central 'scriptural' focus. Here the two planes of the real and the ideal are embodied or 'bound', as Elshtain expresses it. As a Christ-like mediator between religious citizens and God, it takes the place of transcendentalized kingship: 'If, in the older logic, the king dies, Long live the King, in America the "Great Court" never dies – it is perpetually "in session"' (*S*, 154). Elshtain repeats that she does not 'divinize' the sovereign. When she says 'divinization', she has in mind a theocratic absolutism propounded by popes or rulers to the complete exclusion of the ecclesial or political Other. Theocracy is 'all in the interest of a monistic fusion of power, whether into a plenipotentiary state or a plenipotentiary spiritual earthly kingdom' (*S*, 59).[65]

---

[63] Cf. Paul W. Kahn, 'Sacrificial Nation', *Utopian*, 29 March 2010, http://www.the-utopian.org/tagged/Paul_W._Kahn (accessed 30 April 2018) ; see also Kahn's extended Schmittian analysis in *Political Theology: Four New Chapters on the Concept of Sovereignty* (New York: Columbia University Press, 2012); also 'On Political Theology', *The Art of Theory*, http://www.artoftheory.com/on-political-theology-paul-kahn/ (accessed 12 May 2012); Catherine L. Albanese, *America, Religions, and Religion*, 3rd ed. (Belmont; London: Wadsworth, 1999).

[64] NB: Elshtain conflates 'secular' and 'non-believing'. As soon as one talks about 'society' of individuals holding different 'beliefs', one enters sociological analysis. In contrast, see, for example, Karl Barth, *Church Dogmatics* I/2, § 17: 'Revelation as the Sublation [*Aufhebung*] of Religion'.

[65] See also *Sovereignty*, p. 15. Reading Ambrosius, Elshtain sets the 'twinned' identities of earthly rulers and sacral offices against 'theocratic absolutism'. (Cf. also below Chapter 2 on the twin-motif).

However, with America's right to go to war (against terror), Elshtain defends precisely such a plenipotentiary force. The sovereign *will* of the people is once and for all 'bound' in the Constitution. Sovereignty 'of the law', she says, means this law *is* the sovereign. Slightly more than 'political authority', it

> takes on a metaphysical status here – 'it' exists whether an actual political body does or does not. A government may go. But sovereignty endures. Here sovereignty as a metaphysical principle trumps arguments from political necessity or, perhaps better, the two are fused: Political society cannot be insured without a supreme will. (*S*, 155)

So there is a core of will with power at its disposal which is fenced by law, yet answerable to necessities.[66] The Constitution unites and fuses a duality of sovereign will and positive law. At the same time, it is alienated from the modern revolutionary-sovereign political body, the people. This sovereign – both a political *and* supra-political will – is 'bound' in normal times.

Yet Elshtain's opaque formulation of a 'fusion' of 'political necessity' with the 'metaphysical principle' of the sovereign already suggests that the constraints of 'law' can break away to make space for an untrammelled will to survival. 'If ... what is going on is really a war of survival, all bets are off' (*S*, 85). And indeed, in an emergency the sovereign is 'unbound', as she calls it. With Carl Schmitt, the 'sovereign is who decides on the exception'. The executive then can suspend all legal provisions in order to guarantee the continued existence of the sovereign body. The government may unhinge positive law and constitutional provisions in order to preserve the nation and the law itself, violating the very universal human rights it seeks to protect. Crucially though, the emergency does not mark the return of the pre-constitutional popular sovereign. Elshtain is hardly a grassroots-democratic revolutionary. 'An emergency does not create the sovereign power – it has been there all along – but becomes, instead, an occasion for its use.'[67] 'A form of strong sovereignty' follows, a juridical mechanism taken from Jean Bodin (for his part also a 'demonologist'[68]).

This 'monistic' notion of unchallengeable authority has its roots in canon law and the papal *plenitudo potestatis* (Bodin, incidentally, thought Pope Innocent IV knew last what sovereignty meant). In an exceptional case, the government, with all its power, acts according to the dictates of the emergency. And,

> Because at the water's edge sovereignty is one, whether one's internal arrangements are absolutist, or by contrast, the most meticulously calibrated constitutional

---

With the political theorist's focus on the positive decision-making institution, there are only two options: either they merge or they are separate.

[66] Also JWT, pp. 51, 55, 101, 102.

[67] Hence, Paul Kahn's claim that every Supreme Court decision is the exceptional reappearance of the sovereign, and that therefore the Constitution itself presents a Schmittian exceptionalism in America, is misguided. Kahn, *Political Theology*, p. 10. Elshtain's correct analysis, according to which *the government* exercises sovereign power in an exceptional moment even against the Supreme Court, has a historical precedent in Lincoln, an 'absolute dictator', as Schmitt points out.

[68] Cf. Jean Bodin, *De la démonomanie des sorciers* [1580], ed. Virginia Krause et al. (Geneva: Librairie Droz S.A., 2016).

separation of powers, one cannot have dozens of foreign policies declared, nor should presidential prerogative be challenged in a manner during a conflict that undermines significantly the executive's ability to deal effectively with that emergency. (*S*, 156)

As Carl Schmitt demonstrated, such a 'commissarial dictatorship' may become a 'sovereign dictatorship' when the state of exception becomes normality over an extended period of time. This was the case for example during the National-Socialist era, when the Weimar Constitution was partially suspended and de facto rule took its place for twelve years. Elshtain, though lacking enthusiasm, notes that this is the case for America: 'Given that "peacetime" and "wartime" are not so easy to distinguish anymore, a national security apparatus having become permanent, especially so in post 9/11 America, the exception is operating, on some "normalized" level, pretty much all the time' (*S*, 157).[69]

So the political agent, for Elshtain, is the 'strong' sovereign, a 'dictatorial' state, manifestly the United States. But what about – in principle – the moral-political duties of the individual citizen, a potential revolutionary or even tyrannicidal assassin? Elshtain far from suggests that 'dissenting' Christian citizenship in the present City of God may lead a political Christian to overthrow the legal, constitutional order that has become a terror regime in favour of a better one.[70] Elshtain is in fact both a liberal Lutheran and a proponent of a 'conservative revolution'. In its nineteenth-century Catholic version, the latter emphasized the need for religion to maintain social order and hierarchy, a reactive notion of government and above all anti-socialist, anti-revolutionary policies. As both Richard Faber and John Milbank have pointed out, that doesn't require orthodox Catholicism but can be a form of 'secular theology', if not anti-Christian.[71] It is a 'discourse which collapses together empirical discussion of finite realities and invocation of the transcendent', particularly when it comes to state order. Like the conservative Catholics Donoso Cortés, Louis de Bonald or Joseph de Maître, Elshtain abhors revolution 'from below'. The idea invokes the chaotic, anarchic and unordered will of the masses in 1789

> who saw their task as dethroning the semisacred body of the one – the king – the living mediator between heaven and earth, the transcendent and the immanent – and rethroning, via a 'religion of reason' a collective sacral body, *le people* [sic],

---

[69] Elshtain wants to understand the Nazi regime as rooted in Hegel's notion of the state but admits that her analysis lacks the required depth of scholarship. *Sovereignty*, p. 300, n.27.

[70] On the tensions within Luther's work, see, e.g., Peter Blickle, *Der Bauernkrieg: Revolution des Gemeinen Mannes* (München: C. H. Beck, 2006), p. 65f.

[71] Faber, *Political Demonology*, p. 81. See also the early fascist Charles Maurras: 'Je suis athée, mais je suis catholique.' ['I am atheist, but I am Catholic.'], cited in ibid., p. 86. John Milbank, *Theology and Social Theory* (Oxford: Blackwell, 2006), pp. 55–6. Milbank points out that de Maistre's 'mystical materialism' feeds into positivism. This proximity is replicated in Elshtain's seamless movement between Lutheranism, Catholicism and political science.

the people, the general will to which all must pledge 'Amen' without reservation. (*S*, 141–2)

Instead, Elshtain warms herself to Camus's and Benedict XVI's anti- or non-revolutionary stance, their Catholic 'Mediterranean sensibility' (S, 142). In contrast, what is now referred to as 'populist' revolutionaries, Elshtain's sovereign breaks the law from above in order to preserve a stable order, indeed an eternal order with it. In America, it is the constitutional order (or Hobbesian *tranquillitas ordinis*) whose legal principles are violated in the course of securing their continued application. Camus here provides the term 'the rebel' for Elshtain: the (Bush) government itself became 'the rebel' driven by 'love'. Rebellion, or exceptionalist 'revolution', is a *privilege of the government*.[72]

In this respect, Elshtain's drawing on Dietrich Bonhoeffer is less ironic than it might seem.[73] Unlike, for example, the communist would-be assassin Georg Elser, Bonhoeffer and Stauffenberg (not least an admirer of Stefan George) were members of the academic, military and administrative *élites*. If 'with Bonhoeffer we get an ethical account of "the exception"' (*S*, 117), for all his 'anti-totalitarianism', Elshtain goes further and uses him as a mouthpiece for Machiavellian 'free responsibility':

In the course of historical life there comes a point where the exact observance of the formal law … suddenly finds itself in violent conflict with the ineluctable necessities of the lives of men; at this point responsible and pertinent action leaves behind it the domain of principles and convention, the domain of the normal and regular, and is confronted by the extraordinary situation of ultimate necessities, a situation which no law can control. It was for this situation that Machiavelli in his political theory coined the term *necessita* … [These necessities] appeal directly to the free responsibility of the agent, a responsibility which is bounded by no law. (cited in *S*, 116)

I will return to the content of the 'free responsibility of the agent' below. Yet once (with Schmitt) a shared logic of the interplay between legal, moral normality and illegal exception is accepted between George W. Bush and Bonhoeffer, 'tyrannicide' can become a synonym for 'regime change' and invading Afghanistan and Iraq be construed as anti-totalitarian 'resistance'.

Going beyond the Bonhoeffer-Schmitt logic, however, Elshtain argues that the (commissarial-dictatorial) logic of 'anti-legalistic' action extends well beyond the

---

[72] Hence, Elshtain *nolens volens* reintroduces a deeply Nietzschean conception of political authority. In *Sovereignty*, she argues that Nietzsche provided the notion of 'strong sovereignty' only for the individual. It is not clear why only the individual's, but not the state's, 'strong sovereignty' should be Nietzschean. *Sovereignty*, p. 196. Cf. Domenico Losurdo, *Nietzsche, il ribelle aristocratico: Biografia intellettuale e bilancio critic* (Turin: Bollati Boringhieri, 2002). Elshtain and Nietzsche concur in their complete rejection of Hegel to the point of ridicule.

[73] Matthew D. Kirkpatrick, *Bonhoeffer's Ethics: Between Pacifism and Assassination* (Cambridge: Grove, 2011), pp. 4–5.

borders of the sovereign's homeland, especially in war. Here it is Hannah Arendt who, albeit without reference, is to provide support for 'Hobbes *Redux*' and Schmitt's 'sovereign prerogative'. For Arendt, Elshtain claims, 'internally sovereignty is the power to order a domestic arena':

> Externally, sovereign powers function in a system of at least theoretical independence and equality of states whose relations are controlled by principles which are *the reverse* of those that comprise the internal structure of states, at least on the strong construction of sovereignty. *Justice within; force without.* (S, 114–15; italics added)[74]

So while the sovereign's use of violent force in an emergency is restrained by no law, Elshtain can idealize it by continuously pointing to its origin in the American 'foundational principle of moral equality' (*JWT*, 27). This, it should be kept in mind, is still understood as a *realistic* account of political authority. At least conceptually, it has no moral restraints towards external enemies.

American empire of human rights

If the American constitutional state mediates the moral Ought of a transcendent equality, then Elshtain's notion of 'benevolent empire' stretches this confluence beyond national borders. She is often portrayed as having been rather pacific or even anti-imperialist in *Augustine and the Limits of Politics*. But already there she left a moral backdoor to empire:

> One must simply live with this shadow, a penumbra of fear and worry on this earth. But one must not give oneself over to it, not without overweening justification. When one capitulates to this fear, one gets Empire and this in turn has 'given rise to wars of a worse kind, namely, social and civic wars, by which mankind is more lamentably disquieted either when fighting is going on in the hope of bringing hostilities eventually to a peaceful end, or when there are fears that hostilities will break out again'. (*ALP*, 108)

Elshtain here claims (with the 'realists') that one must live within a penumbra of fear. But in fact 11 September 2001 was an occasion to 'give oneself over' to fear and worry so that even when renouncing any *libido dominandi*, it may very well be 'the military brass's *reflexive* empire-building that builds an empire'.[75]

If national defence may be understood as a form of large-scale existentialist subjectivism, then this is further idealized here through the claim that American self-interest and interest for the whole world are harmonious at heart, echoing the

---

[74] Schmitt points out that, despite Locke's domestic precautions against dictatorship, commissarial dictatorship enters as a possibility abroad, apparently without that posing a problem for Locke. Carl Schmitt, *Die Diktatur* (Berlin: Duncker und Humblot, 1994), pp. 40–1; cf. Locke, *Second Treatise of Government*, § 147.

[75] Jonathan Freedland, 'A Black and Disgraceful Site', *New York Review of Books*, vol. 56, no. 9, 28 May 2009, http://www.nybooks.com/articles/22691 (accessed 30 April 2018); emphasis added.

Augustinian principles of rightly ordered self-love and neighbour love: 'The moral imperatives at work here are not pious nostrums that we can ignore when we choose in favour of narrow evocations of national interest. Instead, these ethical considerations are themselves central to our national interest, correctly understood' (*JWT*, 170). American empire is never explicitly a utopia, since for Elshtain it is merely the *continuation* of present praxis. The utopianism to be limited is always that of others:

> Endangered people around the globe will be able to count on us when American enlightened self-interest and the universal language of human rights and civil society come together in significant and robust warp … We cannot follow lines of narrow self-interest to the detriment of global stability. At the same time we must not lose sight of our national interest in favour of a utopian vision of [the] world. (*JWT*, 178)

Here Elshtain unnoticeably transits from (or dialectically reverses) Augustine's mocking of imperialist 'just wars' in the *City of God*, IV.15, into Eusebian praises of the confluence of Rome and Christianity. She would later call it a 'connection between the transcendent and the earthly' the 'messy cobbling together of Jerusalem and Athens' (*S*, 142).[76]

The conceptual identity of the Is and Ought, of the real and the ideal in the state-become-empire, however, is accompanied by an irreconcilable, non-mediated opposition to its enemies. For Elshtain, the antagonistic battle line is drawn between 'us' and 'them'. The War on Terror is about 'confronting political evil' (*JWT*, 102). As 'apocalyptic nihilists' (*JWT*, 103), terrorists become the 'demonic' harbingers of doom. Congruently, Richard Faber notes about Schmitt: 'Political demonology disfigures his talk of "political Christology" back into recognition.' Whether Elshtain talks of Manichaean enemies, as Schmitt and the Bush government did, is a matter of degree, 'but one may or have to talk about a demonization of the enemy'.[77] The war becomes apocalyptic because the state itself takes on the role of Christ, externally battling the forces of evil. This idealized (or rather, transcendentalized) authority finds its unmediated opposition also in its 'idealist' or 'utopian' dissenters. Not only terrorists have 'utopian' aims. 'Utopian' agents – socialists, communists and Christians who pronounce the Kingdom of God to be a present reality – become tacit, 'irresponsible' *collaborators*.[78] This may be one reason Elshtain rejects Origen as 'mainstream'

---

[76] Wilhelm Blum, *Vermittlung und Politik: Untersuchungen zur politischen Philosophie und politischen Theologie in Antike und Gegenwart* (Waldsassen-Bayern: Stiftland-Verlag, 1982), pp. 50–5. Blum points out that Eusebius lacks a trinitarian understanding of Christ the mediator. The authority of the emperor is based on a strict monotheism. But as analogue to Christ and 'friend of God', the emperor *after all* has the role to mediate between God and humankind. See also Jon M. Robertson, *Christ as Mediator: A Study of the Theologies of Eusebius of Caesarea, Marcellus of Ancrya, and Athanasius of Alexandria* (Oxford: Oxford University Press, 2007).

[77] Faber, *Political Demonology*, p. 70; cf. Michael S. Northcott, *An Angel Directs the Storm: Apocalyptic Religion and American Empire* (London; New York: I. B. Tauris, 2004), pp. 154–5; T. Walter Herbert, *Faith-Based War: From 9/11 to Catastrophic Success in Iraq* (London; Oakville, CT: Equinox, 2009).

[78] Cf. Brent Adkins, 'A Review of Jean Bethke Elshtain's Just War against Terror: The Burden of American Power in a Violent World', https://www.elca.org/JLE/Articles/733 (accessed 2 July 2019).

Christianity; he at least argued that their subversive politics do *not* put the empire at risk.[79]

Theologically, an irreconcilable Marcionite juxtaposition of the old God of justice and the new God of love underlies the Elshtainian dichotomy of 'responsible' and 'utopian' politics. In *Political Theology II*, Carl Schmitt makes an important point that links modern sovereign-realist dynamics to a Gnostic dualism:

> The structural core problem of gnostic dualism governs not just every religion of salvation and redemption. In every world in need of change and renewal it is immanently given, inescapably and ineradicably. One cannot remove from the world the enmity between human beings by prohibiting inter-state wars of the old style, propagating a world revolution and trying to turn global politics into a global police [*die Welt-Politik in Welt-Polizei zu verwandeln sucht*].[80]

Similarly, against humanist, internationalist idealists, Elshtain stresses, 'For Christians living in historic time and before the end of time, the pervasiveness of conflict must be faced' (*JWT*, 101). Compare this with Schmitt: 'The Lord of a world to be changed, i.e. a failed world … and the liberator, the bringer of a changed, new world cannot be good friends. They are, so to speak, enemies *of their own accord*.'[81]

Elshtain then resolves this theological dualism between creator and redeemer God by reference to a radically sovereign God, a monistic centre of power.[82] Yet at least for Schmitt, precisely such monotheism generates a logic of *stasis* as upheaval, up to ditheism. Either way, the transfer of divine sovereignty is lifted out of Schmitt, whom Elshtain quotes: 'All significant concepts were transferred from theology to the theory of the state, whereby, for example, the omnipotent God became the omnipotent lawgiver … the recognition of which is necessary for a sociological consideration of these concepts' (S, 30). At the basis of the juristic conception of the 'strong sovereign state' lies 'a monistic conception, i.e., a concentration on a singular, sovereign will [of God]' which 'squeezes out more relational and dialogic understandings' (S, 30). This stands in contrast to a Christological mediation engendering a trinitarian mode of existence. Elshtain's repeated references to Augustine's trinitarian theological unfolding remain without any effect. In *Sovereignty*, it is dropped on historical grounds: 'This dialogic dimension of God's sovereign power fades in late medieval nominalist construal' (S, 35).

The church as a political counter-society?

From this perspective, Elshtain does not need to think the political possibility of reconciling realists and utopians in a trinitarian mode.[83] By simultaneously declaring

---

[79] Peter Brock, *The Roots of War Resistance: Pacifism from the Early Church to Tolstoy* (Nyack, NY: Distributed by the Fellowship of Reconciliation, 1981), p. 11.

[80] Carl Schmitt, *Politische Theologie II* (Berlin: Duncker und Humblot, 1984), p. 120.

[81] Schmitt, *Politische Theologie II*, p. 121. Specifically, this enmity is characteristic of (also modern, anti-revolutionary) Marcionism.

[82] See Chapter 2, Reinhold Niebuhr's 'radical monotheism'.

[83] *JWT*, p. 120.

the God of Old and New Testament identical (while sidelining a salvation-historical unfolding of Creation, Incarnation, Trinity and Resurrection), Elshtain can collapse the salvation-historical moments of BC and AD into one. The Old Testament God of justice is equated with national defence.[84] The notion of neighbour love is then added on to this without any friction: 'Because the God of mercy is also a God of judgment, justice and love go together' (*JWT*, 109).

The church is always already there in Israel,[85] or rather the church is always already part of America's political mission. The nation itself takes the place both of old and new Israel, that is, the church. As the Hebrew desert morphs into the Western prairies of Liberty Valance, 'Elshtain's faith in her own nation marks a shift from the *City of God* to the "city upon a hill".'[86] As a Christological body battling the forces of evil externally, the state *reconciles* a plurality of 'religions' internally.

And yet – to quote Marx – this earthly city has ceased to be theological and become purely political(-economic).[87] Within the constitutional order, the church (or any other religious organization) is a supportive and positive institution of 'civil society' (*JWT*, 29). Behind this lies a two-dimensional concept of church as either 'spiritual', disembodied dimension or as a secular, sociological institution of power. If the 'Augustinian' is 'always a radical *in situ*', as Elshtain says in *Augustine and the Limits of Politics*, then she never fleshes out this 'radicalism' as an ecclesiology. Her 'ideal of the Augustinian maverick who lives "the ethic of the pilgrim" has no concrete collective existence. Like Niebuhr's concentration on the individual soul, Elshtain's Augustine renders the church politically irrelevant, even invisible.'[88]

'The Christian' as an individual is in fact indistinguishable from a liberal citizen. This does not mean a two-kingdoms theology distinguishes 'private' religious and 'public' secular sphere:[89] 'For it is not at all clear that most human beings can seal themselves off into compartments and be believers one moment, good subjects of the king the next.'[90] Rather, the 'bleeding in' of private religion and public politics is an alignment of the believer with the constitutional order, of 'God, state and self', as the subtitle of *Sovereignty* suggests. As Elshtain said in an earlier article, 'Real [constitutional] pluralism *gives all religious believers the space* to be both Catholic and American, Jewish and American, evangelical and American, Muslim and American.'[91]

---

[84] This is also how Kant read it, see Chapter 2.

[85] Oliver O'Donovan, *The Desire of the Nations: Rediscovering the Roots of Political Theology* (Cambridge: Cambridge University Press, 1996), p. 162.

[86] Cian O'Driscoll, 'Jean Bethke Elshtain's Just War against Terror: A Tale of Two Cities', *International Relations*, 21 (2007), 485–92, p. 489; see also T. Walter Herbert, *Faith-Based War: From 9/11 to Catastrophic Success in Iraq* (London; Oakville, CT: Equinox, 2009), pp. 43–59.

[87] Cf. Karl Marx, *On the Jewish Question* (1843), 'Only where the political state exists in its completely developed form can the relation of the Jew, and of the religious man in general, to the political state, and therefore the relation of religion to the state, show itself in its specific character, in its purity.' https://www.marxists.org/archive/marx/works/1844/jewish-question/.

[88] Eugene McCarraher, 'The Enchanted City of Man', in *Augustine and Politics*, ed. John Doody, Kevin L. Hughes and Kim Pfaffenroth (Oxford: Lexington, 2005), pp. 261–96, p. 265.

[89] Without explanation, Elshtain lays this development at the feet of Kant and Hegel.

[90] Elshtain, 'The Bright Line: Liberalism and Religion', *New Criterion*, 17.7 (1 March 1999), http://www.newcriterion.com/articles.cfm/brightline-elshtain-2894 (accessed 12 July 2012).

[91] Ibid.

Similarly, every citizen can benefit from Christian arguments without being Christian, indeed even if they disagree with Christianity (*JWT*, 121). The state is the external reconciler of divisive truth claims, the warrantor of religious freedom. It is perhaps no coincidence that many essentially theological disputes in America tend to centre on the right interpretation not of the Bible but the Constitution.

In this context, Elshtain's use of the word 'sectarian' denotes any specifically Christian ethic: 'many contemporary critics' – whom Elshtain wants to counter – argue 'that an ethic derived from Christianity is sectarian or exclusive' (*JWT*, 100). Sectarian are those 'theological responses' that are 'available in principle only to the company of believers' (*JWT*, 121). 'Sectarian violence' denotes any 'religious war', like those witnessed in Europe in the seventeenth century. Again, a dualism is tangible here: those claiming they are specifically Christian (and/or critical of the Bush regime's policies) are relegated to the sphere of 'pacifism' and thus 'irresponsible', a term Elshtain applies to dictators, utopians and 'anti-American' authors such as Noam Chomsky alike.[92]

If Elshtain smoothly channels the spiritual church into the fabric of state and civil society, the church as a *political* institution must stay out of it. *Just War against Terror* explicitly praises the church-state separation as an advantage of the American constitutional system, indeed something that is 'at stake' in the War on Terror. As already Otto Gierke noted,

> It was ... impossible for natural-law theory, if its conception of sovereignty were pushed to a logical conclusion, to recognize associations as able to exist *side by side* with the State. If the *potestas summa et absoluta* ascribed to the State was to be a real fact, all other associations must necessarily be contained in the State, and they must necessarily be subject to its power.[93]

Similarly, Elshtain mentions in passing that 'religion's exclusion from a visible public role is required under the terms of strong sovereignty' (*S*, 130).

Historically, the great contender to the state for 'earthly dominion' and 'power' was, and to an extent remains, the papal apparatus.[94] Between the earthly and the spiritual, so Elshtain's interpretation, it tended to infringe on the earthly governor's 'responsibility' (*S*, 12). In fact, one must read Elshtain's Gifford Lectures on *Sovereignty*, written at the height of the Iraq War, as a genealogical attempt to show that (American) state sovereignty has been extricated from international, papal, judicial or individual interference. With the Reformation, she notes, 'sovereignty' or the contested ground to 'earthly dominion' irreversibly flowed over to states:

> The upshot is the creation of the *Volkskirche* or *Landeskirche*, the Churches of a particular people, tied to a particular territory. Denying any form of sovereignty to

---

[93] Gierke, *Natural Law Theories*, p. 87.
[94] Cf. again Schmitt, for whom with Hobbes the Reformation had come to a close. 'Die vollendete Reformation: Bemerkungen und Hinweise zu neuen Leviathan-Interpretationen', *Der Staat*, 4 (1965), 51–69. On the 'hierocratic model' of papal supremacy and human-rights idealism, see Chapter 2.

either papacy or empire, sovereign powers flowed into the reservoirs of particular sovereignties and these became what we call 'the state'.[95]

Today's sovereign state therefore also 'rebels' against the crypto-papalist claims of the United Nations to be the final authority on war and peace. In this sense, the Iraq conflict was a renewed flaring up of the Investiture contest. Elshtain idealizes or mythologizes the state, while a legalist (quasi-)papacy instantiates the humanitarian ideal. Both approaches, however – and particularly in their contemporary guises – display a logic of frictionless continuity between political and secularized spiritual or the absolute that relies on the very separation of the two.

Necessity as an act of love

Elshtain's notion of moral action also reflects the dualistic dynamic of the real and the ideal, in this instance the relationship between defence and love. Jesus's ethic 'seems unattainable in principle, save by the few saints among us, and even they are not without sin, as all believers know' (*JWT*, 100). So the 'source' of moral action for Elshtain is not so much Christian faith or worship informing action but the need for rules in 'the earthly city':

> Living an earthly life, what rules should one follow? What is one to do? Temporal peace is a good, whether it is the peace of the body (health and soundness), or fellowship with one's own kind, or 'light, speech, air to breathe, water to drink, and whatever is suitable for the feeding and clothing of the body, for the care of the body and the adornment of the person.' (*ALP*, 95–6)

In order to answer these questions, 'The message of the Christian Savior' requires '*translation* into an ethic of worldly engagement'. Worldly engagement equals good citizenship in the earthly city or the state. Citizens of God are 'sprinkled throughout the earthly cities within which they should be decent, obedient citizens in full awareness that the earthly kingdom is, like the human beings that populate it, finite, partial, incomplete, estranged'. This even 'lifts up the possibility of a secular faith, appropriately relativized, that *all* citizens may share' (*S*, 10). During the *saeculum*, in a Schleiermachian fashion, faith – faith in general, one should add – effects the 'transformation of the self' or of 'feeling' resulting in a general 'community of believers and friends … united by *caritas*' (*ALP*, 11–12). While any specific Christian orientation is renounced, 'secular faith' provides the grounds for political action. 'Secular faith' as opposed to a specific 'religious faith' is a term Elshtain may well have taken from Jacques Maritain's *Man and State*.[96]

---

[95] NB: Elshtain's synonymous use of *Volkskirche* and *Landeskirche* is misleading. The term *Volkskirche*, now simply meaning the church of the majority in a given country, was first introduced by Friedrich Schleiermacher. A fusion of *Volkskirche* and the *Landeskirchen* was attempted by the National Socialists in Germany, as a 'germanicized' mass church to incorporate their ideology.

[96] Jacques Maritain, *Man and State* (Chicago, IL: University of Chicago Press, 1951), p. 110. Notably, Maritain sharply renounces Bodin's political absolutism, i.e. Elshtain's 'strong sovereignty'. See p. 29.

Under the umbrella of 'secular faith', charity and national defence become one. Charity adds a certain benevolence to the use of force as it turns the potentially sadistic joy about violence into a sense of tragedy. Love, one might say with Herbert Marcuse, marks the difference between necessary and surplus repression:

> Politics is erected on the altar of necessity, but not reducible to it. Unfortunately, politics offers a grand canvas on which those who prey on others can paint their gruesome picture. The ruthless leader of the robber band and the avaricious emperor alike need other human beings to work on and to work over. The sin that mars the earthly city is the story of arbitrary power, or the ever-present possibility of such. Within this common mortal life, Augustine offers an understanding of earthly dominion into which love, *caritas*, enters. (S, 9)

At times, Elshtain seems to argue that neighbour love provides the 'limits' of violent force; that the love for one's enemy should prevent belligerents from total war but instead strictly observe the principle of discrimination (*JWT*, 24). The 'just war tradition … shares with pacifism a strong presumption against violence and force, all other things being equal.' But Elshtain not once mentions the love of enemy, arguably an implication of Christ's universal mediation. The 'limits' to political authority and violence merely consist in the 'realistic', *pragmatic* insight that often things will simply not work out the way we want it in a 'fallen world' in which 'perfect justice is not possible'. Elshtain says, 'Augustinian realists are not crusaders, but they do insist that we are called upon to act in a mode of realistic hope with a hardheaded recognition of the limits to action' (*JWT*, 70). Force is deployed within 'necessary limits' (*JWT*, 57).

If love means free and overflowing naturalistic neighbour love, then here, in the state of emergency, it actually results in the loss of freedom, seeing itself surrounded by an abyss of unlawful necessities. Of course, Elshtain would guard herself against the charge that love is a mere benignity: 'Christianity is not an exalted or mystical form of utilitarianism' (*JWT*, 100). With H. Richard Niebuhr, she wants to avoid a Christian flight from the world – evidently against Jesus, who as we heard 'directed [his disciples] away from temporal pursuits' (*JWT*, 99). Her kind of believer 'neither despises the world nor retreats from it'. Here flares up a genuine possibility of transformation: 'Rather, this believer engages the world, sustains it, and seeks to transform it – all at the same time' (*JWT*, 101).

But in the end Elshtain's dualistic dynamic gains the upper hand: either idealistic flight or realistic assimilation. And assimilation it is. Her appeal to the notion of vocation, in Christianity inseparable from repentance and the service of God, becomes indistinguishable from asking people to simply do their job:[97] 'Ordinary vocations are the responsibility of believers. They should not shirk their vocations, including political vocations like soldiering or judging. Such vocations are necessary to sustain a common life' (*JWT*, 101). The freedom of a Christian, potentially opposed to assimilation, is neutralized and reissued as the coinage of political liberty: 'Christians

---

[97] Volker Stümke, *Das Friedensverständnis Martin Luthers: Grundlagen und Anwendungsbereiche seiner politischen Ethik* (Stuttgart: W. Kohlhammer, 2007), p. 158, ff.

must understand that their own freedom is entangled with political realities and possibilities. It follows that Christians as citizens have "an important stake in politics" and in all the institutions that are the warp and woof of a democratic society' (*JWT*, 109).[98] Love, because it is an 'earthly love' for one's children and neighbours, without any tension simply 'goes together' with 'earthly justice': 'As an act of neighbour love and of service, we may at times be obliged to commit ourselves to active intervention in order to prevent evil from having its day, even as we give evil its due' (*JWT*, 102). Indeed, in national defence humanitarian love is 'also implicated', as we saw earlier.

The love added on to consequentialist politics can also be observed in Elshtain's discussion of torture. Utilitarians like Richard Posner advocate and justify the state's use of torture as part of the security apparatus. Elshtain is slightly different. First, she justifies torture on utilitarian grounds: '... a greater moral guilt falls on a person in authority who permits the deaths of hundreds of innocents rather than choosing to "torture" one guilty or complicit person.'[99] But then, since she wants to protect her own children and grandchildren, she sanctions a 'limited' form of torture or 'torture lite'.[100] Her 'religious input', as her reviewer Douglas McCready calls it favourably, is that no 'malice' is involved and that a politician 'can stand before God as a guilty person and seek forgiveness'.[101] McCready explains, 'Forgiveness presupposes the action was wrong, the action transgressed the law, and the action deserves punishment. Moreover, forgiveness can only be granted after the fact.'[102] What this amounts to is that torture is morally wrong, illegal, unjustified and should never be sanctioned. But with a bold leap into the *coram Deo*, divine forgiveness is held out to torturers, a 'deferred repentance'. *Sub specie aeternitatis* the difference between torture victim and torturer is blurred.[103] The confusion of ethical and juridical categories required to uphold such a view is reflected in Michael Ignatieff's summary of Elshtain: 'good consequences cannot justify bad acts, but bad acts are sometimes tragically necessary. The acts remain bad, and the person must accept the moral opprobrium and not seek to excuse the inexcusable with the justifications of necessity.'[104] If Elshtain wants to neither fall into purely utilitarian realism nor deontological idealism (one making torture too easy, the other making it impossible), then indeed this is a 'messy cobbling together' of Jerusalem and Athens (*S*, 142).

This merging of consequentialist politics and (earthly) love is again sustained by a problematic reading of Augustine's *City of God*. David Kim has analysed Elshtain's

---

[98] *Sovereignty*, pp. 80–1, p. 280 n.17.

[99] Elshtain, 'Reflection on the Problem of "Dirty Hands"', p. 87.

[100] Ibid.

[101] Ibid., p. 83.

[102] Douglas McCready, 'When Is Torture Right?', *Studies in Christian Ethics*, 20 (2007), 383–98, p. 393.

[103] See Chapter 2.

[104] Michael Ignatieff, 'Moral Prohibition', in *Torture: A Human Rights Perspective*, ed. Kenneth Roth (New York: New Press; York: Signature Books, 2005), pp. 18–28, 21–2. See also Marnia Lazreg, *Torture and the Twilight of Empire* (Princeton, NJ: Princeton University Press, 2008), pp. 245–50. Lazreg's critique via Hegel seems to me more apt in relation to Elshtain's notion of 'right intention'. Criminality, Hegel points out, lies in objectivizing subjective desires. The act of murder therefore is as random as the 'act of legitimization through declaration'. See Hegel, *Elements of the Philosophy of Right*, § 140.

understanding between making earthly peace and heavenly peace as a form of moralism. He first summarizes Augustine's intention:

> Christians, or the members of the City of God, are called to respond to both [the earthly and the heavenly peace], and not separately, or one at the expense of another. Augustine's genius lies in holding these two contexts in tandem, so that pursuing after earthly peace is the context and referring it to the heavenly peace is the content.[105]

One could say that making earthly peace, and therefore *potentially* using violent force, can be the beneficial 'social' side effect of worship, of the reference of action to God. This reference (or reverence) may or may not result in conventionally 'good' earthly citizenship as it recognizes and brings out the transcendent, eschatological being and destiny of social life.[106]

Elshtain, in contrast, sets up an eschatological *gap* between the 'here and now' of social strife and the City of God. In the twilight of the 'here and now', all cats are grey, all communities stricken by strife. Heavenly peace having been left aside, earthly peace

> is attained fitfully in the *altera civitas* in its earthly pilgrimage; haphazardly, at best, in all earthly cities; and in its full richness only in the city of God, when the time of pressing for the human race in temporality comes to an end. (*ALP*, 94)

This eradicates the dimension of Christianity's eschatological *paradox*, the future Kingdom of God already being here as that to refer to. In 19.20, Augustine says, 'If any man uses this life with a reference to that other which he ardently love and confidently hopes for, he may well be called even now blessed.' But Elshtain never states that through faithful worship one makes earthly peace. On the contrary, while Christians may go to church without disturbance – making use of their 'right to religious freedom' – she calls them to be good citizens of the (American) pluralistic state. 'On this earth there must be compromises "between human wills" if there is to be anything resembling peace; indeed, the heavenly city on pilgrimage helps to forge peace by calling out "citizens from all nations"' (*ALP*, 96).

Political resistance in *Augustine and the Limits of Politics* still seems to be an option. Yet it is not a form of reference to a heavenly peace but born out of a longing for a better earthly peace, an improved liberal *status quo*. As for Reinhold Niebuhr, possibilities and necessities set Elshtain's terms of engagement:

> If the Christian is a disturber of a false peace, he or she yearns for a more authentic representation of earthly peace as that which partakes in the *pax aeterna*. One

---

[105] Kim, 'City of God', p. 132. Note especially Kim's careful and meticulous analysis of *The City of God*, XIX.17, pp. 126–34.

[106] In that sense, consensus is contingent, indeed admirable or a *gift* when it happens, yet suspicious if 'manufactured'.

can hope for what is possible to obtain. An imperfect but nonetheless real earthly peace lies within the realm of the possible. (*ALP*, 105)

Notably, in line with the 'naturalistic morality', the church is not the context for political action but the 'ties of fellowship, in households, clans, and tribes, in earthly love and its many discontents' (*ALP*, 49). Love of God and love of neighbour are portrayed as 'equally valid starting points': 'we must love God and love our neighbour, and the one helps to underscore and animate the other' (*ALP*, 96).[107] The church is again reduced to its social-institutional presence. Elshtain is aware that 'the life of the saint, the life of the citizen, is a social life', but she underplays the church as the *communio sanctorum*, the present spiritual union of the members of the body of Christ (1 Cor 12:13). To be and live accordingly could hardly be understood as 'earthly work' separate from divine calling or a merely 'secular' duty.

Just War theory: Edification and polemic

The specific praxis of Elshtain's just war theory corresponds neatly to this merging of the real and the ideal in loving national defence. It is 'not a meta-ethical theory' but a demonstrative 'account' of reason, statecraft and contingent politics.[108] Just war equally is 'the belief that universal moral reasoning, or what some would call natural moral law, can and should be applied to the activity of war' (*JWT*, 214). Elsewhere, she calls just war 'interpretive political theory'. Philosophers like herself are 'just war analysts'. As Elshtain 'lends the cover of ideational expertise'[109] to politicians in the cataclysmic and critical moment of war, the sovereign state and the loving empire, Elshtain's just war theory functions as a form of *civic edification*.[110] In other words, Elshtain offers reassurance that the United States is doing the right thing.[111]

But what about the fundamentally Marcionite, dualistic orientation of Elshtain's work, which has emerged so far? If civic edification is the inward, domestic task of just war theory as a handmaid of the sovereign, then in relation to dissenters, it is the praxis of *polemics*, verbal antagonism. Indeed, Elshtain's polemic is an 'unsubtle' one.[112] As the intellectual version of decisionism, it separates between friend and enemy. The polemic thrust of Elshtain's just war proposal is determining that she is willing to sacrifice some portion of coherence for it. The work taken from Augustine

---

[107] Kim, 'City of God', p. 147.

[108] Jean Bethke Elshtain, 'Response to Reviews of Just War against Terror', https://www.elca.org/JLE/Articles/719?_ga=2.143439415.349152305.1562075516-1676087201.1562075516 (accessed 5 July 2019).

[109] Lazreg, *Torture and the Twilight of Empire*, p. 250.

[110] On critical philosophy as edification after the Kantian turn, see Georg Wilhelm Friedrich Hegel, *Phänomenologie des Geistes* (Frankfurt am Main: Suhrkamp, 1986), Preface, pp. 11–18.

[111] Daniel M. Bell Jr calls it PPC, 'public policy checklist'. *Just War as Christian Discipleship: Recentering the Tradition in the Church Rather Than the State* (Grand Rapids, MI: Brazos Press, 2009).

[112] Kevin Schilbrack, 'Review: *Just War on Terror*. By Jean Bethke Elshtain', *Journal of the American Academy of Religion*, 74 (2006), 539–43; Brien Hallett also refers to the book as a 'litmus test' and essentially a polemic. 'Review', *Peace and Change*, 29 (2004), 322–4.

is mainly selective, in parts misrepresenting or unreferenced.[113] Authors she prefers are labelled 'distinguished', others 'irresponsible', not knowing 'what they are talking about', 'balderdash', etc. She contradicts herself when she argues that a glance at history deters from concrete present responsibilities but herself continuously refers to the Nazi era. Equally, she refers to international law and America's absolute right to national defence but simultaneously disavows international law and certainly withdraws the right to national defence from America's enemies.

So, quite in line with her 'liberal Augustinianism', Elshtain repeats the anti-revolutionary and dualistic polemic of some 'conservative revolutionaries'. Cortés noted for himself: *Je me trouve constamment entre deux abimes, je marche toujours entre l'être et le néant.*[114] In that sense, Elshtain equally sees no mediating third for Christians as regards their state's politics: 'One way or another, Christians, together with other citizens, face moments when they are asked: Where do we stand? Refusing to answer is itself an answer. But the duty of conscience and of witness demands more from us' (*JWT*, 102). In contrast, the notion of reconciliation – the key work of God's dealings with the world – has no effect on waging war: 'The just war tradition does not discourage acts of forgiveness and reconciliation in political life but does recognize their limits in a world of conflicting human wills, in which the ruthless would prevail if they faced neither restraint nor the prospect of punishment' (*JWT*, 56). Indeed, with Reinhold Niebuhr, reconciliation 'is conceived in terms of pure moral suasion' or 'seeks to avoid conflicts' in inevitably conflictual societies. Again, this is not part of a realistic politics: 'the consequence of such conceptions is to create moral idealists who imagine that they are changing the world by their moral ideals' (*JWT*, 109).

Rather than epistemologically clarifying the nature of and relation between facts, their interpretations, and moral truth, Elshtain's reality-ideology dichotomy repeats what she lays at the feet of her postmodern pragmatist opponents: the amalgamation of facts with descriptions to further a particular political agenda. The Christ of cultural Protestantism, as Bonhoeffer says, in this way 'sanctions the factual'.[115] Where the Christian ethicist might ask, 'What do I do because God is?', the Marcionite public intellectual asks, 'What can we do for you, Mr. President?'[116] It coheres with the genre of myth: 'Where there is only myth, there are no lies' (André Breton). Hence, it was impossible for Elshtain to concede that any government could have lied about Iraq's WMD, even when the evidence became overwhelming.[117] This also elucidates the

---

[113] See e.g. Gregory, *Politics and the Order of Love*, p. 123 n.89; *Sovereignty*, p. 12: 'As Augustine had insisted, earthly rule and dominion and spiritual offices had different ends and were directed toward distinctive purposes.'

[114] 'I constantly find myself between two abysses, always treading between being and nothingness.' Richard Faber, *Politische Dämonologie*, p. 10 [translation my own].

[115] Bonhoeffer, *Ethik*, p. 244, cited in Jürgen Weissbach, *Christologie und Ethik bei Dietrich Bonhoeffer* (München: Chr. Kaiser Verlag, 1966), p. 21.

[116] Jean Bethke Elshtain, 'Religious Leaders Visit the White House', http://www.beliefnet.com/News/Politics/2001/10/Religious-Leaders-Visit-The-White-House.aspx?p=3 (accessed 4 March 2019).

[117] Ken Trainor, 'Just War: Divinity School Professor Jean Bethke Elshtain Considers the Moral Necessities of War', *University of Chicago Magazine*, http://magazine.uchicago.edu/1006/investigations/just-war.shtml (accessed 1 May 2018); Cf. Peter Lee, *Blair's Just War: Iraq and the Illusion of Morality* (Basingstoke: Palgrave Macmillan, 2012).

limitations of para-political post-war enquiries (e.g. Chilcot) or the impossibility to close Guantanamo: the legal-political system can reinforce but not judge itself.

Conclusion

This first chapter looked at a 'realist' just war ethic understood as a 'naturalistic morality' that makes 'use of theological categories' – as an 'Augustinian Christian realism'. In Elshtain's vision the strong sovereign state, specifically the American one, emerges as the point in which realistic human constraints, power and necessities merge with naturalist moral commands and restraints.[118] While the real and the ideal here are identical, a *genuinely* other, unsettling 'ideal' or 'utopia' is portrayed as irreconcilably different, indeed possibly the enemy. Theologically, this Other emerges as a 'revolutionary' Christ. In terms of the logic of war, what is 'realistic' simultaneously becomes an intense idealism: a utopia of benevolent empire, a war that is neighbour love, the catastrophic event as a once-in-a-lifetime opportunity to do liberal good. Following the lead of Richard Faber on modern Marcionism, I read Elshtain as a Marcionite political Catholic and conservative revolutionary in line with Carl Schmitt and Donoso Cortéz – as quite in line with, rather than opposed to, 'liberal Augustinianism'. And if the Marcion-scholar Harnack saw Marcionism as a precondition for Catholicism to take shape, it is perhaps not without significance that Elshtain converted to Catholicism at the end of her life.

As this chapter has been critical of Elshtain and sovereign realism in its imperialist form, we next turn to the diametrically opposed view. Whereas Elshtain invoked the right to national defence, David Rodin dismantles it. Where she appeals to power, he wants to expand institutions of international law. The imperial 'myth' is countered with a proposal for a universal state protecting human rights. As we will see, however, Rodin's thought is subject to the same theo-logic and hence logic of war.

---

[118] Another result of this is the 'ethicalisation of law', which must be understood as precisely a logical *implication* of legal positivism, not only its historical counterposition (as, e.g., between Hans Kelsen and Carl Schmitt).

2

Challenge or twin? The global rule of law

Introduction

David Rodin is credited as being one of the key figures of the so-called revisionist just war theory in analytic moral philosophy. His *War and Self-Defense* (2002) has been hugely influential: it showed that a legal right to national-defence, if it is conceived analogously to the individual right to self-defence, is untenable.[1] Rodin combines influences from Immanuel Kant and the political liberalism associated with John Rawls but also gestures back to Hugo Grotius and Thomas Aquinas. Here we're interested in Rodin's contribution to the ethics of war for three reasons. First, it has presented itself as a counterproposal to Elshtainian and others' 'collectivist' just war proposals associated with (national) sovereignty.[2] Narrowing down the 'Just War' to the discourse after Michael Walzer's seminal *Just and Unjust Wars* (1977) – which itself drew on international law – Rodin even pronounces 'just war theory' dead. Second, in line with his serious commitment to human rights, he seeks to restrict any person's liability to attack to their personal moral responsibility. Moreover, Rodin stands in a long line of arguments in favour of a universal state.[3]

The following pages aim to show that the subtle theological premise, a minimal confinement of 'religion' to a personal, ultimately non-credible horizon of 'belief', continuously at work since the late eighteenth century, engenders a logic of war and conflict that is remarkably parallel to the one we encountered in the previous chapter. The primary mediator between Is and Ought, politics and morality in Rodin's vision is positive law. However, while aiming to cherish and protect the individual, Rodin's approach not only fails to do so but also increases the potential of violence – either theoretically or as it collapses in on itself – and the 'sovereign' takes back over. Most

---

[1] David Rodin, *War and Self-Defense* (Oxford: Oxford University Press, 2002), hereafter *SD*; other key texts: Tony (C. A. J.) Coady, *Morality and Political Violence* (Cambridge: Cambridge University Press, 2008); Jeff McMahan, *Killing in War* (Oxford: Oxford University Press, 2009); Cécile Fabre, *Cosmopolitan War* (Oxford: Oxford University Press, 2012).

[2] David Rodin, 'Personenrechte und die Kriegsrechtsbestimmungen', in *Den Gegner schützen?: Zu einer aktuellen Kontroverse in der Ethik des bewaffneten Konflikts*, ed. Bernhard Koch (Baden-Baden: Nomos; Münster: Aschendorff, 2014), pp. 165–94.

[3] If Elshtain's intellectual trajectory led her out of a difficult Protestantism into a 'Catholic Marcionism', then perhaps Rodin's is equally indicative: he has moved into private ethics consulting and the World Economic Forum.

importantly, Rodin underestimates the mediating and therefore pacifying structures of states and communities.

David Rodin's *War and Self-Defense*

Self-defence

But first, a short recapitulation of Rodin's now well-known argument (readers familiar with it may skip to the next section.) In *War and Self-Defense*, he argued that the right to national defence in international law cannot be upheld. Part I of his book provides the basics. He first examines the individual right to self-defence through the interplay between morality and legality. How far is one permitted to go in defending oneself? What are the constraints to the legal right? In current law, self-defence is not merely excused but *justified*. The defending person can be held fully responsible, and her act is 'right and proper' (*SD*, 30). This is grounded in, first, the basic right a person has *to* a particular good: her life and bodily integrity. Second, the right to self-defence is grounded in the principles of proportionality, necessity and imminence (44–6). Disproportionate, unnecessary self-defence or self-defence without knowing with certainty that an attack will occur is not justified. Third, it is grounded in the 'moral fault' of the aggressor; a person is only justified to defend himself if attacked *wrongfully*.

National defence

If one accepts this concept of individual self-defence, Rodin says, a right to national defence in international law is incoherent. Despite its 'intuitive appeal', the 'domestic analogy' between individual and national defence does not hold water.[4] In this way, he seeks not only to dismantle the 'realism' or, more narrowly, 'statism' in international law but also beyond that.[5]

[4] Reichenbach thinks the analogy is Michael Walzer's (anachronistic) invention. It appears in Hedley Bull, *The Anarchical Society: A Study of Order in World Politics* (London: Macmillan, 1977), pp. 46, 49–51; also Hedley Bull, 'Society and Anarchy in International Relations' and 'The Grotian Conception of International Society', in *Diplomatic Investigations: Essays in the Theory of International Politics*, ed. Herbert Butterfield and Martin Wright (Cambridge, MA: Harvard University Press, 1968); Michael Walzer, *Just and Unjust Wars* (New York: Basic, 1977), p. 58f. Historically, this goes back to the prince being like a *pater familias* but changes with Machiavelli's notion of *lo stato*. With Hobbes's *Leviathan*, the state becomes a person. The claim that Hobbes's *body politic* understood as a person is an analogy in the way Rodin operationalizes it is problematic. Representation is not merely analogizing, even though some of Hobbes's contemporaries may well have conceived it that way. See e.g. Quentin Skinner, *Thomas Hobbes und die Person des Staates*, translated by Christian Neumeier (Berlin: Duncker & Humblot, 2017); cf. also Quentin Skinner, 'Hobbes and the Person of the State', Agnes Cuming Lecture, University College Dublin, 18 November 2015, https://www.youtube.com/watch?v=NKD7uYnCubg (accessed 4 December 2018).

[5] Rodin in *SD* implicitly addresses mainly Michael Walzer's political realism, which drew its strength from international law, but more generally he targets the 'the proposition that politically ordered societies – notably states – have the right to defend their sovereign independence and territorial integrity through war', which has been 'a fixed point' for 'thousands of years'. David Rodin, 'The Myth of National Self-Defense', in *The Morality of Defensive War*, ed. Cécile Fabre and Seth Lazar (Oxford: Oxford University Press, 2014), pp. 69–89, p. 88.

Using the so-called reductive strategy, one *could* understand national defence as a mass movement of individual self-defence.[6] However, soldiers may actively attack enemy forces, defend empty territory or even conquer the adversary's territory. In the domestic individual realm that would be regarded as vastly disproportionate or even criminal. At the same time, necessity, proportionality and imminence are not clearly anchored in international law. Nor can they be observed in the same way as between individuals, especially if we acknowledge the complex interplay between aggression and defence (*SD*, 111–15).

Moreover, whereas national defence might be the state's duty to defend its citizens like parents have a duty to defend their children (129), a humanitarian intervention by a foreign force may actually protect them more effectively (131). In fact, when citizens are the victims of their own state, their neighbours' moral responsibility to protect them overrides that state's right to national defence. At the same time, if there is a 'bloodless invasion', at present the 'defence of persons is not a necessary condition' to exercise the right (132). In short, for Rodin, the personified, but supra-individual entity of the state tied to a distinct territory is only conditionally linked to the protection of its individual citizens – an insufficient basis for international law.

Alternatively, one could ground national defence in the survival of the political community. This would be the analogous strategy.[7] But Rodin points out the mismatch and possible antagonism between individuals and states. He argues that international law requires an objectivity of values which cannot have their basis in the diverse 'subjective' values humans place in their (political) communities that stretch 'beyond a broad consensus of diversity' (151). Only what is objectively and unconditionally acceptable in the first place can be the ground for international law – for Rodin: protecting individuals regardless of cultural and political context (156).[8] Michael Walzer here had argued that every political community has the right to self-determination, including national defence. However, Rodin points out that the outcome of 'working out' who political communities are is often a result of military, not moral superiority. Political coercion is in fact more likely to distort community consensus or identities. So rather than grant an unconditional right to national defence, we need to find another way to 'deal … with the problems of war, conflict, and aggression' (162).

The responsibility of soldiers

Rodin then takes a little detour. On the premise that war is a rights-violating clash between individuals, the moral question is the following: How is a defending soldier

---

[6] NB: The Kantian concept of personhood is not least an attempt to save ethics from political scientism or utilitarianism, the reduction of human persons to atoms in a merciless deluge of inevitable events.

[7] Rodin preliminarily notes that 'many other difficult questions' are 'raised by this approach' (*SD*, 142).

[8] One could argue, as Elshtain does, that the right to national defence is as conditional as the right to self-defence, contingent upon a state's ability to protect human rights. Rodin replies that this would be 'ad hoc and fails to explain how even consistently aggressive states may have defensive rights if they are the victim of unjustified aggression' (*SD*, 148). However, he later argues that there should be principles of subsidiarity and only those states respecting human rights should be regarded as legitimate. Theoretically (arguably a result of the irony I outline below), this amounts to a conditional right to national defence after all.

permitted to kill the soldier of an aggressive state, even though it is states that are engaging in action? It is 'a less than intuitive claim' that soldiers should completely escape responsibility for the unjust wars in which they fight (*SD*, 166). If a soldier neglects his moral duties towards others by taking part in an unjust, that is, 'aggressive' war, he loses his right to not being attacked (*SD*, 165). In Rodin's view, the separation between *ius ad bellum* and *ius in bello* is therefore contradictory. If a war is illegal or 'unjust', violent acts committed by the 'unjust' side are effectively crimes (*SD*, 166).[9] The 'traditional' 'moral division of labour' (independence theory) between governments responsible for deciding and soldiers responsible for fighting should be dropped. There is rather a dependence between *ad bellum* and *in bello* morality: if a government undertakes an unjust war, the participating soldiers become morally liable to attack. With the unconditional authority of nation-states dismantled, soldiers are small-scale sovereign authorities themselves – with no excuses for 'unjust soldiers'.

War as law enforcement in a universal state

So there is a 'moral asymmetry' between soldiers on the 'just' and 'unjust' sides. The wrongdoing of soldiers who take part in an aggressive war justifies the violence inflicted on them as lawful punishment (dependence theory) (173). However, to administer punishment for severe human rights violations, Rodin argues, we require a superior, neutral and impartial authority. And the only conceivable candidate for this would be a universal state. The *ius cosmopoliticum* of the individual world citizen would provide the contractarian basis for it. It would link individuals' agency to an authority they can voluntarily submit to. Such a state would be justified to enforce 'a genuine rule of law against aggressive states and their soldiers' (181). It could use force against 'aggressive soldiers understood as persons, and not simply their state' (180). Although the 'state of nature' is not central to his argument, Rodin uses it to counter sovereign-realists' rejection of a universal state, which he thinks is a reasonable ideal:

> Put in the language of the state of nature (or the original position), the question we must ask is whether the original contractors have greater reason to place themselves within a sovereign commonwealth existing in an international state of nature, or within a non-sovereign political society which is subject to the law of a universal sovereign. (185)

But what should we *do* after Rodin's book? First, work out principles of political subsidiarity that 'would seek to balance the rights and interests of the diverse interlocking communities – … nations, states, regions, cities, as well as the global community of mankind' (*SD*, 187). Second, for now we should 'mitigate and moderate the evils of war in the world as it currently is' (198). Having put just war theory to rest, however, at this point Rodin can no longer resuscitate it.

---

[9]   See also David Rodin, 'Should We Be Free to Criticize Serving Soldiers?', *BBC Magazine*, 14 January 2010, http://news.bbc.co.uk/1/hi/magazine/8457885.stm (accessed 24 October 2012).

The legal cosmopolis – a novel papacy

Several responses to Rodin have extended, amended or rejected his approach. What we are interested in here is the subtle theology undergirding of his argument and hence *how* his proposal works as a result.

Law as mediator: Creating ideal conditions and political (in)action

Interpreting Rodin and analytical moral philosophy *theologically* is to approach it via the seminal shift shaping the 'long 19th-century', one that is after all Christological: Kant's Copernican turn.[10] With this shift, the possibility of participating in a divine logic falls behind the horizon of Enlightened reason. Theological elements become 'regulative ideas' and – particularly in the development of analytic moral philosophy – eventually altogether nonsensical.[11] This fundamental *duality*, and eventually dualism, is a central premise of analytical moral philosophy and underlies the cosmopolitan thought developed in this tradition.

Rodin exemplifies this (*SD*, 67–8) when he talks about 'internal obligations' or 'subjective valuations' that could be religious. A person may 'feel compelled' to act in a certain way. For example, one may have a well-grounded right to self-defence, Rodin says. But it *might* be morally mandated to abstain from self-defence if it entails committing reprehensible acts. Indeed, there may be 'a duty to martyrdom' (*SD*, 67). But this is all based on 'moral reasons operative at an internal level' (*SD*, 68). By no means can such internal convictions constitute external obligations. Instead, 'internal reasons … can be accessed in the objective sphere when we ask ourselves the question: what would we (feel ourselves compelled to) do in the circumstances?' Epistemologically, internal 'intuition' and 'feeling' may feed into (potentially enforceable) law, even if merely as a diffuse sentiment – or a source of moral unease. Rodin and Elshtain are in this sense located within the same modern constellation, despite Elshtain's American-Augustinian liberalism and her invectives against Kantian reason. Both Rodin and Elshtain confine 'religion' to an internal set of convictions that cannot materially shape the constitutionality of the state or the law.

On the grounds of this post-Kantian duality, 'the reality of politics' and (objective) 'morality' for Rodin revert to become *immanent* opposites. In this mode, a perpetual

---

[10] On the crisis of modern Christology, see e.g. Christoph Schwöbel, *Gott in Beziehung* (Tübingen: Mohr Siebeck, 2002), pp. 259–64.

[11] This is to add to, rather than underplay, the varied influences of empiricism, Spinoza and others on analytic moral philosophy; see Michael Beaney (ed.), *The Oxford Handbook of the History of Analytic Philosophy* (Oxford: Oxford University Press, 2013). NB: For example, G. E. M. Anscombe's explicit Catholicism; on Wittgenstein, see Marjorie Perloff, ' "To Become a Different Person": Wittgenstein, Christianity, and the Modernist Ethos', in *Wittgenstein and Modernism*, ed. Michael LeMahieu and Karen Zumhagen-Yekplé (Chicago, IL: University of Chicago Press, 2017), pp. 41–56; the philosopher of religion Jacob Taubes formulates biblically with Wittgenstein that reality is 'what is the case' [was der Fall ist], i.e. *reality is the Fall*; Jürgen Ebach, 'Zeit als Frist. Zur Lektüre der Apokalypse-Abschnitte in der *Abendländischen Eschatologie*', in *Abendländische Eschatologie: ad Jacob Taubes*, ed. Richard Faber, Eveline Goodman-Thau and Thomas H. Macho (Würzburg: Königshausen & Neumann, 2001), pp. 75–92, p. 84.

'eschatological' gap opens up between them. In Rodin's proposal, modern international *law* then takes up the ultimate mediating position between politics and morality, in the tradition of 'secular internationalist utopians' going back to the early nineteenth century. *War and Self-Defense* begins with the commonplace (or Kant's) 'ought implies can'. It means 'what one has a moral obligation to do is limited by what is possible – and this must include what is politically possible – in the circumstances' (*SD*, x).[12] However, 'what is politically possible in a given circumstance is itself affected by moral considerations'. As a result, 'the relationship between moral discourse and politics is complex: one of a dynamic mutual engagement rather than a simple or outright conflict' (*SD*, x). Derived from many treaties and forged in political 'horse-trading, and bully-tactics', international law is yet 'an effective moral framework'. International law

> has acted as a *dynamic intermediary* between the differing and often conflicting demands of morality and politics. The corpus of international law is *a living example* of the attempt to forge a working compromise between what is desirable and what is possible, and as such it is an *indispensable source* for anyone interested in the moral problems of international relations. (*SD*, xi; italics added)

As a living mediator between politics and morality, international law also functions as a proper 'source' of morality.[13] Similarly in the domestic sphere, the right to self-defence is not a legal, morally secondary point of reference. For Rodin, the defensive right *is* a moral orientation. In line with contemporaries such as Nigel Simmonds, for Rodin the law is a 'moral idea', a 'depository' of our 'moral intuitions' (*SD*, 4, 5, 17, 20). Indeed, the political moral *ideal* is 'the rule of law'. Rodin here aligns himself with proponents of a 'juristocracy' or the 'law's empire' – 'we live by the law', as Ronald Dworkin put it succinctly.[14]

Against state-political praxis

Oriented towards what one may call a legalist idealism, Rodin intentionally seeks to override any 'realist', indeed any *political* perspective. Quite in contrast to Elshtain, his approach hardly begins with 'the reality of the situation'. Moral argumentation, Rodin says, 'need not, and indeed ought not, be constrained by the possibilities imposed by

---

[12] This seems to me to be a misinterpretation. Kant seems to suggest that whatever one *ought* to do is something that one *can* do.

[13] Cf. Benedict Vischer, 'Systematicity to Excess: Kant's Conception of the International Legal Order', in *System, Order, and International Law: The Early History of International Legal Thought from Machiavelli to Hegel*, ed. Stefan Kadelbach, Thomas Kleinlein and David Roth-Isigkeit (Oxford: Oxford University Press, 2017), pp. 302–28, p. 307: 'Law provides a means to bridge freedom and nature, mind and world, eternity and time. Thus, it assumes a role of mediation between theory and practice. ... As with other writings, the third Critique associates the cosmopolitan order in the part on teleological judgment with the final end of human existence, envisioning it as the venue of morality's full actualization that reconciles the latter with the empirical world.'

[14] Nigel E. Simmonds, *Law as a Moral Idea* (Oxford: Oxford University Press, 2007); Ronald Dworkin, *Law's Empire* (Oxford: Hart, 1998); also Ran Hirschl, *Towards Juristocracy: The Origins and Consequences of the New Constitutionalism* (Cambridge, MA: Harvard University Press, 2004); Mark Mazower, *Governing the World* (London: Allen Lane, 2012).

local political conditions. This is what I call "aspirational moral argument"' (xiii). It coheres with a moral teleology:

> Indeed, the most significant part of moral advancement often consists not so much in identifying right and wrong acts, or good and bad states of affairs, but in helping to realize the conditions whereby humans are enabled to behave morally and well. (*SD*, xiii)[15]

If the law is progressively fleshed out into institutions, the gap between morality and politics can be eventually closed. Rodin's vision opens up into a global 'utopia' – the opposite of sovereign-realist 'traditionalism' – explicitly Michael Walzer's, implicitly Elshtain's.

However, the excluded Other, the 'realism' of states and war, returns in an *unmediated* confrontation. Rodin doesn't deny the brutality and corruption of politics or history. But we are presented only with a binary Either/Or: an 'impossible dream'[16] of a universal state or a supposed Hobbesian antagonism of states. As a result, Rodin's practical recommendations morally tie politicians' hands. Doing what is *morally* right according to him, they would have to stand by wringing their hands, watching events unfold – 'irresponsibly', as Elshtain would have said with reference to Camus. In response to terrorism and its violations of basic restrictions to warfare, Rodin in this vein has merely argued that the law requires 'normative force'; for that it needs 'moral legitimacy', which is grounded in 'integrity and coherence'.[17]

A concrete case of aggression then dissolves into ethical *dilemmas*, chiefly the dilemma of either failing to protect citizens or to defend the nation (*SD*, 9, 199). Practical deliberation here shrinks down to 'personal moral revulsion' (citing Martin Wight, *SD*, 197) or personal virtue:

> None the less, we must recognize that such a dilemma is not peculiar to my negative account of the ethics of war. It is a very characteristic human problem which arises in many spheres of moral life. Indeed, establishing that the problem of aggression faces us with such a dilemma is itself a useful and important result. For, at the very least, it serves to remind us to maintain a certain moral modesty in our action. (*SD*, 199)

In a later article on 'The War Trap', Rodin sought to address the problem of potentially inactive 'defenders'. He admits that, after all, it may be morally obligatory to continue or contribute to an action that is 'in toto and all things considered wrong'. Nonetheless, political duty remains trapped in the sphere of a 'dilemma'.[18] This conceptual lack of *practical* mediation becomes more evident (and acute) when we look at the political agent Rodin envisions on the grounds of international law.

---

[15] This is very compatible with manipulation or 'nudging' according to 'liberal paternalism'.

[16] See Rodin's (critical) colleague, Henry Shue, *Fighting Hurt: Rule and Exception in Torture and War* (Oxford: Oxford University Press, 2016), p. 428.

[17] Rodin, 'Personenrechte', pp. 191–2.

[18] David Rodin, 'The War Trap: Dilemmas of *jus terminatio*', *Ethics*, 125 (April 2015), 674–95, p. 686. Rodin's example is the 2003 Iraq War, where the allied occupation had to continue to prevent chaos

Universal individual – universal state

Ethical individualism

At the heart of Rodin's legalist proposal lies the individual. *Within the law*, the individual is the central agent and point of concern; hence, it is the violation of individual rights – not of war as a collective enterprise – that requires justification. Rodin's and cognate revisionist proposals thus attempt the moral-political universalization of the individual. Conversely, and consequently, they push for the 'individualisation of war'.[19] If Rodin stands with one leg in the tradition of nineteenth-century legalism, with the other he stands in a legitimacy discourse of individualism, rooted not least the French Revolution. The Declaration of Human Rights, as Werner Hamacher put it, marked the auto-enactment and auto-verification of the human as a judicial essence.[20] In this vein, Rodin has frequently repeated the 'elementary' and 'central' nature of human rights.

The nineteenth century's shift to 'humanity' (though not yet individualism) grew out of a Christian worldview, including Christian humanism. It was a (political-) theological movement, orthodox or not. Certainly, it remained theologically attractive:[21] a mere ten years after the storming of the Bastille, the Pietist *theologian* Friedrich Schleiermacher – both with and against Kant but certainly with Spinoza – suggested his contemporaries 'repair to humanity, that we may find the material for religion'.[22] The 'cultured despisers of religion' in contemplation could still 'rise higher on the wings of religion to an infinite, undivided humanity. Seek it in every single

---

and anarchy after the unjustified invasion. In Rodin's view, the dilemma is that, despite the occupiers fulfilling their duty to prevent anarchy, the 'further period of occupation aggravated the initial wrong of the unjust invasion'. However, this would simply not be a 'dilemma' if Rodin admitted that, in fulfilling their 'stringent obligations' to prevent the descent into anarchy, the troops were *eventually* morally *justified* in continuing their presence, functioning as a 'minimal government'. Rodin's term 'occupation' fails to register this change in the nature of the action. Arguably, due to the Obama administration's subsequent political-military inaction, not least on *moral* grounds, the president trapped in a 'dilemma' contributed to the rise of the so-called Islamic State. See e.g. Michael Kirk and Michael Wiser, *The Secret History of ISIS* (*Frontline*, 2016), broadcast on PBS; in Germany and France as *Von 9/11 zum Kalifat* (*ZDF*, 2016), *arte*, 30 August 2016.

[19] Rodin was co-investigator on the ECR-funded project *The Individualisation of War: Reconfiguring the Ethics, Law, and Politics of Armed Conflict* (2014–19). See https://iow.eui.eu/people/co-investigators/david-rodin/ (accessed 27 March 2018); for a brief trajectory of the debate between liberal individualism and communitarianism in the just war debate since 1946, see Douglas Lackey, 'Book Review: The Morality of Defensive War, Cécile Fabre & Seth Lazar (eds) 2014 Oxford, Oxford University Press', *Journal of Applied Philosophy*, 32.1 (2015), 111–13.

[20] Werner Hamacher, 'The Right Not to Use Rights. Human Rights and the Structure of Judgments', in *Political Theologies: Public Religions in a Post-Secular World*, ed. Hent de Vries and Lawrence Eugene Sullivan (New York: Fordham University Press, 2006), pp. 671–90, p. 672. NB: Hamacher's muted ecclesiology, asking for the expansion of nonjudicial 'zones of indecision'. See Rodin's insistence on human rights as 'essential', 'central', and so on, also in 'Personenrechte', *passim*.

[21] Hence, a Christian/non-Christian dichotomy insufficiently explains the fundamental shift of the late eighteenth and early nineteenth centuries.

[22] This coheres with Tilmann Altwicker's observation that Baruch Spinoza speaks of *confoederati* and a 'league' (*foedus*), though not a '"world state"', a *societas humana* in the way the Spanish Scholastics had contemplated'. Spinoza also speaks of law at least in 'a weak normative sense (and refers to it) as "guidance" or "rule for living"'. Tilmann Altwicker, 'The International Legal

individual, look upon the existence of each as a revelation of [humanity] to you.'[23] Every single individual could be a revelation *of* humanity *to itself*. In the individual, the divine-as-human mediates itself. Effectively, every individual human being becomes a 'prince of peace'. This *gravitas* continues to influence contemporary just war proposals. Cécile Fabre puts it in non-theological terms: 'the individual, as a moral and rational agent, is the fundamental focus for concern and respect.'[24]

Hence in *War and Self-Defence,* (Anglo-Saxon) domestic law functions as a proper 'source' of international law. Similarly to Grotius, for Rodin both kinds of law are initially non-political.[25] On this basis, Rodin then extends the 'intuitions' embodied in domestic law into an a priori morality applicable to all individuals on a global level. So, for example, if a hitman hired by the mafia is responsible for murder, even under duress, then an executioner working for a tyrannous regime, even if under coercion, must analogously know that he is 'something like a murderer' (*SD*, 169). By extension, the same principle applies to all 'unjust' warriors:

> Soldiers characteristically fight for a complex set of reasons including duty, peer pressure, and fear of shame, social stigma or punishment. Though these factors clearly bring great pressure to bear on an agent, they are neither singly nor conjointly sufficient to override the duty not to participate in wrongful killing. (171)

Similar to Augustine's 'idealist', sceptical perspective, a state that violates human rights for Rodin is nothing but a great robber band, a 'criminal conspiracy'.[26] There is no *essential* difference or discontinuity between what each reasonable individual does in self-defence and the limitations of historical, political context. Rodin thus stresses the individual's conscience and rational freedom as the heart of moral agency. The

---

Argument in Spinoza', in *System, Order, and International Law: The Early History of International Legal Thought from Machiavelli to Hegel,* ed. Stefan Kadelbach, Thomas Kleinlein and David Roth-Isigkeit (Oxford: Oxford University Press, 2017), pp. 183–98, p. 191. Altwicker notes, however, that 'Spinoza, in both his works on political philosophy views stable international relations ultimately as a condition of *individual freedom (within a state)*' (p. 198, italics added).

[23] Friedrich Schleiermacher, *On Religion: Speeches to Its Cultured Despisers,* transl. and ed. Richard Crouter (Cambridge: Cambridge University Press, 2003 [1799]), p. 38.

[24] In *Cosmopolitan War* (2012), Fabre, however, keeps significant political elements such as the 'sovereignty-rights'.

[25] Hugo Grotius, *De Jure Belli Ac Pacis Libri Tres,* trans. Francis W. Kelsey, 2 vols (Oxford: Clarendon Press, 1925), I, p. 24: 'These two kinds of law [natural law and the law of nations] I have always particularly sought to distinguish from each other and from municipal law.' John Rawls, in *Justice as Fairness,* p. 19, argues for a 'political', yet 'non-moral' concept of justice: 'Here it is important to keep in mind that justice as fairness is a political conception of justice: that is, it is designed for the special case of the basic structure of society and is not intended as a comprehensive moral doctrine.' John Rawls, *Justice as Fairness: A Restatement,* ed. Erin Kelly (Cambridge, MA: Harvard University Press, 2001).

[26] Cf. Augustine of Hippo, *City of God,* Bk. IV, Chapter 4. O'Donovan briefly mentions Augustine's dichotomy of positivism and idealism in *From Irenaeus to Grotius: A Sourcebook in Christian Political Thought,* p. 108. Cf. Rodin, 'Personenrechte'; Henry Shue, 'Do We Need a "Morality of War"?', in *Just and Unjust Warriors,* ed. David Rodin and Henry Shue (Oxford: Oxford University Press, 2008), pp. 87–111; Ulrich H. J. Körtner, *Evangelische Sozialethik. Grundlagen und Themenfelder* (Göttingen: Vandenhoeck & Ruprecht, 1999), pp. 154–8.

subject is an autonomous originator of his projects (*SD*, 59), whereby autonomy is 'our ability and responsibility to know what morality requires of us and our determination not to act immorally'.[27] But this is no different in war for Rodin: the criminal-legal is effectively political, and the political must become criminal-legal.

Certainly, the idea of an objective 'right' in just war thinking may point back to Fulgosius and Aquinas' natural law and not least to contemporary natural lawyers.[28] For these thinkers, the individual *qua* reason naturally has access to a universal moral imperative. The idea that the international sphere should consist of several sovereign, competing and hence relative (or relativistic) claims to justice makes no sense in this view: 'An objective value is one capable of being recognized as such by all persons universally, irrespective of community membership' (*SD*, 151). Similarly, for Grotius – and to an extent most of the just war tradition – justice in war could only be on one side.[29]

Not least in light of this shared notion of an objective, universal right, Gerhard Beestermöller has repeatedly drawn attention to the structural congruence between the medieval church's crusades and modern humanitarian interventions. In the international sphere, he says, neither vision recognizes merely a 'plurality of enforceable claims to power'; the human rights paradigm attempts to subject power both to truth and law.[30]

> The basic concern of the Thomist political philosophy consists in the realization of an order which is grounded in an absolute truth that works in all spheres of life, is patterned in itself and permeates the whole world, and to which all power must succumb. The aim of the just war is to make objective claims effective everywhere in the world.[31]

The Kingdom of God as all of humankind under the rule of Christ provided the principle of political and spiritual unity that could fuse with international right

---

27. Roger J. Sullivan, *Immanuel Kant's Moral Theory* (Cambridge: Cambridge University Press, 1989), p. 47; Jochen Bojanowski, *Kants Theorie der Freiheit* (Berlin: Walter de Gruyter, 2006), see later in the text.
28. St Thomas Aquinas, *Summa Theologica*, IaIIae, Qu. 94, Art. 2; also John Finnis, *Natural Law and Natural Rights*, 2nd ed. (Oxford: Oxford University Press, 2011); on Fulgosius see *JUW*, 'Introduction', p. 14; Frederick H. Russell, *The Just War in the Middle Ages* (Cambridge: Cambridge University Press, 1975), pp. 218–19. Uwe Steinhoff also complains about the wrong claim that the 'symmetry theory' is supposedly 'traditional'; Uwe Steinhoff, 'Rechte, gerechte Angreifbarkeit und die moralische Gleichheit von Kombattanten', in *Den Gegner schützen?* (Baden-Baden: Nomos; Münstern: Aschendorff, 2014), pp. 195–240, pp. 195–6.
29. *The Two Cities* could be seen as an Augustinian argument for a relative symmetry between soldiers: the human vision of divine *Iustitia* is clouded; hence, political justice on one side is balanced by associative duties on the other.
30. Gerhard Beestermöller, 'Die humanitäre Intervention – Kreuzzug im neuen Gewand? Ein Blick auf die gegenwärtige Diskussion im Spiegel der thomanischen Lehre vom gerechten Krieg', in *Die humanitäre Intervention, Imperativ der Menschenrechtsidee? Rechtsethische Reflexionen am Beispiel des Kosovo-Krieges*, edited by Gerhard Beestermöller (Stuttgart: W. Kohlhammer, 2003), 141–69, p. 143.
31. Ibid., p. 142.

and law.[32] And just as the Pope's claims 'appeared as logical consequences of a legal principle ordained by God himself', so the human rights paradigm, foundational for modern Western political discourse, echoes the *imago Dei* in every human being.[33] Congruently, as any absolute truth is now mediated in 'humanity', for Rodin the visible, large-scale violation of human rights is a universally intelligible 'right', a *causa iusta*. The communal, national and the international spheres merge to become a single universal public legality that identifies private individual, citizen and human being – a phenomenon that could to an extent be observed in the Middle Ages.[34] But again, here it becomes political, as a universal *state*.

The universal state

The individual within a universal order of right provides the context to address the 'problem of aggression' beyond the confines of domestic law. Rodin doesn't believe that states have a Lockean 'natural right to punish' in an international 'state of nature'. Self-defence and war as punishment are simply not the same. Unless we have an authority superior to states, 'it may not count as punishment at all, for the necessary requirement of impartiality could well be absent'. This requirement 'seems to stem directly from the nature of justice itself' (*SD*, 176). Moreover, in Rodin's view, authority requires initial consensual submission; otherwise, it is merely imposed:

> But a system of law, if it is to be legitimate, must express a community's conception of justice and the members of that community must recognize the validity of the rule and processes to which they are subject. … A community's consent is constituted by its recognition of the fairness of the system of law to which it is subject. (*SD*, 177)

Diametrically opposed to Elshtain, he stresses how different both legal retributive and distributive justice are from love and care.[35] The latter are 'private' and 'beneficial' to the offender, as between parents and children (*SD*, 178); Grotius calls this child–parent relationship the 'rectorial law' between unequals. In this 'paternalistic' account of justice, the punishing authority, like a beneficial empire, 'has a natural superiority in knowledge, wisdom, and power as well as having the best interest of the punished at heart'. Because impartiality 'enters only as an instrumental value to [the] broader

---

[32] O'Donovan cites Tertullian's cosmopolitanism in *Ways of Judgment*, p. 121; Otto Gierke, like Beestermöller, points at Aquinas in *Political Theories of the Middle Age* (Cambridge: Cambridge University Press, 1900), p. 107, n. 12.

[33] Ibid., p. 15.

[34] This amalgamation was a conceptual result of the order in which all participated. Martti Koskenniemi, *From Apology to Utopia. The Structure of International Legal Argument* (Cambridge: Cambridge University Press, 2005), p. 76. See also Shue, 'Do We Need a "Morality of War"?', pp. 87–111.

[35] Elshtain had explicitly advocated the notion of 'mothering' in international relations. Randall C. Zachman, 'Jean Elshtain on Mothering and Other Duties', https://www.religion-online.org/article/jean-elshtain-on-mothering-and-other-duties/ (accessed 27 March 2018); Biggar takes a middle ground with the more convincing idea of 'fraternal punishment' in *In Defense of War* (Oxford: Oxford University Press, 2013), pp. 166–7.

end' of the child's welfare and development, 'the notion of punishment explicated by the parental model should perhaps not be seen as part of an account of justice at all' (*SD*, 178). Understandably, Rodin's dismissal is quick: 'The parental model seems to be a non-starter in international relations ... it is difficult to see how the infliction of punishment unto death could ever be justified on a parental model of punishment' (*SD*, 179). Yet Rodin discerns a merely binary choice: either selfish national interest which, as in Elshtain's case, may be potentiated into state mythology; alternatively, the transference of legitimate decision making to a supra-national, positive authority.

International *Recht* [Right] as global criminal law thus requires an authority functioning as a judge. Such an authority should be constituted through individuals contracting by virtue of their humanity (the *ius cosmopoliticum*). Simultaneously (or rather, contradictorily), this authority should stand above states and polities. As the historian Mark Mazower quotes Carl Schmitt, 'the power to decide who is sovereign would signify a new sovereignty',[36] and indeed Rodin eventually mentions that his programme is 'also, and importantly, political' (*SD*, 197). The universal legal state after all *politically* mediates, that is, realizes and instantiates the ethical community, a 'cosmopolitan society' or 'non-sovereign political society' (*SD*, 185), as Rodin would like to have it. This view directly infringes on the powers of the state in the sovereign-realist tradition; Elshtain vehemently opposed it.

In order to theologically understand his move away from the nation-state or empire, Rodin's idealism might be ecclesiologically clarified. As the universal individual is extended and integrated into a universal legal order, Rodin significantly mimics the medieval papal church, which as a 'mediating body' instantiated the moral-political Kingdom of God.[37] Particularly under the 'hierocratic theory' since Gregory VII and subsequent popes such as Innocent III or Boniface VIII, the papacy functioned by a moral-political principle of the unity of all being. And whereas Gregory had desired a *militia sancti Petri*, Innocent III reclaimed for himself the title of *arbiter mundi*.[38] According to the hierocratic model, the spiritual was superior to the material; worldly rulers had no divine authorization of their own at all but were mere 'executives'.[39] The pope ultimately held both the temporal and the spiritual swords. In theory, the pope also stepped in when a 'lapse' occurred and 'it [was] for him to judge and punish Emperors and Kings, to receive complaints against them, to shield the nations from their tyranny'.[40] Moreover, 'the subsidiary arguments touching the Pope's right and

---

[36] Mazower, *Governing the World*, p. 378, citing Carl Schmitt, *Roman Catholicism and Political Form*, transl. G. L. Ulmen (Westport, CT: Greenwood Press, 1996), p. 30.

[37] Cf. Régis Debray, *God: An Itinerary*, trans. Jeffrey Mehlman (London: Verso, 2004), 'The Mediating Body', pp. 131–56; for a classic constitutional history of the papacy, see Walter Ullmann, *A Short History of the Papacy in the Middle Ages* (London: Methuen, 1972).

[38] Rodin tells us that an 'old medieval pun equating *militia* with *malitia* is the central attitude of *ius ad bellum*'; Nigel Biggar rediscovers the pun in Bernard of Clairvaux but informs Rodin that Bernard 'is not here referring to military service in general, but rather to the old, sinful, secular knighthood, which he contrasts with the true *militia Christi* represented by the new Order of the Knights Templar'. Biggar, *In Defense of War*, Chapter 5, n. 203.

[39] Richard H. Helmholz, *Kanonisches Recht und europäische Rechtskultur*, transl. Jörg Müller (Tübingen: Mohr Siebeck, 2013); on the Gregorian hierocratic model as opposed to the model of Gelasius, see pp. 369–97.

[40] Gierke, *Political Theories*, p. 15; Helmholz, *Kanonisches Recht*, p. 373.

title, arguments derived from history and positive law, had no self-sufficient validity, but were regarded as mere outward attestations and examples'.[41]

Congruently, Rodin stresses the 'auxiliary' and 'ultra-minimal' role of the 'universal sovereign' (*SD*, 185). He envisions it as simultaneously political and supra-political (by which he evidently means supra-*state*): 'It may, for instance, consist solely in the establishment of a world monopoly of military force together with a minimal judicial mechanism for the resolution of international and internal disputes'. Rodin envisions it without a 'substantive conception of world government with a broader administrative mandate' (*SD*, 187). This universal body mediating the law also comprises interlocking communities – nations, states, cities 'as well as the global community of mankind'. These should operate under principles of subsidiarity, which balance their rights and interests. Yet ultimately, they are united under one single paradigm: 'A state only has legitimacy within the international system and therefore a claim to recognition by other states if it protects and does not violate the rights of its citizens' (*SD*, 188). Hence, an *institutionalized* international law conceptually mimics the canons of the hierocratic church as 'true Cosmopolis'.[42] Again Gierke states,

> And thus [the subjection of every temporal ruler to the Pope] in fact was derived immediately from the *Ius Divinum*, an ideal comprehending all Mankind, a Constitution which by the universal Sovereignty of the Church thoroughly satisfied the postulate of Unity above Duality.[43]

I stress here that Rodin mimics, echoes or repeats this medieval vision, but this is by no means a complete, explicit or particularly positive continuity. A political-theological recovery of the Thomist order has been underway for some years now, for example (besides Beestermöller's) in the work of John Milbank and Adrian Pabst. However, their (Anglo-)Catholic humanism largely stems itself precisely *against* the immanentist vision of an individualist liberalism as propounded by Rodin. By contrast, if someone like Jürgen Habermas stands behind Rodin – both rely on the post-Kantian analytic distinction between reason and faith – then the difference between religious past and a moral, rational present will be insistently upheld and even policed.

From the Catholic perspective, however, a metaphysical – Christologically warranted – mediation between faith and reason will require both reason and a 'human-rights' order (if at all) to be radically repositioned and transfigured.[44] At present,

---

[41] Gierke, *Political Theories*, p. 15.
[42] Gierke, *Political Theories*, p. 11; cp. Gerhard Beestermöller, 'Thomas Aquinas and Humanitarian Intervention', in *From Just War to Modern Peace Ethics*, ed. Heinz-Gerhard Justenhoven/William A. Barbieri, Jr. (Berlin: De Gruyter, 2012), pp. 71–89; Frederick H. Russell, *The Just War in the Middle Ages* (Cambridge: Cambridge University Press, 1975), pp. 26, 213. On the modern synthesis of Thomistic subsidiarity and liberal democratic principles, see Joan Lockwood O'Donovan, 'Subsidiarity and Political Rule in Theological Perspective', in *Bonds of Imperfection: Christian Politics, Past and Present*, ed. Oliver O'Donovan and Joan Lockwood O'Donovan (Grand Rapids, MI: William B. Eerdmans, 2004), pp. 225–45.
[43] Ibid.
[44] John Milbank explicitly posits 'Ratzinger versus Habermas': John Milbank, 'The Legitimacy and Genealogy of Secularization in Question', in *Radical Secularization? An Inquiry into the*

the European Union comes perhaps closest to the transnational, moral-political entity Rodin envisions, one that also increasingly strives for military centralization. Both John Milbank and Adrian Pabst embrace it only reluctantly and conditionally, *sub specie* a neo-medieval, Catholic-ecumenical empire: 'the European passport is a stepping-stone, if not to heaven, then at least to a more sacramentally mediating earth.'[45] Whether liberal-individualist universalism is ultimately *credible* as a quasi-Catholic vision or whether the two can be merged, tentatively or just pragmatically, remains a matter of intra-Catholic nuance and debate.

Besides these theological tensions, Rodin also misreads Kant in several respects. He goes well beyond Kant's essentially 'Protestant' course when he asserts that good moral behaviour presupposes certain 'conditions' to be created (i.e. engineered). Kant still connected the singular subject's 'private' conscience directly and without any institutional, political mediation to the universal public realm. He upheld – if not discovered – modern individual and always also intellectual freedom. Rodin overtakes this irreducible moment by a theoretical prolepsis into a future 'just state of affairs'. Bernd Wannenwetsch, among others, critically located the origin of this move in the very notion of 'justice as rights': 'Will [it] ... not inadvertently gravitate towards "procedural justice" with its prime interest in *just states of affairs* (to prevail) rather than *just works* (to happen)?' Wannenwetsch points to the difference between a rule of law and the Hebrew writers' notion of political justice: 'But even with regards to ... "doing" justice by way of "making" just laws, the perspective of the Hebrew writers insists that we do not understand ourselves as "producing" justice.' Producing justice means making laws as 'setting up procedures that will *then* generate or even guarantee justice as a result'.[46] And this can be the very point of an immanent legal-institutional understanding of mediation: to foreclose the possibility of political judgement for fear of a bad one. This may explain not least the audible silence in Rodin's proposal on *who* should hold the 'world monopoly of military force' (i.e. the *plenitudo potestatis*).

In this regard, Rodin also *over*interprets Kant as offering a universal political vision in the form of a state:

> Indeed, Kant's conception of cosmopolitan right can be understood as a contribution to precisely this project. It is important to realize that for Kant, the final instantiation of international *recht* [sic] is effective at each of the three possible levels of lawful constitution. It establishes a just regime of law, first, between persons considered as citizens within a political community; secondly,

Religious Roots of Secular Culture, ed. Stijn Latré, Walter Van Herck and Guido Vanheeswijck (London: Bloomsbury, 2014).

[45] See e.g. John Milbank, 'Theologizing Brexit I: Europe, Sovereignty and Nation, ABC Religion and Ethics', 20 Jul 2016, available at http://www.abc.net.au/religion/articles/2016/07/20/4503780.htm (accessed 28 March 2018); Adrian Pabst, 'Commonwealth or Market-State? Europe's Christian Heritage and the Future of the European Polity', in *God and the EU: Faith in the European Project*, ed. Gary Wilton and Jonathan Chaplin (London: Bloomsbury, 2016), pp. 109–28; Therese Feiler, 'Book Review: Jonathan Chaplin and Gary Wilton (eds), *God and the EU: Faith in the European Project*', *Studies in Christian Ethics*, 31.2 (2018), 242–6.

[46] Bernd Wannenwetsch, 'But to *Do* Right ... Why the Language of "Rights" Does Not Do Justice to Justice', *Studies in Christian Ethics*, 23 (2010), 138–46, p. 143.

between states in an international system; and finally between persons and states co-existing in a cosmopolitan community. (*SD*, 187)

What Rodin portrays as interlinked 'levels' are in fact distinct kinds of law, even though they interact. Kant writes, 'By the way, because the duties of virtue always concern all of mankind, so the concept of an ethical communal being always refers to the ideal of the whole of all humans, and in this it is distinct from a political one.'[47] The question whether a world government should be a human institution (or, e.g. merely the permanent possibility of mutual recognition) is therefore much less straightforward than Rodin presents it. Far from a contractual basis, the cosmopolitan law for Kant 'shall be limited to conditions of universal hospitality', not even 'the right to be a guest' but 'the right to visit'.[48] Pace Rodin, Kant does not call for a 'revolution' in international relations, however 'gradualist' (*SD*, 198). Rather, as Vischer notes, a 'strange medium between law and morality, a moral excess within law, cosmopolitan right constitutes an incorruptible, yet ever uncertain element of law'.[49] It certainly has an emancipatory potential that pierces political boundaries. But the idea of 'eternal' (*ewig*) peace 'remains infinitely out of reach because it exceeds time'.[50]

Whether potential ontologically harmonious relations should be reified into an external institution as the representative of a moral (human rights) order remains therefore also a systematic-theological question.[51] Few Christian ecclesiologies – except the Gregorian-hierocratic model mentioned earlier – imply the creation of a universal state under Christ's rule. For 'Protestant Thomists' such as Esther D. Reed, 'the universal church', a spiritual concept, signifies a response to the work of God, the point where human and divine agencies meet in both event and institution. Grounded in revelation, universality is a gift rather than a political project.[52] The liberal-individualist universal state, in contrast, is an immanent ideal originating in human volition. Grounded in self-enacting freedom, it is fully committed to a *judicial humanum*.

Excluding state mediation – the elimination of political form

Rodin's vision of an international, legal order leaves little space for the 'self-authorised' use of violent force for states and communities. Although his aim is to challenge an unconditional, legal right to national defence, he seeks to effectively dismantle the defensive rights of communities altogether. This is only a logical implication of his overall epistemological (and theo-logical) dualism between material, rational humanity and God (whether reduced to diffuse incomprehensibility or a pre-modern, now

---

[47] Immanuel Kant, *Die Religion innerhalb der Grenzen der bloßen Vernunft* (Stuttgart: Philipp Reclam Jr., 2007), p. 122. In seeing that the moral *polis* was the church, Kant remains *theologically* explicit.
[48] Immanuel Kant, *Zum ewigen Frieden* (Stuttgart: Philipp Reclam Jr, 2008), AA, vol. VIII, p. 358.
[49] Vischer, 'Systematicity to Excess', p. 326.
[50] Ibid., p. 310.
[51] Beestermöller, 'Die humanitäre Intervention', p. 143.
[52] Esther D. Reed, *The Ethics of Human Rights: Contested Doctrinal and Moral Issues* (Waco, TX: Baylor University Press, 2007), p. 119. NB: The difference between Biggar and Reed: Esther D. Reed, 'In Defence of the Laws of War', *Studies in Christian Ethics*, 28.3 (2015), 298–304, https://doi.org/10.1177/0953946814565314.

irrational proposition). The goods 'incarnate' and mediated in political communities are a direct challenge to this vision. The highest moral *desideratum* is a regime of international criminal law.

Rodin's scepticism about states and communities can comfortably point to historical experiences of nation-states as monstrous perpetrators of violence. The two World Wars and the Cold War remain classic negative foils but also 'rogue states' such as North Korea or Burma as well as 'nationalism' (or a form of tribalism) in the Balkans. At the same time, Rodin rejects older just war thinkers such as Augustine on governmental authority, shortening or rather distorting him to commanding unconditional obedience to kings in place by divine right.[53] For Augustine, Rodin purports, 'Monarchs rule by divine authority, and even if the ruler in question is an "ungodly king", "the iniquity of giving the orders will make the king guilty while the rank of a servant in the civil order will show the soldier to be innocent"' (*SD*, 168). Either way, these arguments lose their validity as they are premised on the existence of God (*SD*, 169).

But Rodin doesn't merely call political authorities to harness human rights as they fulfil their duties to defend the nation. He rather wholly *discards* four arguments that could legally and morally ground a 'natural' right to national defence. These arguments are (a) the defence of political association as such, (b) the specific character of a common life, (c) communal integrity and self-determination and finally what he calls (d) the 'myth' of discrete communities. Rodin deposits these premises of political realism (or even natural law) into three apolitical dimensions: the amoral-factual, the subjective and the historically contingent. But with this he also discards the communal and institutional forms mediating between the individual and the universal. The political, again in complete reversal to Elshtain, is literally 'utopianized'.

First, Rodin addresses modern sovereignty. Derived from early modern natural law and state theory, it has morphed into a positivist 'legitimate authority' within an international order that grants national defence to any holder of the monopoly of force. In theory, a state's sovereignty comprising 'territorial integrity and political independence' could be an end of national defence. However, Rodin claims, the state or political authorities have no independent 'normative foundation' (*SD*, 115). They have no 'inherent right' (of self-defence) or 'natural right', as the French version of the UN Charter still holds (*SD*, 116). The notion of 'sovereignty' (Rodin explicitly mentions Jean Bodin) is 'incapable … of providing a substantive moral grounding for the right [to national-defense]' (*SD*, 118). Equating legitimacy and power, he simply *asserts* that 'sovereignty is a factual and not a normative concept'. And then why should a state de facto capable of asserting independence and control over a territory 'be seen as possessing the right to them, and, moreover, the right to defend them with lethal force?' (*SD*, 119).[54] In the same sweep, Rodin then rejects the Realist school of International Relations and Military Strategy that 'views states as centres of power in

---

[53] Von Gierke sees in the 'medieval husk an "antique-modern" kernel' that is the basis of 'a newer edifice which was built upon a foundation of Natural Law'. Notably, he points out, both divine right and papal absolutism are 'the first forces to tread the road that leads away from the Middle Age'. Gierke, *Political Theories*, pp. 4–5.

[54] See also, Rodin, 'The Myth of National Self-Defense'.

a dynamic system, continuously asserting and defending themselves against other centres of power' (*SD*, 120).

Rodin then goes further eliminating the 'natural' grounds for political authority or action[55] (*SD*, 141–62). His chapter 'War and the Common Life' throws the baby (the non-contractarian grounds of political authority) out with the bathwater (of contemporary 'statist' international law). The moral opposite of factual sovereignty, the 'value' of community, here becomes purely *subjective*. Rodin's framework again allows only for a binary choice: either a formal liberal individualism or communitarianism and even collectivism.

In this context, Hegel's 'strong organic view of the state' is inacceptable from the start: 'the rights and value of individuals are seen as stemming from their relationship to, or analogy with, the community of which they are part.' For Rodin, this inevitably entails that self-sacrifice for the common good becomes a totalitarian demand and that the individual life has no prior value (*SD*, 143). For Hegel, notably, freedom was *mediated* in the *state*, something even Habermas has readily conceded. Unsurprisingly, as Rodin moves away from Habermas (and Rawls), Hegel's view clashes most fundamentally with international law as the moral-political mediator.[56]

As to his moral grounding, Rodin turns to 'methodological individualism' (*SD*, 147). Specifically, the 'humanistic principle', formulated by Joseph Raz, is 'the claim that the explanation and justification of the goodness or badness of anything derives ultimately from its contribution, actual or possible, to human life and its quality'. The principle

> serves to remind us that all goods and value in human affairs derive ultimately from persons and the valuations they individually and collectively make. An adequate conception of the common life will see it as something whose value is separate from, and irreducible to, the value of the particular individuals that make it up, yet its worth must be seen as deriving from the value it has for them. (*SD*, 144)

The importance of this 'methodological' move can hardly be overestimated: here the liberal-individualist self-mediation of the humanum has been completed. In a constructivist mode, Rodin subjectivizes the political; individuals 'value' something that has no prior intrinsic goodness.[57]

Of course, Rodin concedes that the state *could* be 'a significant centre of moral value'. After all, it provides the basic goods of security and order, protecting individuals from the 'state of nature'. Hence, even a state that preserves order with minimal success could have the right to national defence. This was Elshtain's (Hobbesian) premise to

---

[55] Cf. Chapter 5. O'Donovan's three 'natural authorities' prerequisite for an authorized political act were power, a right and tradition.

[56] Cf. *Philosophy of Right*, mediated to the Anglo-Saxon tradition largely through Russell. For a more differentiated analysis of Hegel on international law, see e.g. Sergio Dellavalle, 'The Plurality of States and the World Order of Reason: On Hegel's Understanding of International Law and Relations', in *System, Order, and International Law*, ed. Stefan Kadelbach et al. (Oxford: Oxford University Press, 2017), pp. 352–79.

[57] Rather than criticising Rodin's view here, Biggar chooses to superimpose a different one on Rodin. See Biggar, *In Defense of War*, Chapter 5.

reclaim national defence, at least for the United States. However, in Rodin's view, the aim of aggression is hardly the destruction of political society as such. The aggressor 'merely' wants to conquer and rule. And since the minimal Hobbesian account does not ask *who* provides rule and order, an act of aggression 'would seem to generate a duty to capitulate swiftly, so as to usher in the new order quickly and painlessly' (*SD*, 147). This would have been the case for many tribes incorporated into the Roman Empire. 'It is difficult to see how such a community could justify a right of defense against invasion in light of an account of national-defense based on the Hobbesian theory of state legitimacy' (*SD*, 147). And of course, American empire as suggested by Elshtain (Chapter 1), operated precisely on those grounds. Similarly, present arguments for a European military centralization merely claim greater 'efficiency' for providing security. An explicit *libido dominandi* is of course nowhere to be seen.[58]

Rodin is well aware that national defence is not just about defending any old order but 'a particular form of order; ... *our* order' (*SD*, 149). Beyond security, 'the character of common lives' may be a good ground for national defence. 'Many of the goods which give meaning to our lives are dependent on our participation in a community' (*SD*, 149). We value the *particular* character of our common life, because beyond security, personal life, judgement and culture requires 'a shared linguistic and conceptual framework' (149). The common life 'stems from our need as humans for an ongoing history or "story" within which we can locate our lives and from which they can draw meaning' (*SD*, 150). Rodin counters this with a breathtakingly facile observation: 'Why should we feel justified in defending a distinctive form of common life when humans are evidently capable of locating their lives within new and different cultural communities, as immigrants often do?' (*SD*, 150).

Rodin's lack of awareness of potentially grave problems with migration (for emigrants, immigrants, countries of origin as well as transit and destination) shows the practical limits of his argument. Additionally, Rodin nonchalantly sweeps away objective grounds for the prohibition of forced displacement, though recently he has somewhat attenuated this implication by including the defence against forced displacement into individual, self-defensive rights against 'genocidal aggression'. Moreover, even if one conceded to Rodin that a particular 'distinctive form of common life' were morally indefensible, then an improved or another one might be.[59]

Yet none of this affects his view on the right to national defence; here, the value of a common life 'principally a subjective, not an objective, value'. It is not necessarily recognizable by someone 'not a participant in that particular common life' (*SD*, 151). It may be 'possible (and even natural)' for members of oppressive communities to value theirs. But Rodin, now drawing on Marx,[60] ascribes that to 'false consciousness':

---

[58] See e.g. https://ec.europa.eu/transport/modes/road/news/2017-11-10-improve-military-mobility_en; Judy Dempsey, 'Judy Asks: Does the EU Need Its Own Army?', *Carnegie Europe*, 10 March 2015, http://carnegieeurope.eu/strategiceurope/59312?lang=en (accessed 17 April 2018).

[59] The recognition of a common form of life as a fundamental human need is evident e.g. in many jurisdictions' restrictions on solitary confinement – applicable also to the 'unjust soldiers' Rodin would like to see tried as criminals.

[60] Rodin here confirms Elshtain's suspicion that liberal internationalism is leftist; both regard Hegel as a common enemy: Rodin sees him as a right-wing statist, Elshtain as a proto-Marxist.

Seeking to ground an objective right to defense (one purporting to have normative force across cultural boundaries) upon such a subjective value judgment (one which is valid only within a particular culture or common life) is a relativist and illegitimate form of argument. (*SD*, 153)[61]

Effectively, the political community here is subjective, private and even relativistic. The determined, intermediate forms in which the 'universal' is mediated and realized may be political facts, but as objective goods they become derivative and in consequence arbitrary. Against the 'symmetry theory' that permits 'unjust' soldiers to attack 'just' soldiers, Rodin reiterates, 'Even if one holds that normative relations in war are necessarily mediated through super-personal entities such as the state or nation, one must still explain why individual soldiers in war no longer possess their ordinary human right not to be killed.'[62]

The ecclesiological parallel is once again tangible here. Shouldn't one give up house, property and country for the Kingdom of God?[63] Should not even the family be looked upon with suspicion since it is 'one of the great sources of idolatry'?[64] In that sense, Rodin denies that a right to national defence has any grounds at all, yet again his humanistic idealism *politically* reifies these moral relations, *over against* even theologically justifiable political goods 'worth fighting for' (the community, the common good, the nation). Again, he goes well beyond both Kant and Rawls here, who, despite a universalist moral perspective, far from override the (state-)political. Both uphold an objective common good whose worth can be legally recognized, including to the point of defence.[65] For Kant, it was certainly possible to regard interpersonal and therefore communal-political relationships as objective as 'humanity' itself.[66]

---

[61] NB: Again the logic of thought here: a non-negotiable *dichotomy* of relativist subjectivism and universalist objectivism.

[62] David Rodin, 'The Liability of Ordinary Soldiers for Crimes of Aggression', *Washington University Global Studies Law Review*, 6 (2007), 591–607. http://openscholarship.wustl.edu/law_globalstudies/vol6/iss3/11.

[63] Matthew, 19, 29. Cf. Francis Lieber to Samuel B. Ruggles: 'Internationalism is part of a white man's religion, for it is the application of the Gospels to the intercourse of nations' (1871). Cited in Mazower, *Governing the World*, p. 67, from Merle Curti, 'Francis Lieber and Nationalism', *Huntington Library Quarterly*, 4.3 (1941), 263–92, p. 249, where it reads 'Gosple'; see also Benjamin Allen Coates, *Legalist Empire: International Law and American Foreign Relations in the Early Twentieth Century* (Oxford, New York: Oxford University Press, 2016), p. 22.

[64] Stanley Hauerwas, *Dispatches from the Front*, cited in Gary Dorrien, *Social Ethics in the Making: Interpreting an American Tradition* (Malden, MA: Blackwell-Wiley, 2009), p. 482.

[65] Rawls suggested a metacommunity of love or solidarity rather than a pure privacy of values, which Dombrowski notes is indeed the Kantianism in his *Theory of Justice*. Daniel A. Dombrowski, *Rawls and Religion: The Case for Political Liberalism* (Albany: State University of New York Press, 2001). Rodin explicitly criticizes Rawls for having states rather than individuals form a commonwealth, since a state's 'interest in its own continued existence which may be in conflict with those of its citizens' (*SD*, 185 n. 39).

[66] Hollenbach makes this point when reading Kant's categorical imperative parallel to Maritain. Kant has the interpersonal relationships in view when talking about humanity rather than individual humans as objective ends. David Hollenbach, *The Common Good and Christian Ethics* (Cambridge: Cambridge University Press, 2002), p. 80. Immanuel Kant, *The Moral Law, or, Kant's Groundwork of the Metaphysic of Morals*, ed Herbert James Paton (London: Hutchinson, 1948), pp. 96–7.

The third argument grounding the right to national defence is also Michael Walzer's. Valuing communal integrity, Walzer thinks every community has a right to self-determination. If that is under attack, they may defend themselves. Citizens also have the right to rebel against their government 'if there is no "fit" between the common life and the state'. Rodin concedes again that 'freedom, autonomy and self-determination are objective transcultural goods in this way' (SD, 155). But for Rodin the 'working out' of this self-determination is 'an eminently political process' and therefore *intrinsically* problematic: 'It involves the manoeuvring of interest groups, the mobilizing of social and economic forces, and, in its most extreme form, civil war' (SD, 157). Rodin implies that the processes of power and violent force undermine a truly moral self-determination; the use of violent force as a continuation of politics itself is suspicious. Hence, he complains that Walzer 'seems to be reducing collective self-determination ultimately to coercion and the balance of force' (SD, 157).

Finally, Rodin attacks what he calls the 'myth of concrete communities'. He correctly notes that '[social] life is not broken into discrete units which might potentially coincide with the boundaries of states' (SD, 159). So why – of all entities – should it be the state to be given a universal (i.e. international-legal) right to defend itself? The individual is tied into several communities ranging from family to country 'and perhaps also the global community of mankind'. There are also other 'horizontally ordered communities' such as classes, ethnic groups, trade unions, and so on. It is perhaps not without significance that Rodin counts the church into this, amalgamating again the political and spiritual. In so far as he targets the legal right to national defence, Rodin's point is convincing:

> Because the present account located the grounding of the right of national-defense
> in the existence of a genuine community capable of exercising a form of collective
> autonomy, it is difficult to see why such groups should be denied an analogous
> right to defend their integrity with force. (SD, 160)

However, a *moral* rather than legal account of the just war would say: Yes, indeed, why not? If a particular community of any kind or size is under special attack – especially an ethnic group or a class – their communal defence is hardly impermissible.

Rodin's logic of legal mediation again proves to be problematic here. He cannot say, 'Legally, only some institutional authorities have the right to self-defend. But morally, it might sometimes be right for non-state communities to fight a defensive war, even if illegally'. Since the law mediates between (power-)'politics' and 'morality', the moral must become legal and vice versa – an understanding that gears towards its own globalized legal positivism.[67] Consequently, Rodin declares communal ties to be historically contingent and therefore politically, that is, enforceable *in extremis*, irrelevant.[68] Because '[in] different contexts any one of these communal associations

---

[67] For some adherents to 'Kantianism', legal positivism becomes possible and necessary since they interpret positive law as a regulator of normative disagreement. See e.g. Jeremy Waldron, 'Kant's Legal Positivism', *Harvard Law Review*, 109 (1996), 1535–66; NB: Joseph Raz bills himself as a legal positivist.

[68] Notably, although Rodin mentions the 'necessary mediation of personal relationships through the state' (SD, 129), his argument against such a mediation later stands on shaky grounds: for people do

may be most important to me and each plays a significant role in defining my identity' (*SD*, 159), *none* of them can be 'objectively', that is, legally, recognized. From Linda Colley he adopts the historicist point specifically about nationhood underlying the nation-state: 'Historically speaking, most nations have always been culturally and ethnically diverse, problematic, protean and artificial constructs that take shape very quickly and come apart just as fast' (*SD*, 161). Rodin's normative alternative to a positivist, totalitarian state is therefore not a demand for a state informed by more *iustitia* but to completely alienate the enforcement of 'human rights' to an enlarged supra-state.

The fact that he finds no potentially political connection between the individual person and her various communities results in an odd distortion of history. A justified collective fight for life (in response to a collectively aimed attack) for Rodin is non-political. Even in obvious cases, he is forced to return to the very individualist 'reductive strategy' of self-defence:

> Thus, when the Jews of the Warsaw ghetto fought against the assault of the German army, they were quite literally fighting for their lives. In such a case it would indeed be possible to dispense with the vocabulary of national-defense, for it is possible to understand their actions as justified wholly within the conceptual scheme of individual rights. (*SD*, 139–40)[69]

Yet this was precisely a political-communal act tied to 'natural ends'. Incidentally, it also provided the very community-shaping narratives Rodin recognizes as an indispensable part of communal existence – in this case a significant part of contemporary Israel's identity. But Rodin's idealist, abstract citizenship cannot account for the historical, political (and narrative) significance of such 'collective acts of self-defense'. Indeed, any historical *meaning* of political action dissolves into the mechanistic interplay between 'aggression' and 'defence'.[70]

In the same vein, the *duties* associated with political citizenship become arbitrary. Universal goods on the one hand and the 'private', political, subjective remain unmediated. Rodin finds particularly the draft simply 'pernicious' (*SD*, 165); for him, there is only a binary choice between statism and moral individualism, between an

---

not seek to defend the specific 'character' of their common lives but their community per se (and its freedom, a term that seems to lose currency). He notes that certain goods (value judgements, art, friendship, value judgements [*SD*, 149]) require a common life. Hence, these goods are obviously universal, encoded also in various international legal frameworks. It is simply a logical fallacy to claim that because of a non-universal *character* of certain goods, these goods themselves are not universal. For example, I may recognize the value of family across cultures (and its defence), even if family structures vary widely.

[69] Again in Rodin, 'The Myth of National Self-Defence', pp. 69–89, p. 80.

[70] Michael Beaney points out that 'the distinction between psychological genesis and logical justification' is 'one of the most fundamental presuppositions of analytic philosophy from which its ahistoricism follows', though, as Beaney shows, the distinction itself has historical origins. Michael Beaney, 'The Historiography of Analytic Philosophy', in *The Oxford Handbook of the History of Analytic Philosophy* (Oxford: Oxford University Press, 2013), p. 58.

all-absorbing militarist machine and everyone fighting a war of their free moral choice.[71] In effect, there is little space for positive duties related to *objective* goods: associates, the community, communal property, the country or neighbouring countries. These objective 'interpretaments [*Interpretamente*] of a fundamental institutionality' contain and elicit responsibility or what Seth Lazar has called 'associative duties'; the human being is essentially inseparable from them.[72] In that sense, Kant still saw political belonging in quite a positive light. While recognizing the belligerence of standing armies, he embraced 'state citizens' voluntary, periodical practice in using arms in order to protect themselves and their fatherland from foreign attacks'.[73] In terms of discrimination, this is reflected in the Grotian 'median guilt' of the soldier: he is *inextricably* part of a community and hence is liable for his material cooperation in hostile activity only.

So the political realism of sovereign states remains the unmediated Other to Rodin's idealism-not-yet fully realized. In a correspondence with Uwe Steinhoff, he argued that states have legitimacy as war-making authorities because they are state institutions: 'The state has an internal set of checks and balances, and in traditional just war theory the authority of the state comes from the fact that it is defending the community and is properly constituted to do so'.[74] If Elshtain had to accept 'utopia' as an ever-recurring world historical nuisance, then it seems Rodin conversely has to accept the existing 'legitimate authority' of the state. He has to concede the extremely limited effect of international legal institutions such as the International Criminal Court and the practical impossibility to try all 'unjust soldiers'. This echoes not least the medieval church's practical effects. Despite a frequent triumphalism in theory, it remained confined to 'tears and prayers',[75] and the canonists expressed frequent 'sadness' about the non-compliance of those wielding the *gladius materialis*.[76]

In short, Rodin's idealist notion of the political agent begins with a Kantian individual and their moral insight. Since morality and politics at the international level are mediated as a legal framework that 'allows people to behave well', Rodin places individuals and especially 'the soldier' within a cosmopolitan universal state. This, I have shown, is akin to the structure and place of the medieval papacy as conceived in the hierocratic model. As supra-political, it is nonetheless fully political, representing all of humankind conceived as subject to a (formerly) divine(-legal), though now immanent legal principle. It blankets out any realist dimension of political authority and hence defensive rights. Moreover, despite frequently drawing on Kant, Rodin fundamentally misreads him.

---

[71] Rodin has recently qualified this approach: western states may well oblige military recruits only to participate in operations that 'have obvious defensive aims' or are 'authorised in a predetermined form'. Rodin, 'Personenrechte', p. 189.

[72] Körtner, *Evangelische Sozialethik*, p. 53; Seth Lazar, 'War and Associative Duties' (unpublished doctoral thesis, University of Oxford, 2009); Seth Lazar, 'Evaluating the Revisionist Critique of Just War Theory', *Daedalus*, 146.1 (2017), 113–24.

[73] Kant, *Zum ewigen Frieden*, p. 5.

[74] Uwe Steinhoff, *Ethik des Krieges und des Terrorismus* (Stuttgart: Kohlhammer, 2011), p. 140 n. 35.

[75] These were the only arms clerics were allowed according to the *Decretum Gratiani*, C. 23 q. 8 c. 3, which paraphrases St Ambrose.

[76] Cf. Helmholz, *Kanonisches Recht*, pp. 397–8.

Anti-war-ism and the cataclysmic event

The methodological individualization of war has a particular aim. If only those people can be legitimately targeted who have done wrong, then war as we know it, with its random deaths, its innocent and non-combatant victims, its unpredictable length and outcome, is irrational and unjustifiable. Rodin explicitly argued in 2010 that the aim should be to eliminate war and armed conflict altogether.[77]

This conviction stands behind his argument that every soldier may see the rightness or wrongness of a war. In this way, responsibility becomes culpability and responsibility combined, that is, being materially and causally imputable. This is expressed elastically rather than precisely: 'But moral responsibility … is a plastic attribute operating along the twin paths of causation and intention that can extend, multiply, and infect various persons, in different ways and for differing reasons' (*SD*, 63).

Rodin widens what Kant calls *Gesinnung* to include consequences.[78] No clear distinction is drawn between, on the one hand, an action's intention and, on the other hand, its consequences and their causation.[79] The 'subjective' soul's standing before God (intention) and one's material 'objective' causation in the world (consequence), that is, the twin aspects of moral agency in theology, are amalgamated here into one singular moral *phenomenon*: visible material causation. One is responsible for fighting an 'unjust war', that is, also guilty, because an act of choosing to do evil implies an immoral intention, however residual.[80] The result is personal, moral responsibility

---

[77] David Rodin, *How We Can Effectively Reduce or even Eliminate Armed Conflict*, Royal Society Showcase 2010, http://www.youtube.com/watch?v=tdOtR54dn5c (accessed 9 February 2018).

[78] Cf. Bernard Williams, *Shame and Necessity* (Berkeley, CA: University of California Press, 1993), pp. 50–2. For the opposite view, see Nigel Biggar, who distinguishes between the culpability for intended effects and the responsibility for accepted external effects. This is opposed to Jonathan Glover, for whom external effects generate responsibility as culpability. Nigel Biggar, *Aiming to Kill* (London: Darton, Longman & Todd, 2004), pp. 63–4. Notably, Glover co-supervised Rodin's DPhil, out of which *War and Self-Defense* grew.

[79] Rodin has recently underlined this again in 'The War Trap' (p. 687), where he gives the fictional example of a 'dilemma': 'If out of malice I dangle a person out of a 12th-floor window for 5 minutes, then even if I have a moral "epiphany", I am culpable *without a change* – even though I now hold on to the person to stop them from falling whilst waiting for a third person to help hoist them up.' 'The continued dangling after the epiphany contributes to my culpability, despite the fact that I am morally required to do it' (p. 687).

[80] With Smith and Hogan, Rodin argues that in domestic law there are no excuses of duress to murder, attempted murder or some forms of treason (*SD*, 126). However, a concept of median guilt for soldiers does not rely on duress as an excuse establishing involuntariness of their actions. If such a concept were to be constructed from criminal law, then one might note that duress *is* a possible defence also in English criminal law: 'threats of immediate death or serious personal violence so great as to overbear the ordinary powers of human resistance should be accepted as a justification for acts which would otherwise be criminal' (*Attorney-General v Whelan* [1934] IR 518, per Murnaghan J. (Irish CCA), cited in David Ormerod QC and Karl Laird, *Smith and Hogan's Criminal Law*, 14th ed. (Oxford: Oxford University Press, 2015), p. 389, see also pp. 387–9, 390–5. The argument for median guilt is not for soldiers to be acquitted of murder (which they may still be held liable for in cases of unwarranted executions, massacres, etc.) but to recognize mitigating factors sufficient to warrant ceasing hostilities against so-called unjust soldiers as soon as there is representative agreement on defeat or victory over their party. Moreover, as O'Donovan will argue (see Chapter 5), the embeddedness in political structures and society is not the same as voluntarily joining a criminal gang (in which case the defence of duress is not available).

and thus liability to be attacked.[81] In this way, Rodin transfers all moral and *then also* political responsibility on the individual as a human being. The protective aspiration of individualism therefore cuts both ways: it extends the scope of concern but also the intensity of judgement. No longer are agents in their role as a soldier under scrutiny but the 'person' (*SD*, 180) as a moral-political whole. The individual human being is a prince of peace – for good or ill.

One attempt to salvage some form of 'median guilt' has been the insistence on the (antagonistic) symmetry between opposing soldiers. Soldiers in a war are conventionally regarded as equals, because both sides will have been subject to propaganda. Hence there is an element of 'invincible ignorance'.[82] As a partial, moral excuse this leaves a space between the subject and the external *Geschehen*, historical events and actions beyond individual control. Most significantly, it means soldiers are liable to attack only in so far as they actually contribute to harm. Rodin certainly recognizes this to a degree. When access to information is limited or censored, then a soldier's moral liability sinks. However, Rodin stresses, individual responsibility cannot be eradicated. Good and evil cannot be historicized or relativized, whether in the domestic or the international sphere.[83] In this way asymmetry is established, and the 'legal permission' for 'unjust soldiers' to fight is transformed into a 'legal prohibition' to participate in a war that is 'unjust' judged by *ad bellum* criteria.

Practically, Rodin's rejection of excuses for soldiers has a specific thrust. If incompetent or in doubt about the justice of a war – a point Rodin concedes to the just war tradition – the soldier should judge himself in the future. But how to judge by standards that evidently fail *in medias res*? Rodin introduces a *calculation*: A soldier has a 50 per cent chance that he is in an unjust war (*SD*, 169). If he cannot judge for himself, and if he is in doubt about the war, he should not fight at all. With this Rodin fosters a quasi-pacifism – or what Soran Reader called 'anti-warism'.[84] The hope is that soldiers' scepticism may bring the fifty-fifty calculation well below the required certainty that a war is just.

---

[81] Cheney Ryan points out that this might actually lead to a 'more adventurous military' in 'Moral Equality, Victimhood, and the Sovereignty Symmetry Problem', in *Just and Unjust Warriors*, ed. David Rodin and Henry Shue (Oxford: Oxford University Press, 2008), pp. 131–52, p. 133.

[82] The term is Dan Zupan's, 'A Presumption of the Moral Equality of Combatants: A Citizen-Soldier's Perspective', in *Just and Unjust Warriors*, ed. David Rodin and Henry Shue (Oxford: Oxford University Press, 2008), pp. 214–25, 202. David Rodin, 'The Moral Inequality of Soldiers: Why Jus in Bello Asymmetry Is Half Right', in *Just and Unjust Warriors* ed. David Rodin and Henry Shue (Oxford: Oxford University Press, 2008), pp. 44–68, 52.

[83] Rodin himself ('Personenrechte und die Kriegsrechtsbestimmungen', p. 178) quotes Michael Walzer on Jeff McMahan, whose proposal he describes as 'a careful and precise account of what individual responsibility in war would be like if war were a peacetime activity'. Michael Walzer, 'Response to McMahan's Paper', *Philosophia*, 34 (2006), 43–5, p. 43. Henry Shue has reiterated the critique: 'In combat you attempt to kill unknown strangers before they kill you, although they do not know you as an individual any more than you know them as individuals. This is unavoidable once one has entered the circumstances of combat because those circumstances of kill-or-be-killed do not allow for the acquisition and thoughtful processing of the detailed information about particular individuals necessary for individual judgements about moral liability. This is why any attempt, such as David Rodin's and Jeff McMahan's, to base the rules for the conduct of war ultimately on individual moral liability is unhelpful.' Shue, *Fighting Hurt*, p. 473.

[84] Soran Reader, 'Cosmopolitan Pacifism', *Journal of Global Ethics*, 3 (2007), 87–103.

At the same time, individual moral liability functions as a comprehensive *deterrent*. Rodin thinks the *post bellum* prospect of punishing 'unjust soldiers' could stop them from fighting wars they consider unjust themselves (*JUW*, 62). Even though a proper punishing authority beyond 'victor's justice' is yet absent in the world, the liability to be punished 'is real but *latent*' (*JUW*, 63). Advocating the principle again in 2014, Rodin thought the prospect of a criminal proceeding for taking part in an unjust war could not only sway those whose loyalty is already shaky. It could also persuade 'unjust' combatants to switch to the 'just' side.[85]

The latency of criminal liability for participating in an unjust war exemplifies the problematic underbelly of Rodin's idealist-legalist proposal. There's dialectical turn here in that his vision of a universal state actually holds out the prospect of being *more* violent than a papally sanctioned crusade. In principle, there is no temporal or spatial limit to war until every single 'unjust soldier' has been found, tried and punished. In the absence of a mediating, partly pacifying body (such as the state), hostilities would in theory continue indefinitely, even if at low-key or subliminal levels. Peace treaties – signed representatively by governments – are of no particular effect here. Neither is 'peace-generating forgetfulness' (*friedewirkendes Vergessen*, i.e. an amnesty) or post-war reconciliation; both are grounded in a modicum of mercy and an awareness that historical situatedness, loyalty and associative duties embed and thus cloud 'objective' judgement in politics and particularly in war. Indeed, Rodin has explicitly rejected the idea that there should be something like a 'morality of war' in which at least minimal moral conventions apply equally to all parties.[86] Instead, the interplay of law and aggression neatly clarifies the 'just' and 'unjust'. In this sense, the 'collectivism' Rodin has chided as underlying the 'traditionalist' just war theory returns even more forcefully.

Moreover, since the moral, legal and ultimately the political are either identical (in the universal state) or separate and unmediated ('subjective'), an *after all* antagonistic notion of politics inheres in Rodin's vision. He shares an essentially conflictual notion of the political.[87] Kant's acceptance of Hobbes's *status hominum naturalis est bellum omnium in omnes* here is as exemplary for this logic, even though he is a little more 'optimistic' about human nature.[88] 'Any moral philosophy must take cognizance of the fact that it is promulgated in a political world, and of the possibilities and limitations that this implies' (*SD*, 188). For Rodin, the continuous

---

[85] Rodin, 'Personenrechte', p. 188.

[86] Henry Shue gives the example of POWs: permitting 'just soldiers' to potentially kill POWs but not permitting 'unjust soldiers' to do so would result in the killing of POWs altogether; instead, it is more convincing to not permit any war party to kill POWs. Shue, *Fighting Hurt*, p. 233.

[87] Rodin identified five 'descriptive' and one 'moral' element of a definition of war: (1) the use of force, (2) contention, (3) intensity and duration, (4) public agents, (5) teleology or ends fought for and (6) a 'normative element'. David Rodin, 'What Is War?', Leverhulme Programme on the Changing Character of War, 27 January 2004, unpublished paper.

[88] Georg Geismann even sees Kant as the 'fulfilment' of Hobbes: 'Kant als Vollender von Hobbes und Rousseau', *Der Staat*, 21 (1982), 161–89. NB: Kant associates the breakdown of law and subsequent war with the Israelites' triumphalism, so a fall back into the 'old age'. Kant, *Zum Ewigen Frieden*, AA vol. VIII, p. 357.

'failure' of politics even provides the necessary and continuous *precondition* for a long-term moral transformation:

> There is a deeply moral response to international conflict which does not seek to contradict the Realist perception that the current mechanisms of international politics are irredeemably devoid of morality, but rather grows out of it. The necessity of a moral critique of international relations derives from an appreciation of the inadequacy, ineffectiveness, poverty, and hypocrisy of the standard conceptions of international morality. (*SD*, 197)[89]

In this sense war is a *cataclysmic* event, both negatively and positively. Negatively, because it is in principle unjustifiable and as mere 'aggression' makes no sense; positively, because the actual foundation of an international order as envisioned by Rodin would require a war to end all wars. Rodin here gestures towards Tolstoy's oscillation between, on the one hand, the 'law of love' – according to which a Christian bears violence without a murmur and thus in martyrdom contributes to the salvation of mankind – and war as 'cataclysm' on the other hand.[90] For Tolstoy, war was a sordid and confused experience wrecking entire consciences; at best, if at all, it made sense between small units of soldiers.

From a slightly different angle, we also have already encountered a version of cataclysm in Elshtain's account in the previous chapter. There, the bucolic urban domesticity of American life was shaken by terrorist attacks, unleashing the defensive forces of the sovereign state and its reactive, albeit supposedly benevolent imperialism. In the absence of a concrete (non-Walzerian) just war proposal, that is, a practical, non-cataclysmic third way integrating political realism and moral idealism, Rodin is conceptually settled on a uniform stance on wars. Not because they are all 'just' but because they are all relatively 'unjust' by his cosmopolitan standard. Rodin and other theorists of humanitarian international law such as Hugo Slim or Jennifer Welsh rarely criticize particular states' wars from the perspective of states as representative political authorities but on the grounds of the damage done to 'human rights' either in general or in the very particular.[91]

Moreover, since consequentialism may sometimes override individual human rights, and national defence be the 'lesser evil', *in practice* legalist idealism may equally lend vocal support to sovereign states that infer the right to national defence on the grounds of human rights. Several liberal human rights theorists, such as Samantha Power or Michael Ignatieff (both also referenced by Elshtain), have painlessly swapped

---

[89] This is the danger of Christian hypocrisy against which Blake set his *The Human Abstract*: 'Pity would be no more/If we did not make somebody poor,/And Mercy no more could be/If all were as happy as we.'

[90] Tolstoy is listed in Rodin's bibliography, but he does not explicitly refer to him anywhere in the book (*SD*, 206). Cf. Walter B. Gallie, *Philosophers of Peace and War: Kant, Clausewitz, Marx, Engels and Tolstoy* (Cambridge: Cambridge University Press, 1978), pp. 100–32.

[91] See Jennifer Welsh, 'How Iraq Changed How We Think about Human Rights', 19 March 2013, https://www.opencanada.org/features/how-iraq-changed-how-we-think-about-human-rights/ (accessed 9 July 2019); 'Cécile Fabre on Cosmopolitanism and War', http://philosophybites.com/2011/01/c%C3%A9cile-fabre-on-cosmopolitanism-and-war.html (accessed 15 March 2012).

internationalist 'impartiality' for the defence of American empire, torture and drone warfare. Absent a universal state, Rodin's internationalist ideal can not only be harnessed to sovereign doctrines drawing on imperial myths, as Elshtain did. The attempt to actually realize it in history has to collapse into imperialism because its 'realization' will always be initiated by some political actors and find considerable resistance.[92] Mark Mazower has shown how the nineteenth-century utopian idea of a world governed by (international) law has been (and continues to be) instrumentalized by states to cast their military interventions and conquests in terms of 'duties of care' or the 'responsibility to protect' (R2P).[93] And while war between 'civilized' states, or those 'protecting human rights' may become increasingly rule-governed and subdued or 'transferred' into legal processes, the sovereignty and protection of weaker, particularly non-Western nations was frequently undermined.[94]

The irony of cosmopolitan ethics

In Chapter 1, we explored briefly what kind of intellectual endeavour Elshtain's just war thinking was. Her theological dualism continued as an antagonistic rhetoric: just war theory was both a polemic directed at her opponents and edification for the American public. As a continuation of the sovereign-realist politics, she offered a 'theoretical account' of American 'statecraft'. As such, however, it was also the jurisprudence for an international, legal order under US tutelage.

Rodin's approach is of an altogether different nature. He claims that just war theory – which he problematically reduces to Michael Walzer – has in fact failed. It has betrayed the promise to 'provide a robust set of principles for effective operation in the political realm' (*SD*, 189). And while Elshtain's strong sovereign state was premised on the very separation from both the Christian and a (supposedly) Kantian *eschaton*, Rodin conveys such a vision of an immanent moral *eschaton* towards which one progressively moves. Indeed, he notes that his suggestions have a 'messianic' character (*SD*, 198).

However, like Elshtain's, Rodin's recommendations are also driven by dualities. The final chapter of *War and Self-Defense* entitled 'Morality and Realism' doesn't dissolve the duality of moral aspiration and 'realistic politics' but rather *reinforces* it. In Rodin's reading, Kant 'suggests a two-tier moral strategy'. The first seeks to mitigate and moderate the evils of war in the world as it currently is. The second represents

---

[92] Koskenniemi, *From Apology to Utopia*, pp. 479–80, n.

[93] NB: Rodin's association with the Carnegie Council; the idealist Andrew Carnegie, like William James, was a member of the Anti-Imperialist League founded in 1889. Arguably, these American and transcendentalist connections further link Elshtain's sovereign-realism and Rodin's legalist-idealism at a deeper level.

[94] The collapse of liberalism into empire is historically well documented; see James Tully, *Rethinking Human Rights and Enlightenment: A View from the Twenty-First Century*, Oxford Amnesty Lecture, 10 February 2010, http://web.uvic.ca/polisci/people/faculty/Tully/publications/Oxford%20Amnesty%20lecture.pdf (retrieved 28 August 2010); Domenico Losurdo, *Liberalism: A Counter-History* (London: Verso, 2011); less explicit perhaps is Karma Nabulsi, *Traditions of War: Occupation, Resistance and the Law* (Oxford: Oxford University Press, 1999), pp. 108 ff.

the attempt to 'develop a measured realistic programme for the achievement of a just system of international relations within which a genuine international rule of law can be realised' (*SD*, 198). The latter, developmental tier is an Aristotelian *bios theoretikos*. The 'need to develop such a programme is the ultimate practical recommendation' of Rodin's work. It comprises developing principles of subsidiarity which integrate states into a global legal order. Rodin in this instance gestures back to the pre-modern Christian tradition even though his premises of Enlightened rationality might initially have suggested: 'Both Augustine and Aquinas argued that war may have a legitimate punitive function. Grotius argued that the world's states constitute a society, in which members are collectively responsible for the enforcement of the law' (*SD*, 174). The idea that military action must be an act of law enforcement against aggressors is of course also enshrined in the present UN Charter, according to which every act of violent force falls into one of three categories:

> Either it is an unlawful use of force, or it is lawful because performed at the request of or with the authorization of the UN, or it is a lawful response to an illegal armed attack and hence an act of legitimate national-defense. (*SD*, 107)

In line with that Rodin does not want to 'justify war'. 'Regular war' or world policing *removes* the antagonistic concept of war, the contention between sovereign, morally equal contenders ever on the verge of cataclysm.

However, first tier of Kant's moral strategy remains a persistent problem for Rodin. As we've heard, it 'seeks to mitigate and moderate the evils of war in the world as it currently is'. That means heeding the realities of injustice, violence and conflict in the absence of procedural mechanisms. But what else would such a 'moral strategy' consist in if not a form of 'just war' thinking? Certainly, the limitations of necessity, imminence and proportionality for the use of violent force emerge indirectly in *War and Self-Defense*; for example, pre-emptive war may be as unjustifiable as pre-emptive self-defence. Yet because these moral restrictions must be legally coherent and apply to all agents equally in international law, Rodin can only acknowledge a 'significant disanalogy between the application [of these principles] in international and domestic law' (*SD*, 111). Aware of the technical abilities and dangers and the nature of warfare as 'intrinsically open-ended on both sides and subject to escalation' (*SD*, 115), Rodin would also need to develop these principles for a universal state.[95] So if the global human rights order could function as the backdrop for a *ius ad bellum* – dealing with 'aggression' – then Rodin's 'realistic tier' still presents the possibility of a kind of independent *ius in bello* for the antagonistic clash of still existing and (perhaps unjustifiably) clashing sovereign states.

Ironically, therefore, in so far as Rodin is not entirely oblivious to the problem of unjust violence, his legalist idealism inadvertently repeats the medieval and early modern inauguration of the very just war theory he is keen to pronounce dead. Notably, these 'theories' were always also responses to concrete political conflicts and embodied goods. For example, the Dominican theologian Francesco de Vitoria (influenced also by conciliarist and Gallican tendencies in Paris) was not a canon lawyer in Rome or

---

[95] Rodin does not use the term 'world policing', though this is what it is commonly referred to.

theorist of the papacy but at Salamanca responded to moral-political questions in early modern Spain conquering the Americas. A Jesuit closer to the Counter-Reformation papacy, Francisco Suàrez several decades later intervened in the controversy between Pope Paul V and James I over the legitimacy of royal power as autonomous in relation to spiritual power.[96] Hugo Grotius' international law emerged as the early modern Calvinist Netherlands sought to justify its overseas trade ventures.

Nigel Biggar noticed this irony in Rodin's work in his *War and Self-Defense*. He accepts the effectiveness of Rodin's critique in so far as it targets an unconditional legal right to national defence and an absolute 'moral symmetry' between soldiers of all parties in a war. But he notes the problematic contradictions: while Rodin seems to be either wilfully oblivious or even opposed to natural law, he 'himself can be found to affirm "objective, trans-cultural goods", even if only the liberal ones of freedom, autonomy, and self-determination'.[97] Rodin also holds that 'it is "absolutely certain" that "consequentialist" considerations sometimes override rights'. But simultaneously he 'asserts that rights "generally override" competing moral considerations, especially "consequentialist" ones that invoke the common good'. Biggar notes that 'this appears to leave open the possibility that the common good may *sometimes* trump individual rights. If so, then the door is shut again when Rodin urges that "[t]he most basic function of a morality of rights is to locate certain extremely important normative considerations [i.e. innocence and guilt] *wholly within the sphere of the subject itself so as to make them unassailable by external contingencies* such as are appealed to by consequentialism"'.[98] In other words, Rodin wants to acknowledge the need to defend the common good but simultaneously cannot accept it. He wants to insist not only that the innocent have an inviolable right to life but also that it may justifiably be taken. His example is from the 1994 Rwandan genocide: the Tutsi Vénuste Hakizamungu was blackmailed to either kill his own brother Théoneste or see the whole family murdered. In this case, though only based on 'internal obligations' Théoneste was right to allow his brother to kill him and to sacrifice his own life. Biggar observes, 'Gingerly [Rodin] concedes that social obligation can justify not only an innocent's self-sacrifice but another's killing the innocent, should he refuse to meet his obligation.'[99]

The irony nestled in Rodin's approach is symptomatic of his own epistemological (and hence theological) premises: where the moral, legal and political come together in one principle of protecting the individual, such mediatory monism is bound to oscillate with its very opposite. Indeed, irony as such may be understood as a lack of mediation made conscious. As Reinhold Niebuhr defined it, irony

> consists of apparently fortuitous incongruities in life which are discovered, upon closer examination, to be not merely fortuitous. Incongruity is merely comic. ... A comic situation is proved to be an ironic one if a hidden relation is discovered in the incongruity. If virtue becomes vice through some hidden defect in virtue; if

---

[96] See e.g. Jean-Paul Coujou, 'Political Thought and Legal Theory in Suárez', in *A Companion to Francisco Suárez*, ed. Victor Salas and Robert Fastiggi (Leiden: Brill, 2014), pp. 29–71.

[97] Biggar, *In Defense of War*, p. 160.

[98] Biggar, *In Defense of War*, p. 184.

[99] Ibid., p. 186.

strength becomes weakness because of the vanity to which strength may prompt the mighty man or nation; if security is transmuted into insecurity because too much reliance is placed upon it; if wisdom becomes folly because it does not know its own limits – in all such cases the situation is ironic.[100]

In Rodin's proposal, moral propositions are persistently haunted by the inadvertent emergence of their opposite: the individual by a collectivist absorption into the 'justice' or 'injustice' of the wars they fight; international law is absorbed by state-centred imperialism, the denial of just war theory by its own emergence.

While Rodin can merely admit discomfort in the light of his moral intuitions, Biggar for his part takes these weak moments as a welcome entry point to clarify not just the just war tradition Rodin mis- or underrepresents but also to show how Rodin's critique of international law ironically vindicates the older Christian tradition. Biggar is free to make this move on *theological* grounds – there is simply no problem for him in embracing earlier Christian approaches. These neither regard positive international law nor the sovereign state as the ultimate, 'living' mediator between politics and morality. And indeed, already Niebuhr noted that 'an ironic smile must turn into bitter laughter or into bitterness without laughter' absent a 'religious sense'. To take Niebuhr further, this 'religious sense' is needed to enjoy (and bear) irony rather than be haunted by it, to consciously disentangle reality and appearance and transpose its incongruent elements into a meaningful mode of existence.[101]

Rodin – perhaps to avoid 'defending war' along the lines of Biggar – seems intent on deepening the irony by repeating his essentially anti-warist position. The Kantian realistic moral tier no longer features explicitly in his work. To Henry Shue's suggestion that a minimal 'morality of war' may still effectively apply to the realities of war, Rodin has responded with an analogy: such a position would be like disapproving of slavery, but instead of advocating its abolition, allowing it to continue in a minimized form as an annual human sacrifice. 'International aggression, even in its non-genocidal, political form is a great evil that demands a robust and effective response. But a self-help regime centred on a presumptive right to conduct wars of self-defence is not that response. Instead, the considerations here introduced compel us to develop alternative ways to prevent and deflect conditional political aggression.'[102] Rodin has focused on advocating changes to international law, particularly with a view to extending the reach of the International Criminal Court.[103] And with a view to incorporating individual criminal liability for fighting an unjust war, he has suggested extending the space for conscientious objection in military recruitment. However, because 'coordinated, lethal, defensive violence against genocidal aggression' – that is 'mass self-defense' – is still permitted, Rodin has claimed a 'new position' he calls 'justified interdiction theory'.[104]

---

[100] Reinhold Niebuhr, *The Irony of American History* (Chicago, IL: University of Chicago Press, 2008 [1952]), p. xxiv.

[101] In the present case, it would be an appreciation both of political duty and international law as distinct, yet in any given case potentially fallible mediators. See Chapters 5 and 6.

[102] Rodin, 'The Myth of National Self-Defense', p. 89.

[103] NB: In 2017, the Assembly of States Parties to the Rome Statute of the International Criminal Court 'activated' the court's jurisdiction over the crime of aggression.

[104] Rodin, 'The Myth of National Self-Defense', p. 89.

With this, Rodin tries to manoeuvre himself out of a dead end, because the traditional name for 'justified interdiction theory' is simply – just war theory.

Conclusion: Elshtain, Rodin and the problem of mediation

We have seen that Rodin's contribution to the ethics of violent force is problematic: the individual is the subject of concern in domestic and international law, which is regarded as the mediator between politics and morality – in contrast and competition to the sovereign national state. Placing this in our overall comparative framework, the logic of Rodin's anthropocentric human rights account is akin to Elshtain's, except that in terms of *content* it is the exact reversal. Like Elshtain, Rodin sees an unmediated duality or a dichotomy of conceptual possibilities: between collectivism and individualism, between subjectivist particularism and objectivist universalism and between state sovereignty and supra-national authority. Rodin consistently prioritizes the latter of these pairs, relying on the objectivist 'rule of law' instead of 'subjectively valued' states as the subject and mediator of international relations. As I argued, he presents the secularized, now conceptually more violent 'papacy' to Elshtain's 'sovereign state'. Both have in common a shared logic. They see these options as exclusive of each other; both suggest a fundamental *separation* from their respective opposite. Elshtain utterly rejects the 'utopian' legalism, whereas Rodin neglects the natural-moral grounds of 'the political'. As a result, each strand *absorbs* or haunts its opposite: Elshtain's state absorbs the juridical ideal of humanity and becomes a mythical 'benevolent empire'; Rodin's juridical ideal of humanity absorbs the state and becomes a 'global non-sovereign political society', though – as noted – this concept, once actualized, is by implication imperialist. Both accounts clash as they champion an essentially positivist, political rule; both, however, also rely on the centrality of the individual human being, a Razian version of humanist self-mediation.

Meanwhile, the foundational, *theological* dualism both of Elshtain's modern Marcionism and Rodin's (quasi-)Kantianism remains unbridgeable. Both authors lack the perspective of a *mediating* Third that accounts for the critical political freedom within a political community. Rodin's idealism certainly echoes Augustine's scepticism and radically deconstructs the sovereign political from a quasi-ecclesial perspective, *including* a supra-political law and individual moral freedom. However, because positive international law reigns in 'law's empire', the implications of this dimension bear no fruit for practical political decisions as history unfolds.

Rodin's and Elshtain's difference reflect the contention between the United Nations and the United States over the authority to enter the Iraq War in 2003 and the persistent differences, collusions and complicities in Western politics since the 1990s. So it may well be interpreted as a renewed Investiture Controversy. With this, we also answer the question in the title of this chapter. Elshtain's and Rodin's positions are *challenging twins*. What sounds metaphorical and perhaps facile is nonetheless a persistent motif in Western political iconography particularly in the Middle Ages. For example, the twins Jacob and Esau in the Genesis story, who 'were fighting wars in the uterus of

Rebecca', were regarded as types for Christianity and Judaism. The canonist Gerhoh of Reichersbach saw Jacob as a priest and Esau as a king; and as the latter had sold his birthright to the former, Gerhoh himself was particularly pained by the imperial ban executed on his abbey. A commentary on the Genesis story ascribed to Thomas Aquinas inferred the *principatus spiritualium super carnales* and the 'impossibility of a twin solution to the relation between *sacerdotium* and *regnum*'.[105]

In Part Two, we will explore two authors who have, each in their own way, challenged the twin solution of papacy and empire, both in their Christian traditional forms and in their post-Christian recurrences. And in this sense they are 'heretics' – with or without quotation marks.

---

[105] Claudius Sieber-Lehmann, *Papst und Kaiser als Zwillinge?: Ein anderer Blick auf die Universalgewalten im Investiturstreit* (Cologne: Böhlau Verlag, 2015), pp. 58–9, 57. Significantly, Sieber-Lehmann altogether de-politicizes and culturalizes the problem of political legitimacy, advocating 'a culture of difference on the grounds of shared origins and a shared wealth of experience'; there is not only 'one's own and the alien, but one's own together with the proximate, familiar Other', p. 166. With such a view, the political questions of the past completely cease to illuminate the present.

Part Two

Heresies: Liberal(-Marxist) and Christian ethics of war

3

Machiavelli for everyone!
Human rights reconsidered

Introduction

The analytic philosopher Uwe Steinhoff (b.1968) has been very critical both of traditional sovereign states' just war theories and cosmopolitanism. His first book, on Jürgen Habermas and Karl-Otto Apel, offered a profound critique of communicative rationality.[1] His second work, *Effiziente Ethik* (Efficient Ethics), demonstrated that a liberal ethic is the most rational choice. It defended a universalist rationality, a realist concept of truth against communitarian and postmodern approaches and – most importantly for us – the autonomous, defensive individual. Venturing into political philosophy, it lay the groundwork for his subsequent contributions to the ethics of war.[2] Published at the height of the American 'war against terror', *The Ethics of War and Terrorism* then pushed the rationalist individual-rights paradigm to its logical conclusions. In effect, Steinhoff's at times libertarian premises provide fertile grounds for the justification of exceptional uses of torture, mercenaries and terrorism – in short, a set of suggestions that gained him a reputation of *philosophe provocateur*.

Apart from being interesting in its own right, in our context Steinhoff's work indicates an alternative way ahead for human rights within the ethics of war. Steinhoff explicitly draws on John Locke, J. S. Mill, Kant and Max Weber; Johann Gottlieb Fichte could perhaps be seen as a 'father in spirit', especially his reflections on the French Revolution.[3] Steinhoff focuses on individual rights, that is, the contractual basis to Elshtain's sovereign state, and the grounds of Rodin's approach. In that sense, the

---

[1] Uwe Steinhoff, *Kritik der kommunikativen Rationalität: Eine Darstellung und Kritik der kommunikationstheoretischen Philosophie von Jürgen Habermas und Karl-Otto* (Paderborn: Mentis, 2006).

[2] Uwe Steinhoff, *Zur Ethik des Krieges und des Terrorismus*, rev. ed. (Stuttgart: Kohlhammer, 2011), hereafter *EKT*. The first English edition, from which some of my translations are taken, was *The Ethics of War and Terrorism* (Oxford: Oxford University Press), 2008, when cited hereafter, *EWT*; Uwe Steinhoff, *Effiziente Ethik* (Paderborn: mentis Verlag, 2006), hereafter *EE*; Uwe Steinhoff, 'Ethics and Mercenaries', in *New Wars and New Soldiers: Military Ethics in the Contemporary World*, ed. Jessica Wolfendale and Paolo G. Tripodi (Farnham: Ashgate: 2011), pp. 137–51.

[3] Johann Gottlieb Fichte, *Beitrag zur Berichtigung der Urteile des Publikums über die französische Revolution* (Hamburg: Felix Meiner Verlag, 1973 [1793]).

self-mediation of humanity together with a modern theological dualism is at work here as well. Yet while a comparable dialectic is also the result, it is so with some positive modifications. Steinhoff's critical work unmasks moralistic pretentions and busts false myths, and in that sense it can be said to bear a prophetic character, departing from the sovereign-cosmopolitan or renewed 'theocratic' constellation presented in Part One. As we will see, Steinhoff's approach also echoes several alternative, heterodox theo-political constellations of the past.

Uwe Steinhoff's *Ethics of War and Terrorism*

But first, Steinhoff's just war proposal needs to be located vis-à-vis the realist and idealist poles of the imperial-cosmopolitan paradigm. *The Ethics of War and Terrorism* aims for 'a thoroughgoing application of a perspective which is enlightened, liberal and oriented to individual rights' (*EWT*, 3). To this end, Steinhoff rigorously revises existing common-sense standards and readjusts the contents of existing just war theories towards an individualist realism.[4]

Legitimate authority

The 'criterion of legitimate authority' easily lends itself to a tautology: a state is a legitimate authority to wage war, because it is the state and therefore legitimate.[5] For Steinhoff, such statism is untenable. Especially if the criterion is 'logically prior' to non-combatant immunity, then 'the theory of just war collapses into an Authorisation Act for "legitimate authorities"' (*EKT*, 16). The mere fact of a 'public monopoly of force' is not a sufficient indicator that a particular state is *good*, even if it formally curbs 'private wars'. 'It may be that the public monopoly of force is a precondition of a "civilised society," but *breaking through* this monopoly is historically and under most circumstances also today an unavoidable precondition for democratisation' (*EKT*, 17). In this reading, the criterion of legitimate authority *formalistically* conceived is absurd. But Steinhoff doesn't deconstruct any state positivism in order to make the state's authority conditional on enforcing justice. Instead, he inflates its currency: he extends the (natural) right to self-defence to a 'right to war'. Everyone naturally *is* an authority for war, since everyone has the right to defend himself against others and a state that violates their rights. One equally has the right to punish others (*EKT*, 24).[6]

So Steinhoff's critical, liberal move is to set the natural rights of individuals against 'legitimate authority'. Nonetheless, some restriction is once again introduced. First, by a

---

4   The exposition of Steinhoff's argument is extensive, so readers familiar with it may skip to the section 'Immanent constellations: Radically reformed (a-)theology, Marxism and unbelieving prophecy'.

5   See Chapter 1 on Elshtain. For a similar criticism, see also Diana Francis, *Rethinking War and Peace* (London: Pluto Press, 2004), p. 88; Anthony Burke, *Beyond Security, Ethics and Violence* (London: Routledge, 2007), pp. 140–6; Andrew Fiala, *The Just War Myth* (Lanham: Rowman & Littlefield, 2008), pp. vii–xi, 70–1.

6   Cf. *Basic Law of the Federal Republic of Germany*, Art. 20, Section 4; *German Penal Code*, Art. 34, 'Justifying Emergency'.

form of *Recht* (right): one can only go to war if one's rights have been violated 'unjustly'. Second, at least for 'public wars' only the community members authorized to decide on war can do so. With this restriction, Steinhoff reintroduces a formal-democratic criterion of legitimate authority, albeit—in comparison to Elshtain—somewhat half-heartedly: 'we don't need a theory of just war for that' (*EKT*, 27). Third, with Francisco de Vitoria, any formal authority still must consult and deliberate carefully.[7] Yet what a public authority is good for, why it should not act privately (*eigenmächtig*) and how it should have the welfare of the community in view are questions not discussed here. Public authority is the sum of its parts; it has a *pragmatic* value.[8]

Just cause and right intention

Steinhoff next turns to the criteria dealing with the cause and direction of violent force. The American Catholic bishops' pastoral letter *The Challenge of Peace* (1983) listed the following causes for permissible war: 'to confront "a real and certain danger", i.e., to protect innocent life, to preserve conditions necessary for decent human existence and to secure basic human rights' (*EKT*, 29). However, in Steinhoff's reading, just war theory is not meant to merely ring fence the scale or reduce the number of wars. What matters morally in a given situation is *justice* and the *adequacy of the means* to achieve it. Adequacy is dealt with in what he calls the 'sub-criteria' of last resort, reasonable chance of success and proportionality. (One could, for example, wage a 'just' but non-bloody war to rescue one's kidnapped pets.) As with 'legitimate authority', Steinhoff here transforms the 'just cause' criterion: 'The only logical and practical thing to do is rather to conceptualise the criterion [of just cause] as a *sufficient* cause and subsume the criterion of last resort, reasonable chance of success and proportionality under it.' More condensed, a just cause and a proportionate response remain standing as interdependent criteria (*EKT*, 31).

'Right intention' remains an independent criterion, but it becomes a quasi-legal externality. Sure, Steinhoff says, if there is a just cause for a war, 'it must also be waged *for* that reason' (*EKT*, 31). If a state effectively intervenes to stop a genocide, it would be illegitimate, impermissible and unjust if it did so only to extend its sphere of influence. But we shouldn't be 'too puritanical'. An agent may *also*, for example, extend his sphere of influence, provided 'his warring does not go further than is necessary to reach the aim defined by the *causa iusta*' (*EKT*, 32). Steinhoff's significant step consists in focussing on the permissibility of actions not 'the moral guilt of the agent' (*EKT*, 31).[9]

---

[7] On these grounds, Steinhoff argues George W. Bush was not a 'right authority' for the second Iraq War, since he refused to talk to churchmen critical of the war. One might wonder: was it really only *that*?

[8] Uwe Steinhoff, 'What Is War – and Can a Lone Individual Wage One?', *International Journal of Applied Philosophy*, 23 (2009), 133–50.

[9] Uwe Steinhoff has frequently critiqued (philosophical versions of) the doctrine of double effect. See e.g. 'The Secret to the Success of the Doctrine of Double Effect (and Related Principles): Biased Framing, Inadequate Methodology, and Clever Distractions', *Journal of Ethics* 22.3–4 (2018), 235–63; 'Wild Goose Chase: Still No Rationales for the Doctrine of Double Effect and Related Principles', *Criminal Law and Philosophy* (Online First, 2018), https://doi.org/10.1007/s11572-018-9456-y; 'Bennett, Intention and the DDE – The Sophisticated Bomber as Pseudo-Problem', *Analysis* 78.1 (2018), 73–80.

The 'right intention' ceases to be a primary moral principle of a war. Congruently, if a sadist takes part exclusively in justified wars, Steinhoff says, 'he respects the rights of others. A liberal cannot ask for more than that.' Anything more would be 'character surveillance', 'sniffing out inclinations and attitudes' (*EKT*, 33). 'Right intention' consists 'not in acting *for* a particular reason' but in agreeing to '*respect* the criterion of just cause as a moral command' (*EKT*, 33).[10]

The remainder of the section criticizes a number of formal just war criteria on which the justice of a war, Steinhoff argues, can hardly depend.[11] War does not have to be the *last resort*, but it must be the last *promising* resort. Going to war might actually be more appropriate than, for example, sanctions, which are also of a military nature but often target the weakest (*EKT*, 34). A *reasonable chance of success* can hardly indicate the justice of a war. Indeed, it can be the 'last flicker of humanity' to fight a lost cause (*EKT*, 35). Steinhoff's example is native American tribes fighting colonial extinction. These two criteria therefore become sub-criteria of general proportionality.

So Steinhoff further dismantles and reshuffles the tick-box list of just war criteria. Any justice to be done requires appropriate and proportionate means. Against that tradition, the 'right intention' remains as a criterion that may limit the scope of an action, but it doesn't define its nature. The justice to be done is not defined by some supernatural standard but the protection of the rights and freedoms of all individuals (*EKT*, 36). The fact that for Steinhoff sometimes 'the rights of some can only be protected by violating the rights of others' entails a substantive analysis of proportionality and the meaning of innocence and guilt.

The innocent, double effect and proportionality

Proportionality is one answer to the question: 'Whom, if at all, may one kill (and why)?' The answer 'may range between "everyone" and "no one" and thus may either almost always permit war or in fact prohibit war' (*EKT*, 36–7). So, Steinhoff also aims for a mediate position between the two. Yet, he goes for a more realist thinking – in an individualist mode.

In the course of discussing proportionality, Steinhoff again dismisses the doctrine of double effect (*EKT*, 31). The bulk of his discussion deals with certain modern versions of the doctrine. These work with a supposedly Christian 'absolute prohibition to kill innocents' (*EKT*, 57), distinguishing between deaths as means or side effects; or

---

[10] Personal 'aims', including vengeance or glory, are morally irrelevant; what matters is the objective, external 'just cause'. Uwe Steinhoff, 'Just Cause and the Continuous Application of Jus ad Bellum', in *The Cambridge Handbook of the Just War*, ed. Larry May (Cambridge: Cambridge University Press, 2018), pp. 80–97, p. 91.

[11] Like O'Donovan, Steinhoff understands these criteria as different aspects of proportionality, not negligible items on a list. See Chapter 5. The *interdependence* of criteria would require further considerations. For example, if one does not have the 'right intentions', then one simply is not the 'right authority' since one wouldn't be doing the right thing; the action performed is therefore not only disproportionate because not related to a good but also morally wrong. Cf. Uwe Steinhoff, 'Just Cause and the Continuous Application of Jus Ad Bellum', in *The Cambridge Handbook of the Just War*, ed. Larry May (Cambridge: Cambridge University Press, 2018), pp. 80–97, p. 81.

they are disguised consequentialist or even utilitarian calculi.[12] Steinhoff rightly notes that these versions leave behind Aquinas's original focus on the intention of an action (*EKT*, 41). But his quest is not to restore the medieval doctrine, 'which cares rather for the salvation of the perpetrator's soul than the physical integrity of the victim' and the 'emotional colouring of intentions and expectations' (*EKT*, 57). Such 'ideal', moral horizons are of no interest to Steinhoff.

One reason is that he is sceptical that we can at all discern someone's intention in the first place. Subjective intention and outward action may be disjointed: 'One can thus often claim that one *did not* intend the negative consequences – and one is presumed innocent.' And in view of 'military necessity', the proportionality principle 'will always tend to be overstretched' (*EKT*, 42).[13] Steinhoff acknowledges the need for judging intentions in domestic law, but intention is somehow left out of the morality of war. For the innocent victim whose 'right to life' is violated, it makes no difference whether they are directly targeted or killed as a side effect (*EKT*, 49, 51, 54, 56). 'What would [they] say to this fascinating distinction? If they haven't lost all humour, which would be understandable, then probably: "Dead is dead" ' (*EKT*, 49).

To qualify the rejected criterion of 'right intention', Steinhoff responds to 'our intuition' that in a given situation the intention of an attacker does matter. The example is a police officer shooting through a person whom a kidnapper of a hundred hostages uses as a human shield. Steinhoff introduces two principles. First, the 'justice' of the action matters: this is 'the (non-absolute) right to defensively attack an unjust aggressor'. People must *deserve* being attacked, like the kidnapper (*EKT*, 51). But this argument – that one person may be sacrificed for the survival of many – has a utilitarian drift; indeed for Steinhoff it tends towards an 'absolute socialism' (*EKT*, 52).[14] It is therefore mitigated by a second principle: certain rights of some cannot be sacrificed for the mere interests of many (*EKT*, 52).[15] With Ronald Dworkin, rights are 'trumps', and they are grounded in a person's ownership of herself. The alternative would be the person as a *socium*, 'in the end a slave (even if only on duty call)' (*EKT*, 53).

However, even the trumps may be trumped. In any given case, the proportionality of the action matters. Steinhoff takes the Allied terror bombing of German citizens in the Second World War as a critical example. It is simply *disproportionate* to kill so many innocents, he says, even if there is a large good looming as a prize, like ridding the continent of fascism.[16] Our 'intuitions' can also be explained with rule-utilitarian thinking. An overall good aim such as stopping a dictatorial regime is insufficient to

---

[12] On the historical development of the doctrine after Aquinas, see Paul Ramsey, *War and the Christian Conscience: How Shall Modern War Be Conducted Justly?* (Durham, NC: Duke University Press, 1961), pp. 46–9.

[13] See Chapter 5. O'Donovan argues that when the damage is excessive and gratuitous, we can *see* that there were no good intentions at work; the claim to 'military necessity' is then hypocritical.

[14] Steinhoff later argued that in exceptional, extreme cases such a rights violation may be justified. Cf. Uwe Steinhoff, 'On Not Believing in Justified Wars without Being a Pacifist', American University of Beirut, 3 May 2010, https://www.youtube.com/watch?v=Mw1bWNzMIwc (accessed 15 May 2018).

[15] Note that the relationship between guilt and intention has important repercussions in contemporary criminal law. For a critique of the merely functional concept of guilt, see e.g. Christoph Johannes Maria Safferling, *Vorsatz und Schuld: Subjektive Täterelemente im deutschen und englischen Strafrecht* (Tübingen: Mohr-Siebeck: 2008), p. 104f.

[16] Cf. Steinhoff, 'On Not Believing in Justified Wars without Being a Pacifist'.

justify huge sacrifices of innocents. In most cases, it does not work and 'any claim to such prescience would be unjustified and irresponsible clairvoyance'.[17] Moreover, it is absurd to think bombs could convince people to change their own government (*EKT*, 55).[18]

In short, Steinhoff's combination of just cause, proportionality and innocents' immunity from attack successfully corrects faulty contemporary doctrines of double effect. But without this doctrine, the logic of rights protection and consequentialism de-absolutizes the 'right' of innocent non-combatants not to be attacked. It becomes a general, objective 'immensely valuable good of right' (*EKT*, 64). And it is hardly the essence of just war.[19] Again, while avoiding the most utilitarian excesses, this 'clash of rights' approach sits on the realist side of just war thinking.

Non-combatant immunity and the definition of innocence and guilt

So the traditional 'absolutism' that forbids intentionally targeting innocent civilians is de-absolutized. Yet a key question must still be answered: How to understand and potentially 'legitimize' war? From this question then emerge the status and rights of innocents.

One could argue that the difference between innocent and guilty corresponds to non-combatants and just combatants on one side, with unjust combatants on the other. This is G. E. M. Anscombe's approach (*EKT*, 65) and in general also Steinhoff's own. However, he points out, (moral) innocence and guilt cannot be equated with combatancy and non-combatancy. A gun-wielding peasant may be deluded or forced to fight, whereas a war-mongering corporate functionary may be guilty without ever holding a gun in his hands. With George Mavrodes, Steinhoff therefore sees non-combatant immunity as a 'useful convention'. There are utilitarian reasons, the best interests of every party involved, to obey these rules.[20] After all, the aim wouldn't be to eradicate each other but to guarantee that human, communal existence is possible after a war (*EKT*, 68–9, 104). In other words, in Steinhoff's critique discrimination becomes a *convention*.

Still, non-combatant immunity may be a result of one's role as a civilian. Against (an effectively totalitarian) Michael Green, who regards even the old, sick and children as liable to attack, Steinhoff invokes John Locke. According to Locke, subjects of an unjust ruler in a war ought 'not to be charged as guilty … any farther than they actually abet it' (*EKT*, 71).[21] At the same time, every citizen has 'a duty to scepticism' since most wars

---

[17] The various versions of the 'Domino Theory' advanced during the Cold War offer good examples of a situation where moral reasoning is replaced with empiricist clairvoyance.

[18] This explains a tendency also apparent in current military strategy: the fact that 'we cannot know' whether terrorizing the innocent works tempts armies that consider themselves 'just' to at least *try* repeatedly and, when failing, try harder – an obvious recipe for escalation. Cf. Carl von Clausewitz, *On War*, transl. J. J. Graham, 3 vols. (London: Kegan Paul, Trench, Trübner, 1908), vol. 1, pp. 4–5.

[19] Pace Ramsey and O'Donovan, see Chapters 4 and 5.

[20] Cf. Henry Shue, *Fighting Hurt: Rule and Exception in Torture and War* (Oxford: Oxford University Press, 2016).

[21] John Locke *Two Treatises*, ed. Peter Laslett (Cambridge: Cambridge University Press, 1988), 2nd Treatise, §179, p. 406. NB: Locke here talks about the power of the conqueror.

just serve the rulers themselves. 'Hence, in a liberal democracy he cannot delegate to a superior his responsibility for supporting an unjust war' (*EKT*, 74). Next, Steinhoff turns to Robert Fullinwider, who emphasizes self-defence. Rights concern things due to a person; their violation entails defence. This refocusing of the notion of war is central, and Steinhoff will neither alienate these self-defensive rights to a state or supra-state. So, he begins with the rule that immediate aggressors may be attacked. Knowledge about the 'moral guilt' of the attacker is not presumed (*EKT*, 75). The epistemological barrier positively limits the range of attack to those enemy combatants who actually fight, those visibly engaged in an attempt to harm or destroy. No one *really* has reliable knowledge about the uninformed peasant (*EKT*, 77–8).

But can individual self-defence, including 'the defence of others' (*Fremdverteidigung*), really carry the weight of a whole war? Steinhoff responds that, after all, individuals shoot and fight: 'The aggressor-soldier shoots the defender-soldier; he shoots back. The aggressor-bomber bombards the fellow citizens of the defender soldier; he shoots him down' (*EKT*, 80).[22] Steinhoff then refutes three major arguments against justifying war as actual self-defence or the defence of others. These refutations of what he, interestingly, calls 'pacifism' significantly contrast with Rodin's approach but also undermine Elshtain's insistence on the sovereign state's prerogative to wage war, so I will briefly sketch them out.

First, one might say that war-as-self-defence often is not worth it. If one country invades another for an oil well or a piece of desert, its inhabitants *could* let go of these things to avoid the carnage of war. Such an 'excess of charity' is always possible. But, 'Right needs not shy away from wrong. On the other hand, one does not always have to insist on one's right' (*EKT*, 81). Appealing to Kant, Steinhoff sharply distinguishes between the juridical duty (*Rechtspflicht*) not to violate innocents' rights and the duty of virtue (*Tugendpflicht*), a 'general command of humanity, of neighbourliness' (*EKT*, 81). If someone attacks me, I do not violate his rights by insisting on my rights. Hence, I do not neglect my juridical duties towards him (*EKT*, 81).[23] This works also beyond a person's bare life: 'Why then should an existing person only be allowed to kill in defence of her existence, but not in defence of a basic life-value of her existence?' (*EKT*, 86).[24] If we take the right to self-defence seriously, one cannot buckle at an arbitrary point.

The same goes for a potentially innocent, because indoctrinated or otherwise non-culpable aggressor. One cannot, Steinhoff says, demand of an innocent defender that he shouldn't save his life (EKT, 83–5). Such self-sacrifice is, again, 'supererogatory, i.e. it surpasses the fulfilling of one's moral duties in an angel-like manner' (*EKT*, 85). If both aggressor and defender are morally innocent, each is in fact at liberty to fight to

---

[22] See Chapter 4 on Ramsey.

[23] For a critical discussion of fully separating juridical and virtue duties, see e.g. John Finnis, *Human Rights and the Common Good: Collected Essays* (Oxford: Oxford University Press 2011), p. 62f.; Konstantinos A. Papageorgiou, 'Kant, ein Rechtsmoralist? Ein Blick auf seine angewandte Ethik', in *Rechtssystem und Praktische Vernunft / Legal System and Practical Reason: Verhandlungen des 15. Weltkongresses für Rechts- und Sozialphilosophie*, ed. Ralf Dreier (Stuttgart: Franz Steiner Verlag, 1993), pp. 198–210.

[24] Steinhoff targets specifically Rodin on this matter in 'Rodin on Self-Defense and the "Myth" of National Self-Defense: A Refutation', *Philosophia*, 41 (2013), 1017–36.

the death.[25] 'The conflict of two equal, general rights [i.e. right to life/self-defence] in a particular case leads to the mutual limitation of the rights and produces two more particular liberties.' Steinhoff argues from intuition: 'it does not seem *acceptable* to demand of anyone to let himself get killed rather than kill an aggressor or a threat (even if they are innocent)' (*EKT*, 85). And later, 'If [an innocent aggressor] can only be stopped through killing, then his right to life must shy away from [the defender's] right to self-defence.' An unlimited antagonism, an unmediated clash of rights, is reined in only by the principle of proportionality.[26]

Of course, in war not only innocents fight. The second justification for fighting back is not derived from the mere fact of the aggressor's attack but from the aggressor's *guilt*. 'The guilt of the aggressor has the consequence that he has no right to defend himself against (proportionate) counter-measures' (*EKT*, 88). Nonetheless, even the *unjust* aggressor has a right to proportionately defend the innocents near and dear to him against becoming 'collateral damage', because it would violate *their* right to life. 'All things considered it may be *justified* to kill them, but it is not *just*' (*EKT*, 96). This lack of justice sufficiently justifies fulfilling associative duties (which Rodin's juridical proposal had effectively neglected):

> Imagine the innocent civilians [of the unjust side] are children. Would their parents not be permitted to intervene on their behalf? And why should third parties not be permitted to intervene on behalf of their spouses, loved ones, friends and, most important in this context, fellow citizens? After all, the cooperative protection against external threats is one of the major advantages (and duties) of common citizenship. (*EKT*, 98)[27]

Because such defensive coordination is justified, Steinhoff moves from mere immediate self-defence to a justification of self-defence on a larger scale, albeit without discussing international law. What matters here is the *actual* exercise of natural defensive rights. In that sense, he remains much closer to the sovereign 'realism' of Elshtain and does not need to justify a legal right to national defence.

Steinhoff far from refutes the third argument against war as individual or collective self-defence. This argument says that most killings in war have nothing to do with just self-defence, not even on the justified side. No army waits until it gets attacked (*EKT*, 100). So, he turns to criminal law. A 'justifying emergency' or 'necessity' legally justifies a defender to avert a grave danger to 'life, body, freedom, honour, property or another legal good [*Rechtsgut*]' even before an attack has actually taken place. In just-war terms, one could perhaps understand Steinhoff as arguing for pre-emptive self-defence.[28] '[The] exercise of the emergency right against an illegitimate and otherwise

---

[25] Steinhoff emphatically distinguishes between liberties and claim rights: the latter entails a claim towards the other that he not attack me; the former entails no duties for others. Uwe Steinhoff, 'Rights, Liability, and the Moral Equality of Combatants', unpublished manuscript, 2011.

[26] Steinhoff made this explicit in a Q&A session in 2011.

[27] For a political-philosophical discussion of associative versus cosmopolitan duties, see e.g. Jonathan Seglow, 'Associative Duties and Global Justice', *Journal of Moral Philosophy*, 7 (2010), 54–73.

[28] Steinhoff's example is a father in the woods, who, with five escaped mass murderers roaming about, sets out to kill them in order to protect his family.

not avoidable threat is permitted not only to save oneself, but also others' (*EKT*, 101). Here he finally adds that in view of the 'unjust side', discrimination is made between combatants and non-combatants (EKT, 102). Nevertheless, sometimes a danger to life, body or freedom cannot be averted but by attacking non-combatants in so far as they are *guilty* of causing the danger. The question of attacking innocent non-combatants may then also 'cause grave dilemmas' (*EKT*, 102).

In brief, how one discriminates between innocent and guilty depends on how one justifies war. For Steinhoff, four theoretical approaches and their inherent principles work together: guilt, convention, self-defence and emergency. First, the innocent are immune from attack. Second, this is a convention for which there are rule-utilitarian reasons. Third, a person may defend herself against illegitimate attack and, finally, a person is justified in attacking in an unjustified emergency. Each principle is intrinsically valid. They are all interdependent, restraining each other, even when they collide:

> In case of such a collision the 'subordinate' principle recedes, gives more space to the other, but at the same time upholds certain limits: up to here and no further! The continuous validity of the principle of guilt or innocence is apparent in so far as the use of violent force is allowed *only to the extent that* is necessary to avert the danger (whilst one could repay the aggression to the aggressor 'with interest', that is punish it). (*EKT*, 103)

The 'guilt-principle' in combination with an emergency principle largely corresponds to the traditional just war approach. However, it only works in connection with a doctrine of double effect, which Steinhoff has rejected. Instead, his move towards *effective* rights protection rests on the interplay between several restraining, regulative principles. One inference is that in a supreme emergency of self-defence one may break the convention and attack non-combatants. This amounts to the possible justification of terrorism.

The ethics of terrorism

In the final section of his book, Steinhoff wrestles the concept of 'terrorism' from its 'double-standard, propagandist' uses, 'preferably for the actions of others, not one's own' (*EKT*, 111). He systematically defines terrorism to see whether it may be morally permissible. Again, his critical move is an analytical readjustment and clarification, a logical testing of our 'linguistic intuitions' (*EKT*, 121) in light of a consequently liberal paradigm.

Terrorism is primarily a form of action: 'Whether an act is terrorist is to be determined by the action itself, not the agent' (*EKT*, 112). After a discussion of other definitions, he arrives at his own:

> *Terrorism* is the strategy of influencing the behaviour, perceptions, beliefs or attitudes of others than the immediate victims or targets of its violence by the threat, made credible by a corresponding act or series of acts, of the repeated killing

or severe harming of innocents or the repeated destruction or severe harming of their property. *Terrorist acts* are such severe attacks on innocents or their property that are part of such a strategy. (*EKT*, 123)

In this sense, many cases commonly labelled terrorism are actually something else; for example, some cases in which Palestinians target civilian Israelis. The latter, Steinhoff argues, democratically voted for their government. But 'terrorism' should only apply to *morally* innocent civilians: 'Direct attacks on school buses, kindergartens and similar targets would of course be terrorist, since those children, of course, have not voted' (*EKT*, 132). Certainly, there would be genuinely innocent victims when Israeli cafés get bombed, but these would be ' "collateral damage", which happens in the course of an attack on an aggressor' (*EKT*, 132). Of course, saving innocents still remains prior to the 'liberal right to punish an aggressor'. The *arbiter* between non-combatant immunity and punishment therefore is a utilitarian calculus: 'The Palestinian attacks on Israeli civilians entitled to vote are justified or not depending on the prospects of success one can assume after responsible calculation.'

In a 'justifying emergency' or indeed a 'state of exception also used by the apologists of state emergency' (*EKT*, 136), the convention of non-combatant immunity may be breached. For Steinhoff, such a case is 'the arbitrariness and brutality of the stronger one' (*EKT*, 134). If a militarily weak, small people are repeatedly attacked by an overwhelmingly larger, militarily superior aggressor, there may be no other strategic possibility left but to target the aggressor's innocent civilians. Such attacks do not breach the utilitarian rule calculus for non-combatant immunity. But it leads to a different 'emergency rule', valid when aggressors get away with impunity: 'If a community can only protect a large number of their innocents from an aggressor by attacking a smaller number of his innocents, this is permissible *unless it can be expected that a number of aggressors sufficient for deterrence will be punished for their attacks*' (*EKT*, 135). Even if the prospect of success is low – a point Steinhoff admits – such attacks would still be justified as a form of punishment. In other words, if successes do not materialize, the (terrorist) defendants are permitted to keep on trying harder.

Because of the duty to protect innocents, terrorism is only rarely justified. But unless one has an 'ethic of conviction' (which would be 'absolutist') as opposed to an 'ethic of responsibility', it is impossible to argue that terrorism can *never* be justified (*EKT*, 136). This repeats a distinction Steinhoff made earlier between duties of right and duties of virtue or supererogation. He decidedly casts his lot on the side of law as regulated struggle, individual defensive rights and associated responsibilities as opposed to pious 'convictions'. Finally, however, a cosmopolitan order of sorts appears on the horizon. In order to overcome subnational terrorism, or the need for it, Steinhoff suggests giving up double standards and state terrorism, the 'criminal prosecution of aggressors' and 'the inclusion of the excluded' (*EKT*, 137).[29]

---

[29] In a scathing review of Cécile Fabre's *Cosmopolitan War* (Oxford: Oxford University Press, 2012), Steinhoff qualified this claim: 'Self- and other-defense, after all, are not only about defending individual rights, but also about defending the legal or moral order.' *Notre Dame Philosophical Reviews*, 30 March 2013, online at https://ndpr.nd.edu/news/cosmopolitan-war/#_ednref (accessed 15 May 2018).

In short, Steinhoff's ethics of war mark an alternative path between the sovereigntist (imperialist) and the cosmopolitan (quasi-papalist) legalism approaches we encountered in Part One. He critically readjusts just war criteria in light of individuals' natural rights to defend themselves and those associated with them and thus presents a kind of individualist realism.

Immanent constellations: Radically reformed (a-)theology, Marxism and unbelieving prophecy

How does Steinhoff ground his ethics of war? Why should we believe that his approach is legitimate? Steinhoff's contribution is firmly grounded in his previous work on rationality, concepts of truth and the foundations of ethics. From this perspective, he also presents a particular theo-logic. There is an irreconcilable, unmediated gap between the reality of differing interests on the one hand and (possible) ethical *ideals* on the other hand. These are confined to a private, voluntary, though potentially substantial *Sittlichkeit*. As a result of this separation, the real and the ideal here fall together in an immanent liberal 'ethical' paradigm. In that sense, individual human beings are again the foundational 'princes of peace'. Unlike Rodin or Elshtain, however, Steinhoff sharply siphons off any religious or utopian dimension, whether immanent or transcendent. Nonetheless, his proposal retains some of the logical implications of sovereign realism. Considering Steinhoff's frequent critique of US hegemony and Elshtain's appeals to religion, this is striking. The reason, however, is not that he suggests an altogether different ethic but that he transposes sovereign state politics to the individual level – or as he says, 'Machiavelli for everyone' (*EE*, 15).

Reality: Nature – science – truth

Ethics are inevitably intertwined with what we believe to be true. What we recognize as 'reality' indicates a fundamental order of things as well as the possibilities of action. In that sense, locating Steinhoff theologically needs to be done inferentially. Epistemologically, he is a dedicated rationalist: the Christ event here falls behind the horizon of Enlightened reason. This is ultimately *theologically* warranted, or – to rephrase Wolfhart Pannenberg – it derives from an 'a-theology from below'. When defending radical liberalism in *Effiziente Ethik*, Steinhoff directly addresses theodicy 'after Auschwitz'. He accords to the Christian God the same kind of existence, will and 'responsibility' as any other person (*EE*, 52). The idea that such a God is almighty and good is pure mockery, he notes, even *more so* than Holocaust denial: 'with a denial one at least recognizes that something like the Holocaust *is simply incompatible with* the moral imperfection of those responsible – and whoever fails to render assistance, like God did, is responsible' (*EE*, 115). In that sense, traditional religion is akin to the belief in fairies and spirits mocked by Hobbes. But while Hobbes envisioned religion within the Leviathan, Steinhoff's God – if existent – is altogether a failure; transcendence is either a subjective choice or a blank space.[30]

---

[30] Thomas Hobbes, *Leviathan*, ed. Richard Tuck (Cambridge: Cambridge University Press, 2010), pp. 18–19, 83.

Nonetheless, the New Testament may well be a useful tool to promulgate a liberal ethic: 'certainly one can deny the existence of angels, demons, God and his son without denying the significance of the New Testament and its moral beliefs and moral standards and without abstaining from drawing on them' (*EE*, 109). Revelations are not needed though, since they merely 'repeat conventional moral wisdom with great pomp' (*EE*, 52). This again recalls Kant, for whom scripture falls apart into 'practically' relevant sections and sections that are 'theoretical, proclaimed to be holy, but surmounting the grasp of (even moral) reason'. This includes notions such as the Trinity, Incarnation, Ascension, etc. What one might call Steinhoff's sceptical-atheist Jesuology guarantees that the mediation of the real and the ideal in Christ becomes impossible.[31] Morality is transferred to human rational capacity and its propensity for advantageous choices.

Against any moral realism, which presupposes a form of revelation, Steinhoff begins from a more immediate epistemological point. 'The truth' is hardly a *tertium* both beyond and holding together empiricism and ideal vision, a truth that 'enlightens reason' (St Augustine). Steinhoff rejects any such ambitions: '[since] the mind cannot just produce reality and hence truth, it has to *find* it. ... In rationalism, rational thinking and rational argumentation is the best (although not infallible) method to find out truth understood as the congruence with reality' (*EE*, 27). Similarly to Elshtain, he defends the quest for truth against postmodern rhetoricism, albeit in favour of an empirical (rather than moralistic) quest (*EE*, 27–48). Pace the rhetoricists, reality is independent of human linguistic constructions – natural entities like snow are simply *there* and can be 'adequately described' (*EE*, 46). Any truth(quest) emerges and evolves between scientific hypothesis and empirical verification. There is nothing metaphysical about it; indeed, metaphysics should be critiqued (*EE*, 47, 109). Finding truth thus is like uncovering a crime or predicting the weather. Importantly for the present project, this is independent of any moral truths, indeed facticity *preconditions* morality. Steinhoff emphasizes that we need to be aware of the 'facts' in order to make moral decisions. *Science* supplies data on both the practical feasibility of our projects and the rational ends to be pursued (*EE*, 11–15, 49–56, 192–3). What is 'good and what is to be believed to be good for oneself ... depends on the real nature of the world' (*EE*, 48). Hence, one should try to find out about it. Since rational actions must be 'based on information grounded in a rational search for truth' *Effiziente Ethik* defends the scientific quest as ethically relevant (*EE*, 49). Steinhoff is quite upfront about the fact that there is no 'ultimate truth available'. *Wissenschaft* (science broadly understood) justifies its theories and theses by supporting them with facts. In this way, the 'belief in these theories and theses becomes rational'.

---

31 Immanuel Kant, 'Der Streit der Fakultäten', in *Kant's Gesammelte Schriften*, vol. VII (Berlin: Georg Reimer, 1917), pp. 38–44. See Steinhoff's own use of Jesus's saying thou shalt recognize a tree by its fruit (Mt. 7.15–20; Lk. 6.43–4); this was not least one of the most significant emphases of the 'radical' Reformation; see Hans J. Hillerbrand, *The Division of Christendom: Christianity in the Sixteenth Century* (Louisville, KT: Westminster John Knox, 2007), p. 109. NB: If a Cartesian separation between inner morality and external causality is moot before the 'public' view of God, Steinhoff in contrast cements it with his 'ethics of efficiency'.

The truth of nature and science becomes a secular *analogon* to revelation. In line with the Enlightened juxtaposition of faith and reason, Steinhoff directly sets reason against believing in God (*EE*, 52).[32] And whereas the church may witness to truth in God (and be the locus of 'Christian ethics'), Steinhoff's turn to 'the world' as empirical nature entails an analogous realization or positivization. Scientific 'truth' manifests itself as, is *mediated by*, 'institutionalised *Wissenschaft*'. Institutionalized science is the 'eminent embodiment of epistemic rationality' (*EE*, 56). And the scientific community explicitly represents a secular alternative to the church. It is less dogmatic, more self-critical and more principled in the search for truth: 'The principles of religion and the church ... support, indeed demand uncritical belief, the genesis of dogmatism, wilful ignorance of contradictory evidence' (*EE*, 56). In that sense, we can already see the outlines of an alternative mediator between Is and Ought besides the Leviathan (Elshtain) or international law (Rodin), though politically, science ends up with a largely auxiliary function.

Steinhoff's promotion of science is of course a welcome attack on 'para- and pseudo-sciences or New Age belief systems' (*EE*, 56). It safeguards the value of rationality and prudence, reminiscent of Machiavelli's *virtù*.[33] Empirical reality is then a source of political ethics, albeit negatively. Natural science can hardly tell us what we *should* do.[34] From an 'is' one cannot derive an 'ought'. But certainly one can infer a 'non-ought' from an 'is' (*EE*, 190), Steinhoff says. 'Facts (like the empirical fact of a physical or practical impossibility) can prove commands wrong (if one cannot realise heaven on earth, then one has no duty to do it)' (*EE*, 191). The factual *Can* is a litmus test to all *Oughts*. And since the scientific paradigm knows no Kingdom of God, there can be no such morally commanding reality.[35] Unsurprisingly, *pace* Rodin's view, international law cannot absorb or sidestep the practical demands of any given real-world situation. At the same time, any political decision must pass the tests of rational deliberation and the interests of those involved.

Empirical *social* science feeds into Steinhoff's just war thinking both as analysis and prediction; his academic background in psychology resurfaces at several points. For example, he uses the psychological 'Terror Management Theory', which focuses on the innate human fear of death and people's innate inclination to obey authorities. If soldiers are constantly reminded of their mortality, as they were in Abu Ghraib, it can be predicted that out of fear they will gradually descend into 'barbarism'. Such social facts then provide the basis to arrange new social facts: 'How barbaric a war is depends on how well these basic psychological dynamics are held at bay or even manipulated.'[36]

---

[32] It is beyond the scope of our work here to investigate the premises of this juxtaposition, but one problem may be the analysis of faith as a psychological operation. See, e.g. Robert Audi, *Rationality and Religious Commitment* (Oxford: Oxford University Press, 2011), pp. 248–85.

[33] Cf. Quentin Skinner, *Machiavelli* (Oxford: Oxford University Press, 1981), pp. 37–40.

[34] Pretensions to such projects are essentially forms of physical or chemical manipulation of humans as *objects*, as for example in Transhumanism or neuro-philosophy.

[35] As a side effect, of course, the origins of a moral judgement are at stake, hence intuition – potentially *irrational* in its own way – plays a central role in analytic philosophy (e.g. the 'intuition' that intention matters to the morality of an action).

[36] Uwe Steinhoff, 'Why There Is No Barbarization but a Lot of Barbarity in Warfare', in *Warrior's Dishonour: Barbarity, Morality and Torture in Modern Warfare*, ed. George Kassimeris (Aldershot: Ashgate, 2006), pp. 101–11, 106.

In terms of *political* ontology, there is no preconceived political sphere or a given international sphere already ordered by *ius gentium* or natural law. It is contingent upon individual contractual choice. Indeed, any ('created') sociality is fundamentally questioned.[37] For example, Article 28 of the Declaration of Human Rights says that every human has a right to a social and international order in order to realize his rights. But for Steinhoff such 'amassments' are merely the result of a large human population. Only 'amassment fanatics' could demand of people, and thus potentially force them, to live in society. This, Steinhoff claims, would mean violating Article 20 of the same Declaration (EE, 181).

For Steinhoff, political reality thus begins with a 'state of nature'. It forms the backbone of his just war proposal: 'Following John Locke, in the "state of nature", that is before the individual confers certain rights to a community, every individual has the right to punish someone who violates natural law, i.e. every aggressor.' This right persists also in the community and resurfaces 'when the state cannot help an individual up against an aggressor' (*EKT*, 55). The great Other to this vision – the contents of religion or any residual social insights drawn from that tradition – is confined to an 'absolute' sphere beyond reason. Leaving aside Elshtain's grounds in myth, Steinhoff shares important elements with her – not only in their vision of the 'state of nature' but also in rejecting as politically formative what Elshtain called 'sectarian' religion.[38] Power-politically neutralized, revelation as 'religion' can thus be mocked or tolerated – or both simultaneously.

Expedient choices

Alan Padgett has pointed out that 'the practical-nature bias of the natural sciences ... has nothing in fact to do with a full-blown ontology as a philosophical worldview' and that 'it is just too easy to think of methodological naturalism as simply acting in the practice of science as if naturalism (full-blown) were true'.[39] However, in Steinhoff's case, it seems that the method of enquiry and the basic naturalist assumption about 'the world' do go together, at least in so far as the social and political sciences *already* prefigure a certain normative order. It is the conflicted interplay between individuals and 'society' according to gradually unfolding, observable regularities. Scientific and instrumental rationality are intertwined as they become the tools of an individual person's 'success'. 'Ethics' is less a reflection on, or practical representation of, an

---

[37] Cf. Uwe Steinhoff, 'Is There a Duty to Militarily Intervene to Stop a Genocide?', in *Military Interventions: Considerations from Philosophy and Political Science*, ed. Christian Neuhäuser and Christoph Schuck (Baden-Baden: Nomos, 2017), pp. 59–80: Steinhoff argues that there is a permission to militarily intervene, but a duty only exists if there is a prevenient contract. If there was a duty, omission to act would result in owing a compensation to victims.

[38] The military-industrial complex marks the marriage of Steinhoff's 'embodied rationality' and Elshtain's sovereign security, including its own 'prophets'. Peter Goodchild, *J. Robert Oppenheimer: Shatterer of Worlds* (London: British Broadcasting Corp, 1980); Lynda Walsh, *Scientists as Prophets: A Rhetorical Genealogy* (New York: Oxford University Press, 2013).

[39] Alan G. Padget, 'Practical Objectivity', in *Blackwell Companion to Science and Christianity* (Oxford: Wiley-Blackwell, 2012), pp. 93–102, p. 96.

alternative vision or reality. For Steinhoff, it is rather a 'functional thing', 'motivating agents to act morally' (*EE*, 91, 180).

One reflex may be to ask: What is the moral standard for 'acting morally'? Steinhoff remains consistently sceptical. There is no objective moral standard for 'good' or 'good life': 'Even if an objective measure [of moral goodness] did actually exist and we somehow discovered it, it may very well be that it supports norms that we reject, like the norm "You should kill at least one person per month!"' (*EE*, 92).[40] In the absence of such an objective standard, ethics has two aspects. One is the externally functional one just mentioned. As something 'to propagate' – a neutral term here – ethics functions so as to 'regulate society' (*EE*, 93). The other aspect appeals to the individual subject. Similar to Foucault, whom he identifies as a regular liberal, Steinhoff advocates an 'ethic of the care of oneself as a *praxis* of freedom' (*EE*, 164). For example, a serial killer may be reluctant to internalize a liberal ethic, because it would mean he would have to stop killing people. But he might be happy to propagate it to others.[41] Others' well-being, of course, may very well be a part of one's own interests. Such 'enlightened self-interest' was already an element of Elshtain's American empire. Here, it returns as an individualist version of the realism (familiar in International Relations theory of states): the moral aim (and aim of morality) is to *successfully safeguard subjective interests*.

For Steinhoff, a personal cost-benefit analysis is then the criterion for a choice of one's moral conviction:

> As a rational agent I will propagate (internalize) an ethic of which an epistemically rational examination proves that to propagate (internalize) it goes hand in hand with the best possible ratio between the benefits of the expected outcomes of propaganda (i.e. internalisation) on the one hand, and the probability of the result that is to be expected. (*EE*, 94; also 99)

So one chooses an 'ethic' because it is expedient, because it directly promises the greatest advantage to oneself (which includes a regulated society) (*EE*, 14, 90, 94). That Steinhoff's preferred ethic is liberal or even 'radically liberal' may be unsurprising, since he redoubles and reaffirms the presumed social-liberal paradigm of differing private interests: 'Is it good for me, is it in my interest to be a liberal?' A subtle oscillation is at work here: on the one hand, the 'choice' of ethic presupposes an absolute voluntarist freedom. On the other hand, the (Weberian) paradigm with its duality between a (social-)scientific reality and certainly worthy 'ideals' (*EE*, 191) is beyond dispute. A transformative, and hence mediating, potentially revelatory event questioning this

---

40 This argument is a non sequitur. The moral realist would simply say we recognize an objective measure of moral goodness. Steinhoff himself implies that killing a person a month *cannot* be a moral objective. Paradoxically, while this is obviously clear, the truth of such a morality claim must remain opaque. Perhaps Steinhoff is aware that it finally requires the same realm of 'absolute truth' that is also inaccessible for science; at least John Locke still recognized that individual human beings were creatures of God.

41 Against the claim that one can hardly justify morality through egotistical-prudential reasons, he argues, 'Although the person has made a moral system her own out of extra-moral reasons, [having internalised a moral system] she then still acts morally (also) out of moral reasons' (*EE*, 100).

order of secular reality as such is impossible. Ethics is identified as social manipulation, even self-regulation.

Steinhoff's liberalism here should be understood as a naturalized, politically realizable *ecclesia*, a *polis* in which the value of each individual is recognized.[42] Liberalism has the advantage that it allows for the 'free development' of one's personality and recognizing others as such personalities. This includes the freedom to change one's morality (i.e. rules or dogmas, if one finds them to be untrue). Moreover, unlike deontological ethics, a liberal ethic emphasizes *rights* (*EE*, 104).[43] Steinhoff's act of generosity in 'rights' is to grant to everyone the Machiavellian maxime: *mantener lo stato*. This view may not be groundbreaking, and Steinhoff makes no claim to that. But it renews the liberal human rights approach in between the Habermasian and some of its postmodernist detractors.

Notably, even if one did not believe in human rights as 'moral facts', Steinhoff says, a liberal ethic 'warrants a large part of that freedom, which has always been before the senses as an attractive temptation'. The 'ideal of a liberal ethic' is a rule of compromise, a 'Kantian formula of Right, the conceptual sum of conditions under which the arbitrary will of one can be united with that of another according to a general law of freedom'. Whatever people do beyond that is morally irrelevant, 'as long as they agree' (*EE*, 103).[44] This formula of Right is the maximum 'moral ideal' Steinhoff can commit to.

In practice, the oscillation between interests and formal curbing drives Steinhoff's rejection to question the relevance of inner attitudes and intentions. It throws the (traditional) doctrine of double effect into disrepute, subverting the idea of thinking politics in terms of personal integrity. These are simply dimensions that fellow humans cannot adjudicate as they cannot drill windows into other people's hearts. Simultaneously, morality here is already a *judicial* law rather than a practical reference to truth (theologically reflected on).[45] Law and morality are assimilated 'by specifying enforceability as their common feature' so that the greatest autonomy is guaranteed

---

[42] At least in so far as he draws on Locke, cf. e.g. Winthrop S. Hudson, who notes that Edmund Burke and John Adams 'were both aware of the pit from whence the political principles of Locke had been dug, and the cartoons of the time made it evident that the general populace was equally clear in its understanding that Locke and Sidney and Calvin were representatives of a single tradition'. John Locke, 'Heir of Puritan Political Theorists', in *Calvinism and the Political Order*, ed. George L. Hunt and John T. McNeill (Philadelphia: Westminster, 1965), pp. 108–29; for a discussion of Locke's liberalism in the contemporary American debate, see esp. John Perry, *The Pretenses of Loyalty: Locke, Liberal Theory, and American Political Theology* (Oxford: Oxford University Press, 2011), pp. 165–200.

[43] On the pragmatic usefulness of human rights ethics as opposed to their foundationalist grounding, see also Michael Ignatieff, 'Human Rights as Politics and Idolatry', in *Human Rights as Politics and Idolatry*, ed. Amy Gutmann (Princeton, NJ: Princeton University Press, 2001), p. 55; Diane F. Orentlicher, 'Relativism and Religion', in *Human Rights as Politics and Idolatry*, ed. Amy Gutmann (Princeton, NJ: Princeton University Press, 2001), pp. 141–58.

[44] On David Richards' (mis)reading of Kant in that regard, see Finnis, *Human Rights and the Common Good*, pp. 53–60.

[45] Cf. Luther's reading of the meaning of the law as Adam changes with the Fall: it becomes *alia lex*, a mere letter (*lex litterae*), an external code arbitrarily imposed and therefore a 'merely moral matter' (WA [Weimarer Ausgabe, *D. Martin Luthers Werke*, 120 vols. Weimar: 1883–2009], 40/I, 413). The law itself, however, remains the same (WA 42, 82). Bernd Wannenwetsch, 'Luther's Moral Theology', in *Cambridge Companion to Martin Luther*, ed. Donald K. McKim (Cambridge: Cambridge University Press, 2003), pp. 120–35, 125–6.

to everyone.[46] This is also where the just war criteria-as-conventions come in: not so much a result of any transformative or ontological peacefulness but as the tentative regulation of fundamentally clashing interests.

Steinhoff's ethic thus repeats Elshtain's realism at significant points. It relies on a fundamental dualism between the empirical and 'religion' in the sense of a propositional faith in Christian revelation. This correlates with (an ultimately impractical) Jesuology. Ecclesiology here has collapsed into a (quasi-ecclesial) liberalism and also political egalitarianism geared towards successful rights enforcement. In terms of political-theological precedents, the Lockean and – further back – the sixteenth-century Calvinist struggles with the Libertines are significant.[47] Calvin marks an essential break with the papal-imperial consensus, but in his struggle with Michael Servetus he also clashed with an alternative 'reformation of the Reformation'.[48] A medical doctor and (proto-)scientist, Servetus formulated a decisively non-Trinitarian theology, discerning the spiritual workings of God within the material workings of the body and creation as a whole. Jesus was the son of the eternal God, though not the eternal son of God. Calvin, for his part, regarded Servetus as varyingly guilty of Arian and Sabellian heresies. After Servetus's spectacular demise (burnt twice: once at the stake, once in effigy), his legacy fed into various unitarianisms that would become influential in the United States; his avid defender, the humanist Sebastian Castellio, made a case for religious tolerance; Voltaire in his *Essais sur les mœrs* (1756) adduced Servetus as an example for Calvin's violent intolerance.[49] As for the present comparison, we may note that Elshtain with (an after all Calvinist) Lincoln steers a Hobbesian path to state sovereignty, alongside the *Eusebius redivivus* Schmitt. For his part, Steinhoff seeks to *defend*, preserve and improve the individual and individualist elements within that (still liberal) scheme (*EE*, 191). Both stand against a (quasi-)Catholic legal(ist) order as proposed by Rodin.

Analogous to Elshtain's view, Steinhoff's realism also has its own (potentially violent) utopian implications. While a divinely authorized state is 'utopian', literally without a conceivable space, such a morally indefinite space and time promises unlimited opportunities to pursue one's desires and ethical projects. This will become clearer when we look at how Steinhoff conceives the moral agent.

The defensive individual – against the ideological state apparatus

In line with his conception of reality, Steinhoff rejects 'the great portion of metaphysics' required to argue, for example, that only the community has the right to punish but not 'the individual as an individual' (*EKT*, 26).[50] In so far as he draws on Locke (and,

---

[46] John Stuart Mill, *On Liberty and Other Essays* (Oxford: Oxford University Press, 1998), pp. xv, 5.
[47] Cf. Hillerbrand, *The Division of Christendom*, pp. 306–14.
[48] Hillerbrand, *Division of Christendom*, p. 108.
[49] See e.g. Sebastian Castellio's De haereticis an sint persequendi (1554); see *Das Manifest der Toleranz: Sebastian Castellio: Über Ketzer und ob man sie verfolgen soll: De haereticis an sint persequendi*, ed. Wolfgang Stammler (Essen: Franz Steiner Verlag, alcorde Verlag, 2017); Voltaire, *Essai sur les mœurs et l'esprit des nations*, edition Garnier, vol. 12 (Paris: Garnier, 1878), pp. 306–10.
[50] Brian Rosebury has convincingly shown how a purely retributive notion of justice becomes hard to distinguish from revenge. Brian Rosebury, 'Private Revenge and Its Relation to Punishment', *Utilitas* 21 (2009), 1–21. See Steinhoff above, *EKT*, 103; also *EE*, 125–6.

concomitantly, his empiricism and proto-liberalism), Steinhoff embraces the 'sovereign self' that Elshtain – albeit unconvincingly – rejected.[51]

Natural rights – shearing off state metaphysics

As we heard, whatever rights a communal authority (conceived as a positive institution) has, it does so by the contractual rights conferral of its individual, naturally free constituents. Political authority is simply the institutional sum of alienated rights. If it 'fails', all authority returns to each citizen. There is no *categorical* change from particle to whole, private to public, subjective to objective: 'Contrary to the church fathers it is the view of a *liberal* theorist like Locke that a community can only have the rights that its members confer to it.' Steinhoff's mockery is hard to miss: 'There is no miraculous representative rights-increase' (*EKT*, 26). *Pace* the Hobbesian tradition of the state as a fictional person, a qualitative leap from private to public would be 'obscure metaphysics of numbers' or 'metaphysics of collectives'.[52] This does not diminish the fact that states or groups may go to war. If attacked aggressively, they are *at liberty* to respond.

When it comes to a body politic worth or even commanding defence, Steinhoff's individualism is more entrenched than in many other contractarianisms. This has partly to do with his moral epistemology: not everything right or rational can be justified to everyone. Contractarianism 'aims to answer [the] question: "The institutionalisation of which normative system is good for everyone (in a society or a territory)?"' But it is 'an idle longing' to attain a general justification of authority or a public good. That leads to 'ignoring the differences between individuals, to inadequate idealisations and models that abstract from reality rather than help us to deal with it' (*EE*, 94–5). Without qualitative add-ons to these differences but rather *in respect of them*, political authority is no more than a pragmatic, reactive apparatus of organized restraint and defence.[53] It ceases to be in any way necessary representative, communal mediation. Hence, echoing Rodin, Steinhoff turns away from a particular kind of just war theory:

> Contrary to just war theory, individuals – or more or less unorganized groups, for that matter – do not at first need the mediation of a representative (as in Catholicism) in order to attain legitimate authority for waging war; rather, they bear this authority in themselves. If, under certain conditions, a *right to war* comes into operation, it is, or is based upon, an *individual right*. (EKT, 27)[54]

In other words, individual defence and political authority on the other hand become *identical* by the *fact*. Steinhoff here redoubles on the level of the individual a Weberian

---

[51] Elshtain, *Sovereignty: God, State and Self* (New York: Basic, 2008), pp. 181–201.

[52] Steinhoff, 'Lone Individual', pp. 137–8.

[53] For Locke, the duty of self-preservation still rests on the fact that the individual is a creature of God, not merely the will to survival. *Second Treatise*, Chapter 2, § 6.

[54] While there are congruencies with traditional just war theory, and Steinhoff affirmatively refers to e.g. Vitoria or Molina, he sharply criticizes Rodin and others for misrepresenting the tradition. See e.g. Uwe Steinhoff, 'Personenrechte und die Kriegsrechtsbestimmungen', in *Den Gegner schützen?: Zu einer aktuellen Kontroverse in der Ethik des bewaffneten Konflikts*, ed. Bernhard Koch (Baden-Baden: Nomos; Münstern: Aschendorff, 2014), pp. 165–94, pp. 165–6.

definition of the state as the factual monopoly of force: 'the authority of an individual to wage war ... results from the fact that the individual defends his individuality and his individual rights and is legitimated to do so by those very rights, his rationality and his moral autonomy' (*EKT*, 140, n. 35). The self-mediation of the humanum here is probably most obvious.

At least in *Effiziente Ethik* Steinhoff appears to ground his aversion against 'representation' in it being a mere concept of elitist ruling and empirical findings. Domestically, he positively alludes to Switzerland's direct democracy – an affinity alone that in the current political climate frequently gets attacked as 'populist' (and hence theological-political 'heresy'):

> But a certain part of the elite, for example the governing elite can, as empirical research shows, also be less liberal or democratic than the mass as a whole. Hence representation ... is an insufficient instrument to minimize what [Sartori] calls 'external costs' (i.e. oppression), whilst participation, in contrast, does not undermine democracy but ensures it. (*EE*, 185)

There should of course be formal institutions to decide for the community, Steinhoff adds. But this is merely pragmatic; there is no *moral* reason why it should be wrong for everybody to go to war. Thus, absent a transcendently qualified Other such as the 'metaphysics of the state' or other 'miracles', Steinhoff's individualist realism mediates and legitimizes itself – or idealizes itself. Everybody is a would-be politician by virtue of their interests.

Steinhoff again provides the 'revolutionary' underbelly of Elshtain's liberal-democratic imperial(ist) state. Notably, some authors associated with Radical Orthodoxy and other 'new traditionalist' Catholics had rejected empire but equally such (participatory) socialist and grass-roots democratic alternatives. William T. Cavanaugh, for example, denounced the modern state as 'a source of an alternative soteriology to that of the Church ... the body of the state is a simulacrum, a false copy, of the body of Christ'. In contrast, the 'Eucharist, which makes the Body of Christ, is ... a key practice for a Christian anarchism'.[55] So also in this respect Steinhoff stands in a tradition of (theological-)political 'heresy'.

Besides the Catholic traditions, secular *cosmopolitanism*, especially Habermas's version, has been one of Steinhoff's explicit targets.[56] Habermas found a 'critical theory of society' on 'discursive' rationality' as a form of consensus.[57] The universal moral vision, the 'world society' to be politically constituted, then encounters a particular

---

[55] Cited in Michael Horton, 'In Praise of Profanity: A Theological Defense of the Secular', in *Evangelicals and Empire: Christian Alternatives to the Political Status Quo*, ed. Bruce Ellis Benson and Peter Goodwin Heltzel (Grand Rapids, MI: Brazos Press), pp. 252–66, p. 254.

[56] Critical also of Cécile Fabre: Uwe Steinhoff, 'Review: Cécile Fabre, *Cosmopolitan War*, Oxford University Press, 2012', *Notre Dame Philosophical Reviews*, 30 March 2013, available at https://ndpr.nd.edu/news/cosmopolitan-war/ (accessed 7 December 2018).

[57] For an analysis of the movement from philosophy to social theory specifically in the work of Hegel, see Herbert Marcuse, *Reason and Revolution. Hegel and the Rise of Social Theory* (London: Routledge & Kegan, 1955), p. 251f.

given reality of conflict.[58] Habermas eventually warmed to the possibility that such an ethic could stand on religious foundations, a position that Steinhoff, for his part, chides as 'regression'.[59] He thinks that such a universal ethic – and here he notes a dialectical turn – ends up being 'provincial and inefficient', since Habermasian 'internalised conscience controls' are de facto absent in many societies (*EE*, 90).[60] Against 'the powerlessness of the pure "ought"' Habermas merely posits the 'need for a certain congruency' between 'moral universalism and *already given* political and societal institutions as well as *existing* ways of conscience formation' (*EE*, 88). Steinhoff correctly considers this, if not inconsistent, then at least untrue to the facts. Hence, he disposes of Habermas's 'utopian' cosmopolitan ideal. With this, utopian, ideal political institutions are no longer defensible.

In the present framework, Steinhoff effectively naturalizes the former 'priesthood of all' of Reformed or, rather, radical Protestantism. The latter's ecclesial discipline is fully politicized here. The spiritual distrust of external authority becomes a radical individualism; the emphasis on individual faith is a radical voluntarism. Of course, a certain *pacific mindset* undergirds the fundamental, politically foundational recognition of each individual's (inalienable) rights (Steinhoff is everything but a militarist). Yet historically, the radically Reformed tradition was associated with schism and potential insurrection – an option Steinhoff defends at least in theory.[61] Either way, both Steinhoff and Habermas avoid the question of a *practical mediation* between the real and the ideal, between politics and morality. Either a problem of impracticability arises (Habermas) or the moral-metaphysical possibilities of public political authority shrink away (Steinhoff), and we are left with (un)regulated, potentially indiscriminate self-preservation. The latter, as we will see later, is after all 'bound' in the liberal constitutional state. That the two authors are matching '*counter*-parts' may not be surprising.[62]

In Steinhoff's scepticism about authority, one may also detect a hint of Pierre-Joseph Proudhon or Louis Althusser wrestling with ideology.[63] Not that for him 'property is theft' – Steinhoff is after all a Lockean. In the spirit of J. S. Mill, it is something like 'claims to authority are tyrannical'. This is a radical scepticism not quite unfamiliar to Augustine:

---

[58] See e.g. Habermas's formula of a 'world society to be politically constituted', in e.g. 'Europa am Scheideweg', *Handelsblatt*, 18 June 2011, http://www.handelsblatt.com/politik/international/essay-europa-am-scheideweg/4298474.html (accessed 7 December 2018).

[59] Uwe Steinhoff, *The Philosophy of Jürgen Habermas – A Critical Introduction* (Oxford: Oxford University Press, 2009); Jürgen Habermas and Joseph Ratzinger, *Dialectics of Secularization: On Reason and Religion* (San Francisco, CA: Ignatius Press, 2006).

[60] Cf. Chapter 2 cosmopolitanism collapsing into subjectivism and empire.

[61] See Alistair McGrath, *Reformation Thought: An Introduction* (Oxford: Basil Blackwell, 1988), p. 10; Huntston Williams, *The Radical Reformation*, 3rd ed. (Kirksville, MO: Sixteenth Century Journal, 1992), p. 359 f.

[62] Cf. the way that Methodism and Roman Catholicism work together in Ramsey's *War and the Christian Conscience*; see Chapter 4.

[63] Louis Althusser, 'Ideology and Ideological State Apparatus (Notes towards an Investigation)', in Althusser, *Lenin and Philosophy and Other Essays* (New York: Monthly Review Press, 2001), pp. 85–126, esp. p. 89f. Steinhoff in *EE*, p. 119. Christianity questions and sublates this dichotomy of external world and ideology.

That medieval thinkers, for whom a civilised life obviously consisted in an authority [*Obrigkeit*] supposedly appointed by God telling a subservient mass [*Untrigkeit*] what to do, put great emphasis on the principle of legitimate authority is probably owed to their own interests rather than the public interest. (EKT, 26)

Steinhoff's scepticism here also subtly shifts the meaning of 'public'. Not that publicity (in the Kantian, Protestant sense) equals the individual conscience's immediate access to a universal public reason, whereas state authorities are 'private'. Rather, the universality of *private* authority *is* true publicity. Claims to authority as public per se are more likely to be self-interested pretence. Authority is an intellectual faculty grounded in rational capacity and will rather than the point of public communal representation.[64] On these premises, it remains consequently unclear why a state authority or experts (who are also limited) should make any better decisions than individuals. Or indeed how they could be anything else but cunning criminals in disguise (*EKT*, 140, n. 35).

Again, one should not miss Steinhoff's mention of Catholicism (*EKT*, 13, 40; *EE*, 176–7). The 'metaphysics of the state' as a totalitarian entity and that of the church become indistinguishable if one understands them as equally posited institutional manifestations of an imagined social or communal idea (the Kingdom of God, the mystical body of the *Volk*, etc.). Thus conceived, both Christian universalism and the 'metaphysics of numbers' can indeed function as ideologies. They are 'imaginary orders' or 'constructed realities', as Althusser would say, with a will-to-power at their root. Steinhoff says this explicitly: in propounding a 'just war theory' instead of its original pacifism, 'historical Christianity' transformed into a 'ruling ideology'.[65] The 'metaphysical social visions' of state and church imply a 'bad positivity', to use a Hegelian phrase.[66] They are the harmful, practical manifestations of irrational beliefs, as each individual submits to institutions obliterating their agency, authority and rationality.[67] Hence also his mockery of the 'higher blessing of the U.N.'. Yet in terms of the logic of authority in war, as for Rodin, political authority can only choose between collectivism and individualism. Either it devours the individual in the name of a social agency or it merely formalizes the reactive liberal right to resistance (viz. *EE*, 180).[68] The latter then becomes clearly preferable. A possibility to think authority and citizenship springing

---

[64] This parallels also the Lockean shift from a previous understanding of personhood as ontological to psychological, as 'consciousness'. John Locke, *Essay Concerning Human Understanding*, Bk. II, Ch. 27, §§ 9–12.

[65] That Christianity *can* become a state ideology was demonstrated by Eusebius and Elshtain in Chapter 1. Cf. Oliver O'Donovan, *From Irenaeus to Grotius, From Irenaeus to Grotius: A Sourcebook in Christian Political Thought* (Grand Rapids, MI: William B. Eerdmans, 1999), p. 56. Steinhoff's sense is correct here: disconnected from revelation (and an adequate witness), these things are no more than ideologies. Nevertheless, he suggests something comparable when 'using' the Bible.

[66] Hans Küng, *Menschwerdung Gottes; Eine Einführung in Hegels theologisches Denken als Prolegomena zu einer künftigen Christologie* (Freiburg i. Br.: Herder, 1970), pp. 123–5.

[67] Max Weber, *Wirtschaft und Gesellschaft* (Tübingen: J. C. B. Mohr [P. Siebeck], 1947), pp. 142–8, 642: 'It is the fate of charisma throughout to ebb away as it streams into the permanent formations of communal action in favour of the powers either of tradition or rational socialization. Its waning means, all in all, that the significance of individual action is pushed back.'

[68] See also Bernd Wannenwetsch, *Political Worship* (Oxford: Oxford University Press, 2009), p. 3.

from a mediate and *transcendent* point between individual 'natural right' or liberty and 'ideology'[69] is suspicious in this dichotomous, modern constellation.

Nevertheless, such a metaphysical, teleological and 'alien' moment of political authority remains lingering in Steinhoff's proposal.[70] Steinhoff leaves open the possibility that direct democratic decisions could be *more* representative and go beyond individual interest by 'solving the problems of the community' (*EE*, 187). Despite Steinhoff's polemics, this community (and more recently, the defence of the 'moral' and 'socio-legal order'[71]) is certainly there. Similarly, an individual going to war to defend his rights, which may include tyrannicide, may very well act representatively, even if that is no *necessary* requirement.[72] Although leaving a certain opening, the dangling question of community and representation remains problematic. Steinhoff chides a 'totalitarian democracy à la Rousseau', in which all adult citizens of an unjustly attacking democratic country are liable to attack. But later he regards citizens of an aggressive, yet democratic state such as Israel as morally guilty based on the fact that they have voted for the Sharon government. Non-combatant civilians become liable to attack as 'morally guilty'. Arguably, this is an effect of failing to consider what he called the 'miraculous representative rights-increase' of political authority, a morally 'objective' quality of authority beyond citizens' subjective 'choices'.

Other metaphysical questions remain open. Steinhoff requires some normative content for his Kantian formula: 'The [radically liberal] principle, understood as abstract and "pure", cannot be realised at all, but only in a form in which substantial pre-decisions about the recognisability [*Anerkennungswürdigkeit*] of certain *façons* have already been made' (*EE*, 115). Any given liberal order already embodies an arrangement of substantial normative decisions about the good life and thus mediates abstract universals or 'values'. Steinhoff even recognizes that the 'flame of freedom' actually *depends* on such decisions for substantial goods (*EE*, 116).

Yet without debating such contents, Steinhoff can hardly go beyond radical suspicion:

> In [every liberal order] there is always an asymmetry between *façons*, between possibilities of individuals to develop, so that one always has to factor in the possibility that the existing asymmetry is an unjust one. (*EE*, 116)[73]

This echoes Augustine's (and Rodin's) gloomy, but essentially anti-positivist, moment in the *City of God*: a *res publica* without *Iustitia* may as well be a robber band.[74] Steinhoff's

---

[69] For this option, see Chapter 5 on Oliver O'Donovan.
[70] This is opposed to a (paradoxical) mutual reflection of the individual and the universal to each other.
[71] See Steinhoff, 'Rodin on Self-Defense'.
[72] Steinhoff, 'Lone individual', p. 138. See Bernd Wannenwetsch, 'Luther's Moral Theology', p. 126. The law demands an agent or subject no longer there, which implies an inherently representative scope. See also the 'just war' of Heinrich von Kleist's *Michael Kohlhaas* (1811).
[73] The term *façon* echoes Frederick II of Prussia's proto-liberal dictum: 'Everyone may seek Heaven in his own fashion.'
[74] City of God, IV, 4, 1; on Augustine as anti-positivist, see e.g. John Milbank, *Theology and Social Theory: Beyond Secular Reason*, 2nd ed. (Oxford: Blackwell, 2006); Pope Benedict XVI, *Speech before the Reichstag* (Visit to the German Federal Parliament), 22 September 2011; Emile Perreau-Saussine, 'Heaven as a Political Theme in Augustine's City of God', in *Paradise in Antiquity: Jewish*

radical scepticism for a moment occupies the same spot as Ramsey's (Nietzschean) agapism, which we will examine in the Chapter 4. Analogous to Steinhoff, Ramsey rejects sovereign states as well as papalism as 'atheist' to then plunge into a *critical* freedom that is *Christian* beyond positive institutions. Appealing to the same critical freedom, Steinhoff also rejects these as oppressive institutions. However, at this juncture, the two authors go separate ways. For Ramsey, *agape's* generous freedom by Christ's kenotic standard can wage a crusade *for* the neighbour. Steinhoff, getting rid of all metaphysical pretence on rationalist grounds, cuts himself short from naming any good *façons*. There has to be some sort of incorporation of the good, but that's as far as he can go. Steinhoff's *Iustitia* has to remain mute.[75]

The political agent extended: Ideology, liberal empire and the state of exception

For this reason, Steinhoff's moment of transcendent freedom is prone to collapse into a progressivist human rights idealism. In that sense, Steinhoff suggests furthering liberalism itself as an ideology.[76] The neutrality principle as to normative content, for example, is a basic 'ideologeme'. Once a person has found liberalism to be the most advantageous view to internalize, Steinhoff argues, the question of which ethic to propagate arises (a term used without the negative connotations of 'propaganda' in mind) (*EE*, 106).

The 'spreading of liberalism' may not always be helpful, for example when it effectively threatens the lives of those one wants to liberate. A 'weighing of goods', that is, successful results, is always necessary (*EE*, 107). Steinhoff then gives advice reminiscent of manuals for *missionaries*. When justifying liberalism to others, one must appeal to their 'cultural sensitivities'; one must 'package' it attractively. Like pagan residues, it remains inevitable that the pure 'liberal principle' is 'tainted by *Sittlichkeit*', the substantive normative contents mentioned above. Nevertheless, step by step, one should get 'the liberal train moving' and politically support other liberal movements, especially dissidents. The strategy needs to be flexible (*EE*, 117).

In this voluntarist vein, liberalism is hardly a persuasion to be shared or to grow by itself 'like a mustard seed'.[77] As an ideal, after all juridical system that grows out of natural-individual rights, it has to politically (and frequently militarily) impose the conditions for its own success. If legal, political and economic institutions are a *prerequisite* to the exercise of human rights, as they are here, these institutions must

---

and *Christian Views*, ed. Markus Bockmuehl and Guy G. Stroumsa (Leiden: Cambridge University Press, 2009), pp. 179–91, 185.

[75] In fact he criticizes Jean-François Lyotard's 'antagonism', which cannot distinguish between 'women, blacks, native Americans, homosexuals, philosophers and others in themselves acceptable, but more or less marginalised groups' as rightful complainants as opposed to 'child abusers, racists, chauvinists, mass murderers, fascists, etc.' (*EE*, 142). Steinhoff appears to ground the difference between them in common sense.

[76] See also Michael Freeden, who argues that ideologies are positive and 'essential' to political life. *Ideologies and Political Theory* (Oxford: Oxford University Press, 1998); *Ideology: A Very Short Introduction* (Oxford: Oxford University Press, 2003).

[77] Mark 4: 26–9; Cf. O'Donovan, *The Desire of the Nations: Rediscovering the Roots of Political Theology* (Cambridge: Cambridge University Press, 1996), p. 95.

be spread first. As James Tully has pointed out, a military-expansionist tendency is inherent in the 'high Enlightenment tradition of human rights'.[78] The logical, indeed ideological outgrowth of Steinhoff's realism is not entirely dissimilar to Elshtain and Rodin (albeit the latter's inadvertently so) (*EE*, 119). On its frontiers the spread of liberalism

> should be accompanied by flanking measures: to this belongs political pressure (which includes threatening military intervention, to be realised if necessary), economic pressure on dictators and their clientele, as well as economic and developmental support that sidesteps their pockets and actually helps the populace. (*EE*, 118)

However, Steinhoff explicitly goes down a more Marxist route, thus marking another 'heretical' divergence from the sovereign-papalist paradigm.[79] For Steinhoff, liberal freedom requires an equal redistribution of power to individuals, which goes hand in hand with economic improvements. As a 'Reset' button on the material conditions of liberty, he suggests an egalitarian 'land reform' and 'popularisation of property'. In terms of the underlying theo-logic (self-mediation of the humanum in an individualist or imperial[ist] mode), one may argue about whether this is a secularists' version of Liberation theology or radically reformed socialism. Either way, it qualifies the (moral) 'freedom of a Christian' to 'do right' in the form of a(legal) individual negative liberty and material claim rights.

In that sense, Steinhoff's proposal works within the material, interest- and power-focused premises of those whom power and wealth are to be wrestled from. Liberal ideology here does not lead to a Christian charitable overfulfilment of the law but rather an immanent, potentially material revolution. As a political self-mediation, it guarantees the continuation and survival of a naturalist-individualist order. The best institutional basic arrangement to secure this order both abroad and at home is 'liberal-democratic ..., an institutional order in which the majority principle is reined in by the principle of the rule of law [*Rechtsstaatsprinzip*] and especially a catalogue of individual rights, which is protected by an independent constitutional judiciary'. Steinhoff advocates the exchange of 'the *current* liberal-democratic constitutional order for *another* liberal-democratic institutional order'. He neither claims to be conservative nor progressive nor radical (*EE*, 196). From a religious-philosophical or indeed theological point of view, Steinhoff's moral 'new age' is therefore the 'old age' of law.

Moreover, *in extremis* the sovereign exception we encountered in Chapter 1 may also re-enter at an individual level. One might call this an inverted 'metaphysics of numbers'. We can in fact short-circuit Steinhoff and Elshtain on the grounds of their Enlightened dualism. At the forefront of spreading and protecting liberal rights the Is and Ought collapse into the sovereign agent, since he both factually asserts and

---

[78] James Tully, 'Rethinking Human Rights and Enlightenment', in *Self-evident Truths? Human Rights and the Enlightenment: The Oxford Amnesty Lectures of 2010*, ed. Kate Tunstall (London: Bloomsbury, 2012), pp. 3–35.

[79] In terms of the theological-political constellation, this turns into the direction of Thomas Müntzer.

reasserts himself in an emergency. This is the logic at work in Steinhoff's justification of terrorism but equally in 'the right to torture'. The 'state of exception' relies on the shared realist and revolutionary-democratic traditions. Here, first a fundamental gap arises between realistic power politics, or the 'metaphysics of difference' on the one hand, and the impossible 'Kingdom of Heaven' (Elshtain) or, for Steinhoff, any 'objective moral standard' altogether on the other.[80] In this gap the sovereign operates, at times with mythological splendour. In an exceptional political scenario, it then oscillates between public law and political fact, breaking the law and creating facts in order to safeguard the law.[81] The sovereign then mediates between criminal facts and the positivist juridical form of the liberal state. That is the highest moral-political 'ideal'. Despite Elshtain's 'use of theological categories', her Augustinian sovereign differs from Steinhoff's Machiavellian individual only in terms of the 'size' of the agent. Both are equally sustained by a liberal ideology.[82] Elshtain favourably compared the executive decisions of Abraham Lincoln ('an absolute dictator'[83]) and the post-9/11 American government which act under the auspices of necessity. For Steinhoff, 'necessity' is the *Notstand*.[84] Absent in both cases is an 'extrademocratic law of natural justice' as *Iustitia* is mute.[85] The only 'natural law' inheres in the facts of the emergency itself, the defensive rights following the aggression. That liberal human rights are therefore compatible with or become the civil religion of a sovereign imperial state ceases to be contradictory. (And as we saw in Chapter 2, this oscillation also underlies Rodin's suggestions.)

Ironically, Steinhoff also defends the very liberal-positivist constitutions whose exceptionalist human rights violations during national defence he criticizes. Steinhoff is somewhat aware of this tension when it comes to the expansionist wars of the United States. The US-NATO military alliance fires missiles from far away, risking higher 'collateral damage' in order to protect their own soldiers, he points out, and 'it is unclear how this tribalism squares with the universalist values the USA, Great Britain and other European nations purport to defend'. Steinhoff does not outrightly condemn terrorism and contemporary Western liberal warfare. His chief complaint at that point is that it is contradictory and hypocritical to call terrorists 'barbarians' but not those states. The same goes for the 'state of exception'. He claims its policies for individuals to the point of justifiable terrorism, arguing that statists *also* invoke the 'state of exception'.

---

[80] The lack of possibilities for understanding 'naturally' is equally pointed out by Augustine. Letters 55 and 232. O'Donovan, for example, shows how the *pneuma* precisely knits and redefines this gap between subjective imagination and objective external world. RMO, 102: 'the Spirit makes the reality of redemption, distant from us in time, both present and authoritative; secondly, … he evokes our free response to this reality as moral agents'. Whereas theology may fuse the cleavage between 'world' (Jacques Lacan: the Real) and imaginary constitutions of ideology, philosophers such as Judith Butler escalate the scope of linguistic, performative construction to the very subject itself.

[81] Giorgio Agamben, *State of Exception* (Chicago, IL: University of Chicago Press, 2005), p. 1.

[82] On Carl Schmitt's specifically ideological method, see e.g. Jan Müller, 'Carl Schmitt's Method: Between Ideology, Demonology and Myth', *Journal of Political Ideologies*, 4 (1999), 61–85.

[83] Agamben, *State of Exception*, p. 20.

[84] This includes a positive right to torture. Uwe Steinhoff, 'Legalizing Defensive Torture', *Public Affairs Quarterly*, 26 (2012), 19–32.

[85] John Milbank, 'Paul against Biopolitics', in *Paul's New Moment*, ed. John Milbank, Slavoj Žižek and Creston Davis (Grand Rapids, MI: Brazos Press, 2010), p. 25.

Elshtain's 'strong sovereignty' above was precisely such a case. Steinhoff has no intrinsic problem with it as long as it is a *coherent* liberal-imperial logic.[86]

To summarize Steinhoff's moral conception of the political agent: with a modern scientism in the background, the individual natural rights paradigm gains primacy. The notion of political authority oscillates between innate, individual authority as a capacity to decide and enforce one's rights and the institutionalized framework of the liberal-democratic state as the maximal moral-political ideal. While normative content, or *Sittlichkeit*, ideally would be left outside a radically liberal order, metaphysical residues and spaces remain in Steinhoff's approach, even if unexplored. In fact, our liberty depends on them; recently Steinhoff seems to have developed much greater sense of this necessity, particularly as he critiques Rodin.

With the closure of the moral-juridical order, authoritative dimensions of an 'ideal' (theological/metaphysical) kind are rejected as incoherent: the 'metaphysics of state' and church are rather oppressive, stopping the individual from breathing freely. Nevertheless, liberalism becomes an ideology in its own right, including a liberal imperialism. *In extremis* and for the sake of self-preservation, it allows the autonomous individual to violate just war conventions analogous to Elshtain's sovereign state.[87]

The similarity between Elshtain and Steinhoff, both realists in their own way, is the lack of a specifically Christological *tertium* that would be politically effective in analogical action, mediating between the ideal and the real.[88] There is no 'referral' of all earthly action to a 'substantial' peace or to the *salus hominum*.[89] This point, then, leads to the final section on the nature of political action.

Conceptual necessities of self-defence

Realistic, secular praxis

The basic dualist pattern in Steinhoff's proposal manifests itself also in terms of moral action: effective individual rights protection on the one hand and *supererogatory* actions on the other.

Steinhoff's liberal moral praxis quite consciously springs from a (pre-incarnational) *saeculum* that is not *essentially* different from postmodern paganism. This comes into view in his critique of the postmoderns, who he thinks are either contradictory or have nothing to add to liberalism (*EE*, 134–6; *EE*, 214, n. 38). Jean-François Lyotard, for example, is torn between the ' "pagan" imperative … to maximize as much as possible the multiplication of small narratives' or 'multiple justices' – and a Kantian conception

---

[86] Steinhoff, 'Why There is No Barbarization but a Lot of Barbarity in Warfare', p. 105–6; at the same time, since revolutionary rights are bound into the constitution, Steinhoff's revolutionary rights merely remain theoretical, analogous to Ramsey's Methodist *agape* bound by Catholic 'natural law'.

[87] Agamben, *State of Exception*, pp. 5, 25–26.

[88] Analytical moral philosophy as Steinhoff practices it finds such metaphysical enquiries beyond its purview, since it 'starts from scratch' by clarifying concepts. See especially Steinhoff, 'Lone Individual', p. 134. NB: Absent a non-empirical truth, this positivist epistemology ('We here believe in human rights') may well turn into a renewed authoritarian dogmatism. Cf. Nietzsche above: the truths of the Enlightenment are now *irrefutable*.

[89] Agamben, *State of Exception*, p. 25; Augustine, *De Civitate Dei*, Bk. XIX, Chapter 4.

'in which the whole of reasonable beings as well as a "principle of a multiplicity" function as regulative ideas'. Not only does the latter sound an awful lot like Kant's concept of Right, Steinhoff points out. Kantianism positively *limits* the 'terroristic maximum demands' of such multiple justices. As a result, there is no contradiction between the two. 'Instead, [Kantianism] lies in paganism itself' (*EE*, 135). Not multiple justices but the 'justice of multiplicity'. Moreover, 'celebrating otherness' with J. S. Mill may as well be read as 'celebrating individuality' (*EE*, 128); and Lyotard's 'activating of difference' as a guarantee of freedom Steinhoff thinks is best solved by the non-conformist model of 'different parties allowing to each other spheres in which one lets the other do what he wants – the liberal concept' (*EE*, 145). In this way, through avoiding an ancient *agon* – rather than 'witnessing to it', as Lyotard suggests – we can at least guarantee a kind of 'peaceful coexistence' or, as Fichte would have said, a 'temporal felicitousness'.

In this vein, the law of liberal democracy '*unites* the *togetherness of differences* with the *reduction of injustice*' (*EE*, 146). Justice is simply neutral non-interference; injustice is aggression. The law fulfils an *usus politicus*. It is not one *usus* out of two or three,[90] a reflexive turning back against crime in view of the possibility of its overfulfilment or transformation. Rather, as noted, the law itself is 'the ideal of a liberal ethic'. *Within* its framework, we have 'private freedoms' to do whatever we want.[91] Nobody is entitled to interfere with these choices (*EE*, 145).

Steinhoff's intention to limit the scope of law through withdrawing certain areas from a public-punitive gaze certainly echoes a Christian move to end judgement.[92] Yet here that is chiefly effective as a *separation* of the spheres. *Sittlich* generosity has to remain confined to a private, a-political sphere or will. A fusion and hence *mediation* between minimal restraining political action and charitable praxis is thus prevented. The praxis of religion conceived as private leaves the formal framework of public law untouched. Israel and Babylon, to put it in biblical terms, have to coexist. For critics, it may be a 'Babylonian captivity'; for others, it might be the option still preferable to assimilation into Babylon.[93]

Frequently, Steinhoff is very upfront about how liberal moral action is completely distinct from any action grounded in faith:

> For liberals it is not important to praise values or to bear witness to God, Providence or the spirit of world history, or to abide by their alleged commands; it is rather important that the rights and liberty of individuals are protected as much as possible. (*EKT*, 36)

As the inner moral posture of the agent ceases to be relevant, outward conformity to 'the law' matters. Echoing Machiavelli and Plato's Thrasymachus, Steinhoff suggests that it is sufficient to resemble a good person. 'The liberal concept of law leaves the thoughts and feelings untouched. Only the actions of individuals are limited by the freedoms

---

[90] That is, the *usus legis civilis* as opposed to the *usus elenchticus* or *theologicis* (Luther) or, additionally, the third use Melanchthon introduces, i.e. the *usus in renatis*, approximated not least by Calvin.

[91] Cf. Immanuel Kant, *Zum Ewigen Frieden* (Stuttgart: Reclam, 2008), p. 31.

[92] Mt. 6.7.

[93] See Chapter 5 on O'Donovan for the theological debates on this.

of others' (*EKT*, 56). In fact, *God himself* is a spy, snooping into people's convictions. The quality of an action does not depend on (objectively) right or wrong intentions; repeated intentions form habits and therefore future actions, yet this is not 'relevant for the moral judgment of the agent'. These considerations are altogether distinct from the 'question whether [a person] violates the rights of those he knowingly kills, hurts or does not so' (*EKT*, 57). Moreover, one may well manipulate others, considering there may well be a complete difference between 'ethics for myself' and 'ethics to propagate to others'. Steinhoff is well aware that this 'may give birth to monsters' and serial killers. His response is pragmatic: 'a lot of potential avengers (which will in all likelihood be more numerous than the serial killers), because of these thoughts [the liberal proposal] will decide to give to those rapists and serial killers what they probably deserve' (*EE*, 126).

In short, *successful praxis* here is the effective, regulated exercise of one's free will in addition to the most basic need (and will) to survive. In war, as the most extreme form, all other principles like punishment come into view from the exercise of a moral and legal right to self-defence against unjust aggression (*EKT*, 55). The antagonistic clash of rights between the innocent attacked and the innocent non-combatants of an overpowering aggressor becomes a *phenomenon* where people from all sides shoot at each other, a series of events never far from the pure facticity of chaos. Again, an alternative to Rodin, for whom war is ideally international law enforcement or a cataclysmic trap but also an individualist alternative to Elshtain, for whom war was either liberal-imperial expansion triumphant or antagonistic tragedy. Where both these authors neglect the implications of individual rights, either because their 'incarnation' in political forms lacks practical consequences or because of an anti-individualist reflex, Steinhoff adheres to the principle of individual defence.

Supererogation?

Since the question of ethics as such is 'What kinds of behaviour can people demand of other people?', they become voluntary options, while morality in itself is a form of *legality*. From this perspective, it is of course impossible (or unnecessary) to morally think the law 'from the other side'; philosophy here can only identify the locus of the *possibility* of revelation.[94] This is not to suggest that for Steinhoff moral values or ideals disappear. Arguably, he shears off that dimension in order to *clarify* them. Ironically, Steinhoff repeats a pre-Reformation Catholic distinction between *praecepta* and *consilia*.[95] It makes the breaking-in of superabundant love and lasting social-legal

---

[94] Philosophy here can only identify the locus of the possibility of revelation. For example, Alain Badiou, *Being and Event* (London: Continuum, 2005); Karl Barth's Christological prolepsis identifies in Christ both the possibility of revelation and its fulfilment, thus, to use an insight from O'Donovan, collapsing the AD and BC. *CD*, I.2, p. 25f.

[95] An observed structural parallel between supererogatory actions (*consilia*) and *Tugendpflichten* pushes Kant into a rather Catholic corner. This parallel, which allows us to map Steinhoff closer to Elshtain on the idealism-realism divide, is also noted by Ulla Wessels, *Die gute Samariterin* (Berlin: De Gruyter, 2002), p. 161. Nonetheless, for Kant only those actions that are done according to duty and out of a sense of duty are good. Therefore, there are no actions that are good and *not* a duty. So, strictly speaking, there are no supererogatory actions as Steinhoff suggests when appealing to Kant's *Tugendpflichten*. Wessels, *Die gute Samariterin*, p. 162. Another example of someone who

effect of the universal through the individual a *higher form* of virtue. All forms of generous charity are certainly praiseworthy. However, they are 'supererogatory', an add-on to moral duties, far from a social praxis effectively informing – dialectically or paradoxically – the law, in this case the law of conflict. Love remains, in a sense, a monastic ideal. For example, there may be no *need* to scoff at people or to despise them. But nobody has a 'right not to be scoffed at' (*EE*, 114) or a 'right to emotional minimal regard' (*EKT*, 56).[96]

Together with other modern theorists, Steinhoff also implies that supererogation tends towards selfishness: the agent concerns himself with his own salvation rather than the protection of the victims. This Nietzschean reading allows secular theories of supererogation to present themselves as interested in *true* selflessness.[97] The *paradox* of gaining all through losing all[98] – for example in martyrdom – would obviously require a horizon of faith, love and hope. (Nietzsche precisely talks about this when he says, 'Harshness and terror in morality can be a consequence of the surplus of life: for in this case much can be ventured, much challenged, much *squandered*, too.'[99])

A concrete example for how the moral-legal praxis of choice and rights remains untouched (and 'ideals' unmediated) is that of mercenaries and citizen-soldiers. Tony Coady, a revisionist author Steinhoff frequently criticizes, rejects mercenaries on the same grounds as prostitution (viz. *EE*, 114). For Coady, it is the external performance of fighting for the sake of money, absent good motives: 'the solidarity with and stake in the well-being of the community under threat that would provide appropriate motive for killing on its behalf.' In response, Steinhoff points at the *fact* that paid citizen soldiers often also have purely monetary interests. Mercenaries are in fact freer to choose to fight in just wars only, for example to protect their reputation. Moreover,

> Coady's view of the good sex – the ideal of mutual enjoyment which has the character of a gift – is romanticised; he postulates an ideal case in relation to which prostitution is compared and found wanting, which simply ignores the fact that much, if not most, non-prostitutional sexual activity does not live up to this standard. ... A parallel romanticism exists in his analysis of war motives.[100]

In the interplay between facts, legitimacy and contract, there is no space for the 'romanticism' of noble motives. Hence, Steinhoff finds nothing particularly objectionable about private military contractors. Primarily, of course, no one could

---

prefers Kant to modern supererogationism is Marcia Baron, 'Kantian Ethics and Supererogation', *Journal of Philosophy*, 84 (1987), 237–62.

[96] Where the distinction between morality and law completely falls away – and Steinhoff's option of a moral 'supererogation' successfully stems itself against this trend – this tendency comes to fruition as a criminalization of speech and impoliteness, as can be seen in the proliferating legislation against 'hate speech', and condemnation of even inadvertent (!) 'micro-aggressions'.

[97] See also Wessels, *Die gute Samariterin*, pp. 158–9.

[98] Cf. Mt. 10, 39; 16, 25, Mk 8, 35; Lk. 9, 24; Jn 12, 25.

[99] Friedrich Nietzsche, *Twilight of the Idols* (Oxford: Oxford University Press, 1998), p. 63.

[100] Uwe Steinhoff, 'Ethics and Mercenaries', in *New Wars and New Soldiers: Military Ethics in the Contemporary World*, ed. Paolo Tripodi and Jessica Wolfendale (Farnham: Ashgate, 2011), pp. 137–51, p. 139, n. 1.

morally *forbid* the voluntary commercial contract between an individual and the hiring party. The possibility that Steinhoff would like to discard is that 'motive' and 'action' enter a distinct unity.[101]

Steinhoff remains, to use Milbank's interpretation of Kant, 'in the Old Testament': 'morality is legally "over against" our natural desires.' In Milbank's reading, Kant cannot envisage 'a transfigured natural desire for peace and harmony ... which no longer requires either prohibitions or commandments'.[102] An authoritative, moral transformation of the 'secular' praxis of coercion is not possible for Steinhoff: 'irrational' revelation clashes with the epistemic rationality of his analytical liberalism. At the same time, however, the freedom of contract and conscience and the freedom of *Sittlichkeit* is safeguarded. Steinhoff is neither (fully) absorbed into the liberal-imperial myth nor the cosmopolitan legalist credo. As a focus on the essentials of liberal ethics, this marks a significant departure.[103]

Steinhoff's delicate separation between 'rights' and 'acts of supererogation' is not without difficulties. For example, if 'Django'[104] is threatened with a gun and told to hand over a single dollar, could he defensively shoot-to-kill? Steinhoff wants to have his moral cake and eat it: 'It seems to me that he [rather] *should* hand over the dollar, but at the same time has the *right* not to do it.' The duties of right may be legally enforced, he says, but a violation of the duties of virtue may only be answered 'with rebuke, outrage, rejection and so on'. One could not, he claims, 'treat Django like a murderer or manslayer' (*EKT*, 81). But how can one say someone should do something, while saying he does not need to do it? Steinhoff's somewhat artificial separation therefore has to collapse in favour of an insistence on the duties of law and rights. The duties of virtue are merely *sittlich* liberty. One may relinquish one's right to self-defence as much as one may blame and rebuke someone who excessively kills for the sake of a dollar. And while the right of an innocent to self-defence is inalienable, one is certainly at liberty not to defend oneself against an innocent attacker.

Steinhoff here goes further than many jurisdictions that are (still) infused with the duties of virtue. If one unnecessarily kills in self-defence, then legal punishment is in fact mandatory. Some would not merely call Django 'brutal', they would punish him based precisely on the grounds of 'humanity' and neighbourliness demanded in law. For example Rodin, still more deontological and Kantian, also thinks the law does and can expect innocent people not to lethally self-defend when it is excessive, as for the single dollar, or against innocent and incapable victims. For Rodin, since morality can

---

[101] Not only can a state turn its citizens into mercenaries, one can equally make a prostitute out of one's wife by 'using' her. But if one only looks at their voluntary, contractual engagement and their de facto habitual fighting for money without any visible, external damage being done, the difference between citizen-soldiers and mercenaries is indeed moot. In *EKT*, notably, Steinhoff uses a much more 'traditional' view of citizenship, which is the duty of protection of one's neighbours.

[102] Milbank and Žižek, *The Monstrosity of Christ: Paradox or Dialectic?* (Cambridge: MIT Press, 2009), p. 121; Immanuel Kant, *Metaphysic of Morals*, 2 vols. (London: William Richardson, 1799), p. xiii. Milbank tends to overmodulate here.

[103] Again, Cavanaugh's neo-traditionalist critique casts the state as a 'parody' of the Body of Christ.

[104] The fact that Steinhoff shares the Wild West imagery with Elshtain is indicative of a parallel and, in the American case, certainly mutually dependent elements: 'sovereign state – sovereign self', a liberal oscillation between absolute state and libertarian counterpart.

eclipse the mere necessities of survival, there are certain actions that we should not perform, even at the risk of death. Steinhoff has consistently argued against these views by appealing to the legal principle: 'Right need not shy away from wrong.'[105]

In short, an unmediated disjunction between the politically real and the moral ideal (or even the divine) manifests itself as, on the one hand, a judiciable, legal praxis of rights and restraints which for a liberal like Steinhoff is all that ethics can do. The liberal law *is* the moral ideal. On the other hand, there is what he labels 'romanticism', morally praiseworthy ideals or religious *topoi*, which may flourish mostly in a private (and thus the subjective) sphere as well as actions beyond duty. In this regard, Steinhoff echoes the radical Reformation: the separation of religion from political powers, the beginnings of religious tolerance in the light of individual, subjectively experienced faith (whether heterodox or none at all) was rooted in, but also diverged from, the Protestant consensus – often with biographical connections to Catholicism as much as humanism.[106] In modernity, Max Weber, who in many ways informs Steinhoff's approach, makes the disjunction most explicit (italics added):

> But there is *an abysmally deep difference* between acting under a conscious-ethical maxime – religiously said –: 'A Christian does right and ascribes all success to God' –, *or* acting responsibly-ethical: that one is liable for the (predictable) consequences of one's action.[107]

Weber proposes a separation of the inward, spiritual and excessively charitable from the praxis of external law, rights and duties. In this spirit, Steinhoff's realistic, 'Machiavellian' praxis weaves an autonomous moral-political social corpus of its own – a 'parody' of the body of Christ for its most acerbic critics, a liberal, albeit (joyfully) heterodox alternative to the imperial-sovereign paradigm, stopping short of any transcendent horizons.

Just war theory – analysis and critique

What kind of endeavour are the ethics of war? Arguably, the underlying theo-logic – the immanent, a-theological self-mediation of the human and the natural – is also reflected in the way Steinhoff goes about doing ethics of war. In lieu of the Christ-event (but analogously judging and discerning), Steinhoff performs a *critical-analytical revolution* to existing common-sense standards. Rejecting any moral romanticism, he explains why controversial practices may be morally legitimate – at least if individual rights are taken seriously, as many contemporaries claim to do. Here he shows a fine sense for residual Christian traces in the current ethics of war that cannot be accounted for without recurrence to these sources. Finally, he readjusts the criteria according to a *consequently* liberal principle. The 'sources', as for Rodin, are intuitions here, the muted

[105]　See Chapter 2 and Steinhoff's critical response: 'Rodin on Self-Defense'.
[106]　Cf. Hillerbrand, *The Division of Christendom*, pp. 132–3.
[107]　Max Weber, *Politik als Beruf* (München: Duncker & Humblot, 1919), pp. 57–8.

depositories of a (formerly Christian) *Iustitia*, though without being moored in the latter and thus always prone to atrophy.

In this paradigm, 'useful conventions' such as non-combatant immunity are now non-absolute; the 'Kantian faithfulness to principles' is weakened. Particularly, non-combatant immunity can be trumped when the will-to-life, the 'last flicker of humanity', is at stake against an overpowering aggressor (*EKT*, 134). To an extent, this vision marks the return of Achilles' *agon* as described by Spariosu, at least on the battlefield. Its rules

> are based on mutual agreement, which remains in force only as long as it is perceived as being advantageous to all parties involved. Neither is playing by the rules, or 'fair play', a moral exigency; it is merely the result of cooperation among almost equally powerful contestants, guaranteeing the continuation of the game.[108]

Steinhoff's 'just war theory' is not totally dissimilar to Elshtain's (and Rodin's inadvertent embrace of it). The aim of the just war theory is '(or at least today should be) to limit war and not to promote self-righteousness or to give unlimited licence' (*EKT*, 136). Instead of triumphalism, the fact that war is an evil may 'lead to a more modest and thoughtful attitude towards the tragedy, which may add to more and more limit the evil' (*EKT*, 63). This broadly repeats the reading of Christian realism's just war tradition, an effect of a comparable vision of the fundamental 'tragedy of politics'.

Nonetheless, Steinhoff's liberal version is much more attuned to the necessities of self-defence and the defence of those one cares about. While Elshtain moved between polemics and legitimizing a particular war for the religious edification of the (American) public, Steinhoff's political leanings only occasionally surface in an overall systematic, analytical quest for coherence. The fact that he seems to side with the Palestinians in the Israeli-Palestinian conflict may not necessarily be owed to Islamic (or even Islamist) sympathies but rather the result of a rejection of any religiously laden state formation – in favour of logical coherence.[109] At least in the latter regard, an unmasking critique – whether Nietzschean or libertarian – may not least function as an indispensable *prophetic* endeavour: it is a lineage that begins with the 'Zwickau Prophets' around Thomas Müntzer (regarded as a proto-socialist in the twentieth century) and continues in Marx's radical critique. Both were read together not least by Ernst Bloch – on the most anti-trinitarian, because Marcionite and hence absolutely dualist premises.[110]

---

[108] Mihai Spariosu, *God of Many Names: Play, Poetry, and Power in Hellenic Thought from Homer to Aristotle* (Durham, NC: Duke University Press, 1991), p. 8.

[109] The German connection between Enlightenment and Islam (the 'Orient') reaches back at least to J. W. Goethe. In 1898, the (Calvinist) German emperor Wilhelm II, visiting the grave of Sultan Saladin in Damascus, assured 'all Mohammedans' of his perpetual friendship.

[110] Stuart Jeffries, *Grand Hotel Abyss: The Lives of the Frankfurt School* (New York: Verso, 2016); Eugene McCarraher, 'Prophecy in Unbelieving Form: Stuart Jeffries, *Grand Hotel Abyss*', *Hedgehog Review*, 19.1 (Spring 2017), available online at http://iasc-culture.org/THR/THR_article_2017_Spring_McCarraher.php (accessed 5 June 2018); Ernst Bloch, *Atheismus im Christentum*, transl. J. T. Swann (New York: Verso, 2009); in his Introduction (p. xvii), Peter Thompson cites Ernst Bloch, *Freiheit und Ordnung* (Frankfurt am Main: Suhrkamp, 1972), p. 464: 'Marxism therefore is not a non-utopia, but the genuine, concretely-mediated and processually-open one.'

Like Bloch opposed to any collectivism, Steinhoff for his part would most likely reject this interpretation of his work. But this should not deter theological ethicists on the grounds that it is non-Christian, liberal or otherwise secularist. What matters is that intellectual coherence and critique, particularly as it questions the 'just war theory' of the last forty years, have a theologically identifiable locus. Here, it has been located on the cusp of a revelatory horizon, disturbing the edifices of contemporary political, ethical and theological-political orthodoxies.

Conclusion

Instead of a Christological mediation, Steinhoff sees a stark distinction between the world as a natural, scientific materiality and the (im)possibility of any 'absolute truth', even the absurdity of God in the Christian tradition. His central reference point was the individual human being, the point in which the Is and Ought merge; each person is a 'prince of peace', the master of their own individual ethic. Steinhoff thus began with the same, essentially humanist premises as Rodin and to an extent Elshtain. What matters here, however, is what is scientifically coherent, possible and feasible. Steinhoff is as 'anti-Catholic' as he was critical of Rodin's or Habermas's cosmopolitanism, and anti-imperialist in so far as empire implies the sovereign state's 'metaphysics of numbers'. Instead, his liberalism was effectively the 'revolutionary' underbelly of Elshtain's (American-)Schmittian state. He repeated and transferred the sovereign politics of the state onto the individual level.

Steinhoff's ethics of war are a *consequently* liberal and Enlightened enquiry. The core of it is the right to self-defence and the defence of others near and dear to oneself; equal individual rights are regulated by convention, whereby the conventions were subject to be overridden in extreme cases. 'Conventional war' is certainly a possibility for Steinhoff, but he points out that if one actually takes human rights seriously, then terrorism may be a possible strategy.

Nonetheless, we saw that some logical implications noticeable in Elshtain and Rodin return. The moral and the political, the statist and the ecclesial, love and law collapse into immanent, albeit formalistic, unities. Although any substantial moral 'idealism', whether Christianity or humanism, is rejected, the politically real becomes idealized and turns into its own opposite. The liberal's 'earthly beatitude' oscillates between innate individual defensive rights and a contractually established institutional state order to enforce these rights. However, even though radical liberalism promises radical freedom, Steinhoff's liberalism takes on the role of yet another ideology. Not only does this contain its own 'doctrine of sovereignty' and the adjacent politics of the 'state of exception', it also requires an expansive imperialism. In the revolutionary-democratic tradition, the gloves can come off and human rights can be violated in order to protect the rights of others. Absent an order of Right, a transcendent equity, we are left with an escalating antagonism.

While a moral substantial *Sittlichkeit* was given up in favour of an ethic of success, such an ethic of success may always become a substantial morality of its own, effective through manipulation and self-regulation. Moreover, ethics, in so far as they are already understood as legality, remain distinct from *Tugendpflichten*. Nonetheless, the values and contents of *Sittlichkeit* still linger around the argument, since Steinhoff takes them for granted: community, representation, love, truth. They are possibly related to the absolute, but they may as well be irrational. More seriously, one should add, the equation of morality with legality, even though intended to restrict the former's intrusive reach, can lead to a contrary effect (albeit explicitly not intended by Steinhoff): the law may become increasingly moralistic, policing even *perceived* intrusions, feelings or basic affects. Concerning political *praxis*, a dualistic dialectic repeats itself. Political praxis falls apart into the restrictions and forces of law and the voluntary, optional (and indeterminate, indefinable) possibilities of love and humanity. However, because only that which is judiciable counts as morality, guaranteeing the legal rights of non-interference trumps our ability to see for *ourselves* how a freedom of love can transform the paradigm of those rights.

In short, in the absence of a mediating, ontological-redemptive revolution in Christ, Steinhoff's proposal presents a critical bump, albeit a significant one on the road of sovereign-papal paradigms. With analytical, interferential fire, the rationalist author applies the prevailing scientist-individualist perspective more thoroughly – the liberal 'gospel' inaugurates a more coherent *agon*. Steinhoff's atheism, or at least an anti-trinitarian, residual Jesuology is scientific and critical, and for this reason he stands in the tradition of different strands of the radical Reformation. In itself a 'heretical' 'reformation of the Reformation' (Hillerbrand), these strands of the tradition were no longer Catholic but also beyond the Protestant consensus, while imbibing and transforming the humanist impulse.

Chapter 4 will turn to a Christian ethicist who at times, similarly to the authors examined so far, came close to a Marcionite dualism. Like Steinhoff initially rejecting the sovereign-papal paradigm, also in its modern guises, Paul Ramsey then moved to carve out the possibility of a contemporary Christian ethics of war.

Christian ethics: Paul Ramsey's theo-logics of war haunted by Hegel and Nietzsche

Introduction

Paul Ramsey (1913–1988) was a sceptic quite different to the ones encountered so far. As a decisively Christian ethicist, he combined theological acumen with an acute awareness of how the modern mind works. He intervened into many political and societal debates of his time; the Cold War as well as the civil rights movement set the tasks for his theological-ethical reflections. A charismatic teacher, Ramsey also left a lasting impression on his students. As the political philosopher and theorist Jeffrey Stout once aptly put it, 'First comes a moral awakening, with its youthful attachments to great causes or charismatic heroes; next an initial encounter with Ramsey; and then an unending and ambivalent struggle with his arguments … Ramsey did not win you over all the way, he just changed your life forever.'[1] Besides his engagement with medical ethics, he is credited with introducing the just war doctrine into twentieth-century Protestant thinking.

Throughout his prolific career, Ramsey underwent a significant intellectual movement: from idealist pacifism, via 'transformism' or 'conversionism', to a more conservative, perhaps hard-headed, realism. A particular theological constellation holds together not only his ethics of war but to an extent is reflected in his intellectual trajectory altogether. It is the connection of a *totaliter aliter* revelatory, yet *im*-mediate *agape* with an idealist sensibility for the divine that unfolds and is mediated in history. On a bipolar axis 'moral man' stood between *agape* – a divine self-giving and neighbour-oriented love – and the world of systems, including modern philosophical systems of thought.

Here I will look at a particular period in Ramsey's intellectual evolution: the movement from Christian scepticism to realism. In order to overcome the impractical or even unsavoury implications of a potentially disordered *agape*, Ramsey developed his own version of Christian 'transformism', heavily drawing on philosophical idealism.

---

[1] Cited in Adam Hollowell, 'Paul Ramsey (1913–1988)', in *Just War Thinkers: From Cicero to the 21st Century*, ed. Daniel R. Brunstetter and Cian O'Driscoll (Abingdon: Routledge, 2018), pp. 137–44, p. 137.

At this point, a practical, political logic of mediation became a brief possibility, though theologically underarticulated. Not least because of that, Ramsey believed the Christ event had no transformative effect on the political sphere.[2]

For some perhaps too flippantly, I am including Ramsey into a section on 'heresy' or heterodoxy. There are two reasons for that. First, Ramsey's nominal Methodism represents a historically dissenting theological position. As we heard from Jeffrey Stout, despite the admiration Ramsey elicits from his readers, the reception of his thought was and to an extent remains ambiguous, comparable to the reception of early twentieth-century dialectical theology. Second, Ramsey directly confronted both the claims to absolute sovereignty by modern theories of the state and the Catholic and liberal-internationalist claims to mediate or even implement a kind of theological-political reconciliation. But before I go into the details of theo-logic as Ramsey presents it, a brief overview of his thought on war will be given, as in the previous chapters.

At this point, a brief note on this chapter's structure is necessary. After the exposition of Ramsey's work on the ethics of war, I will examine the underlying theology in three distinct subsections that reflect what I think are important phases in his thought. Moreover, I have included what I think Ramsey means by 'the ethics of war' within these sections in order to avoid breaking up the timeline of his intellectual trajectory.

Ramsey's evolving thought on war between love and the world of systems

During the mid-1930s, while at Millsaps College and seeking to become a pastor, Paul Ramsey was a committed pacifist. In line with the liberal Methodism at the time, he advocated conscientious objection, the abolition of the munitions industry and the institutions of international law in place of war. Concerned with the very disposition to combativeness, Ramsey even opposed intercollegiate football. In the attempt to transform a militaristic, warring society, an ethic of Jesus and of neighbour love could only mean non-violence and non-resistance.[3]

His views began to change once he had read Reinhold Niebuhr, who highlighted the irony of liberal pacifism: its *ex ante* passivity inadvertently props up tyrants and dictators.[4] In Ramsey's first book *Basic Christian Ethics (BCE)* (1949), reviewed by Niebuhr, the notion of love then yielded quite different results. Violent force is now a viable possibility.[5] While never resisting an attack on himself and his rights, Ramsey argues, the Christian may change his 'action to resistance by the most effective possible means, judicial or military, violent or non-violent, when the needs of more than one neighbor come into view' (*BCE*, 165). If the Good Samaritan had come to the scene of

---

[2] Sections from this and the next chapter on Oliver O'Donovan have been published in Therese Feiler, 'From Dialectics to Theo-Logic: The Ethics of War from Paul Ramsey to Oliver O'Donovan', *Studies in Christian Ethics*, 28.3 (2015), 343–59.

[3] D. Stephen Long, *Tragedy, Tradition, Transformism. The Ethics of Paul Ramsey* (Eugene, OR: Wipf & Stock, 2007), pp. 7–23.

[4] Cf. my interpretation of Rodin in Chapter 2.

[5] Paul Ramsey, *Basic Christian Ethics* (London: SCM Press, 1953). Hereafter BCE.

the robbers while they were still at their fell work, then Jesus might have approved of him fighting back (*BCE*, 170). Participating in war is a change of Christian *tactics*. But the *strategy*, the first principle, remains the same: loving service for others who suffer injustice or harm (*BCE*, 172).

War and the Christian Conscience (1961) shows more concretely how *agape* bears upon warfare.[6] In between nuclear pacifism and 'those who speak recklessly of "preventive war" and of "massive retaliation"', and equally a kind of Niebuhrian consequentialism, Ramsey injected the 'just-war doctrine'.[7] Ramsey understands it specifically as the result of a transformative Christian *agape*. In the same year as *War and the Christian Conscience*, Ramsey published 'What Americans Ordinarily Think about Justice in War' (*JW*, 42–69). Here he critiques the so-called aggressor-defender doctrine. This doctrine oscillates between antagonistic, indiscriminate defence and quasi-pacifist, indiscriminate humanitarianism.

However, Ramsey somewhat abandoned this transformism. As we will see again later in more detail, his later writings were chiefly concerned with national security and anti-communism to the point that discrimination took a decisively consequentialist slant. So eventually he would travel to the realist camp, though not without having questioned and corrected the ethics of modern sovereign states. In order to understand and explain these dichotomous travels between pacifist idealism and just war realism, but particularly his movement from scepticism to practical transformism, I will now turn to Ramsey's theology between God's love and the world of systems.

Basic Christian Ethics – *agape* and Christian scepticism

Once an essential part of the subject's syllabi in American universities, Ramsey's first book *Basic Christian Ethics* (1949) was somewhat neglected for several years. Nonetheless, it represents an essential moment in American and British Christian ethics, both in terms of Ramsey's influence and in terms of the theo-logic it describes.[8] Influenced by his explorations in idealist philosophy, Karl Barth, Reinhold Niebuhr and, significantly, Nietzsche, Ramsey here interprets Christian ethics through *agape*, divine (neighbour) love. My thesis here is that, as Ramsey is drawn into the wholly other dimension of *agape* and the 'strange new world of the Bible', he develops what one might call a modern Christian scepticism. Both in terms of its theo-logic and its practical implications, it results in an oscillation between divine-human duality and identity. It implied something like a 'crusade for the neighbour' – albeit one that has to remain hypothetical. In that sense, there is a moment of overlap with Rodin's liberal-internationalist conditional pacifism but one that Ramsey would soon clarify.

---

[6] Paul Ramsey, *War and the Christian Conscience: How Shall Modern War be Conducted Justly?* (Durham, NC: Duke University Press, 1961); hereafter *WCC*.
[7] Foreword by John H. Hallowell, *WCC*, p. vii.
[8] Ramsey, *Basic Christian Ethics*.

A just war theory of love?

Practically, an antinomian love as Ramsey interpreted it is alien to 'just war theory'.[9] He is highly sceptical towards any such 'excuses'. With Augustine, he thinks 'generally self-defense is the worst of all possible excuses for war or for any other form of resistance or any sort of preference among other people' (*BCE*, 173). He then criticizes Augustine and Ambrose for their 'unqualified acceptance of public protection', because it amounts to *private* self-defence and a lack of impartiality: 'Even in his vocation, where multilateral neighbor-relationships intersect, an individual finds himself drawn not by neighbor-love alone or by considerations of justice alone but by selfish preference or personal affinity for these persons rather than those' (*BCE*, 175).

Ramsey doesn't say war is murder. But he concludes with confident scepticism that it always could be. Thus, the mediate, practical space between unrestrained neighbour love and public duty-turned-selfish gets lost. One can never discern *which* war is murder. As a result, the possible loving use of force collapses into pragmatism, one that can in the end well be harnessed to any political interest: *whatever* serves the neighbour needs to be done.[10] Christians may change their 'action to resistance by the most effective possible means, judicial or military, violent or non-violent, when the needs of more than one neighbor come into view' (*BCE*, 165). D. Stephen Long points out that Ramsey also completely omits discussing non-combatant immunity. Effectively, he permits a 'crusade for the neighbour's sake', as Long neatly puts it.[11]

Vis-à-vis this oscillation between crusade and scepticism, Ramsey's rejection of Hegel's notion of love is significant (*BCE*, 303–4). Hegel precisely suggests a mediating love or rather love *as* mediator. Love 'implies a distinguishing between two' who are actually 'not distinguished from one another'.[12] A person's self-consciousness is not in herself but in another; 'but this Other in whom alone I find satisfaction and am at peace with myself', 'just because it is outside of me, has its self-consciousness only in me'. Love *is* the medium between humans but equally between the dual choice of logical separation or identity. To love means to know and feel this duality-unity: 'Thus the two are represented simply by this consciousness of their being outside of themselves and of their identity, and of this perception, this feeling, this knowledge of the unity of love'(*BCE*, 303).[13] But instead of seeing love as a mediator – loving as knowing the logic of not-self – Ramsey misunderstands Hegel's 'unity' to mean a postulated 'identity' between self and neighbour. In that case, of course, love is the brainchild of 'idolatrous

---

9 Long, *Tragedy, Tradition, Transformism*, p. 49.
10 Robert W. Tuttle, 'All You Need Is Love: Paul Ramsey's "Basic Christian Ethics" and the Dilemma of Protestant Antilegalism', *Journal of Law and Religion*, 18 (2002–3), p. 436. In that sense, Ramsey is still very close to Niebuhr's realism, which centred on *proportionality* so that almost everything was permitted to defeat an evil (a particularly pressing question during the Second World War). So, Ramsey here shares with Steinhoff a sense of pragmatism, even if 'fuelled' from opposite poles of the (ultimately dialectical-theological) world-God dichotomy.
11 Long, *Tragedy, Tradition, Transformism*, p. 53.
12 Cf. Ella Csikós, 'Zu Hegels Interpretation des Skeptizismus', in *Hegels Phänomenologie des Geistes: Ein kooperativer Kommentar zu einem Schlüsselwerk der Moderne*, ed. Klaus Vieweg and Wolfgang Welsch (Frankfurt am Main: Suhrkamp, 2008), pp. 270–85.
13 See also Hegel, *Phänomenologie des Geistes* (Frankfurt am Main: Suhrkamp, 1986), IV B, 'Skeptizismus und das unglückliche Bewußtsein', pp. 163–4.

spirit'; by identifying the neighbour's needs with my own, I subtly serve myself. In response, Ramsey settles for the fundamental duality of self and neighbour. Both God and neighbour, as he expresses it, 'stand over against us' (*BCE*, 303).

Unsurprisingly, at this point, Ramsey and Hegel are no less politically at odds. Hegel famously wrote with regard to the French Revolution that the 'merely negative freedom of the understanding', once it turns to reality, 'becomes the fanaticism of the destruction of all existing social order', and what is 'in itself an abstract imagination' in its realization is 'the fury of destruction'.[14] For Ramsey, *agape* always retains this revolutionary posture. Covenant obedience, 'the conviction that man's ultimate loyalty transcends every earthly system or center of human power', only 'gives man whereon to stand in opposing the present shape of the world' (*BCE*, 387). Certainly, such a sceptical No recognizes and 'actively performs ... the infinity and freedom of thinking' itself.[15] Understandably, Ramsey never wanted to significantly revise his first book.[16] But how to 'fulfil' this agapeic scepticism, risking the 'embarrassment of involvement', remains an open question.[17] It may collapse right into (pragmatically) doing what one was supposed to do in any case (*BCE*, 162). This brings us to Ramsey's endorsement both of idealism and democracy.

Idealism – the immanent logic of mediation and the metaphysics of democracy

Ramsey was aware that reasonable decisions in politics had to guard against a (revolutionary) nihilism inherent in *agape* (*BCE*, 68–9). Hence, the Christian always searches for the 'best possible social ethic in which Christian love may incarnate itself' (*BCE*, 326). Notwithstanding his sweeping critique of Hegel, he was convinced that 'Christian ethics must make common cause with the ethics of philosophical idealism' (*BCE*, xiii). Idealism's emphasis on 'the vast "difference" between finite and infinite' and then their 'identity' (*BCE*, 304) could be 'salvaged for Christian thought' (306). Idealism was therefore the most viable vehicle to practically conceive of a theologically grounded mediation of *agape*.[18] Ramsey's Barthian theo-logic thus was given a (post-)Lutheran operationalization. Vis-à-vis the unmediated relationship between the faithful individual and God, the pivotal point of political mediation between Is and Ought, between divine love and 'the world of systems' is then *anthropology*. With Bernard Bosanquet, Josiah Royce and not least T. H. Green in mind, Ramsey argues that in every human the absolute is incarnate, the infinite in the finite, the divine in the human – 'the Absolute is a teleological whole that requires individuals be "concrete universals" for the Absolute's intrinsic purpose'.[19] Mediation-as-incarnation between

---

[14] Georg Wilhelm Friedrich Hegel, *Grundlinien der Philosophie des Rechts*, ed. Bernhard Lakebrink (Stuttgart: Philip Reclam jun., 2009), p. 78.

[15] Csikós, 'Zu Hegels Interpretation des Skeptizismus', p. 273.

[16] Adam Edward Hollowell, 'Revising Basic Christian Ethics: Rethinking Paul Ramsey's Early Contributions to Moral Theology', *Studies in Christian Ethics*, 23 (2010), 267–83.

[17] Csikós, 'Zu Hegels Interpretation des Skeptizismus', p. 278.

[18] Ramsey knew Hegel via the British idealists, having written a dissertation on Bernard Bosanquet and Josiah Royce that drew heavily on T. H. Green. I thank an anonymous reviewer of *Studies in Christian Ethics* for pointing out Ramsey's connections to Green.

[19] Long, *Tragedy, Tradition, Transformism*, p. 28.

divine and human is a historical human essence and practice.[20] Love 'must take on the flesh of some specific social order'.

And who is the political subject? Ramsey draws on Reinhold Niebuhr's dictum that 'man's capacity for justice makes democracy possible; but man's inclination to injustice makes democracy necessary'.[21] While love pertained to the infinite aspects of individuals, its finite social and political realization had to be democracy:[22]

> All are but men, apt to make exceptions of themselves if allowed to do so. Sin must be checked in every one, ruler and ruled alike. For this reason, both the external procedures of democracy and the fundamental definition of a just political order should take account of man's inclination to sin even while building upon man's capacity for doing right. (*BCE*, 331)

Christian love '[making] common cause with' idealism also entailed a derivation of human rights, because 'a conception of self-Other relationship is ... essential to idealism's understanding of man's nature'.[23] But against any understanding of inherent or natural rights as claims and counterclaims – so *pace* the authors we have looked at so far – Ramsey derives them from an overarching duty towards the neighbour (*BCE*, 353).[24] They 'arise from the fundamental conditions of good community life'. 'A man cannot claim a right for himself alone, just because he likes things that way; rather he claims it as a member of society contributing to the general welfare' (*BCE*, 359). In brief, 'Any right is also a duty' (361). In this way, individual freedom is neither subsumed under the 'general will' nor is the common good dissolved into a multitude of subjective claims.

A (dis)embodied church?

The effect of Ramsey's idealist anthropology is far-reaching. Despite or because of an ultimately 'formless' notion of *agape*, he recognized the necessity of a communal mediation and contextualization of love (far from a ubiquitously dreaded collectivism):

> Although their independent reality must be assumed, selves cannot be endowed with such isolation and caprice as to be able to make anarchy out of the 'City

---

[20] For a juxtaposition of Hegel's logic and 'the Chalcedon', see Martin Wendte, *Gottmenschliche Einheit bei Hegel: eine logische und theologische Untersuchung* (Berlin: Walter de Gruyter, 2007).

[21] Paul Ramsey, 'The Theory of Democracy: Idealistic or Christian?', *Ethics*, 56 (1946), 251–66, p. 251.

[22] NB: Ramsey's dissertation at Yale had shown that Niebuhr's realism is not that different from philosophical idealism. This is important once the anti-Hegelian reflex of Christian realism gets examined closer (see also below). See R. Paul Ramsey, 'The Nature of Man in the Philosophy of Josiah Royce and Bernard Bosanquet', Dissertation, Yale University (1943); for a more detailed study of Niebuhr's pragmatism and Ramsey's idealism, see Kevin Carnahan, *Reinhold Niebuhr and Paul Ramsey: Idealist and Pragmatic Christians on Politics, Philosophy, Religion, and War* (Lanham, MD: Lexington, 2010).

[23] Ramsey, cited in Long, *Tragedy, Tradition, Transformism*, p. 26. This is also pace Elshtain on idealism.

[24] Cf. John Milbank, 'Against Human Rights: Liberty in the Western Tradition', *Oxford Journal of Law and Religion*, 1.1 (2012), 1–32.

of God'. … Finite selves in community are individuated by their purposes and deed, but, in so far as they form a united life, one can more truly affirm 'Thus the community acts in and through me', than he can say, 'I act thus'.[25]

The City of God is mentioned here, but 'community' so far is a generic term. In 'civilization' which unfolds teleologically and under divine providence in history, freedom and morality are equally lived out and embodied in constitutions, empires or churches. For D. Stephen Long, such political mediation is theologically highly problematic; from the church's point of view, 'the differences between these communities are obliterated'.[26] Tuttle also complains,

> The incarnation is not a once-and-for-all event that gives us a specific form for Christ, but rather one among many times in which the universal becomes particularized. The particularizations of the universal are purely contingent, and should not be seen as anything more than temporary resting places for the universal, which is utterly free to leave them behind in search of a better way to 'become incarnate'.[27]

The notion of democracy as a living social-political body of anthropological mediation is supported by Ramsey's notion of the church. Similar to Elshtain's, Ramsey's ecclesiology casts the church as either social institution or subjective experience. The church as a (highly problematic) *political* society or agent cannot develop here, which is owed to a notion of the eucharist reminiscent of Zwingli's:

> Strictly speaking, the Christian church is not a community of prayer, but a community of memory. When Christians pray they pray 'in Christ's name'; prayer thus is set decisively within the contexts of grateful remembrance of the God who put forward Christ. Strictly speaking Christians are not lovers of God; they are *theodidacti*, 'taught of God.' (*BCE*, 132)[28]

---

[25] Cited in Long, *Tragedy, Tradition, Transformism*, p. 28. NB: This is a marked difference from Elshtain's liberal insistence that God created Adam as one individual human being. See Chapter 1.

[26] Long, *Tragedy, Tradition, Transformism*, p. 30. The fault line between Long's Methodist-evangelical approach and a more Lutheran Hegelian embrace of historical political incarnation should not go unnoticed. Hollowell counters Long's critical reading of Ramsey by demonstrating his continued *theological* commitments in Adam Edward Hollowell, *Power and Purpose: Paul Ramsey and Contemporary Christian Political Theology* (Grand Rapids, MI: William. B. Eerdmans, 2015); essentially agreeing with Hollowell but suggesting a more positive reading of Ramsey as both theologian *and* idealist: Therese Feiler, 'Review: Adam Edward Hollowell, Power and Purpose: Paul Ramsey and Contemporary Christian Political Theology', *Studies in Christian Ethics*, 30.2 (2017), 244–6.

[27] Tuttle, 'All You Need Is Love', p. 435, n. 41.

[28] Daniel M. Bell Jr., 'The Reformation and the Wesleys: A Complex Relationship', *Interpreter Magazine*, September/October 2017, available online at http://www.interpretermagazine.org/topics/the-reformation-and-the-wesleys-a-complex-relationship (accessed 13 July 2018). Bell argues that the Wesleyan 'reformation of the Reformation' (an expression H. J. Hillerbrand uses for the 'radical Reformation') was also a kind of counter-Reformation; this is a dialectical turn, though Bell doesn't call it that.

Tuttle also criticizes Ramsey's idealist Christology-turned-anthropology specifically from an ecclesiological perspective: 'both the ordered form of Christian community and the Christian moral life come to be seen as arbitrary, disconnected from the life of the incarnate one whose image they are called to reflect.'[29] However, for Ramsey this is not a problem. Rather than ecclesiology and a spiritual-practical community, his Christian 'metaphysics of democracy' provide an alternative, critical theory.[30]

> Christianity is not, like Judaism and other forms of religious ethics, a 'religious civilization', it is rather a criticism of any civilization, religious or otherwise, and of any customary code of conduct, on behalf of the welfare of the neighbor, which all civilizations and codes of conduct are absolutely bound to serve in obedient love. (*BCE*, 44)

Moreover,

> Christian ethics may claim to be relevant in criticism of every situation precisely because its standard derives from no particular situation and is not accommodated to man's continuing life in normal, historical relationships. (BCE, 44)

Essentially a Christian democratic theorist, Ramsey far from claims that democracy is fully realized in the United States. Like Hegel, he seeks to identify a *sittlich* polity. In that sense, Ramsey's Christian 'metaphysics of democracy' politicize loving individuals now fully outside the context of Jesus's apocalypticism. Eventually, democratic politics can be seen as embodying love and so gain quasi-ecclesial status. Inadvertently, Ramsey set himself up to reach what McWilliams once said about Niebuhr: 'The Heavenly City of Reinhold Niebuhr retains a distinctly modern form in which to cast its eternal perfections. In fact, the best state in the world – as opposed to the heavenly ultimate – seems strikingly to resemble the United States.'[31]

The problem here is not Ramsey's idealist democratic theory itself, since, as noted in Chapter 2 above, the key deficiency of conditional pacifism is that it cannot recognize that abstract 'values' or goods are always incarnate in a particular time, place and indeed legal system.

Rather, the problem is that once 'love' (or such values) lose their ecclesial and theological moorings, philosophical idealism can turn into statism. Historical incarnation vis-à-vis an effectively dualist Christology certainly opened up the path for Ramsey's Christian-realist Yes to the necessities of the international 'Hobbesian

---

[29] Tuttle, 'All You Need Is Love', p. 435 n. 41.
[30] Conversely, that means 'social theory' after Hegel may potentially claim ecclesial dimensions for itself, not least also pretensions. Hollowell similarly sees Ramsey as a 'theoretician'. Adam E. Hollowell, *This Side of the Ploughshares: Concepts of Covenant and Repentance in Paul Ramsey's Political Theology* (PhD thesis, University of Edinburgh, 2009), p. 162.
[31] Wilson Carey McWilliams on Reinhold Niebuhr, cited in Eric Gregory, *Politics and the Order of Love: An Augustinian Ethic of Democratic Citizenship* (Chicago, IL: University of Chicago Press, 2008), p. 18.

bad weather'.[32] Eventually, the love embodied in liberal democracies generated national defence as the primary political imperative. Meanwhile, *agape* turns into an 'ideal' once its apocalyptic 'mystery' and faith are suspended.[33]

In *Basic Christian Ethics*, Ramsey stopped short of these implications. As regards the ethics of war, the sceptical rather than the idealist-pragmatist posture prevailed. What *could* be extracted from the individual's love vis-à-vis God in connection with the 'metaphysics of democracy', however, was a pre-political communal *corpus*. It was conceivable through God's covenant with Israel; 'it was the "covenant with Yahweh by which the community came into existence."'.[34] Ramsey expounds in a chapter (added to the book upon Reinhold Niebuhr's request):

> The covenant, to the Hebrews, served as a kind of charter or national constitution. When the laws are thought of together with the covenant, it is referred to as the 'nature of the kingdom' (1 Sam. 10.25) ... It may be compared with a basic contract making possible all such specific agreements, a 'contract of contracts' logically prior to all law. (*BCE*, 367–8)

The covenant established God's fidelity and righteous sovereignty, and it established the nation of Israel as a people with a common voice (*BCE*, 375). Ramsey here sought to raise a bulwark against various modern forms of 'single-contract' state sovereignty. 'Beside the covenant there could be none other. It was impossible to conceive of any public contract with other gods or rulers that would not be a violation of the first' (*BCE*, 379). This is a notable counterpoint to Elshtain's view of the state, a 'limited sovereignty' in Bodinian, Schmittian or Hobbesian terms (whereby these 'limitations' were unhinged *in extremis*).

Ramsey doesn't provide a biblical theory of politics here.[35] One cannot derive democracy from Israel's covenant, he insists. But 'we would be better advised to confront there the asserted and "ratified" sovereignty of God' (*BCE*, 384).[36] The divine authority or 'sovereignty' established in this covenant cannot be claimed or 'transferred from God'. Rather, so the line of 'double-contract theories': '[the] justification of earthly authority ... must be reduced to a simple corollary of the idea of "covenant"' (*BCE*, 386).

Most significant in terms of the theo-logic of mediation is the fact that, by referring to the covenant, Ramsey carves out an alternative position – more or less explicitly 'heretical' vis-à-vis a papal-sovereign paradigm (in its more traditional

---

[32] Paul Ramsey, *The Just War: Force and Political Responsibility* (Lanham, MD: Rowman & Littlefield, 2002), p. xxiii.

[33] Chapter 6 will address this problem.

[34] Cited in Hollowell, *Power and Purpose*, p. 20.

[35] Cf. Chapter 5, where O'Donovan turns Ramsey's negative conclusions from Israel's politics into a biblical ground for authority.

[36] The sovereignty of God was the key doctrine that Ramsey's doctoral supervisor H. Richard Niebuhr had defended in *Radical Monotheism and Western Culture* (1960); it was then on the point of the radicality and status of the doctrine that Ramsey fell out with James M. Gustafson, who had 'radicalised *Radical Monotheism*' – Jeffrey Stout, Paul Ramsey 100th Birthday Celebration, Millsaps College, 2 December 2013, available at https://www.youtube.com/watch?v=XdH1AAmWQps (accessed 13 July 2018).

form[37]). The covenant, Ramsey says with Emil Brunner, stems itself against 'atheist' notions of modern sovereignty:

> The biblical covenant stood, and stands, against both politically atheistic worlds, both the modern world of monolithic dictators and omnicompetent states and the Roman Catholic world in which the pope claims to be, if he does not always act like, Christ's vicar on earth in such fashion as to make Christ his vicar in heaven. (*BCE*, 385)

In consequence, neither vision is tenable: 'The current conflict between these two politically atheistic worlds is a war of religions which are not ours' (*BCE*, 385). So the agapeic position of man before God may not generate an authority calculus. But its positivity is politically negative: 'covenant-obedience holds firmly onto the conviction that man's ultimate loyalty transcends every earthly system or center of human power'; and this at least 'gives man whereon to stand in opposing the present shape of the world' (*BCE*, 387).

As indicated previously, Steinhoff's radical scepticism and Ramsey's agapism for a moment occupy the same spot. If Ramsey rejected sovereign states as well as papalism as 'atheist' and plunged into a critical freedom beyond positive institutions, Steinhoff demands the same critical freedom, rejecting them as institutions based on ideological fictions. However, at this juncture the two authors go separate ways. For Ramsey, democracy was Christian *agape* – proximate, incarnate in democratic structures. For Steinhoff, *Iustitia* had to remain mute; hence he cut himself short of naming any good *façons* for liberal democracy. The right to self-defence and right to self-development provided the basic formal structures.[38]

Political reality: An ontology of tragedy?

Once he had taken more conservative political positions, the later Ramsey had to face the criticism that his realism was too negative. It deprived politics, as a sphere or reality, of freedom and the potential to do *good*. Did this critique, if at all, hit the target when we look at Ramsey's earlier work?

Because the pivotal, mediating point in Ramsey's theology was an anthropology, a theologically unbridged incommensurability remains between the realm of irredeemably sinful human creatures and a realm of divine ideals or 'supernatural standards'. Nonetheless, human beings' 'capacity to do justice, but their inclination to sin' implies that there is both an aspect of opportunity, of freedom to do good, but equally the persistent sting of sin. So on the one hand Ramsey's anthropology provided

---

[37] Christian love is also different from 'simple humanitarianism': 'ethical humanism is grounded on the infinite inherent value of *human* personality in general, while the view here suggested proceeds on the inherently more Christian principle of infinite preference for the *neighbor's*' (*BCE*, 259; cf. 355–8). Ramsey's generation of Christian ethicists could still function without a (theological) philosophy of secularization, not least since the post-war crisis of Christian theology as Christian *and* political was still under way.

[38] See Chapter 3.

the 'structural' basis of what D. Stephen Long calls an 'ontology of tragedy'. It begins with the sheer monstrosity of war, both of what happens to the afflicted, but more importantly the things people *do*. Ramsey says, 'By faith in God the young man in the service himself may be reconciled to the evil that he suffers and does (not that it is evil but that it has to be done).' Long relates this to the 'radical monotheism', which Ramsey had learnt from H. Richard Niebuhr, in particular the continuity between BC and AD in the biblical exegesis of love, the 'strange world of the Bible'. 'Radical monotheism', Long argues,

> provided a unity to earthly, political existence, which goes beyond making tragedy understandable, it makes tragedy unavoidable. The soldier is reconciled not to the evil he does, but to the fact that given the historical circumstances in which he has been thrown, he must do evil.[39]

As a result, Long points out, 'The soldier's culpability dissipates into the unavoidable structure of tragedy.'[40] This tragic fabric continues to set the political coordinates: 'politics can never escape force, violence and coercion. ... While Ramsey may allow for the purpose of political society to be a just order, it could never be a peaceable order.'[41] From this perspective, the more alien, the more wholly different *agape* is conceived as divine-ethical action or mode of being, the more *negative* its counterpart, the more 'human, all too human', political reality becomes. And indeed, the 'unavoidability' of war, or at least its permanent possibility, remained a recurring theme for Ramsey's notion of the political.

On the other hand, several commentators have emphasized the notion of freedom inherent in *agape*. Ramsey's lifelong efforts themselves are proof against a quasi-deterministic acceptance of 'the reality of politics' as tragic, antagonistic necessity.[42] These opposing scholarly positions, however, once seen through Ramsey's idealism, are not necessarily contradictory. After all, philosophical idealism precisely sought to overcome a Kantian dualism between nature and freedom, between morality and politics. Reformulating a theodicy, Ramsey saw the abysmal cracks of darkness in history as evidence of human freedom and the possibility of good. The ambiguity of human nature is therefore not a moral judgement. Nonetheless, Long is correct to point out that in a structural sense the ontology of tragedy has the potential to become fundamental.

Love beats the law

Like in his early pacifist days at Millsaps, Ramsey in *Basic Christian Ethics* continued to expound the meaning of neighbour love. The 'central ethical notion or "category"' in

---

[39] Long, *Tragedy, Tradition, Transformism*, p. 47.
[40] Ibid.
[41] Ibid., p. 146.
[42] Adam E. Hollowell and James F. Cubie, '"Where Have We Been? Where Are We Going?" – Paul Ramsey, Paul Lehmann, and Karl Barth's Doctrine of God', in *Explorations in Christian Theology and Christian Ethics: Essays in Conversation with Paul L. Lehmann*, ed. Philip G. Ziegler and Michelle J. Bartel (Farnham: Ashgate, 2009), pp. 79–101, p. 116 n. 56.

Christin ethics' is '"obedient love" – the sort of love the gospels describe as "love fulfilling the law" and St. Paul designates as "faith that works through love"' (*BCE*, xi). However, he now sets an ethic of love *against* the immanent historicism of those who equalled Christianity with social and political reform. Ramsey now thinks that Jesus's strenuous teachings are wrongly understood as 'a method for making all the world a kingdom of God' (*BCE*, 37). He thinks this view misunderstands Jesus's unique apocalypticism: 'God's final judgment was expected to separate the sheep from the goats; whereas in the crisis of our time, at Bikini, both sheep and goats were killed' (36). Moreover, the idea that Jesus's 'strenuous teachings' was a method to create God's peaceful kingdom misunderstands the nature of God's work:

> The reverse was the case: the kingdom of God was already effective in the present age and for this reason [Jesus] believed the strenuous teachings could be lived out. Since 'it is God's good pleasure to give you the kingdom', men may now 'fear not', their love and forgiveness be unrestricted, themselves meek. (*BCE*, 37)

Since for Jesus the Kingdom was already here, 'two directions in which Christian thought and decision may move' were equally alien to his mind. Despite God's reign, both paths take human initiative too seriously, even though in opposite directions. Either one 'can say that to love, to suffer and to do good in the face of armed injustice is "God's method of dealing with evil" in its entirety'. But if we do that, 'we say something Jesus would not have said; he did not attribute such power to love and non-resistance' (*BCE*, 38). Equally, Jesus would have rejected the opposite. And with this, Ramsey *removes* the grounds for all just war thinking:

> The other alternative is to justify the employment of force in dealing with tyrannical structures of evil. This involves the substitution of human power-controls for divine power and, it may be, humanly directed violence for the divine violence entailed literally in Jesus' eschatological expectation. God's coercive intervention to deal with general evil may be replaced by concrete legislative measures, governmental institutions, and other responsible human arrangements, which then stand in exactly the same relation to the love-ethic as did the divine intervention which Jesus expected. (*BCE*, 38)

So what was the third way between these two paths? Ramsey points at a truly unsettling possibility. One 'must have the courage to look squarely into the mystery of how ideals were manufactured in this Christian world', he quotes Nietzsche (who recurs frequently in BCE). From the Christian mystery, 'the late-Jewish Messianic world-view' springs *agape*, a love beyond good and evil, one that could be meek but equally deal with the not-so-meek.[43] *Agape* was a love that comprised everything and was still 'primitive',

---

[43] As far as I can see, only D. Stephen Long has highlighted the influence of Nietzsche on Ramsey (see Long, *Tragedy, Tradition, Transformism*, p. 53), though this is not least transmitted via Karl Barth. With Nietzsche, Ramsey questions a Pharisaic code morality (*BCE*, 74) as well as humility as an 'additional value' (*BCE*, 220); on the fundamental transvaluative upheaval of Christianity see also *BCE* (247). NB: Steinhoff and Ramsey (at least during this Christian-sceptical period) reject, with

a love much more than Jesus's voluntarist interpreters –including the early Ramsey himself – could have envisioned. And here 'we can, after a fashion, watch revelation taking place' (*BCE*, 40).

So, if the modern rationalist critical project meant that human reason breaks *out* of the theocratic option (as encountered in Chapter 3 on Steinhoff), then here, in Ramsey's understanding, the divine breaks *into* the world. It is worth quoting Ramsey at length on the nature of *agape*, since the concept – and its theo-political implications – would remain relevant throughout his life:

> In face of the in breaking kingdom, moral decision was stripped of all prudential considerations, all calculation of what is right in terms of consequences which in this present age normally follow certain lines of action. Not only all prudential calculation of consequences likely to fall upon the agent himself, but likewise all sober regard for the future performance of his responsibility for family or friends, duties to oneself and *fixed* duties to others, both alike were jettisoned from view. Preferential loves, even those justifiable in normal times, were supplanted by entirely non-preferential regard for whomever happened to be standing by, friend or enemy, bullying sergeant or indigent beggar. All that mattered was perfect obedience to God. All that mattered was complete readiness for the kingdom to come. All that mattered was the single individual a man happened to confront. All that mattered was unhesitating, total love. (*BCE*, 39)

Ramsey acknowledges Jesus's unique apocalypticism as an eschatological paradox and the 'inbreaking' divine horizon that frees up obedient, kenotic neighbour love. This is *agape*'s distinct 'perspective' (*BCE*, 21, 101). The individual's direct, immediate position vis-à-vis God, a *sola fide*, makes possible a Christ-like kenotic love for everybody.

Nevertheless, Jesus's unique vision cannot be replicated. Less so negotiating the terms of the Incarnation, Ramsey's apocalyptic Jesuology remains grounded in history after all: 'This has to be said, so let it be said forthrightly: few contemporary Christians accept the kind of kingdom-expectation Jesus considered of central importance, and rightly they do not' (*BCE*, 35–6). For Ramsey, the present world of responsibilities 'must be viewed largely in non-apocalyptic terms' (*BCE*, 42). It remains separated from God's kingdom by an 'eschatological gulf'. There is a 'rift' between the present age and the hereafter; and nobody should try to 'overleap the abyss between the ages' (*BCE*, 133). So the *im*-mediacy of *agape* in faith stands eye to eye with a practically dichotomous eschatology, decisively distinguishing between this age and the next.[44]

But because divine–human immediacy and separation are spliced together rather than mediated here, Ramsey's early ethics oscillated. He was pulled into two directions. He had to explicate *agape* as moral without marring its purity. And he had to do ethics

---

Nietzsche, any 'self-regarding concern for others' (see Chapter 3): 'whoever gives even his body to be burned in order to save his own soul loves only himself' (*BCE*, 103–4).

[44] For a focused analysis, see Shaun A. Casey, 'Eschatology and Statecraft in Paul Ramsey', *Studies in Christian Ethics*, 21 (2008), 73–193.

without losing sight of *agape*.[45] Thus, on the one hand, the Reformation's (particularly Luther's) de-secularizing notion of vocation replaced the Catholic 'counsels of perfection', indeed any culture of supererogatory virtue.[46] Now everyone within their worldly vocation is called to serve God, in line with their gifts and the neighbour's need. 'Every Christian everywhere, no matter what his function in society, is obliged ... to measure his life by non-resisting love, and not only his inner disposition but his outward action as well' (*BCE*, 189). *Agape* could operate without any gaps, a complete *Christ*-ianization. For that reason, the Methodist scholar Shaun O. Casey still discerned a genuine drive for 'progressivism' in the early Ramsey.[47]

On the other hand, the work of *agape* was 'incommensurate' with ethics, incommensurate with 'the world of systems' (*BCE*, 17), even anti-legalistic.[48] Jesus's words, that 'not an iota, not a dot, will pass from the law until all is accomplished' (Matt. 5.18), for Ramsey 'are either not the original words of Jesus or else they are sorely in need of a loose interpretation'. He understands Jesus 'fulfils the law' to mean that he 'completes in such fashion as entirely to annul the law' (*BCE*, 54). Jesus's verdict not only nullifies the Mosaic Code but also 'any ethic of conventional respectability, any customary code of conduct into which at least every man is born, any more or less philosophic definition of good and evil'.[49] Love is indeed *alien* and irreducible to any 'natural' rules or laws:

> Instead of measuring love for God and man against other parts of the code and declaring the love commandments to be more important than all or any one of the remainder, Jesus in effect affirms the love commandments to be *incommensurable* with all the rest and declines to measure their importance by comparison with any other legislation. (*BCE*, 65; italics original)

Love is not without 'abundant content' but simultaneously – and this is the key difficulty – love remains without 'determinate content' (*BCE*, 338). Hence also the doctrine of vocation 'recognizes a large area of relativity in ethics, disclaiming any hard-and-fast absolute principles or rigid laws' (*BCE*, 188). In short, 'Unmediated love demands freedom from the law.'[50] On the grounds of this 'anti-legalism', Robert W. Tuttle much later levelled the charge of Gnosticism and *Marcionism* against Ramsey.[51] Marcionism entirely spiritualizes and hence disembodies Christ.[51] While the historical

---

[45] Ramsey corrects Augustine, for whom the neighbour is to be employed to obtain the only proper object of desire, i.e. the union with God: 'If, then, both a Christian and his God have a love born of plenitude, not out of need, God may love man for his own sake and the Christian love his neighbor for his own sake ... The neighbor is never the ultimate object of aspiring *caritas*-love; he is always the end-term of *agape*-love' (*BCE*, 124). Tuttle, 'All You Need Is Love', 427–57, p. 431.

[46] Cf. Chapter 3, section on supererogation.

[47] Casey, 'Eschatology', p. 176.

[48] Cf. Long, *Tragedy, Tradition, Transformism*, pp. 10–12. From the perspective of love, as Bonhoeffer and Barth note, ethics is always already a *problem*. And although Ramsey cited Niebuhr precisely along those lines during his pacifist phase, this came only to fruition in BCE.

[49] Tuttle, 'All You Need Is Love', 427–57, p. 443.

[50] Tuttle, 'All You Need is Love', supra n. 14, p. 436. Adam E. Hollowell artfully retraces Ramsey's (significantly later) arguments against situationism in *Power and Purpose*, pp. 83–102.

[51] Tuttle, 'All You Need Is Love', pp. 445–7.

Jesus has very limited ethical authority, the Christ is both alien and everywhere already. Notably, the charge of Marcionism was levelled also against Barth after first publishing his *Römerbrief* (1919). Dialectical theology (not least Brunner's *The Mediator*, though not mentioned by Ramsey) forms the backdrop of Ramsey's discussion, though now under the auspices of the Second World War.

More systematically, however, and in terms of the theo-logic of mediation at stake here, we may now reconnect the early Ramsey to the authors in Part One. He repeats their essentially modern paradigm from the opposing side: he explicates the very *totaliter aliter* love springing from a dimension the previous authors had rejected as dangerously sectarian and/or transformed into an immanent humanitarianism. Steinhoff had approximated it but turned away from it as relevant for a liberal ethics, not to mention the ethics of war.

Christian transformism and the dialectics of the political act

Love transforms the law

Ramsey was aware of the practical problems implicit in *Basic Christian Ethics*. In order to safeguard the possibility of his Christian ethics, he had to pick up the loose ends of that book. The altogether biblically grounded, non-naturalistic *agape* had to be reconciled with natural moral reason. This could prevent a Kierkegaardian teleological suspension of the ethical, which he knew could 'countermand human conscience' (*BCE*, 338). So in 1953 he wrote, 'Of late my thought has been much concerned with the various types which H. R. Niebuhr delineates, and so I would phrase my present point of view as "love transforming justice." '[52]

This was not a merely scholastic debate. The question was how Christian love related to any humanistic ethic, which '[derived] the standard for man solely from man and the structures immanent in human society', as he wrote a few years later in *Nine Modern Moralists* (1961). Between the 'Egypt' of such a 'natural law' and Christian ethics in a mode of 'Exodus' ('taking note only of the demands upon men who live in the immediate presence of God' [*NMM*, 181]), Ramsey sought to clarify a mediate position. And it was signified by a dynamic and creative relationship between the two: Christ 'transforms, renews, reshapes, and redirects the natural law'. And, 'where Christ reigns, *agape* enters into a fresh determination of what it is right to do; yet Christ does not reign over a structureless world or over men who are bereft of any sense of natural injustice'.[53] This transformism could address the oscillation, the fundamental dualism and simultaneous (even if hypothetical) 'identity', between the spiritual and the political, between formless *agape* and sovereign legality grounded in natural law. It was a way of thinking Christo-logical mediation. But was it a success?

---

[52] Cited in Long, *Tragedy, Tradition, Transformism*, p. 54.
[53] Paul Ramsey, *Ramsey, Nine Modern Moralists* (New York: University Press of America, 1961), p. 5. Hereafter NMM.

In *War and the Christian Conscience* (1961),[54] first an unbridgeable difference between political justice and Christian love comes into view, now seen through St Augustine's eyes in *The City of God*. Augustine's sceptical view of earthly justice led Ramsey to conclude that Christian faith working through love could never question that city's ways. Ramsey here sharply criticizes Ernest Barker's reading of Augustine – relevant for us since it reflects Elshtain's view. Barker mistakenly suggests a 'smooth Christianisation of Classical politics' by suggesting there is a 'limited *iustitia*' in the earthly city. But for Augustine, Ramsey says, there is no such thing as earthly 'relative justice'.[55] And where there is no true justice (*iustitia*) there can be no right (*ius*); hence, Augustine's claim that there was never a 'Roman republic' (*WCC*, 24).

The earthly city can merely offer a *pax-ordo* void of *iustitia*, divine justice. Augustine 'is not calling for a mere religious addendum, or for a State that goes further than its existent, intrinsic justice to become a denominationally Christian State'. Instead, Augustine 'demoralizes *res publica*' (*WCC*, 25), even deconstructs it. Within the earthly city, any 'just war' therefore has little to do with Christian love: 'It is *a lively sense of man's common plight* in wrong-doing and of *the judgment of God* that overarches the justified war, and not – except perhaps as an incidental implication of what Augustine says – a sense of or clarity about the universal ethical standards that are to be applied' (*WCC*, 28; italics added). Self-love 'may be *absent* when the public good is in question; but whether it is love that is *present,* governing the Christian in what concerns the public good ... may be questioned' (*WCC*, 38). From the perspective of divine *iustitia*, not to mention divine love, all earthly cities and wars are therefore equally (un)just (*WCC*, 28).[56]

Rather than highlighting the fundamental difference between an Augustinian 'conversionism' (or the possible 'transformation' of war) and Barker's ideology of empire, Ramsey first fully compartmentalizes 'earthly justice' and *agape*. The latter, now absent the 'mystery' of Jesus' apocalypticism, has become equal to an 'idealism' – to be avoided at all cost. To make a political point out of love only poses the threat of idealizing the real: 'An unrectified *nisus* toward the eternal disturbs every people's purpose: that is why they see in their good the Good, in the laws of their peace the conditions of universal peace and are resolved that this too shall not pass away' (*WCC*, 31). Ramsey saw his scepticism confirmed by a modern world that was a 'vast concentration camp' (and it was never enough for Ramsey to merely oppose the Nazis; the Allied obliteration bombing was equally totalitarian).[57] With both sides of a war suspiciously unjust, a Christian cannot add anything meaningful to the (democratic, earthly) *ad bellum* criteria (*WCC*, 32).

[54] Ramsey, *War and the Christian Conscience*.
[55] A term Elshtain used as well, see e.g. 'Paul Elie, Jean Bethke Elshtain, and Robin Lovin, "Moral Man and Immoral Society: Rediscovering Reinhold Niebuhr"', *On Being with Krista Tippett*, https://onbeing.org/programs/paul-elie-jean-bethke-elshtain-and-robin-lovin-moral-man-and-immoral-society-rediscovering-reinhold-niebuhr/ (accessed 11 July 2019).
[56] William Werpehowski, *American Protestant Ethics and the Legacy of H. Richard Niebuhr* (Washington, DC: Georgetown University Press, 2002), pp. 56, 69; Paul Ramsey and Stanley Hauerwas, *Speak Up for Just War or Pacifism: A Critique of the United Methodist Bishops' Pastoral Letter 'In Defense of Creation'* (University Park: Pennsylvania State University Press, 1988), pp. 89–90.
[57] Ramsey, *Nine Modern Moralists*, p. 19.

However, since Christian 'participation in war' (31) may be justified, *agape* enters as it determines the 'right *conduct* of war' (*WCC*, 32). And here, Christ's universal *agape* provided the absolute standard for discrimination. Christ had died for the godly and the ungodly so that individuals are surrounded by immunity from *direct* killing (*WCC*, 55). As the Christian loves God in the neighbour, it is the moral impossibility of 'killing Christ anew' that guarantees the inviolability of life from direct attack.[58] As we will see, Ramsey showed that discrimination would transform the paradigmatic 'aggressor-defender doctrine', which continues to structure just war thinking and international law today. Before I explicate this, I will briefly look at how love-transforming law impacted on authority.

Between the priesthood of all and the 'earthly city'

Basic Christian Ethics had left the individual vis-à-vis God in a critical position towards all institutions and authorities. But how does or can this 'Christian perspective' transform the 'justice' of modern state sovereignty and any Catholic (or catholicizing) authorities? In *War and the Christian Conscience*, Ramsey located political form now *between* the agape of the Calvinist 'radical reformation' of Geneva on the one hand and the legal limitations and 'restraints' of violent force provided by Catholic canon law on the other. The chapter on 'Justified Revolution' in *WCC* makes this particularly clear. Beginning from Aquinas to Calvin, whatever rung in the ladder of the social hierarchy was permitted to revolt, 'it was not an incitement to riot or to unlimited revolution' (*WCC*, 122). *Agape* may be a noble motive, but it has to be channelled. The fact that it is limited by a 'theory' is even a precondition for Christians to approve of revolution. In other words, for Ramsey it may be an act of Christian conscience (and thus potentially *agape*) to limit popular, enthusiastic *agape* in response to social and political injustice (*WCC*, 124). What follows is a 'theory of "constitutional" or "official" revolution'.

> It means that an abstract and universal justice, or its serious violation within a nation, is never sufficient to warrant an appeal to arms. ... Instead, one must wait – long past the point where simple justice began to be violated – until there arises someone or some group capable of representing a better *pax-ordo*, and capable of bringing this to pass without letting worse befall. (*WCC*, 124)

Ramsey's notion of revolution here draws on two sources: First, individuals' recognition of God's sovereignty *per vocationem* of magistrate or citizen. Vocation is again the vehicle for God's 'sway [to] be felt in every crevice of the kingdom'. And, 'consequently, not only inner faith and books but social relationships and social justice are religious matters and just as important as the freedom of faith'. The fact that 'the private consciences of free men become the fundaments source of political authority' is 'the practical extension of the priesthood of all', the sense in which everyone is a king (*WCC*, 126). In other words, here we have the possibility of radical, Christian

---

[58] Oliver O'Donovan, 'Karl Barth and Ramsey's "Uses of Power"', *Journal of Religious Ethics*, 19 (1991), 9.

democracy: spiritual and political are identical; love and law, church and state may become one.

However, Ramsey precisely does not want to make possible is a politically 'heterodox', Calvinist Geneva challenging an Augustinian empire. The second source therefore – a matching *counterpart* to Ramsey's often vocally anti-Catholic Methodism – limits this revolutionary *agape*: 'the continuing importance of Roman Catholicism is that, with its tradition of natural law still intact, it instructs these new magistrates as it did the old ones in what is just and not alterable merely by their "sovereign" will, and in the law to which their decisions should conform' (*WCC*, 126). Since for Ramsey the political community was a matter of the nation-state (rather than the church), it is not surprising that he uses the juridical paradigm of liberal democracy as a compromise between 'making [revolutionary] chaos of the Kingdom of God' and the law of an institutional church.[59] Since the late eighteenth century, the possibility of chaotic 'disordered' revolution has been brought to a final close by a legal, constitutional apparatus. So, Ramsey stays on familiar territory: 'What then is democracy but *bellum iustum*?'[60] The democratic paradigm and Christian *bellum iustum* become congruent: when 'democracy as "regularized struggle" breaks down, then people may need to be "directly coerced".[61]

Theologically, Ramsey's transformist turn from an alien, biblical agape to democracy-as-mediation (and *bellum iustum*) remains predicated on the Christological duality described earlier. Before that backdrop, D. Stephen Long observes that an unacknowledged 'epistemological rupture' occurs in *War and the Christian Conscience*, one that pulls Ramsey away from 'confessional ethics' to 'natural law' and 'natural rights'.[62] The taboo to target the children 'to get at their fathers' now becomes an insight of *natural reason*. According to Long, it was not that the analysis of (indeterminate) love led Ramsey to develop the norm of discrimination. It was Father John C. Ford and the Roman Catholic moral tradition. And at least Ford moved the just war tradition into the realm of international law, the law of humanity and natural law; for Ford, discrimination was unrelated to 'the confessional' and a matter of natural moral insight.

Ramsey's shift (with Ford) marks an alternative to a Christologically grounded political mediation, since it is a *shift* from love to 'non-confessional' natural law. Love of neighbour by the standard of Christ determines the absolute duty of discrimination. But that remains potentially confined to subjective experience, while its explications (such as the principle of order) and *ad bellum* criteria are derived from natural law.[63] Much later, Ramsey conceded that the switch from love to 'non-confessional' natural law could not perform the transformist task as well as he had envisioned. He

---

[59] Cf. Giorgio Agamben, *State of Exception* (Chicago, IL: University of Chicago Press, 2008), pp. 1–31; John Milbank, 'Paul against Biopolitics', in *Paul's New Moment: Continental Philosophy and the Future of Christian Theology*, ed. John Milbank, Slavoj Žižek and Creston Davis (Grand Rapids, MI: Brazos Press, 2010), pp. 21–73.

[60] Ramsey, *War and the Christian Conscience*, p. 126.

[61] Cited in Long, *Tragedy, Tradition, Transformism*, p. 67; Ramsey, *War and the Christian Conscience*, p. 126.

[62] Long, *Tragedy, Tradition, Transformism*, p. 77.

[63] Hollowell has unearthed a letter from 1965, in which Ramsey underlines, 'My treatment of warfare does NOT rest upon a natural law basis; it rests rather on a prior demonstration that non-combatant immunity was and is a rule and work of charity – Christ illuminating the meaning of justice.' Cited in Hollowell, *Power and Purpose*, p. 186.

described it as 'thinking in one direction only between altogether separate sources of ethics (a possible reading of my "love transforming natural justice")'.[64] And despite the overall reigning Christ in his vision, which would become Oliver O'Donovan's central theological focus (see Chapter 5), only much later he came to the conclusion that Christology is 'the real issue'.[65]

The emergence of a modern Christian just war doctrine

Nevertheless, Ramsey's transformist period yielded three fruitful entry points for a political theo-logic of mediation, one that also shifted politics from the agent to the political *act*. Ramsey's approach thus further corrects some of the problematic implications of the authors we've looked at in the previous chapters.

Discrimination

First, as noted, *War and the Christian Conscience* (1961) shows how *agape* bears upon warfare.[66] In between nuclear pacifism and 'those who speak recklessly of "preventive war" and of "massive retaliation"', and equally in contrast to Reinhold Niebuhr's pragmatism, Ramsey injected the 'just-war doctrine'.[67] It is not the case that the Christian 'adopts (and "seasons" with love) a rigorous alien natural-law principle … but that he finds himself still required to do only what love requires and permitted to do only what love allows to be right' (*WCC*, xx).

If the duty to protect the neighbour justified participation in war, then now severe *limits* have to be placed on warfare. This limit is the prohibition of indiscriminate killing; that is the essence of Christian just war thinking. The 'little ones' must be surrounded with moral immunity from direct killing (*WCC*, xx), even if Ramsey remains vague: 'We only have to know *that* there are non-combatants, not exactly *who* or *where* they are, in order to know that warfare should be forces and counter-forces warfare, and attack be limited to legitimate military targets' (*WCC*, 68). Yet the point is that once discrimination is actually intended (and here the moral integrity of the agent is one central element), strategies like deliberate carpet-bombing, 'counter-population warfare' or the terrorist targeting of innocents are impermissible and condemnable.[68]

The 'absolutism' of non-combatant immunity can only function if it goes hand in hand with a doctrine of double effect, because not to harm or kill any non-combatants is only something one can *aim* for. For Ramsey, the doctrine is a direct result of *merging agape* with the consequentialist pragmatism of his time: 'The good or the best or the lesser evil among the goals of action is to be chosen, yet by action that is

---

[64] Cited in Hollowell, 'Revising Basic Christian Ethics', 267–83, p. 277.
[65] Hollowell, *This Side of the Ploughshares*, p. 168.
[66] Ramsey, *War and the Christian Conscience*.
[67] Foreword by John H. Hallowell, *WCC*, p. vii.
[68] NB: Ramsey also rejects the (almost ridiculous) suggestion that a bomber pilot might press the button to carpet-bomb a city without 'intending' to kill indiscriminately. Intention and action (a) cannot be clearly isolated from each other and (b) one action cannot be analysed in clear isolation from its surrounding actions. An intention *does* transform the action.

not intrinsically and from the beginning wrong in itself' (*WCC*, 4). And even in war the primary aim should never be to kill the enemy soldier but to incapacitate him, to terminate his status as a combatant.[69] In order to avoid any subjectivism as regards an individual's intention, the military act must be objectively proportionate: 'The evil, secondary effect only allowed must not be out of proportion to the good effect one intends to obtain' (*WCC*, 43). And, 'the good must be not only willed directly but also done directly, if the agent is not to be held directly accountable also for the foreknown evil consequence of his action' (*WCC*, 55).

If *BCE* had focused on individuals' love, then here the notion of political authority comes into better view. The use of force is only morally justified for the sake of a public good (keeping in mind also the idealist derivation of individual rights). Only in acting for the common good, a Christian may be permitted to kill an unjust assailant (*WCC*, 41). Ramsey injects one further qualification here: it is the common good 'to which one has allegiance more than for the public good of another' (*WCC*, 41).

In contrast, self-defence is never a *moral right* for a Christian. That implies two things. First, of course, it could never be prohibited legally. Second, unselfish neighbour love cannot *morally* fully *justify* killing even a criminal for one's own sake. In other words, there is a serious point in the anguish about killing someone; it reflects the infinite aspect of the human being. Ramsey connects this with the 'transformative' accounts of Augustine and Aquinas. Augustine, who is thinking of 'justice radically transformed by supernatural charity', says, 'But I see not how these men [who defend themselves privately], while not held guilty by law, can be without fault: for the law does not force them to kill, but leaves it in their power' (*WCC*, 36). Aquinas, more of a natural lawyer, regards self-preservation as a natural impulse. Still, Ramsey says, 'he thinks about these questions from the point of view of love, or of love-transformed justice' (*WCC*, 42). Aquinas' consequence is a doctrine of double effect: 'Subjectively, the Christian must never intend to kill a man, since love refuses to allow that motive, and countenances only the intention of saving life, even one's own' (*WCC*, 43).[70] Killing

---

[69] Although often regarded as unrealistic romanticism by soldiers and military personnel, this consideration should not diminish military effectiveness. It rather grounds the principle of necessity, guarding against an unrestricted shoot-to-kill policy not merely on the grounds of pragmatism. Cf. Ryan Goodman, 'The Power to Kill or Capture Enemy Combatants', *European Journal of International Law*, 24.3 (2013), 819–853, doi:10.1093/ejil/cht048 – Goodman identifies the following maxim in the Laws of Armed Conflict: 'If enemy combatants can be put out of action by capturing them, they should not be injured; if they can be put out of action by injury, they should not be killed; and if they can be put out of action by light injury, grave injury should be avoided'; Michael N. Schmitt, 'Wound, Capture, or Kill: A Reply to Ryan Goodman's "The Power to Kill or Capture Enemy Combatants"', *European Journal of International Law*, 24.3 (2013), 855–61, https://doi.org/10.1093/ejil/cht049. Schmitt sees no legal duty to capture rather than kill where possible but notes that it is usually preferable, maybe 'ethical' and pragmatic (e.g. avoid alienating the locals).

[70] The right to self-defence is elaborated on to contrast it with Steinhoff's and Rodin's understanding above. The contrast between the *moral freedom* to not kill the enemy and the *legal right* to self-defend is most important. For Ramsey, the latter is de-absolutized by the duty to retreat from the attacker if possible (on the grounds that the defending agent may not want to kill or avoid an escalation to the point where killing the assailant is necessary. Steinhoff is more likely to interpret avoidance of such an escalation as 'right shying away from wrong').

the attacker may nevertheless be a side effect of self-defence.[71] The moral *duty* (which Ramsey keeps more distinct from the law than Steinhoff's liberalism) is rather to retreat in order to avoid killing, at least as far as possible. In that sense, both Augustine and Aquinas for Ramsey represent a 'transformative' Christian political ethics.

Transforming the 'aggressor-defender' doctrine of war – discrimination and order

Second, in the same year as WCC Ramsey published 'What Americans Ordinarily Think about Justice in War' (*JW*, 42–69). In this article, he critiques the so-called aggressor-defender doctrine. This is worth a closer look, since this implication of Ramsey's transformism marks another point of departure from the contemporary sovereign-internationalist paradigm we explored in Part One.

In Ramsey's interpretation, the 'aggressor-defender doctrine' – which we might understand as a non-mediating theo-logic unfolding – focuses on the *inception* of war. Initial aggression justifies the act of defence, because war is always presumed to be unnecessary and superfluous. This voluntarist conception of politics regards 'aggression' as a combination of bad will and miscalculation (or a *libido dominandi*). The 'aggressor' is the one who shoots first; therefore, he is always wrong. Since at that point all necessary justification for the war is provided, there are then no principled limitations in the objectives of a war. If the aims are broad enough ('the war to end wars', 'spreading democracy', 'war against terror', 'war against fascism'), any kind of warfare, even nuclear, is possible. Only acts of 'wanton destructiveness', such as massacres committed by individual soldiers, are exempt (*JW*, 58). However, if the war objectives are unlimited, very few instances count as genuinely wanton – because disproportionate – in the first place. The voluntarism in the run-up to the war is in fact complemented by a determinism in war. The conduct of war is exclusively understood in terms of military necessity. It is regarded as disastrous and tragic but hardly morally wrong. This logic is then acerbated by the idea that war signifies the *breakdown* of all order and ordered action. With the realms of war and peace so disjointed, despite 'ethical limitations', a war's objective and conduct are *effectively* unlimited.[72]

As a 'transformative' response, Ramsey makes non-combatant immunity central to his argument and notes how it coheres with other limitations. He objects to the type of humanitarianism that protects inherent rights of individuals *qua* individuals. Rather, non-combatant immunity is also 'the parent of the principle of order' (*JW*, 60, 163). Put differently, the 'principle of order' is the corresponding 'natural law' to discrimination (*JW*, 60) or a 'helpful supplement' (*JW*, 163). Combatants and non-combatants are always members of states (a point corroborated by his Christian-idealist theory of democracy). If one discriminates between them, a form of order should also to be guaranteed for the survivors of attacks. Therefore, the elimination of states and social

---

[71] This killing then is excused rather than justified (pace Steinhoff and Rodin, though the two differ as to the extent to which retreating from an attacker is a duty). Ramsey draws on 'excusable homicide', where the defender 'does not share with this other man a mutual murderous intent' (*WCC*, 42).
[72] See Chapter 2 on war as a 'trap' or a form of cataclysm.

orders is impermissible; it is 'total war' (JW, 163). The 'vital interest of states ought not to be at stake in the course or on the outcome of war' (*JW*, 60–1). Ramsey here seeks to keep at bay a kind of warfare that is apocalyptic (and thus dualistic) itself, whether in secular or Christian guises. Reconstruction cannot happen out of chaos, let alone be dependent on it.

The uses of power

Third, in his seminal essay *The Uses of Power* (1964), Ramsey developed the dynamics of the political act.[73] Again, *theologically* the discussion remains framed by his eschatological dichotomy.[74] The cross' dark shadow falls into the Babylonic *polis*, which remains untouched by salvific events; Adam and Eve face the 'No-Returning' to paradise and start their 'agricultural economy' from 'a social platform of friendly competition, cooperation, and mutual respect', as Ramsey ironically fabulates.[75]

However, despite the gloomy eschatological abyss, Ramsey's 'political act' relies on the categories of *continuous mediation* between opposites: on 'coincidence', 'but not entire congruency', an ongoing attempt to reconcile what could fall into duality and violent opposition.[76] In this vein, the state's responsibility is 'defined by the national ... and international common good', national interest and humanitarian duty.[77] Although there is 'to say the least, a dialectic, a tension, a polarity, if there is not an actual or irremediable conflict' between the two goods, Ramsey insists that the responsibility of the politician 'is defined by the area of incidence, or overlap, between them'. The politician should try to 'envision and if possible establish a larger area of incidence between his nation's good and the international common good'.[78] Put differently, 'every responsible political decision involves some precarious determination of how the circles of the national and the international common good are to be drawn'.[79] Ramsey also identifies what he calls the 'terminal political values' for 'government' or 'political agency'. The ends of political action are *ordo*, the order (of power); *iustitia* or justice as 'the regulative ideal of "humanitarianism"'; and *lex*, positive law.[80] 'The magistrate' will continuously weigh these goods or 'values' against another and should increase their overlap: 'Whether justice warrants a disordering action or order warrants the permission of some injustice, nobody can say in advance of statesmanship which rules by what it decrees.'[81]

---

[73] 'The Uses of Power', in Ramsey, *The Just War*, pp. 3–18.

[74] Cf. Casey, 'Eschatology'.

[75] Ramsey, *Just War*, p. xxvii. Such explicit irony is not least a way to counter the mere irony of inadvertency. In that sense, Rorty's praise of irony has its place.

[76] Ramsey, 'The Uses of Power', p. 12. NB: Finding *common* ground closely relates to 'communication', not as the occupation of the 'chattering classes' but as holding 'in common' or 'participation'; the particular implications this has for the development of 'the common good' cannot be developed here, but see e.g. Oliver O'Donovan, 'The Common Good – Does It Amount to a Political Programme?', Baylor ISR Lecture, 17 September 2018, https://www.youtube.com/watch?v=aNRsWbHJqtA (accessed 6 March 2019).

[77] Ramsey, 'The Uses of Power', p. 9.

[78] Ibid.

[79] Ibid., p. 10.

[80] Ibid., p. 12.

[81] Ibid., p. 11.

Ramsey remains curiously formal here, with seemingly 'abstract' conceptual analysis: '*Lex* and *ordo* and *iustitia* stand in a dialectical relationship in all responsible agency.'[82] For all the emphasis on continued responsibility, even the politician's (aesthetic) duty to 'envision' a larger area of coincidence, the geometry of overlapping circles is incongruent with his powerful biblical images of Fall, darkness and the cross's shadow. These themes rather underline Christ's decisive, irreversible Not Yet to what Ramsey calls the 'post-evil' and 'post-political' humankind. To use a Hegelian dichotomy, the *conceptual* dynamics of the political act are potentially much more fruitful, dynamic and practical than the *Vorstellungen* (images) seem to suggest.

While critics mainly targeted Ramsey's realist tendencies, *The Uses of Power* remains an intriguing piece of writing. And precisely, the notion of the political act became central for Oliver O'Donovan. In *Desire of the Nations* (1996), concerned with showing how 'divine rule confers authority on [political] acts', he acknowledges Ramsey:

> The political act was not bounded by institutions. At home in the city, it could extend itself into open spaces across the boundaries erected by civilized institution-building. It was impossible for Ramsey to conceive politics as an island-kingdom, washed on all sides by the trackless ocean of a state of nature. The Lockean liberalism that conceived it that way had placed the abstract political institution at the core of political theory, in the place where political action belonged.'[83]

In *Ways of Judgment* (2005), O'Donovan restated his by then well-known theorem that political authority 'arises where power, the execution of right, and the perpetuation of tradition are assured together in one coordinated agency'. He added, 'The source of this triad [power, right, tradition], as I now realize, was Paul Ramsey's analysis of authority as *lex*, *iustitia*, and *ordo*.'[84] In the Chapter 5, we will see how O'Donovan for his part has theologically transformed Ramsey's idealist transformism. For Ramsey, mediating logic of the political act was possible only vis-à-vis a theological duality between a new 'humanity' and the shadow of the cross over the polis.

Political reality: The transformation of Babylon?

As Ramsey continued to wrestle with moral idealism and utopianism (a category into which *agape* as a political term would eventually retreat), a potential transformation of 'Babylon' became less easy to envision and even a security risk.

Already 'The Uses of Power' was developed in contradistinction to Karl Barth, whom Ramsey charges with stipulating a 'post-evil, Christ-formed man'. O'Donovan clarified later that Barth's 'Christological root of the state ... has to do with the proper location of the political order within the covenant of reconciliation between God and man. ... "In this authority we are dealing indirectly, but in reality, with the authority of

---

[82] Ibid., p. 12.
[83] O'Donovan, 'Karl Barth and Ramsey's "Uses of Power"', 1–30, 23; *The Desire of the Nations: Rediscovering the Roots of Political Theology* (Cambridge: Cambridge University Press, 1996), p. 21.
[84] Oliver O'Donovan, *The Ways of Judgment* (Grand Rapids, MI: William B. Eerdmans, 2005), p. 142.

Jesus Christ."' Jesus Christ 'is represented to us in different ways both by the state and the church but by the church more inclusively since it "contains the state in itself"'.[85] As O'Donovan reads it, '[central] to Barth's conception here is the collapse into one theological moment of the traditionally differentiated moments of God's preserving providence and his saving atonement, the collapse of B.C. into A.D.' So, Ramsey actually misread Barth as stipulating a 'post-evil, Christ-formed man'. Yet the collapse of BC and AD for Ramsey was simply sufficient to locate Barth in the 'idealist camp' – that is, an early form of 'conditional pacifism'. And indeed, many Barthians and Barth scholars in subsequent decades have read him that way. For Barth, the use of violent force was abnormalized, though in a supreme emergency, when the state's 'very existence and autonomy are menaced and attacked', then Barth envisions an exceptional war. *Ironically* (though logically), he ends up with a 'zone of politics which can be viewed only "soberly" and not with evangelical faith or hope'.[86] O'Donovan continues, 'Barth situates politics, as it were, in the Gospels, while Ramsey throws it back into the depths of the Old Testament, somewhere in the middle of the Yahwist's primal history: the expulsion from Eden, perhaps, or the city of Cain, or the post-diluvian covenant, or the Tower of Babel'.[87]

So for Barth, state and church are summed up in Christ – the use of force is abnormalized. For Ramsey, state and church are summed up in the Old Testament –*agape* is abnormalized. The *esse* of politics is the use of force. Not that 'higher values' are impossible in politics or that only a positivist legal order matters. But even the *bene esse* of politics is always related to a *possible* use of force. The state as the Lutheran *Notverordnung* ('order of necessity') is currently the only relevant moral subject of political action.[88] For now, the state is the 'proximate solution to human sacrifice'. Pace Ramsey's disappointed 'idealist', 'agapist' or ontologically optimist critics to this day, this approach still *limits* rather than extends the possible use of force: 'nations might better renounce the use of war as an instrument of *anything but* national policy' (*WCC*, 29).

In short, two simultaneous theo-logics are at work in Ramsey's transformist period. On the one hand, he thinks within the dichotomous paradigm of a 'realistic' earthly politics as opposed to 'utopianism'. Such a fundamental – theological –dichotomy, at

[85] O'Donovan, 'Karl Barth and Ramsey's "Uses of Power"', 5.

[86] Ibid., p. 14; Ramsey's reading of Barth as a liberal underlines the fact that modern Christian ethics, in so far as they rely on Enlightened premises, are either indistinguishable from liberal-revolutionary democracy or confirm it through opposition. See Slavoj Žižek, John Milbank and Creston Davis, *The Monstrosity of Christ: Paradox or Dialectic?* (Cambridge: MIT Press, 2009), p. 6.

[87] Ibid., p. 9.

[88] Considering the divergent, at times conflicting political-theological positions Ramsey drew on (e.g. Barth and Thielicke; see also below), Hauerwas read Ramsey 'partly as a person in search of a theological position that would do justice to his basic intuitions. And I'm not sure he ever found it'. 'Paul Ramsey 100th Birthday Celebration', Millsaps College, 2 December 2013, available at https://www.youtube.com/watch?v=XdH1AAmWQps (accessed 13 July 2018). Already in 1989, Oswald Bayer called the investigation of the relationship between Barth and Luther an 'epochal task'. Oswald Bayer, 'Barmen zwischen Barth und Luther', in *Luther und Barth: Veröffentlichungen der Luther-Akademie e. V. Ratzeburg*, ed. Joachim Heubach (Erlangen: Martin-Luther-Verlag, 1989), pp. 21–36, p. 26. Taking the opposite position to Bayer: Rustin E. Brian, *Covering up Luther: How Barth's Christology Challenged the deus absconditus that Haunts Modernity* (Eugene, OR: Cascade, 2013).

times dualism, drives the just war theorists we have encountered so far. On the other hand, besides the transformative effects of discrimination, Ramsey sharply defended a political practice transformed by Christian love, the incidence of the national and international common good and *lex-ordo-iustitia*.[89] Stephen Long thus rightly notes that 'Ramsey's use of the transformationist motif neither collapsed the "sphere of the Church" with the "sphere of the state" nor created a disjunction between them'.[90] Christology always played *some* role in it; for Ramsey 'it is precisely Jesus Christ through whom we can and may and must act within the world' (*WCC*, 113). Arguably, the 'transformist' motive in itself is one of Ramsey's lasting legacies, overcoming the idealist-realist dichotomy (e.g. in its form as the aggressor-defender doctrine). Nonetheless, because of Ramsey's antinomian notion of agape[91] and his philosophical idealism's drift towards political tragedy, the next logical step was a much greater sense of realism.

Realism – 'this side of the ploughshares'

Without a Christological context, the transformist mediating logic was unstable. Not least in light of the developments in Vietnam, increasing political divisions within the United States during the 1960s, but also his work on medical ethics, Ramsey's interest in different 'sources' of ethics was accompanied by an increasing awareness of the embeddedness and the professional skills of what is now blandly called 'decision makers'. More decisively than previously, Ramsey separated Christian ethics and political prudence, state and church as well as the Gospel age and the age of Babylon. He then *mythologically* (but always with a sense of humour and irony) explicated the intrinsic logic of division, opposition and force particularly in the international sphere. Dogmatically, this was necessitated by Ramsey's renewed insistence on the eschatological gap: 'There is more than a slash between the words "already/not yet." There is more than a momentous slash. The slash is *aeonic*.'[92] In that sense, the later Ramsey returns to the dichotomies we have encountered in the previous chapters, albeit with great theological sophistication.

Charity: Scientific expertise and national defence

By the mid-1960s, Ramsey saw greater political awareness in 'magistrates' relying on secular reason. In 1967 he wrote, 'The owl of Minerva (political wisdom), which rested for three decades upon a spokesman of Christian truth … dwells now with secular analysts, such as Robert E. Osgood and Robert W. Tucker' (*JW*, 261). The central virtue for political ethics is prudence, and that was best lived when *distinct* from Christian faith or works of neighbour love. For Ramsey, 'the engine of religion

---

[89] NB: Ramsey referred to Augustine as a 'conversionist'.
[90] Long, *Tragedy, Tradition, Transformism*, p. 81.
[91] Hauerwas points out that Ramsey always remained haunted by John-Howard Yoder's Christology, cf. 'Paul Ramsey 100th Birthday Celebration'.
[92] Ramsey and Hauerwas, *Speak Up*, p. 37.

or morality cannot be placed behind any person's prudential political diagnosis, or behind the opposite opinions about Vietnam'. An analysis may be mistaken, but –pace, for example, Karl Barth – it cannot be a direct implication of one's particular faith (*JW*, 506). Ramsey regards 'counting the cost' as the politician's proper task, though he never supported mere consequentialism; indeed, he saw Niebuhr's consequentialism (or rather, pragmatism) as a form of 'doing evil to achieve good'.[93] Now quite in line with Steinhoff's rationalist approach, politics is a 'science, not prophecy'.[94] Political reason can, and should, make use of scientific models and techniques of analysis. In that way, Ramsey sharpens the critical edge against liberal internationalism both in its secularist and ecclesiastical-institutional forms. Even stronger, 'in connection with the principle of discrimination, members of ecclesiastical councils should listen to experts in the political and military sectors and … learn to know the meaning of a present application of the principle of discrimination' (*JW*, 455).

One of the 'secular' tools of analysis was 'opposed-systems analysis' of Albrecht Wohlstetter, whom Ramsey cites in a later chapter on 'Strategic Thinking'.[95] Based on rational choice theory (most prevalent in modern economics), it views the human as essentially and only rational, in possession of the necessary facts to make preferred choices according to a calculation of cost and benefit. As Angie Keefer expressed it, rational choice is 'underpinned by models of predictable fundamentally invariable norms of human behaviour unmediated by historical contingencies'.[96] The theory posits a 'methodological individualism' (ironically – see above Chapter 2 on David Rodin) that can hardly explain 'altruistic choices' unless they are a form of self-interest. Mutual assured destruction (MAD), one strategy of rational choice, is based on

> a mathematical model of human behaviour that excludes the probability of irrational moves or of cooperation among subjects. Nash equilibrium – the concept underlying MAD – posits players acting in hyper-rational self-interest against entirely hostile opponents. … The possibility of trust among adversaries is excluded.[97]

In this spirit, Ramsey emphasizes 'the need for independent analysis'. There is a 'collision in interpretations between a trust-system ("the church") and an opposed-system (of states)'.[98] In the book of Genesis, he then finds 'mythopoetic warrants' for the opposed system, a perpetual antagonistic play-off between centres of power. 'The story of the Tower of Babel is a myth of the origins of a world of countervailing constellations of political power, which we call the multi-national system'.[99]

---

[93] A remarkable point, considering Obama regarded Niebuhr as the philosopher who had the most impact on him.

[94] Paul Ramsey, 'Politics as Science, Not Prophecy', *Worldview* 11 (1968), 18–21.

[95] Paul Ramsey, 'Appendix: A Political Ethics Context for Strategic Thinking', in Ramsey and Hauerwas, *Speak Up*, pp. 183–212.

[96] Angie Keefer, 'The Sky Is Not the Limit', *Dot Dot Dot*, 18 (2009), 58–67, pp. 64–5.

[97] Ibid.

[98] Ramsey and Hauerwas, *Speak Up*, p. 190.

[99] Ibid., p. 184.

In the Cold War stand-off between East and West, for Ramsey the West could claim ostensibly more embodied justice than the latter. The ethics of national defence and 'love' – though now it is 'charity' rather than *agape*[100] – cease to be contradictions; charity and national defence are continuous. A passage from 1964 summarizes well the political analogies of charity:

> It was a work of charity for the Good Samaritan to give help to the man who fell among thieves. But one step more, it may have been a work of charity for the inn-keeper to hold himself ready to receive beaten and wounded men, and for him to have conducted his business so that he was solvent enough to extend credit to the Good Samaritan. By another step it would have been a work of charity, and not of justice alone, to maintain and serve in a police patrol on the Jericho road to prevent such things from happening. By yet another step, it might well be a work of charity to resist, by force of arms, any external aggression against the social order that maintains the police patrol along the road to Jericho. (*JW*, 142)

The liberal Catholic theologian Charles E. Curran complained that Ramsey's political ethics 'do not connect the redemptive work of God to political activity after Jesus has come into the world and sent his spirit'.[101] Instead, all political action now remains *before* the Christ event.[102]

> A Christian will think politically in the light of Christ, and he will think politically in the light of the revealing shadow thrown by the cross of Christ over our fallen human existence. This darkness does not envelop that light. Neither does the light diminish, it rather throws, the shadows. So it will be to the end of time. (*JW*, 529)

This marks the mature reversal of both Ramsey's own idealism and his agapeic scepticism. Politics remains in the shadow; its preservative, negative function against anarchy prevails. Precisely because 'the king' and 'modern democratic man' are 'there in the shadows', their political offices 'must serve to preserve the world against the destructiveness to which otherwise we all would be driven' (*JW*, 530). *Pace* O'Donovan, Ramsey's later ethics were less about 'in-principled love' than the defence and preservation of 'embodied justice' or 'politically-embodied justice'.[103] In a letter to James Childress (1977), Ramsey tried 'to get away from the "juridical model", of declaration as a sentence from an impartial court'. He writes, 'Still one does the *ostensibly* just thing without subjective guilt. So there not only can but must be relative judgments of justice *ad bellum*, without the claim to encompass objective justice.'[104]

---

[100] Namely, *BCE*, 124 – the two are not the same: 'The neighbor is never the ultimate object of aspiring caritas-love; he is always the end-term of *agape*-love.'

[101] Charles E. Curran, *Politics, Medicine, and Christian Ethics: A Dialogue with Paul Ramsey* (Philadelphia, PA: Fortress Press, 1973), p. 14.

[102] See Hollowell, 'This Side of the Ploughshares', p. 280.

[103] *JW*, pp. 132, 390, 428, 444, 465, 482.

[104] Hollowell, 'This Side of the Ploughshares', pp. 83–4.

The state versus church politics and idealism

As he moved to the realist end of the idealist-realist paradigm, Ramsey also emphasized more decisively the state's authority in contrast to 'utopian' or 'liberal' alternatives. He wrestled especially with contemporary 'liberals' promoting the United Nations as a new international agent. The free, political act functions as the *katechon*, restraining the destroyer of the world over against political romanticism:

> A man must take care that his zeal and idealism is not a matter of high-minded rebellion against the governor and preserver of the existing world. This means that a political order is worth something only if it is real, and not merely ideal. Any order is better than none at all. Since God in His governance of the fallen creation desires in His mercy to keep at bay chaos and disorganization and the destruction of every human political dwelling place which would be the final consequences of sin, men must preserve politically embodied justice and even a peace of sorts. (*JW*, 390)

States are ordained as a ' "garment of skin" (Gen. 3.21) in which human nakedness may be clothed, and in which men may together find a tolerably secure dwelling place' (*JW*, 530). The 'myth' of the state is provided by Ramsey's reading of the Lutheran Helmut Thielicke (who was also a critic of Barth): 'The Noachian covenant means that, among fallen humanity, "arbitrary and unlimited power is to be restrained and limited by further power" … That means that power must be limited by further power, else it is bound to become arbitrary and unlimited.' Ramsey doesn't think people are *condemned* to set up states, as Thielicke says, but they are 'condemned to do no more than govern one another through an opposed-system in which power is restrained by further power'.[105]

The church here is hardly a transformative force. As Hollowell put it (not unproblematically), 'The fact that Christ has changed everything does not mean everything has changed.' Christianity in a Lutheran key is a way to think politically. It is derived from an awareness of the Fall and the abysses of human evil in the first place.[106] When explaining this, Ramsey at times echoes – or rather, precedes – Elshtain's anti-Enlightenment reflex, not sufficiently differentiating between various philosophies-as-theologies:

> No church of the Reformation, no church coming in the wake of the Reformation, *indeed no church before the Enlightenment*, NONE put its faith and hope or deed of discipleship in context with such *elision* between this world and the next.[107]

---

[105] Ramsey and Hauerwas, *Speak Up*, p. 186. NB: Again the tension between the Lutheran and Barthian notions of the state.

[106] Cf. Hollowell, *Power and Purpose*, p. 67 and my response, Feiler, 'Review: Hollowell, *Power and Purpose*', p. 245.

[107] Ramsey and Hauerwas, *Speak Up*, p. 37.

Critical of a humanistic political (self-)mediation, Ramsey here remains equally suspicious of the Catholic institutional mediation of the universal in the church –'good works' of institutions. But since immediate obedience to God can always descend into anarchy, it is *the state* that mediates and embodies neighbour love. On those grounds, William Werpehowski criticized Ramsey's excessive deference to political authority that 'may operate to mask or marginalize realities of killing, injury, and human suffering' and 'leaves to the state the embodiment of "Christ", the highest ideal feasible among the options in political life'.[108] Nonetheless, it is precisely the reference to the Old Testament and the ultimately Lutheran rather than Hobbesian or Schmittian political theology – both dualist or dichotomous in their own way – that prevents Ramsey's realism from becoming a triumphalist monism. And it is precisely with a view to the prophecy (e.g. Isaiah) and the future of a Christ-to-come that the political in Ramsey's view never descends into despair.

Political reality: Babylon versus 'utopia'

Ramsey's later shift of perspective, from spiritual *agape* onto 'realist grounds', repeats the juxtaposition of the 'reality of politics' and utopia we already encountered in previous chapters. In 1973, he writes, 'The verdict at Babel only suppressed man's "vertical" aspiration to high heaven; it did nothing to allay the resulting chaos on the horizontal plane'.[109] The transformative force of *agape* recedes into the background, and 'the necessary always becomes more basic than the possible'.[110] Ramsey saw a theory of opposed systems in the Old Testament, in particular the constellation of the prophet Isaiah and King Ahaz. Ahaz, in fixing the waterworks to make them withstand Israel's attack, 'acted responsibly within an opposed-system'. The prophet Isaiah 'gave him this sign of the trustworthiness of the action in all the action the king was preparing to face': the prophecy that a virgin would bear a son and by then Ahaz' enemies would be gone.[111] As power can be limited only by power, there is no bemusement from 'one or another of the utopianisms or gradualisms of the modern mentality'.[112]

Unsurprisingly, he saw the international sphere as 'largely in a "state of nature" (or "state of war," if this means a perpetual inclination thereto, like Hobbes' "bad weather")' (*JW*, xxiii). There are the inevitable 'facts of power' and it is futile to deny them. 'The nation-state is surrounded by arbitrariness on all sides: the other is always a stranger and a potential enemy where there are no dependable structures through which identification may pass' (*JW*, 498). In such an *essentially* opposed, or antagonistic, system, war is an 'unavoidable tragic arbitrament of arms', even though it makes possible a future peace (*JW*, 489). The 'if' and 'when' to go to war is largely determined by forces and pressures beyond specifically Christian moral decision making. As Charles E. Curran paraphrases Ramsey,

[108] Werpehowski, *American Protestant Ethics and the Legacy of H. Richard Niebuhr*, p. 62.
[109] Ramsey and Hauerwas, *Speak Up*, p. 185.
[110] Long, *Tragedy, Tradition, Transformism*, p. 62.
[111] Ibid., p. 190; Isa. 7.8, 14, 16.
[112] Casey, 'Eschatology and Statecraft', p. 185.

We cannot put the engine of the Christian religion behind these positions which do not have specifically Christian bases. Different opinions about the war in Vietnam, for example, arise because of different interpretations people have about the domino theory. However, there is nothing the church as such can and should say about the domino theory precisely because such a judgment lies outside its competency.[113]

On the practical front, both Ramsey's support for the Vietnam War and his eventual demand that it be ended were an application, or rather an implication, of these principles. Subsequent critical (Clausewitzian) analyses of the Vietnam disaster have noted that the aims in the war, but never the *end* or *point* of the war, were clear. This systematic *lack* a theologian could have highlighted without proposing an aim with which to fill that gap.

When analysing the counter-insurgency in Vietnam, Ramsey also revised again the principle of discrimination. He distanced himself from his earlier 'absolutism' and approached it more pragmatically. 'Non-combatancy is a function of how the nations or the forces are organized for war, and of military technology' (*JW*, 502). If Vietnamese 'insurgents' live among the people 'like fish in the water', then one 'needs to withdraw the water' to see 'what happens to the fish' (*JW*, 481).[114] If underground strongholds and supply lines are the way insurgents are organized, he thinks airstrikes against villages, fields, and so forth, cannot be regarded as indiscriminate. After all, they *aim* at military facilities. It is the guerrillas who have 'deliberately enlarged the extent of foreknowable but collateral civil destruction in the attempt to gain a privileged sanctuary through a military posture that brought more of his own population into range' (*JW*, 508). In this way, he argues that the 'insurgents' *themselves* have brought the bombing campaigns upon their villagers.

Ramsey's anti-Communist sense of America's liberal-democratic supremacy literally went nuclear.[115] The enemy also has no immunity from nuclear counter-attack just 'because he had the shrewdness to locate his missile bases in the heart of his cities' (ibid.). The only limitation to this is the proportionality principle: over all, such an attack may cause an overall greater evil than it averts. As Richard B. Miller summarizes,

---

[113] Curran, *Politics, Medicine, and Christian Ethics*, p. 45. In this regard, also note Ramsey's distinction between *in bello* and *ad bellum* thinking.

[114] This was Ramsey's preferred phrase around the time that US defence secretary Robert McNamara resigned, having complained that by 1967 the Air Force had dropped more bombs on Vietnam than throughout the whole of the Second World War – without a military effect. The idea of irregular fighters being like 'fish in the water' stems from Chapter 6 of Mao Tse-Tung's seminal *On Guerilla Warfare* (1937), not least a counter-tactic to the 'acceleration of war' since Napoleon aiming at a long-term corrosion of the military and psychological capacities of the enemy. See Herfried Münkler, *Theorie und Gewalt: Das Denken des Krieges, seine modelltheoretische Hegung und die Sprengkraft von Ideen und Innovationen*, Vorlesungsreihe Johannes Gutenberg-Stiftungsprofessur, lecture series 2018: *Das politische Denken. Politische Ideengeschichte und die großen Herausforderungen unserer Gegenwart in zehn Erkundungsschritten*, Lecture, 19 June 2018, available at https://www.youtube.com/watch?v=YvRPBXgmbtk (accessed 19 August 2018).

[115] In the 2002 preface to *Just War*, Hauerwas also noted that this was the result of the fundamental architecture of Ramsey's thought.

Ramsey's brand of political realism imperils his argument about the morality of nuclear deterrence, for the subordinate, prudential concern for preservation finally prevails in his attempt to conceive of a morally justifiable nuclear deterrent, overriding the implications wrought from the protection paradigm, deontically construed.[116]

Again, once Ramsey regarded justice and love as *already* embodied in the United States – an 'absolute state', as it were – the themes of defence and preservation 'took precedence in his grand concerto of Christian ethics'.[117]

Realist(ic) just war thinking

As one aspect of Christian 'action', just war thinking itself changed its character in Ramsey's more mature thought. As mentioned, Ramsey played 'prophecy' off against political science. Rather than love-imbibed transformations of the fundamental political tasks, Christianity now offers consolation to politicians engaging in counting up the costs: 'There is no reason why Christians should withhold this consoling word from political leaders in all their dealings with "outcomes"' (*JW*, 529). In *Speak up for Just War or Pacifism*, Ramsey commends 'espousing the virtues of a mythopoetic understanding of the actors and the interactions going on in the international system'. By 'looking at ourselves through the synoptic "pre-historic" culture myths in the first book of the Hebrew Bible named "In the Beginning" (Genesis, as the Greeks called it)', one can gain 'a rapid sketch of insights into and perspectives upon mankind's existence in political communities'.[118] Elsewhere, Ramsey called himself a 'mythologist'. Myth and revelation are hardly the same categories; 'myth' rather helps to understand the *conditio politica*; any transformative influence of faith fall behind rationalist-technological reason, prone to become an ideological superstructure. As Jeffrey Stout pointed out, due to his social conservatism (and his support for the Vietnam War, I would add), Ramsey came to be seen as the 'poster-boy of the religious right'.[119]

Nonetheless, Ramsey's lasting Christian 'input' to politics remained the notion of discrimination. In 1966, he bemoaned the fact that 'Christian comment upon foreign policy evidences but little concern to press relentlessly the requirements of discrimination as these may be shown ... to bear upon modern warfare' (*JW*, 456). The 'common wisdom' and 'the principle of proportionality', which 'defines right action altogether in terms of consequences', could function quite well without any specific Christian competency. They also didn't require additional input from ecclesiastical councils: 'the churches are able to predict the good and evil consequences and to propose policies falling under the principle of proportion about as well as any other group within our society'. Hence, any moral statements along *those* lines would be a confusion of the realms of church and state, 'of moralist and magistrate' (*JW*, 456).

---

[116] Richard B. Miller, 'Love, Intention and Proportion: Paul Ramsey on the Morality of Nuclear Deterrence', *Journal of Religious Ethics*, 16 (1988), 205.
[117] Miller, 'Love, Intention and Proportion, 201–21, p. 206.
[118] Ramsey, 'Appendix: A Political Ethics Context', p. 183.
[119] 'Paul Ramsey 100th Birthday Celebration'.

So although Ramsey considered the possibility that Christian instruction could lead to substantive conclusions, the realm of state, technological expertise and calculation had to remain independent and recognized for their specific competency. In so far as the 'moralist' watched politics from the sidelines, his political-philosophical impact somewhat declined. The aim remained to improve the arguments of public debate – and here Ramsey was largely successful.

Conclusion

Ramsey's realism was the last logical step in a long and productive career, the final stage of a long journey from one end of the theological and political idealism-realism divide to the other. This movement presupposed a stark division, a *bipolarity* between Christian faith, the 'strange world of the Bible' and the secular world of systems so characteristic of the twentieth century. As a theo-logic, it entailed a division between the historical, human Jesus, incredibly difficult and impractical to imitate, and a formless, spiritual Christ always in search of some kind of form. This division was an essentially modern condition, one that Ramsey had learnt not least from dialectical theologians.

Throughout his works, Ramsey wrestled with the gap between *agape* and the 'world of systems' as well as possibilities to mediate these contrasts. In his early liberal-pacifist phase, to act as if the Kingdom of God was already here for Ramsey meant to imitate Jesus over against the war machines of the early and mid-twentieth century. Under the influence of Niebuhr and Nietzsche, his understanding of love changed. Agape was a genuine breaking-in of the supernatural that could truly shake the foundations of the 'world of systems'. Hence, he relentlessly chided the efforts to ignore or elide the gap between the aeons. Philosophically, Ramsey then drew on Hegelian idealism and its concerns with mediation. Here, the Christian possibility of ultimate, divine mediation between 'the secular' and God was understood as an immanent, rational continuity unfolding throughout the civilizations in history. This became the point of his ethical transformism. Yet the 'aeonic rift' at the heart of his theology – always a possibility in the Augustinian dichotomy of the Two Cities – was never to be mended. Although Ramsey did come to see Christology as 'the central issue', his idealist logic of mediation, that is, the dialectic of the political act, had no transformative effect on the political. Indeed, any attempts to do so were highly problematic, if not dangerous.

We may now put both Ramsey and Steinhoff into perspective. In contrast to the paradigm Elshtain-Rodin – and the vying for authority that repeats the imperial-papalist tensions of old – Ramsey and Steinhoff (together with similar authors) offer alternative, partly 'heterodox' impulses that ground their ethics of war. Against legal or state positivism, the individualist-rationalist as well as the agapeist options preserve the possibility of rational, free action – whether before a Marcionite or secular-liberal, even liberal-Marxist horizon. While Steinhoff exercises merciless conceptual critique, Ramsey pushes for the (messianic) option of kenotic neighbour love. To an extent this should be appreciated as prophetic, in so far as that means critically challenging an establishment that vies for theocracy. Yet their theo-logics of *breaking* – human reason breaking out of the theocratic or the divine breaking into the world – also affirm, even if negatively, both the sovereign-cosmopolitan paradigm *and* the possibility of theological-political mediation in Christ. In Ramsey's work, this last appears as the political act, presenting the possibility of mediating praxis between conflicting ends and values. However, practical differences between Steinhoff and Ramsey are also stark. More than Steinhoff, Ramsey insisted on the absolute prohibition to directly target non-combatants; the transformative horizon (though not the transformative effect) remained always in sight. Whereas Steinhoff had swiftly rejected a Christian (or Jewish) notion of God in light of egregious human suffering, Ramsey sees a theodicy formulated in the light and shadow of the cross over the political sphere (echoing not least a Hegelian theodicy). Although this theo-logic grounded a prohibition to target innocent non-combatants 'so as not to kill Christ anew', Ramsey's later realism saw this principle contextualized – some would say, watered-down – by overarching considerations of effective, prudent defence of the nation-state, itself embodying justice.

I have argued here that, absent a systematically reflected theo-logic of mediation, Ramsey's transformist just war thinking retreated to more realist grounds. This brings us to Part Three, in which several aspects and implications of such a theo-logic of mediation will be considered. We will see first how, starting off with insights from his one-time teacher Paul Ramsey, Oliver O'Donovan for his part transforms transformism, turning it into an evangelical just war proposal – grounded in Christ mediating all antagonisms.

Part Three

Theo-logics of mediation

5

An eschatological fusion – Oliver O'Donovan's evangelical political theology

Introduction

So far, we have examined a number of possible theological-political constellations that each generate distinct ethical approaches and logics of war. On the one hand, there was a realism (Christian or secular), producing marked idealist, but also ideological undercurrents; on the other hand, wholly separate, a 'utopian' idealism that collapsed into violent realities. These moments could be ironical reversals, inadvertent results or accepted with a shrug in the face of tragedy.

Chapter 4 noted that in his transformist writings Paul Ramsey beyond this impasse opened up the systematic and ethical door for a Christian *locus operandi*. The author of the present chapter, Oliver O'Donovan (b.1945), now opens that door widely and pulls in an integrated biblical vision. O'Donovan, one of the most influential and eminent Anglican evangelical theologians of the later twentieth and early twenty-first century, has consistently sought to rediscover political concepts from historical theology as well as the Bible. O'Donovan's project has always sought to be a *sui generis* theological rather than philosophical, and specifically philosophical-idealist, endeavour: 'the exploration of Christian moral concepts must always, in the first place, be the work of theology.'[1] Indeed, 'theological ethics is metaethics', where the church is a 'metaethical community of discourse'.[2] Consequently, any political theology must begin from an (political) account and position of the church.[3]

In what follows, I aim to show that O'Donovan's Christology re-sublates the Idealist dialectics of mediation into biblical specificity. As he relocates Hegel's question of mediation (and the sceptical oscillation Hegel sought to overcome) within exegesis, O'Donovan incorporates the Ramseyan-Hegelian mediating logic like a *fetus in fetu*. Precisely in that way, he walks through the door to the *totaliter aliter* opened by Ramsey/ Nietzsche and gives extensive biblical-theological content to Ramsey's political act.

---

[1] Oliver O'Donovan, 'How Can Theology Be Moral?', *Journal of Religious Ethics*, 17 (1989), 81–94.
[2] Oliver O'Donovan, *Resurrection and Moral Order: An Outline for Evangelical Ethics*, 2nd ed. (Grand Rapids, MI: William B. Eerdmans, 1994), p. viii. Hereafter *RMO*.
[3] Oliver O'Donovan, *The Desire of the Nations: Rediscovering the Roots of Political Theology* (Cambridge: Cambridge University Press, 1996), p. 159. Hereafter *DN*.

For O'Donovan, mediation (a term he rarely uses) means the final unity of political and spiritual, political and moral or Is and Ought in Christ which, before the end of the *saeculum*, generates a merely residual duality. This theo-logic is crystallized in the tension-filled narrative of Israel's politics before and after the Christ-event. Ethics itself then discloses, proclaims and responds to the reality of revelation in participatory action. In that regard, O'Donovan both practically and dogmatically corrects key points of the previous authors, integrating and transforming viable elements both of just war realism and idealism. But first, I will show how he affirms an 'evangelical' just war thinking and how this transforms the idealist-realist dichotomies.

An evangelical Just War proposal

Like the first three authors in Parts I and II, Oliver O'Donovan's *The Just War Revisited* (2003) intervened in the debate on the 'War on Terror' and not least the imminent invasion of Iraq. But rather than a partisan defence or sweeping critique, his contribution was a clarification of 'evangelical counter-praxis'.

Evangelical reality and counter-praxis

God's will is *peace*, O'Donovan begins, which is an 'all-determining truth' (*JWR*, 1).[4] Three propositions follow from that. Peace is (a) the original ontological truth of creation and (b) the end of history. Thus, it is (c) a practical demand.[5] So from the outset, just war praxis depends on an evangelical reality, that is, the working out of the statement that God *is*.[6] However, God's will, peace, is neither a utopian 'ideal' nor does the frequent violation of peace in politics present a 'challenge' to it.[7] Instead, the peace of creation is a reality that engenders the 'counter-praxis' of *reconciliation*. Reconciliation discerns peace while describing and judging crime. This peace, and not merely any kind of 'political stability', also generates the *recta intentio*.

Reconciliation is not merely announced, however, but 'staged missiologically against a backdrop of unbelief and disobedience'. And so it 'assumes the secular form of judgment' as 'the interim provision of God's common grace, promising the dawning of God's final peace' (*JWR*, 6). For O'Donovan, politics as 'the act of judgment' is the 'exercise of Gospel faith' in the 'theatre of war' (*JWR*, 6). It becomes a 'provisional witness to the unity of God's rule in the face of the antagonistic praxis of *duellum*' (*JWR*, 7). Judgement is both extraordinary and ordinary. It is extraordinary in its means,

---

[4] Oliver O'Donovan, *The Just War Revisited* (Cambridge: Cambridge University Press, 2003), hereafter *JWR*. Michael Haspel begins with the same statement but channels it into cosmopolitanism. *Friedensethik und Humanitäre Intervention: Der Kosovo-Krieg als Herausforderung evangelischer Friedensethik* (Neukirchen-Vluyn: Neukirchener, 2002).

[5] Cf. *Aus Gottes Frieden leben – für gerechten Frieden sorgen. Eine Denkschrift des Rates der Evangelischen Kirche in Deutschland*, 2007, pp. 11, 28. http://www.ekd.de/download/ekd_friedensdenkschrift.pdf (accessed 13 December 2018).

[6] Bernd Wannenwetsch, 'Just War', in *Cambridge Dictionary of Christian Theology*, ed. Ian A. McFarland et al. (Cambridge: Cambridge University Press, 2011), pp. 255–7.

[7] Bernd Wannenwetsch, *Political Worship* (Oxford: Oxford University Press, 2009), p. 26.

using the same weapons as criminals. But it is ordinary in its guiding and limiting principles. So, the *No* to war is not a *No* to violent force. O'Donovan has no problem with Clausewitz's dictum that war is the continuation of policy by other means. The problem with Clausewitz is rather that he assumes that vitality and will are the truest realities (*JWR*, 92).

Significantly, O'Donovan's notion of reconciling praxis marks a *via media* between idealistic or realistic praxis. Before the Christ-event, he says, war was conceived as a *duellum*, an occurrence separate from times of peace, a crisis to engender heroism and social renewal. The fundamental 'rejection of war' only followed from the cross and exaltation of Christ (*JWR*, 5). Since then, 'unmediated conflict' has to be rejected. It would be a 'crime against peace ... [to make] antagonistic praxis a goal of politics, whether as means or end; that sin consists in cultivating antagonism as a form of self-perfection' (*JWR*, 2). Equally, if survival, national or individual self-defence or even self-aggrandizement at the cost of one's neighbour has the last word, then 'paganism is restored' (*JWR*, 9). These are therefore no *causae iustae*. So although 'making war possible' (Paul Ramsey), evangelical counter-praxis transforms ritual, periodical as well as excessive, heroic warfare.

Reconciliatory praxis equally avoids just war idealism. In its ecclesial form, this suggests non-violence as the only viable form of politics. It is the 'waging of peace *against* violence' as a response to God's will (*JWR*, 5). Specifically Christian pacifism not so much reifies a quasi-Kantian ideal but 'limits the range of possible political action' to imitating the Jesus's non-violent *exemplum* in the Kingdom already come.[8] Patience is to prevail in the face of conflict, crime and evil. However, in line with Ramsey and before him Reinhold Niebuhr, O'Donovan notes that by waging peace, pacifists indirectly (one could also say, dialectically) *authorize* a sphere of violence. This gestures towards the logic of the excluded, unmediated Other that returns more forcefully. Pacifists warp the Christian conviction that evil is a form of not-being, *privatio boni*.[9] However, the political sphere is not an *a priori* negativity:

> A certain 'statism' is implied in the pacifist position, which will not contemplate the *improvisation* of judgment where it is not provided for within a state structure, and to that extent cannot treat international politics wholly seriously as politics, a God-given sphere of peaceful interaction. (*JWR*, 8)

---

[8] O'Donovan notes that the category 'idealism' applies to pacifism only as a 'religious synthesis with idealist rationalism'. There is a difficulty in associating Hauerwas with moral idealism, since his pacifism focuses on the lived narrative of the church as the very challenge to Enlightened reason. However, one could argue that Hauerwas' fideism has transported Enlightened progressivism onto a theological and ecclesiological plane, albeit in a postmodern mode. From that perspective, James Gustafson's claim that Hauerwas is a 'twentieth-century version of Marcion' may be defensible. Cited in Gary Dorrien, *Social Ethics in the Making: Interpreting an American Tradition* (Malden, MA: Blackwell-Wiley, 2009), pp. 481–4; see also Stanley Hauerwas, *The Peaceable Kingdom: A Primer in Christian Ethics* (London: SCM Press, 2003), p. 72 f; Emmanuel Katongole, *Beyond Universal Reason: The Relation between Religion and Ethics in the Work of Stanley Hauerwas* (Notre Dame, IN: University of Notre Dame Press, 2000).

[9] Especially with St Augustine; see also John Milbank, *Theology and Social Theory: Beyond Secular Reason* (Oxford: Blackwell, 2006), p. 317.

Steering between a violent reality and a moral(istic) ideal, O'Donovan's political sphere and act are anything but religiously neutral or pluralistic.[10] The theologian, speaking *per definitionem* out of the church, calls upon states both as political and subject to God.[11] In that way, the idealist *No* to 'secular politics' is transformed into a provisional, 'cautious' *Yes* under God's reign and law.[12]

Authority – government as judgement

With reference to Suárez and Vitoria, O'Donovan then explains the act of judgement outside a country's borders and outside ordinary judicial procedures. How can the same person be judge and plaintiff at the same time? This happens in an emergency, O'Donovan argues, precisely when an arbitrator is absent – as is frequently the case in the international sphere. Unlike, for example, David Rodin (Chapter 2), O'Donovan is not out to design the institution of a global(ist) arbitrator. He investigates the moral possibility of arbitration precisely when it seems to have run out. With a focus on the flexible *act* of judgement, O'Donovan's concept of 'legitimate authority' stands on the 'realist' grounds of already existing governmental structures and natural instincts. But authority also gestures towards an 'ideal judgment'. In that way, the political act falls between – or rather, goes beyond and sublates – both an unmediated realist antagonism and an institutional or individualist idealism. What he later says about institutional *forms* remains tenuous, especially in light of their historical contingency.

O'Donovan's insistence on 'authority' repeats a classical concern about private violence. 'Privacy' is merely a form of *interest* based on factual existence. Sovereign states or individual persons can be 'private'.[13] In contrast, authority is the *sine qua non* for violent force to be genuinely political, which means pertaining to the common good:

> Only public acts may legitimately call upon the use of force. Only governments may make war, for the same reason that only police and magistrates may arrest and only judges sentence, namely, that they require representative persons, acting for the community, to perform them. (*JWR*, 22)

Such representative publicity excludes terrorism; terrorists use violent force indiscriminately, as a strategy without politics. They merely 'nudge historical necessity' (*JWR*, 31). Still, government as public judgement by no means bans 'ordered', 'responsible' rebellion or revolution (*JWR*, 26, 30). An evangelical proposal needs to recognize these as genuine possibilities, because authoritative institutions depend on the 'relations of right', not the other way around (23). Those who judge as public

---

[10] Reality does not *depend* on this recognition, which is what O'Donovan's 'realist principle' among other things means. This is the classical Reformed *extra nos* Luther develops in the *Commentary on the Letter to the Galatians*.

[11] The just war proposal itself is evangelical, pastoral praxis, not distinct from decisional praxis but located elsewhere, i.e. in the church. In any case, it is not a *theory*.

[12] Robert Song, *Christianity and Liberal Society* (Oxford: Oxford University Press, 2006), p. 214.

[13] St Augustine, *Answer to Faustus* (New York: New City Press, 2007), p. 49; Aquinas, ST IIaIIae, Qu. 40, Art. 1; Grotius, *De Iure Belli Ac Pacis*, Bk. 1, Chapter 3.

representatives *are* 'the government'. As O'Donovan expresses it, the act of judgement *is authorized* by being representative and acting in defence of the common good.

How can there be 'publicity' in the international sphere without formal authority? (*JWR*, 22–3) O'Donovan here first peels away realism (including Elshtain's) which recognizes no authority between sovereign states. 'Who are you to judge me?' says one sovereign to another. Post-Kantian internationalist federalisms also rely on this notion of sovereign *raisons d'état* competing in a tense sphere (*JWR*, 22).[14] On these premises, O'Donovan concurs that international publicity is unthinkable. War becomes private, from which 'arises the modern tendency to reduce the causes of war to the single cause of national self-defense' (*JWR*, 22). But the interest of natural entities in their own survival is not the sole ground of authoritative judgement. Nation-states are not authorities merely because they exist.[15]

A specifically evangelical proposal, O'Donovan proposes with Vitoria, is not the enforcement of national interest or human rights in a violent world but charitable 'authorised arbitration' (*JWR*, 22). An evangelical *judicial* proposal requires the victor (F. de Vitoria) or all belligerents (O'Donovan) to 'act […] as though one is not merely defending one's own interests but deciding an issue between claimants'. The belligerent takes the role of a *third party*: 'Acts of war carry with them the responsibility to care for the right of both parties equally. A belligerent has to act for "the" right, not "our" right' (*JWR*, 25).

This right is always already governing the international sphere. Doing justice becomes a reordering upon a wrong done. Yet international right-as-order is neither a legal nor even utopian ideal. It is itself the objective, existing moral order corresponding to any international judgement which refuses to descend into a 'private' antagonism. A multitude of political entities participate in or disobey this order. Hence, 'the just belligerent is supposed to venture, informally and with extraordinary means, the judgment that *would* be made by a formal court, *if* there were a competent one' (23). In this way, O'Donovan argues, international judgement is genuinely *public*.

Here he clarifies the notion of 'ideal judgment'. For once, it is present in public sentiment. While, curiously, not mentioning the public's loud *opposition* to recent wars in various contexts, O'Donovan thinks public sentiment 'sows the dragon's teeth from which an authorised army springs to life' (*JWR*, 23). Here the first 'idealistic' door could open: critique and protest 'from below', where every citizen is an authoritative judge on the war *as a whole*.[16] But O'Donovan closes this door quickly. He thinks public trains of thought are 'indefinitely open to contest; and that is why

---

[14] Immanuel Kant, *Zum ewigen Frieden* (Stuttgart: Philipp Reclam Jr, 2008), p. 10: 'Der Frieden ist kein natürlicher Zustand, er muss gestiftet werden.' – 'Peace is not a natural state of affairs; it has to be founded.'

[15] This I take to be the meaning of the possibility of a government's self-delusion about its own righteousness: 'the idea of an ideal judgment which would or would not authorise this act of war must be a coherent moral idea. If the hypothesis of the ideal judge is unthinkable, the self-deception is impossible.' Only by a standard transcending the judge himself can he judge and be judged. If no such moral reality exists, then an agent is right simply by being, which amounts to a kind of existentialist totalitarianism. Subsuming all morality under a state's 'unconditional right to existence' is an example of this.

[16] NB: In Chapter 3 on Steinhoff, I interpret this primarily as a form of realism.

where formally constituted authorities exist, it is they, not the ideal ones, that must be obeyed' (*JWR*, 24). This rejection of ideal authorities explains his distance from pure 'criticism' or 'ressentiment' which unmask the 'true reasons for war' (*JWR*, 42–3). Nevertheless, he adds, one may *after all* ask whether a war is just. Public reflection is in fact the very essence of authorization (*JWR*, 25). In any case, there remains room for 'informal pronouncements which carry moral authority' (*JWR*, 24). So, the individual's judgement is not altogether dismissed but made concrete and requires working out in the specific vocational setting (*JWR*, 17).

O'Donovan perhaps consciously encourages two interpretations of this section. On the one hand, he can be read as empowering citizens to sympathetic, constructive deliberation instead of a constant, though merely intellectual overthrow of the authorities in place. From this angle, he criticizes a public cacophony that presumes omnipresent popular authority but ignores the real mechanisms of power, albeit quickly exhausting itself and remaining ineffective.[17] On the other hand, his stance against protests and demonstrations may give rise to the suspicion that he is a patrician defender of the *status quo*.[18] His scepticism about scepticism makes it difficult to identify and criticize, for example, warring quests for resources (he mentions the thirst for oil) which he has renounced a few pages earlier.

In a similar way, O'Donovan deals with the idealism of international legalists. Also touching on a contemporary tendency to reduce wars to their 'legality', he deprives international law of its moral ultimacy – albeit without dismissing it. Invoking the *ius gentium*, he recognizes the United Nations as an authority, since its formality is grounded in treaty. A belligerent should defer to it, 'even if it sometimes rules in a way that a truly impartial and well-informed judge would not have ruled, for courts have authority even when they are mistaken in particulars' (*JWR*, 24). Nevertheless, the United Nations remains flawed, so here too remains room for informal international judgement (*JWR*, 25).[19]

In this context, O'Donovan again clarifies what he means by 'settling of a right'. The duty to act for *the* right rather than one's own right is limited to settling a particular cause. 'Victory is not a title of conquest' (*JWR*, 25). One may settle a cause but never rule or govern the other party. Somewhat vaguely, one can discern here how O'Donovan identifies the grounds for government: 'the right to govern depends not solely upon force and the exercise of judgment, but upon the tradition of the governed' (*JWR*, 26). An authority must be rooted in the community it claims to represent: power, right and tradition are what he calls the natural grounds of political authority.

---

[17] Cf. Interview with Slavoj Žižek, *Believer*, July 2004, http://www.believermag.com/issues/200407/ ?read=interview_zizek (accessed 25 July 2012). Arguably, this has morphed into a digital 'shitstorm democracy', which loses interest quickly and remains ultimately a-historical.

[18] See Chapter 6. Interestingly, there is no treatment of tyrannicide here, though this may possibly be grouped under O'Donovan's treatment of 'targeted assassination'. Tim Gorringe, 'Authority, Plebs and Patricians', *Studies in Christian Ethics*, 11 (1998), 24–9.

[19] For Nigel Biggar, the informality of judgement *is* the marker of an evangelical proposal. 'Review Article: The Just War Revisited', *Studies in Christian Ethics*, 19 (2006), 223–32. It seems to me that in O'Donovan's case, it is the paradoxical recognition of *all* authorities, both formal and informal. The evangelical approach requires a discernment of right in the given situation.

To a large extent, he takes this from Paul Ramsey (*DN*, 20–1), fleshing out the latter's transformative perspective. I quote again from *Desire of the Nations* (1996), concerned with showing how 'divine rule confers authority on [political] acts':

> The political act was not bounded by institutions. At home in the city, it could extend itself into open spaces across the boundaries erected by civilized institution-building. It was impossible for Ramsey to conceive politics as an island-kingdom, washed on all sides by the trackless ocean of a state of nature. The Lockean liberalism that conceived it that way had placed the abstract political institution at the core of political theory, in the place where political action belonged.[20]

As we will see later, however, O'Donovan's notion of authority is differently grounded, preventing Ramsey's drift towards realism.

Nonetheless, O'Donovan also heeds the 'natural intuitions about war' and so gives limited recognition to 'realism'. These intuitions are actually antagonistic, hence initially un-evangelical. For example, wars of national defence to O'Donovan at first seem more 'common sense' than interventions and 'we instinctively find armed revolutions more difficult to justify than war against external powers' (*JWR*, 26). One may debate which convictions are 'instinctive' or what he means by claiming that some wars are 'instinctively' difficult to justify. In any case, the 'radically evangelical' interpretation of war as judgement concedes a certain legitimacy to 'apparently statist sentiments in favour of existing authorities'. Decisively distinct from an overall antagonistic 'statism', they guard against idealism or 'enthusiasm':

> The formal authority of political structures, on which the task of judgment depends, must not simply be swept away by an enthusiasm to improvise judgement whenever and however it appears to be needed. Judgment has need of its settled institutions, too, and we must mind that they are properly respected. (*JWR*, 27)

By generally heeding traditional, institutional settlements, O'Donovan's evangelical proposal keeps faith with St Paul's limited endorsement of 'authorities that exist'. Nonetheless, his consistent focus on the political act rather than the institution allows for a dynamic history of peoples. As the confluence of power, right and tradition continues, the new must not be a *krisis*-driven overhaul of order but an ordered taking of responsibility.[21] This strongly echoes not only Ramsey's transformism, especially the notion of 'constitutional revolution',[22] but also Hegel's rejection of nihilist revolution.

O'Donovan then turns to the representative aspect of international judgement. In 'classical' theory, 'the aggressor, by injuring another people, put itself under the

---

[20] Oliver O'Donovan, 'Karl Barth and Ramsey's "Uses of Power"', *Journal of Religious Ethics*, 19 (1991), 1–30, p. 23; *Desire of the Nations*, p. 21.

[21] See Chapter 2. David Rodin subjectivizes these natural inclinations so that they may be replaced by a subsidiary grid of legal arbitration. See also, Michael Walzer, *Arguing about War* (New Haven, CT: Yale University Press, 2006). If anything, O'Donovan's idea of informal arbitration highlights the legalist incapability to think *legally* outside positive law.

[22] See Chapter 2.

jurisdiction of that people's prince' (*JWR*, 27). Put differently, the government of an injured people 'projects, as it were, its general responsibility for the causes of its people into a situation where the opposing party is a foreign people'. It temporarily extends its own jurisdiction. Hence, such judgement is an 'extraordinary act of love, providing, in the first place, the judgment of which the injured neighbour stands in need, but not excluding love for the injured neighbour's enemy at the same time' (*JWR*, 28). Judgement 'in the name of the people' effectively *includes* the Other (*despite* and *in spite of* their crime) into those it represents.[23]

This raises the question whether an injured people's government is their only legitimate authority. O'Donovan permits 'humanitarian intervention', covering the case when a people's government is the very perpetrator of injustice. Still, this is a far cry from making universal human rights the essence of his proposal (*JWR*, 29). Moreover, international law must never be a 'doctrinaire posture' but appears to be a moral-legal casuistry 'to be developed in relation to cases'. The intervening belligerent must be 'a credible representative' and not driven by self-interest.[24] 'Altruistic interest' comes from kinship, neighbourhood or from cultural ties. 'Regional interests', O'Donovan adds, 'are not to be despised as a ground for moral authorisation' (*JWR*, 29). Still, it is not clear at what point for O'Donovan 'the cause lies *outside* [a belligerent party's] sphere of authority' (*JWR*, 21). The lack of further discussion may indicate that the act of judgement has few geographical limitations.

O'Donovan's mention of 'nation-building' is noteworthy here. 'Nation-building' for Elshtain was the prominent moral imperative of sovereign 'mothering', an aspect of 'enlightened self-interest'; similarly, Ramsey in his more realist phase regarded it as the 'business' of the United States for its own security. O'Donovan readjusts this: a law-giving act of judgement merely makes sure the other party is ruled. 'Nobody could undertake to depose the Taliban, in however worthy a cause, without taking serious steps to enable the emergence of a representative government for Afghanistan.' What is required is 'government by law, which is the will of God for both'. This cannot be subsumed under an ulterior, selfish interest on the side of the intervening party.[25]

In short, in terms of authority, O'Donovan renounces a straightforward realist sovereigntism as well as an idealist enthusiasm or liberal-internationalist institutionalism. Paradoxically, he recognizes both formal and informal authorities, be

---

[23] More concisely, the judge also represents the criminal *to* the criminal (without his crime), not merely the victims or the families of the victims (cf. Oliver O'Donovan, *The Ways of Judgment* (Grand Rapids, MI: William B. Eerdmans, 2005). Hereafter WJ.). The same goes for the international sphere.

[24] In response to O'Donovan, Nigel Biggar has pointed out that national interest must be there to provide the motivation for why *our* sons and daughters should lose their limbs and lives. Nigel Biggar, 'Regime Change in Iraq: A Christian Reading of the Morals of the Story', in *The Authority of the Gospel: Explorations in Moral and Political Theology in Honor of Oliver O'Donovan*, ed. Robert Song and Brent Waters (Grand Rapids, MI: Wm. B. Eerdmans, 2015), pp. 64–6, p. 66. Note also p. 65 n. 30: pace O'Donovan on humanitarian interventions – '*self*-interest … is, at best, irrelevant, but altruistic interest' (*JWR*, 29) – Biggar notes that 'self-interest is not the same as selfishness and need not be an alternative to altruism'.

[25] Perhaps Albania in the early 1990s is another good example. When anarchy broke out after the government had collapsed, international passivity allowed for weapons formerly owned by the government to fall into the hands of what would later be the UÇK and for organized crime to grow exponentially.

they individual, national or international. What matters is that the *act* of judgement requires a right, a representative status and the publicity of international law as it gears towards an 'ideal judgment'. This implies the dynamic possibility of taking unexpected forms.

Discrimination

With these basic structures in place, the remainder of O'Donovan's lecture series deals with the intricacies of the act of judgement. Here O'Donovan again carries Ramsey's torch.

Judgement per se is discriminating, so one must break with the antagonism of 'our' self-defence against 'their' hostility (one could also say: the aggressor-defender doctrine). The discriminative principle 'is the greatest moral safeguard we have against totalitarian claims to loyalty made on behalf of the nation-state or of any other popular formation' (*JWR*, 33). Discrimination is defined by the *intention* to make a distinction between guilt and innocence. But if 'excessive damage may be expected, it may be assumed intended; if intended, then indiscriminate' (*JWR*, 35).

As to 'guilt' and 'innocence', the judge must take into account the opponents' political communality – again, an echo of Ramsey. Crucially, corporate responsibility incurred in war is neither personal guilt nor innocence of the soldier as a mere 'tool'.[26] What Grotius calls *median guilt* lies in between the two. The crime of a *mafioso* is unlike that of a soldier – an important corrective to the recent individualization of war.[27] 'There are different ways of being implicated in a common guilt incurred by the society as a whole.' Grotius's natural law, which includes the ties of birth and civil membership, trumps Augustine's idealist-sceptical comparison of Rome with a large band of robbers. As a result, the soldier's 'liability arises quite particularly and exclusively while he is *actively engaged* in hostilities' (*JWR*, 37). The duty to spare the surrendered is one consequence. For Grotius, this is also a natural law; for O'Donovan, it is evangelical.[28] 'Direct collaboration' also applies to material targets, but essential life sustenance must not be made impossible.

---

[26] Moral philosophy at this point cannot imagine a *tertium* between the soldier as criminal or tool, so chooses 'personal guilt' as the basis of discrimination. See Chapters 2 and 3.

[27] See especially Chapter 2. Notably, individualization also happens in many police forces.

[28] O'Donovan's interpretation of Grotius is unusual compared to the more philosophical ones, e.g. Richard Tuck, *The Rights of War and Peace: Political Thought and the International Order from Grotius to Kant* (Oxford: Oxford University Press, 1999), p. 78f; *Hugo Grotius and International Relations*, ed. Hedley Bull, Benedict Kingsbury and Adam Roberts (Oxford: Clarendon Press, 1990); Dieter Janssen, 'Bellum iustum und Völkerrecht im Werk des Hugo Grotius', in *Krieg und Kultur: Die Rezeption von Krieg und Frieden in der Niederlandischen Republik und im Deutschen Reich 1568–1648*, ed. Horst Lademacher and Simon Groenveld (Münster: Waxmann Verlag, 1998), pp. 129–56. O'Donovan also stresses the relevance of 'De veritate religionis'. This Augustinian interpretation (and appropriation) of Grotius's international law is indebted to two fundamental theological decisions: (a) to discern God's will *through* the created order (*RMO*, 134) because of (b) the real presence of the Kingdom of God. *From Irenaeus to Grotius: A Sourcebook in Christian Political Thought*, ed. Oliver O'Donovan and Joan Lockwood O'Donovan (Grand Rapids, MI: William B. Eerdmans: 1999), p. 789; See also Christoph A. Stumpf, *The Grotian Theology of International Law* (Berlin: Walter de Gruyter, 2006), pp. 5, 68 f.

If median guilt limits the liability of the individual person as a criminal, does that mean conscripts incur less guilt? For O'Donovan, that seems to be the case: conscription incorporates the understanding that 'armed forces act *only* as their society's representatives'. This echoes Ramsey's insistence that it must be attempted to incapacitate the soldier, not to eradicate the individual human being. Conscription 'has the socially desirable result that societies must study the price-tag on their policies' (*JWR*, 38). In any case, it does not change the balance of median guilt, which reflects the duties and ambiguities of citizenship.

Further on the individual level, the concept of median guilt also affects so-called targeted killing. O'Donovan suggests its impermissibility in the customary law of war: *assassination* 'lacks the degree of public accountability that is present even in a summary trial' and 'it attacks leaders as individuals rather than through the militias of which they are the representatives' (*JWR*, 74).[29] His diagnosis of the problem here flags up the very antagonistic/idealistic oscillation to be overcome. Absent the notion of counter-insurgency as war and that of median guilt, liberal society (or international law) can only choose between criminal law and downright murder (*JWR*, 74). I will revisit this topic in Chapter 6.

On the social level, median guilt means that righting a wrong does not permit one society to 'prevent another from existing, nor from engaging in the normal self-sustaining activities of life' (*JWR*, 39). One may take offence against the hostilities of military structures, not the other society. The route of total war 'denies the right of peaceful social existence, a right in which we and our enemy both share' (*JWR*, 40).

The intention to distinguish is 'the only one "just intention" in armed conflict'. This is not moral purism but implies that all other intentions in war 'should be subordinated to its demands and restraints'. It does, however, imply an endorsement of the principle of double effect, albeit 'well understood' (*JWR*, 44). In short, with the notion of median guilt and a doctrine of double effect O'Donovan's steers discriminating judgement between two poles. The antagonistic one makes no distinction at all, setting 'our right to survival' against 'theirs'. The other pole does not discriminate either, but on seemingly unselfish grounds: all individuals are essentially of equal worth (*JWR*, 47).

Proportion

According to O'Donovan, the tendency to regard proportion as merely the ordering principle of violent means to any given end actually turns the principle on its head. If the end is broadly defined, then hardly any means are disproportionate. Ramsey pointed out this danger of the 'ordinary doctrine of war' in his transformist writings, and O'Donovan is equally aware of it. In response, he broadens 'proportion' to govern the whole act of judgement, without dismissing certain aims as 'utopian' or 'unrealistic'.

---

[29] Median guilt roughly corresponds to the distinction between the 'corporate' persons of soldiers as combatants and their 'individual' status as humans in international humanitarian law. See Caroline Kennedy and Nicholas Rengger, 'The New Assassination Bureau: On the "Robotic Turn" in Contemporary War', 2012, http://www.carnegiecouncil.org/publications/ethics_online/0075.html (accessed 13 December 2018); Nils Melzer, *Targeted Killing in International Law* (Oxford: Oxford University Press, 2008).

Proportion is both forward- and backward-looking. The prudent gaze spans the field of wrong done and right to be restored.[30] In 'retrospective proportion', judgement looks at the just cause. Does whatever happened warrant the use of violent force? For O'Donovan, a cause of war must be a *iniuria accepta*, though not an *iniuria perfecta*. 'Preemptive war' is antagonistic self-defence and hence impermissible (*JWR*, 49). According to Grotius, the threat must be 'immediate'.

Contesting this, not least with the Iraq debate on 'preventive war' in mind, Nigel Biggar distinguishes between an ontological dimension ('what is the case') and an epistemological dimension ('what we have good reason to believe is the case'). He thinks the epistemological dimension is *primary* in determining whether to go to war: 'what may justify pre-emptive war is a threat that we have good reason to suppose is substantial and serious and that could not be deterred by other means. Whether such a threat is mature or emergent is strictly beside the point.' However, one could argue that what 'we have good reason to suppose' is always dependent on 'the ontological dimension': there must be visible, tangible evidence in order for us to have good reason to believe something is the case. Otherwise, one would intentionally introduce the possibility of insincerity. This is where 'immediacy' comes in.[31] So, perhaps the legal distinction between 'risk' and 'danger' is more helpful. To fight risks engenders a utilitarian chase of counterfactual claims, domino theories and myriad other possible scenarios.[32] When a political party chases a fiction, striking the enemy before he can even become a 'threat', pre-emptive antagonism arises. At least, Grotius finds the (self-)deceptive moment of pre-emptive war justifications shows a lack of faith in divine providence (*JWR*, 49). O'Donovan's insistence on *inuria accepta* thus gestures towards a median path between both utilitarian scenario fighters and 'defense-only' strategists. Both display the same fault with the same logic: instead of encountering the situation at hand, they oscillate unsteadily between survivalist defence and survivalist prevention. In the end, both positions are two sides of the same coin.

O'Donovan then differentiates the single *causa iusta*, 'wrong done', into three elementary aspects. To only think of attack and defence, associated with the sovereign rights tradition, just leads to 'mortal combat'. But in an 'international community of right', by contrast, the three causes of defence, restoration and punishment come together in order to install the right order between social entities:

---

[30] A purely reactive understanding is impossible, since all acts of judgement set the terms of new action: judgement implies new law. Several authors have noted O'Donovan's reluctance to name positive goods, even if it is prudence, which distinguishes O'Donovan from libertarianism. Nigel Biggar, 'On Defining Political Authority as an Act of Judgment: A Discussion of Oliver O'Donovan's Ways of Judgment (Part I)', *Political Theology*, 9 (2008), 273–93; Jonathan Rist, 'Judgment, Reaction and the Common Good', *Political Theology*, 9 (2008), 363–72; David H. McIlroy 'The Right Reason for Caesar to Confess Christ as Lord' (2008), http://klice.co.uk/uploads/EST08McIlroy.pdf (accessed 15 January 2013).

[31] Biggar, 'Review', p. 226 f. O'Donovan's and Biggar's difference is a matter of nuance: 'An adversary far advanced on the road towards biological weapons is worth a very great deal more loss to stop than one who presents no comparable hazard' (*JWR*, 60).

[32] David Rodin, 'The Problem with Prevention 1', in *Preemption: Military Action and Moral Justification*, ed. David Rodin and Henry Shue (Oxford: Oxford University Press, 2007), pp. 140–74, pp. 144–6.

We need the idea of *penal* desert to restrict the potentially elastic permissions of defence and reparation. A *defensive* objective is necessary, because without real and pressing danger one cannot justify exposing the world to the dangers that war itself brings with it. A *reparative* objective is necessary, for without actual loss to be redressed the combination of malice and danger does not amount to an actual wrong. (*JWR*, 53)[33]

At first sight, of course, 'retribution' clashes with an evangelical perspective. But the aim of this conception is simply to limit the act of judgement. The tripartite form of judgement under law fosters the possibility of reconciliation as it presents the possibility of *adequate* settlement: 'To require a penal objective guards against the resort to war as a response to non-culpable injury, and prevents the subtle expansion of defensive war-aims into further goals, such as colonisation' (*JWR*, 58). Hence, 'readers can glean that evangelical retribution aims at (just and therefore lasting) peace – not an equality of suffering – between victim and wrongdoer'.[34]

'Prospective judgment', finally, concerns the prospect for the settling of the right. This is a difficult task, because armed conflict 'is a venture outside the given sphere of government, and the only means available run the risk of breach in the banks of practical rationality that could release a flood of absolute antagonism'. Most importantly, the end of war must be peace, rather than victory – only then it is political and not just military (*JWR*, 59, 61). Winning the war is not even the *sine qua non* of peace: 'whether it is necessary or not in any given case depends on whether peace can be made first' (*JWR*, 59). Second, there are the criteria of 'last resort' and 'prospect of success'. The first one weighs up alternative possible actions; the second measures the risk of failure. As such, they guard against 'sins against practical rationality': 'a precipitate rush to arms, and a stubborn refusal to count the cost'. But the criteria should not be used to declare *every* military action disproportionate from the start. 'Like the stopped clock telling the correct time twice in 24 hours', it is easy to insist on a war being disproportionate until that becomes true. The specifically practical nature of O'Donovan's proposal becomes most evident here. Although serving as critical tools, the principles do not make up an impractical counterposition. Equally, they rest on the primacy of politics over the military, of peace over victory. There is an element of risk, 'hazarded upon God's providential provision' at work here (*JWR*, 19). Principled venturing of judgement neither proclaims ideological supremacy nor does it recline in critical and loving non-violence.

In short, O'Donovan's evangelical, practical proposal lies between the premises and proposals of antagonism and idealism but also between sovereign realism and liberal

---

[33] Cf. Walter Benjamin, 'Critique of Violence', in *Continental Ethics Reader* (London: Routledge, 2003), pp. 113–26, p. 119. In so far as neither Elshtain nor the mature Ramsey conceive of an international, legal order (with a positive moment), their concept of punishment is determined by expansive national defence. O'Donovan notes an imbalance to that effect in the US National Security Strategy (*JWR*, 132 f).

[34] Biggar, 'Review', p. 224. A lack of distinction between punishment and revenge in current debates may be noted; it seems the representative perspectives are increasingly difficult to understand. See e.g. David Luban, "War as Punishment" (2011). *Georgetown Law Faculty Working Papers*. Paper 145. http://scholarship.law.georgetown.edu/fwps_papers/145 (accessed 25 August 2011).

internationalism. Steinhoff's critical points against these two and the fruits of Ramsey's transformist period are given further nuance and structure. Evangelical counter-praxis is the service of reconciliatory judgement. It must be charitable and refrains from totalizing the opposite belligerent, whether positively or negatively. The political agent targets, yet discriminates, proportionate to a concrete injury. The 'logic' of war envisioned here is restrained, yet effective, corresponding to Right, yet tied neither to a distinct political agenda nor ideology.

Christ the ruling mediator

Broadly speaking, O'Donovan's ethics of war go beyond the 'idealism-realism nexus', as he calls it in a slightly different context.[35] Yet this outlook, like the previous authors', is deeply moored in theological assumptions. If – as Graham Ward suggests with a view to the early Hegel – 'dialectic is a working out of a Christological and philosophical principle',[36] then in terms of theological systematics, my suggestion here is that O'Donovan's Christology re-sublates the idealist dialectics of mediation into biblical specificity. O'Donovan relocates Hegel's question of mediation (and the sceptical oscillation Hegel sought to overcome) within a theological framework and biblical exegesis.[37] To rephrase Marx, he turns Hegel 'back on his head' – a theological head. Precisely in that way, O'Donovan steps through the door opened by Ramsey, whose thought and intellectual trajectory was (still) an unfolding philosophical-idealist logic.

The move beyond post-Enlightenment and idealist philosophies was an important point of departure already for the early O'Donovan (not least, perhaps, a form of resistance against the Marxist political philosophies influential in the West before 1990). Already in his first major work, *Resurrection and Moral Order*, he sought to identify 'an integrally evangelical ethics which rejoices in the heart and gives light to the eyes because it springs from God's gift to mankind in Jesus Christ' (*RMO*, 12) – between and beyond both *libertarianism* and *legalism*.

O'Donovan's ethics of war are then the practical result of unfolding the systematic understanding that the ruling Jesus Christ is the mediator between God and humankind. In religious-philosophical terms, mediation in O'Donovan's work appears as the final closure of all duality. This determines O'Donovan's understanding of 'reality' (including political reality), political agency and authority, and finally political action, specifically the tension between law (including positive law) and 'love'. Christ, so O'Donovan's emphasis, is the *objective* centre of all being and striving, the 'desire

---

[35] O'Donovan himself uses this term in *DN*, p. 121, also linking it to a Jesuology to the detriment of Christology.

[36] Graham Ward, 'How Hegel Became a Philosopher: Logos and the Economy of Logic', *Critical Research on Religion*, 1 (2013), 275. See also Graham Ward, *How the Light Gets In: Ethical Life I* (Oxford: Oxford University Press, 2016), pp. 298–303. Cf. Introduction above.

[37] O'Donovan, *Desire of the Nations*, pp. 9–15; O'Donovan, 'The Future of Theological Ethics', *Studies in Christian Ethics*, 25.2 (2012), 186–98; for a sustained engagement with O'Donovan's exegesis see *A Royal Priesthood? The Use of the Bible Ethically and Politically: A Dialogue with Oliver O'Donovan*, ed. Craig G. Bartholomew (Carlisle: Paternoster Press, 2002).

of the nations'.[38] As we will see, his emphatically evangelical-theological view then also transforms and reintegrates the implicit or explicit theological presuppositions encountered in the previous chapters.[39]

Evangelical reality and politics

For O'Donovan, the first and primary reality is the one that is affirmed in faith: God reigns in Christ. *Tu rex gloriae, Christe* – the *Te Deum* introduces his seminal 1996 *Desire of the Nations*. This divine 'conclusion', so to speak, *crowns* the world as the mediator between God and man. O'Donovan's political theology thus begins with the divine Kingdom; it is towards this *reality* (rather than other categories such as 'ideals' or 'values') to which his evangelical just war ethic is oriented.

Going through Ramsey's transformist door and making the 'leap of faith', O'Donovan significantly shifts the 'aeonic rift' Ramsey had discerned between this age and the next. The 'two kingdoms' of spiritual and political power, paradoxically, are now two *contemporaneous ages*:

> The doctrine of the Two was, before all else, a doctrine of two ages. The passing age of the principalities and powers has overlapped with the coming age of God's Kingdom. The confrontation of the two societies, the more attenuated balance of the two rules and the inner dynamism of the two persons are all generated by this eschatological fusion. (*DN*, 211)[40]

Pace post-Humean empiricism, the 'will of God as peace' is an *ontological* truth and the end of history (*JWR*, 3) as well as the content of moral intention. As a result, just war thinking is based on the 'evangelical rejection of war' rather than a factual, predetermined reality or phenomenon.

The reality of divine rule constitutes the architecture of the world and subsequently any ethical proposal. From the outset, there is no duality between a utopian or immanent ideal and a naturalistic sphere of politics. Such differentiations rather come into view before a unified horizon that is the history of the people of God with its climax in Jesus's life, death and resurrection. O'Donovan's theo-logic is thus crystallized in the tension-filled narrative of Israel's politics before and after the Christ-event. From this pivotal point, the paradigmatic history of Israel is the repository of political concepts,

---

[38] See also Augustine, *The City of God against the Pagans*, ed. Robert W. Dyson (Cambridge: Cambridge University Press, 1998), Bk. XVIII, Chapter 35; Hag. 2.6.

[39] This 'summing up' is comparable to Barth's 'sublation of religion in revelation', though a sustained comparative reading of O'Donovan and Barth is beyond the scope of this chapter. See e.g. Karl Barth, *Church Dogmatics*, I/2, paragraph 17, and comparative discussions in *Commanding Grace: Studies in Karl Barth's Ethics*, ed. Daniel L. Migliore (Grand Rapids, MI: William B. Eerdmans, 2010), esp. Eric Gregory, 'The Spirit and the Letter: Protestant Thomism and Nigel Biggar's "Karl Barth's Ethics Revisited"', in *Commanding Grace: Studies in Karl Barth's Ethics*, ed. Daniel L. Migliore (Grand Rapids, MI: William B. Eerdmans, 2010), pp. 50–9; and William Werpehowski, 'Karl Barth and Just War: A Conversation with Roman Catholicism', in *Commanding Grace: Studies in Karl Barth's Ethics*, ed. Daniel L. Migliore (Grand Rapids, MI: William B. Eerdmans, 2010), pp. 60–82.

[40] Also *DN*, p. 82, 90–1, 117, 124.

which O'Donovan investigates with the formal dichotomy of political institutions and the church in mind. Crucially, the turn to Israel gives extensive theological *content* to Ramsey's dialectical political act: 'Failure to attend to Israel is what left Christian political thought oscillating between idealist and realist poles'.[41] Israel – because the church is Israel too – links contemporary life to the universal divine narrative. We will revisit this more closely in the section on political authority.

But first, why should the evangelical reality be morally authoritative? After all, as Bernard Williams famously observed, even a believer would be obedient to God for moral reasons. 'Either one's motives for following the moral word of God are moral motives, or they are not.'[42] Even in arguing for moral commands from God's goodness, one would apply an a priori concept of goodness. Along those lines, contemporary ethics of war, particularly in analytical philosophy but also a generalized 'naturalistic' 'religious' ethic such as Elshtain's, appeal to perceived rational presuppositions or intuitions. O'Donovan responds that Jesus appears as *the* moral teacher and example, 'where someone exceptional is needed to show people things which, however universally true these may be, they are not capable of recognizing otherwise'.[43] Beyond a mere *imitatio*-Jesuology, in Christ the moral order has also *come to be*, as O'Donovan points out.[44] Whatever is then said about Christian morality has to be said 'in Christ', since 'the universal meaning which lies behind all our moral perceptions has been given a concrete and irreplaceable embodiment'. Christ is the one in whom the restored creation 'is summed up' (*RMO*, 150).[45]

Epistemologically, the Christ-event, as O'Donovan presents it, contrasts also with the dichotomous or dualistic epistemological frameworks encountered so far. What Elshtain regarded as 'sectarian' belief, Rodin and Steinhoff as atavistic, here is the starting point for a systematic conceptual unfolding. O'Donovan frequently adds that everybody is free to renounce belief or to suspend their unbelief. But *if* one believes, he points out, one must also derive one's moral concepts from the redeeming reality of Christ's life and work. Moral thinking is commanded by the Christ-event as in itself authoritative. In this event, 'power' and 'word' become one, which O'Donovan argues is the very meaning of authority.[46] Moving from the Kingdom of God to 'core' political concepts for him then offers new analogies and the 'liberation to an imprisoned political culture' (*DN*, 119).

The very question of moral theology also shifts: from an ethical, analytical-neutral 'What should we do?' to 'What does one have to do because God *is*?'[47] O'Donovan's is neither merely Christianized nor Christian 'realism' but an 'evangelical realism'.

---

[41] O'Donovan, *Desire of the Nations*, p. 27.

[42] Bernard Williams, *Morality: An Introduction to Ethics* (Cambridge: Cambridge University Press, 1972), p. 78f.

[43] *RMO*, p. 19, 89.

[44] See Jon. 14.6.

[45] Cf. note above on Barth's 'sublation', see footnote 39.

[46] The variety in morality is a matter of the historical contingency of standpoints, not of the content – the standpoint of 'an obscure Jewish rabbi of the 1st century', 'Response to Peter Scott', in *A Royal Priesthood?*, pp. 374–6, p. 375.

[47] Karl Barth, *Ethics*, Lectures at Münster (1928) and Bonn (1930), trans. Geoffrey W. Bromiley (Edinburgh: T&T Clark, 1981), p. 25.

The 'reality principle' of O'Donovan's ethics finds a metaphysical correlation between an 'is' and an 'ought'. This is possible, however, only together with what he calls the 'evangelical principle'. What is true and thus to be done is constituted by what God has done for the world and humankind in Jesus Christ.[48] A passage from Bonhoeffer might further clarify this as a determination of any quotidian reality by the ontological-redemptive reality of Christ:

> In Jesus Christ the actuality of God has gone down in the actuality [*Wirklichkeit*] of this world. The place in which the question for the actuality of God as well as the actuality of this world finds its answer is signified only by the name: Jesus Christ. In this name God and the world are concluded. In him everything has its continued being (Col. 1, 16). From now on neither God nor the world can be spoken of rightly without speaking of Jesus Christ. All concepts of actuality which turn away from him are abstractions.[49]

God's *basileia* is thus not merely a set of commands occasionally flashing into the world like lightning bolts.[50] Rather, the evangelical commanding reality, the Kingdom of God, is *present* as a vindicated creation order.[51]

Vindicated creation order – integrating 'utopia'

This leads to the perhaps more tangible aspect of reality, the kind of world that political action encounters and implies. In O'Donovan's approach, Christ announces the fulfilment of the time; he redeems a previously unfulfilled creation. The *new creation* together with God's providential action in history becomes the moral horizon for all action.

Dogmatically, the central theological moment that establishes the connection between evangelical reality and the created natural order is the *resurrection*, both as the backward-looking death and forward-looking triumph of Christ. In O'Donovan's reading, it is a 'double event' rather than a revolutionary watershed between Old and New; it holds both old and new age together in Christ.[52] This is highly relevant as a meta-politics: as a theo-logical moment, the resurrection subtly de-authorizes revolution, anarchism –but also the faceless, only apparently natural determinism of bureaucratic technocracies or hedonistic repetitiveness.

---

[48] Cf. *COL*, p. 10.

[49] 'In Jesus Christus ist die Wirklichkeit Gottes in die Wirklichkeit dieser Welt eingegangen. Der Ort, an dem die Frage nach der Wirklichkeit Gottes wie die nach der Wirklichkeit der Welt zugleich Beantwortung erfährt, ist allein bezeichnet durch den Namen: Jesus Christus. In diesen Namen ist Gott und die Welt beschlossen. In ihm hat alles seinen Bestand (Col. 1, 16). Von nun an kann weder von Gott noch von der Welt recht geredet werden ohne von Jesus Christus zu reden. Alle Wirklichkeitsbegriffe, die von ihm absehen, sind Abstraktionen.' (Dietrich Bonhoeffer, *Ethik*, ed. Ilse Tödt et al. (Munich: Kaiser, 1992), p. 39).

[50] *DN*, 132; O'Donovan, 'How Can Theology Be Moral?', p. 88.

[51] See *RMO*, xv, on the foundation of ethics in the resurrection 'embracing the partial truths' of Kingdom and Creation ethics.

[52] *RMO*, 56–7; *DN*, 128, 130.

As death and sin are overcome with the resurrection, creation is affirmed both in its created goodness and its *telos*, its destination towards the promised final fulfilment in God's eternity: 'all shall be made alive' (1 Cor. 15.22). Moreover, Christ is *the* representative, 'expressing a reality which has an independent and prior standing, but in the way that a national leader is representative when he brings about for the whole of his people whatever it is, war or peace, that he effects on their behalf' (*RMO*, 15).[53] Thus, in this 'double-event' the reconciliation, and hence the *mediation*, between creation and Kingdom takes place. Mediated by the Christ-event, they can no longer be thought as separate. The new creation, however, is not an altogether different world but a creation order that is vindicated. 'Christian morality is [the human being's] glad response to the deed of God which has restored, proved and fulfilled that order, making man free to conform to it' (*RMO*, 76).

In O'Donovan's view, the resurrection entails an objective, natural-teleological order, an ordering towards God in which one may freely and creatively participate. Not only is God's kingdom linked with the cosmic order, as it says in the Psalms (*DN*, 34). With *tsedeq*, divine righteousness or justice, 'we are in a fully public realm of a world court' (*DN*, 37). Creation as an order now discernibly points towards its fulfilment as it is always already partially fulfilled in the revealed rule of God. With this, O'Donovan reconnects not least to Augustine, for whom natural orders have a pointing or eidetic character. As he puts it in *Desire of the Nations*, 'To judge politics in the light of the divine rule is to be assured of its world-affirming and humane character' (*DN*, 19).[54] Humankind under God's authority is now the authorized 'ruler' of the ordered creation restored to take its authoritative and beneficent place in this order (*RMO*, 55). Humans do not have to install or generate 'new world orders' of various kinds, nor do they have to 'warrant' (Elshtain) the one that exists (*DN*, 30). They are 'free to interpret God's law in a way that realises God's purposes for mankind's welfare' (*DN*, 104).

Effectively, O'Donovan here re-'assumes' or reintegrates what in early modernity became 'utopia', which, as we saw in Part One, has been haunting politics and moral conceptualizations of war and anti-war in a new mode since the nineteenth century. Yet the sublation of 'utopia' into a 'vindicated creation order' also hoists the mature Ramsey's 'politics' as wholly 'under the sign of Babylon' into a more positive position. On the international level, the new ordering *post Christum* takes the form of the *ius gentium* as part of the *ius naturale* 'revealed in new clarity by the Gospel' (*WJ*, 129).[55] Pace liberal-internationalist suggestions of a world government, 'the appropriate unifying element in international order is law rather than government' (*DN*, 72). Notably, in *Just War Revisited*, O'Donovan is less rigid as to the differentiation between evangelical and natural law than in his earlier work (*RMO*, 85–7). On the one hand, the

---

[53] 'Independent and prior' does not mean independent of the world but rather independent of human experience – *pace* e.g. Meillassoux's 'correlationism'. Quentin Meillassoux, *After Finitude: An Essay on The Necessity of Contingency* (London: Continuum, 2008).

[54] Oliver O'Donovan and Joan Lockwood O'Donovan, *Bonds of Imperfection: Christian Politics, Past and Present* (Grand Rapids, MI: Eerdmans, 2004), p. 2. Hereafter, BI.

[55] *Ius naturale* is not necessarily the same as *ius gentium*, the latter having a 'positive moment' according to Dieter Schwab, 'Der Staat im Naturrecht der Scholastik', in *Naturrecht und Staat: Politische Funktionen des europäischen Naturrechts*, ed. Diethelm Klippel (Munich: Oldenbourg, 2006), pp. 1–18, p. 3.

epistemology is the same – all moral knowledge of the created order must flow from the central point of Christ (*RMO*, 85).[56] On the other hand, the *ius naturae* or Natural Right is simply there – even if humanity ignores it.

At the same time, O'Donovan rejects contemporary individualist human rights paradigms, continuing a strand of thought already begun by Ramsey. At least where subjective and *original* to the individual, rights are an unreconciled plurality of 'primitive endowment[s] of power' (*DN*, 262).[57] Instead, O'Donovan argues that there is an objective order of Right, since rights must have their place 'within a discourse founded on law'. Here, one might say with Hegel: the ordering performance of justice precisely reconciles subjective and objective perspectives.[58] External order and subjective claims cease to be at odds.[59] (Incidentally, for O'Donovan judgement also does not fall apart into 'making' and 'enforcing' law.)

O'Donovan's notion of a 'vindicated creation order' underlying political authority and action marks a significant contrast to the sovereign-internationalist paradigm and the heterodox approaches in Part Two. These had sought to overcome or subtly reinforced an oscillation between a 'mere' realism and utopian proposals. For the state-sovereigntist, the destruction of (artificial) state structures *after all* meant a descent into a chaotic state of nature, because sociality required such structures to maintain its *esse*.[60] By contrast, evangelical reality in O'Donovan's understanding (with Augustine) generates also a moral (and subsequently political) realism: the order of Right is *there*, irrespective of human construction, even recognition, and as such authoritative, inviting free response.

Theologically, by focussing on the resurrection event as both elevating and confirming creation, O'Donovan settles between Milbank's Catholic 'counter-ontology' (against the Roman Empire and liberalism) and Grotius's proto-secularist

---

[56] Cf. Aquinas, ST IaIIae, Qu. 107, Art. 1; J. Cole noted a tension between the 'creationist' and 'providentialist' ontologies of political authority in *RMO* and *DN/WJ*, respectively, with O'Donovan appearing to have settled on the latter: politics is an order of history, not of nature. Noting the subtle difference between politics as prelapsarian (*RMO*) or postlapsarian (*DN* and O'Donovan's later works), Cole gives no clear reason why political authority, if existing due to divine providence in history rather than as part of the created order (which is after all 'vindicated'), *shouldn't* be able to 'evoke the free and intelligible collective human response that it so clearly does'. Jonathan Cole, 'Towards a Christian Ontology of Political Authority: The Relationship between Created Order and Providence in Oliver O'Donovan's Theology of Political Authority', *Studies in Christian Ethics*, first published online, 6 May 2018, 1–19, p. 12.

[57] Cf. Chapter 3 on Uwe Steinhoff. The debate on rights versus Right continues; besides O'Donovan, see Joan Lockwood O'Donovan, John Milbank, 'Against Human Rights: Liberty in the Western Tradition', *Oxford Journal of Law and Religion*, 1.1 (2012), 203–34; Nicholas Wolterstorff, *Justice: Rights and Wrongs* (Princeton, NJ: Princeton University Press, 2008); see e.g. Nigel Biggar, *What's Wrong with Rights?* (forthcoming) again critically: Nicholas Wolterstorff, 'Modern Protestant Developments in Human Rights', in *Christianity and Human Rights: An Introduction*, ed. John Witte, Jr and Frank S. Alexander (Cambridge: Cambridge University Press, 2010), pp. 155–72.

[58] See *WJ*, 118–9; *RMO*, 102–9 on the mediate role of the Spirit. In *WJ*, O'Donovan explicitly heeds Hegel's notion of punishment as 'bring[ing] to theoretical completion the scattered insight of patristic Christianity' but bemoans its lack of 'relating penal practice to the wider range of practices that constitute political and social life'. *WJ*, 321. See again Chapter 6.

[59] See below on 'just war action'. *RMO*, *DN*, 246 f.

[60] Except in the domestic sphere.

international order of Right *etsi Deus non daretur*.[61] He corrects Milbank by finding the positive in contemporary politics as part of God's 'common grace'. He corrects (the classicist) Grotius by stressing the double event of the resurrection: the new life under Christ must be a service to divine righteousness, participating in the triumph of Christ, which is the 'reign' of grace (*DN*, 128).

A 'violent world'? Realism and fallenness

O'Donovan's early work lacks the classical Protestant, incisive sharpness about the abject depravity of humanity Reinhold Niebuhr and Ramsey skilfully drew their readers' attention to. There is something other-worldly particularly to *Resurrection and Moral Order* that makes it difficult to connect to the experiences of crime, injustice and injury frequently prompting engagement with the ethics of war in the first place.

At least in *RMO*, O'Donovan shifts the understanding of the postlapsarian 'reality' of politics to a more prelapsarian idea of creation as the ground of political authority (his view is thus perhaps more Aristotelian than Augustinian, or rather he doesn't see them as necessarily opposed).[62] As part of the vindicated creation order, 'politics' is not a separate sphere, the summary of negativity that arises in judgement on innocent and guilty.[63] Politics is the 'sphere' in which rulers are summoned to facilitate – by the means available to them – the participation in the restored world order with its distinctly eschatological *finis*.[64] As Jonathan Cole highlights,

> By making the ontological distinction between an *esse* of political authority grounded in the created order and a *bene esse* of political authority founded in the work of divine providence in history, O'Donovan actually possesses a powerful theological explanation for the existence of oppressive and unjust regimes that does not make God complicit in their existence … As a special conjunction of natural authorities in the created order, political authority is there to be discovered and used, or, as the case may be, manipulated and abused, by all humans.[65]

With the recognition of an all-embracing teleology, an ordering towards God, there is no fundamental 'ontology of violence' (to use a phrase from 'Radical Orthodoxy'), since all difference is subject to a supreme *ens*.[66] Hence,

---

[61] Cf. *DN*, 128. Grotius partly succumbed to the Western tendency to isolate the death of Christ and 'thereby radically depoliticising the central saving event of the Gospel'.

[62] Cf. Jonathan Cole, 'Towards a Christian Ontology of Political Authority'; Cole explicitly sees 'a great deal of synergy between Aquinas's conception of the function of authority in the prelapsarian "state of innocence" and the role O'Donovan sees for natural authorities in the created order' (p. 15).

[63] See *WJ*, 238, against Hannah Arendt on 'politics unclouded by philosophy'.

[64] Bernd Wannenwetsch aptly translates the Greek passage: rather than 'for your good', suggesting the political self-alienated will of the constituents, 'for the good' means the divine good. 'Soul Citizens: How Christians Understand Their Political Role', *Political Theology*, 9 (2008), 373–94, p. 381.

[65] Cole, 'Towards a Christian Ontology of Political Authority', p. 18.

[66] Milbank, *Theology and Social Theory*, p. 305.

The unification of all rule in [Christ's] rule, the subordination of all sovereignty under his sovereignty, forbade [Christians] to think that sheer unmediated antagonism could, in however carefully defined circumstances, be admitted as a possibility. Since every opposition of hostile parties was subject to the throne of God and of his Christ, there could be no outright duality. Antagonistic praxis was superseded by the climax of salvation history. (*JWR*, 5)

Evil becomes now a form of 'disobedience' to God as a form of (yet) failed vision.[67] By contrast, the 'analysis' of evil in terms of scientific models (such as Wohlstetter's) is insufficient as their neutral *epistemes* point to various forms of anthropocentrism or human(ist) self-mediation.

Consequentialism is notably absent in O'Donovan's proposal, not least avoiding a 'scenario'-thinking as cultivated during the Cold War and even more dominant today. If politics were only a negative order against evil, 'all necessary means' could be justified by the ends, which – in a climate of fear rather than the knowledge of divine providence – is defined as preventing complete annihilation and destruction or defeating evil.[68] Ramsey had recognized this danger when he rallied against the aggressor-defender doctrine in his transformist phase. O'Donovan again connects to this here.

To summarize this section, 'evangelical reality' for O'Donovan can challenge the dialectic between sovereigntist realism and an optimistic, even idealistic liberal internationalism. Under the rule of Christ, there is an ontological peacefulness of order and Right. The dualism between (fallen) creation and future kingdom is alleviated. Fallen reality is recurring human disobedience but does not constitute a pre-incarnational Babylonic sphere. Where following the Aristotelian-Thomist tradition, O'Donovan sees a pre-political sociality and society which coheres with the 'natural', created authorities of might, right and tradition (i.e. the grounds of political authority, see next section). To the new creation corresponds an order of Right, part of which is the *ius gentium*. This is then the transformed context and 'ontology' for political action to take shape.

Government-as-judgement: From dialectics to theo-logic

In many ways, what has just been said about reality and order has been a preliminary to understand O'Donovan's notion of the political agent. Indeed, many commentators have argued that the core of his project has been the recovery of political authority, drawing on a wealthy pre-modern Christian tradition. The thesis to be defended here is that O'Donovan's notion of political authority theologically sublates Ramsey's idealist-philosophical transformist project and in this way simultaneously rejects and integrates the notions of legitimate political authority we have encountered in Parts I and II.

---

[67] Namely, *RMO*, 19.
[68] For example, Christopher Hitchens, 'In Defense of Endless War', *Slate Magazine*, 19 September 2011, https://slate.com/news-and-politics/2011/09/endless-war-a-decade-after-9-11-civilization-must-still-defend-itself.html (accessed 4 December 2018).

The question of who or what is a legitimate authority for O'Donovan centres on the nature of the political act. As we noted, in *Desire of the Nations* (1996) he acknowledged his former teacher Paul Ramsey for liberating the question of political institutions.[69] In *Ways of Judgment* (2005), O'Donovan restated his by then well-known theorem that political authority 'arises where power, the execution of right, and the perpetuation of tradition are assured together in one coordinated agency'. He added, 'The source of this triad [power, right, tradition], as I now realize, was Paul Ramsey's analysis of authority as *lex, iustitia*, and *ordo*.'[70] This intellectual-historical movement is not without theological *irony*. It is a reverse, *more evangelical* break of Anglican liberalism with the older generation influenced by idealist-philosophical, residually dialectical theology. So how does O'Donovan theologically transform Ramsey's transformism?

Christ the mediator and the mediating task of government

Already in his *Resurrection and Moral Order* (1986), O'Donovan emphasized the *distinctiveness* of evangelical ethics, advocating 'an integrally evangelical ethics which rejoices in the heart and gives light to the eyes because it springs from God's gift to mankind in Jesus Christ' (*RMO*, 12).[71] In the same work, he decisively rejected Hegel and idealism's notion of (Christological) mediation, voicing Tuttle's critique of Ramsey.[72] Idealist incarnation '(without the definite article)' means that 'the meaning of the whole has been focused in a representative one'; so eventually 'any concrete being may … be an "incarnation" of universal meaning in this sense'. In contrast, however, 'Christ's particularity belongs to his divine nature, his universality to his human nature. As the one whom God has sent he is irreplaceable; as the new man he is the pattern to which we may conform ourselves.'[73]

Via this distinct theo-logic, O'Donovan averts the Niebuhrian incarnation of the Kingdom of Heaven taking immanent form in any concrete state, social order or conglomerate of states.[74] Further down the line, just war and 'democracy' are therefore not synonyms by default. 'What is remarkable', O'Donovan goes on in *RMO*, 'and what only *the* incarnation can tell us of, is not the representation of universal order in any one being, but the coming within universal order of that which belongs outside it, the one divine Word which gave it its origin and which pronounces its judgment'.[75]This critique of idealism, and beyond Hegel the Marxist and liberation-theological project,

---

[69] O'Donovan, 'Karl Barth and Ramsey's "Uses of Power"', pp. 1–30, 23; *Desire of the Nations*, p. 21.
[70] O'Donovan, *The Ways of Judgment*, p. 142. This may also answer the question as to the hermeneutical principles.
[71] See e.g. 'Il problema della mediazione', in Carlo Galli, *Genealogia della Politica: Carl Schmitt e la Crisi del Pensiero Politico Moderno* (Bologna: Il Mulino 1996), pp. 3–178.
[72] See Chapter 4.
[73] O'Donovan, *Resurrection*, p. 143.
[74] Earlier he had compared John of Patmos' reference to Nero with Hegel's remark that the universal and homogenous state would first come into being in America – Oliver O'Donovan, 'The Political Thought of the Book of Revelation', *Tyndale Bulletin* 37 (1986), 61–94, p. 68.
[75] O'Donovan, *Resurrection*, p. 144

runs through O'Donovan's work, and we will return to it in Chapter 6. Suffice to say here that it went hand in hand with a significant reconception of political authority.

In *The Desire of the Nations* (1996), the evangelical-theological dislodgement of idealism was an introductory remark to an altogether positive 'rediscovery' of political theology. First, O'Donovan's prolegomena revisited the scepticism characteristic of modern political theology: the fundamental *separation* of politics from theology – 'morality' being theology's surrogate – as opposed to (divine) unitary rule. Already in Augustine's more sceptical moments (without Justice, all kingdoms are really bands of robbers), it finds a modern expression in Kant's suspicion of the 'political moralist' (*DN*, 7). In 2005, O'Donovan again wrote, 'A *cordon sanitaire* between politics and theology, or between politics and philosophy, cannot claim intelligibility to be a *precondition* for thought, but only an *imposition* on it, and therefore has within itself the character of tyranny'[76] (*WJ*, 237). Not least this *cordon sanitaire* was the precondition both of Niebuhrian 'realistic politics' as opposed to Christian 'universal niceness' (Elshtain) as well as Ramsey's 'world of systems' as opposed to a formless *agape* searching for incarnation (Ramsey). And it was a premise of both Rodin's and Steinhoff's approaches. Theologically, I suggested, these could be understood as subtle forms of modern Marcionism.

Investigating the political meaning of Christ's mediation of the divine rule, O'Donovan turned to *Israel*: 'The hermeneutic principle that governs a Christian appeal to political categories within the Hebrew Scriptures is, simply, Israel itself' (*DN*, 27).[77] As the 'new Israel', the church links contemporary life to a divine narrative. Its development is a *figura* (a term O'Donovan doesn't use to avoid any sense of 'myth') for the subsequent tension between political institutions and the church. In that sense, the very turn to Israel was already a 'step of faith on the theologian's part' (*DN*, 28). Throughout *Desire of the Nations*, O'Donovan shows that speaking about Israel, salvation, the church and the Trinity makes it possible to '[reclaim] for faith what scepticism surrendered to mechanistic necessity' (*DN*, 3). Overcoming 'necessity' together with its adjacent voluntarism – especially in its post-Kantian epistemological dualism – had been not least one of the promises of Ramsey's transformism.[78] Throughout the biblical narrative, the nature and extent of divine–human mediation shifts and turns, each moment unlocking subsequent historical theological-political constellations. Most importantly, in the Christ-event, the mediation between God and humanity in Christ fundamentally and irreversibly transforms the mediating task of political institutions.

But that means there is a *two-part* story particularly also to political authority. First, the OT narrative of Israel yields the *grounds* of 'government-as-judgment': the 'natural authorities' of power, injured right and tradition. As mentioned, O'Donovan took this hermeneutical triad from Ramsey's *formal* analysis of authority as *lex*,

---

[76] O'Donovan, *The Ways of Judgment*.
[77] Cf. *DN*, 125.
[78] Cf. Bernd Wannenwetsch, 'Just War', in *The Cambridge Dictionary of Christian Theology*, ed. Ian A. McFarland, David A. S. Fergusson, Karen Kilby and Iain R. Torrance (Leiden: Cambridge University Press, 2011), pp. 255–7; Alain Badiou, *Ethics: An Essay on the Understanding of Evil* (London: Verso, 2001), esp. 'Ethics as the servant of necessity', pp. 30–4; O'Donovan *pace* Kant and Hume, *RMO*, 46.

ordo and *iustitia*. In O'Donovan's exegesis, Yhwh's authority was first established by accomplishing Israel's victorious deliverance from its enemies, which brings the need for *power* into focus. Second, the presence of judicial discrimination in Israel sets the doing of justice, the settling of *right*, as a ground for authority. 'Right' again invokes both public representation and a social order rather than individual rights only. Third, a *possession* to be handed down through the generations provides clarity about God's judgements, which give order and structure to the community 'and sustain it in being'. O'Donovan added faith or 'recognition' to these three. Notably, people's recognition of a government is not constitutive of authority. It is rather *demonstrative*: if the people do not recognize someone as an authority, that person has merely seized power[79] (*WJ*, 128).

In the Old Testament, political authority under Yhwh could still claim transcendence. Moses's role in the Book of Exodus 'corresponds to the same [tripartite] pattern: he leads the people out of Egypt to the victory of the Red Sea; he judges their cases in the wilderness; he lays before them the pattern of their new life in possession of their land at Sinai' (*DN*, 52). However, 'whereas Moses is conceived as the unitary mediator of divine rule in its three aspects, the prospect for the future is a diffused and differentiated mediation'. War as a sacral performance – God giving *immediate* directions in warfare – develops in the wake of Moses (who is never a military commander). Moreover, 'the Deuteronomic law developed the sacral conception in the direction of an elementary "just-war" code' (*DN*, 54).[80]

Yet such holy wars, O'Donovan argues, are done away with. The second part of the story is initiated by the watershed of the Christ-event, which is bound up in the history of Israel.[81] The appearance of *Christ's* authority in Jerusalem, and especially when he ascends to the Temple, is one of several key moment of the *eschatological fusion* between the old and new age. It 'meant the unity of political and religious spheres under the rule of God. Obedience and worship were to be one and the same. But that is to say: the Kingdom was the Lord's! The Two Kingdoms period, in which Temple without power and *praetorium* without worship coexisted in some kind of parallel, was declared closed' (*DN*, 117).

An account of secular political authority then requires Christology to show how 'the independence of the individual believer ... arises from the authority of another community, centred in the authority of the risen Christ' (*DN*, 123). Christ had two roles, O'Donovan explains. He is the mediator of God's rule, 'the role focussed centrally upon the Davidide monarch, though also borne in lesser and partial ways by other authorities in Israel, priestly and administrative'. Second, he is the 'representative individual, who in lonely faithfulness carries the tradition of the people, its fate and its

---

[79] This provides effectively a much stronger and continued challenge to governments than one might assume. If recognition or consent is constitutive, as in liberal democracies, *tacit* consent can always be assumed, if not to the government in question, then at least to 'the system' that put it in place. If recognition is demonstrative, however, then the *actual* authority of a government can be scrutinized and challenged at any point in time.

[80] *DN*, 49, 51–2, 55–7.

[81] Cf. O'Donovan's sermon, Church of the Incarnation, Dallas, TX, 2017: 'the whole truth of Jesus Christ was bound up for [St. Stephen] in the truth of the history of God's chosen people.'

promise, in his own destiny' (*DN*, 123). And 'when to this formal duality [of roles] is added the eschatological presence of God's Kingdom ... [we] must then speak of Christ as the *decisive* presence of God and the *decisive* presence of God's people' (*DN*, 123–4). So before Christ, God's rule had been mediated 'through the judicial tasks of angels and kings in all the nations'. But now divine authority 'is irreplaceably immediate in the dying, rising and future disclosing of Jesus' (*DN*, 124). In short, Christ is the *immediate mediator* of God.

The representative role of Christ marks a decisive moment in the history of Israel. He is the one to represent first Israel and eventually humanity. 'Christ's death, ... takes place within the sphere of the old authority; it represents the point at which the old is confronted and challenged; in the resurrection the challenge issues in the assertion of the new' (*DN*, 128). Here a dichotomy *within* Israel emerges through God's dealings with it: 'Jesus' death was the overthrow of God's cause at the hands of rebellious Israel; his resurrection was the reassertion of God's triumph over Israel' (*DN*, 129). Notably, 'he it is who *is* Israel, "the root"', and 'Israel must learn to see itself in terms of him; and when it does so, the struggle for Israel will have borne fruit' (131).[82] So what will eventually illuminate the relationship between state and church is a question of Israel's recognition of itself, its old and new ways vis-à-vis God.

Because of the not-yet of the full Kingdom, the simultaneity of the two ages, the material *polis* cannot be dismissed: 'The continuing Israel, which does not yet believe ... is not to be dismissed as an irrelevant survival from the past: "God has not rejected the people whom he foreknew!" (Rom. 11.2)' (*DN*, 131).[83] Israel's public tradition is not *nullified* by faith (a point we will return to later). The 'old' Israel persists in its 'public tradition', O'Donovan reminds the reader with Paul (Rom. 9.4). 'So until the last reconciliation the two communities must coexist, the one with the witness of public institutions, the other with a witness founded on and attesting faith, the community of circumcision and the community of baptism' (*DN*, 132). In short, 'In the Christ-event we found the elements of God's rule: an act of power, an act of judgment and the gift of possession. But these elements are presented in the narrative account of a decisive act, an act in which God's rule was mediated and his people reconstituted in Christ' (*DN*, 133).

With 'Christ's triumph', Israel's military victory is no longer sacred, neither is the possession of land and law. Christ marks victory and salvation; *he* is now the possession of Israel. In light of that transformative, mediating Christ-event, however, the mediating task of government has been transformed too:

> But secular authorities are no longer in the fullest sense mediators of the rule of God. They mediate his judgments only. The power that they exercise in defeating their enemies, the national possessions they safeguard, these are now rendered irrelevant by Christ's triumph. This is what might properly be meant by that misleading expression, the 'desacralisation' of politics by the Gospel. No

---

[82] NB: 'In the mean time the "grafting" of the Gentiles onto Israel's root [by faith] cannot change the fact that it is Israel's root that they are grafted onto.'

[83] Also *DN*, 132.

government has a right to exist, no nation has a right to defend itself. Such claims are overwhelmed by the immediate claim of the Kingdom. There remains simply the rump of political authority which cannot be dispensed with yet, the exercise of judgment. (*DN*, 151)

Now, the authorized political act, this rump of political authority, contains elements both of 'natural authorities' and divine authorization. We saw that O'Donovan derived the grounds of government – power, right and tradition – exegetically, though this is also a *theory* of political authority: '...one whose possession of *might* is in accord with the *established order* of a society takes responsibility for the *righting of wrongs* within that society' (*RMO*, 128). Genuine political authority 'cannot arise except where one and the same agency can dispose of all three' (*WJ*, 142). Power without right and tradition is mere violence. If one has a right but no power, such right has no effect. In that sense, natural disasters threaten the *polis*, and no statesmen can rule without arms or ink in their pen. Equally, tradition on its own is evidently not political. So authority is grounded in creation or three distinct 'natural authorities'; these are realistic foundations of authority, though without being 'realist' (viz. *RMO*, 62).

As part of a 'theistic' political theory,[84] the political act mediates Right. But the act itself holds a mediate position between the 'natural authorities', its grounds, and a divine 'energy' in order to come into actual being. In other words, power, right and tradition require what others call *historical luck* to come together. This recalibrates contractarian political theories and accounts for the 'alien', 'non-reciprocal' character of political authority as something that is not only our self-alienated will.[85] In conjunction with human cooperation (viz. Ockham), authority comes to be through the 'providential gift of authority' (*WJ*, 129). Providence marks the point at which the theory of political authority turns into *actuality*.[86] Notably, this is not 'a *special* intervention of the divine to appoint a particular ruler, but a *general* provision of non-reciprocal relations under which we may flourish' (*WJ*, 129).

Joan Lockwood O'Donovan has explicated this 'dual authorisation' by natural authority and 'divine energy': the authorization both from below and above avoids overemphasizing either.[87] With that in mind, O'Donovan's reading of authorities as 'angelic' becomes intelligible: 'The political rulers of the world are angelic and spiritual precisely because they are representative; and they are political rulers precisely because they are angelic and spiritual. In the cross they meet the final representative identity of mankind' (*WJ*, 231–2).[88]

---

[84] Cf. *DN*, 31–2, where O'Donovan juxtaposes the 'humanist' with the 'theistic' 'families' of political theories.

[85] Cf. Hegel, *Elements of the Philosophy of Right*, § 324 (Cambridge: Cambridge University Press, 2003), p. 361.

[86] Reminiscent of the left-wing legal theorist Costas Douzinas, who said at a public lecture in 2012: 'The revolution is like falling in love: it happens to you, it slaps you in the face and sweeps you off your feet.'

[87] Joan Lockwood O'Donovan, 'Political Authority and European Community: The Challenge of the Christian Political Tradition', *Scottish Journal of Theology*, 47 (1994), 1–18.

[88] Critical about O'Donovan's often idealized reading of the Christian past is Gorringe, 'Authority, Plebs and Patricians', 27.

Because of their 'angelic' – that is, representative and Christ-analogous – character, authorities may also become *demonic* when they usurp the place of Christ's present authority. This moment occurs when political and the transcendent become *identical*: 'When believers find themselves confronted with an order that, implicitly or explicitly, offers itself as the sufficient and necessary condition of human welfare, they will recognise the beast. When a political structure makes this claim, we call it "totalitarian"' (*DN*, 274). A more subtle form of such an imposition on Christ's rule is to propose 'self-interpreting doctrines which define metaphysical parameters for thought and action' or indeed the disavowal of metaphysics altogether, a characteristic of modernity. At least in *Desire of the Nations*, where O'Donovan is careful to note that neither Rome nor the old Israel have been 'deauthorised', 'modernity' suggests itself a 'Antichrist, a parodic and corrupt development of Christian social order' (*DN*, 275).[89] Whether this is an entirely justified claim or not, O'Donovan's critique of alternative conceptions of 'political authority' draws much of its strength from a genealogy of modernity (*DN*, 275). Significant for our project here: it refrains from a conclusive authorization of any *institutional form* of government and hence legitimate authority to use violent force.

O'Donovan's theo-logic thus engenders a matrix for critique, readjustment but also *tentative endorsement* of the just war proposals examined previously. All rule unified in Christ, the eschatological *not yet* effects a 'transitory duality' (*DN*, 93) between the remaining 'structure of Israel' and the new Israel of the Church. Moving again beyond Ramsey, O'Donovan starts from the ecclesial locus. After the Christ-event, he says, God's people are gathered in the church.[90] The church is the social and political presence of the fulfilment of the Kingdom of God and the promises made to Israel. It is in itself a political society in which one participates by faith (*DN*, 166). The identity of the church and the believer's identity are primary to all other political ones: 'Identified with him in his baptism, the believer is identified with Israel present in him, and so with the church which is Israel baptised with the Holy Spirit' (*DN*, 178). In that way, political government cannot be absorbed into the church.

Against idealist scepticism and liberal internationalism

This transforms the approaches to political authority we have encountered so far and their theo-logics of mediation. First, what one might call a *political* enthusiasm or idealism – in the form of *scepticism*.[91] Here, all become just war authorities. In O'Donovan's reading, in this form the liberal idea itself has drifted away from its ecclesial moorings and has become utterly politicized. Originally, the liberal idea presupposed the Christian triumph over all kings and authorities: 'It is a paradigm for the birth of free society, grounded in the recognition of a superior authority which

---

[89] Cf. Bruce Ward, *Redeeming the Enlightenment: Christianity and the Liberal Virtues* (Grand Rapids, MI: William B. Eerdmans, 2010).

[90] On Augustine's tendency to conflate the 'ideal with the actual' church, cf. John M. Rist, *Augustine: Ancient Thought Baptized* (Cambridge: Cambridge University Press, 1996), p. 253.

[91] This we have encountered particularly in Rodin and Ramsey, most strongly in his agapist-sceptical phase, though Steinhoff draws on this tradition most extensively.

renders all authorities beneath it relative and provisional' (*DN*, 252). After all, 'Where the Spirit of the Lord is, there is liberty' (2 Cor. 3.18). Here is the political society and fellowship, the 'free and worshipping embrace of God's rule'. True political freedom (paradoxically) is that of the believer in Christ. However, the modern connection between individual reason and 'totalized politics' turns this ecclesial principle into ubiquitous judgement, albeit one that has no power. O'Donovan relates this to a wrapped-up global assent to or dissent from a war: 'The worst crimes in war tend to be committed later in its course, when patience and discipline have worn thin. But by the time the leaders of the nations are driven to resort to the worst excesses of wickedness, the public has so exhausted its rhetorical resources that it is liable to let the fact pass without notice' (*JWR*, 18).

Indeed, a case can made that something like this has actually happened in the past decade, a collective, drowsy settling into the 'militarization of peace',[92] mixed with simultaneous oblivion as to what is to be done in Afghanistan, Iraq and more recently Libya and Syria. This is frequently mixed with a rejection of political responsibility altogether.[93] So the politically realized ideal of individual authority, formerly rooted in the *ecclesia*, is rejected by O'Donovan as impractical or at least less effective than the approach might seem.[94]

The second possibility of *political* idealism is equally unacceptable for O'Donovan. It consists in realizing a universal humanistic/humanitarian ideal as a global authority. This can take two forms: accepting the pope as the highest moral arbitrator between states, one that can even step in as a 'king'.[95] We encountered this kind of (quasi-)papal global mediating institution in Chapter 2 on David Rodin. For his part, O'Donovan locates this acute possibility between two theological-political currents: on the one hand, a Christian idealism, for which John Wyclif is exemplary: the concept of secular 'dominion by God's grace' meant that '*ius* must flow from the fountain-head of *iustitia*' – human law should rest on evangelical law. This, however, makes the notion of *natural* political authority inoperable.[96] On the other side stands the Salamanca School's search for political order in creation and the natural human capacity of justice; 'a Christian secularism'. O'Donovan argues that this tension requires 'mediation' – 'a political order which *itself* discloses and reveals the judging presence of God in society' (*DN*, 27). His turn to Israel is then precisely the turn away from claiming 'that role for the church – as the medieval papalists did, and as it is now fashionable to do once again'. The reason is that 'the church's bona fides as a political structure cannot simply be taken for granted.

---

[92] Reza Negarestani, 'The Militarization of Peace: Absence of Terror or Terror of Absence?', *Collapse* 1 (2006), 53–92.

[93] In that regard the differences between John Howard Yoder and Oliver O'Donovan rightfully merit continuous attention. See e.g. P. Travis Kroeker, *Messianic Political Theology and Diaspora Ethics: Essays in Exile* (Eugene, OR: Cascade, 2017), p. 8; Kroeker rightfully points out that what is at stake is not merely 'pacifism' or not but a question of the pattern (or *nomos*) of communal discipleship.

[94] Nigel Biggar has taken issue with this (see also Chapter 6).

[95] Honorius Augustodunensis, *Summa Gloria de apostolic et augusto* 3 in *DN*, 163; Otto Friedrich von Gierke, *Political Theories of the Middle Age* (Cambridge: Cambridge University Press, 1900), p. 117, n. 32; James of Viterbo, *DN*, 168.

[96] NB: theologically qualified idealism refers to what Elshtain called 'utopian' or 'sectarian' versions of Christian politics.

It has to be shown to arise out of the church's relation to Israel, a relation which itself safeguards the church against dangers of theocratic tyranny and inauthenticity that arise, as history shows, from its flexing of political muscle' (*DN*, 27).

As I argued in Chapter 2, the post-Napoleonic version of medieval-papalist mediation is international legal institutionalism. O'Donovan certainly highlights that the United Nations differs from papal authority. One is ostensibly secular, the other spiritual; one accepts the givenness of states and is constituted by them, the other pronounces on their legitimacy. Nonetheless, 'The claims of papalism at their best anticipate those which have driven the search for international authority in later times, and, indeed, were the original inspiration for them' (*WJ*, 216). From his theological perspective, O'Donovan senses the flicker of conflict as they both have 'humanity' as their subject: 'The word of God is abroad on the earth; the community of God tastes of the life of heaven on earth. There is no vacancy for a substitute for these, and if there were, it would not take the form of a politically constituted organ with juridical, parliamentary, and administrative organisation' (*WJ*, 218).

From a practical perspective, the international community remains 'an abstract universal' (*WJ*, 217); it is not a real community.[97] It cannot claim authority and dispose of authority in the same way a representative government can. Hence, O'Donovan explicitly criticises the tendency to view the United Nations as 'a temple enclosed in its sacred *temenos*, kept apart from the profane compromise of political action in order to give voice to a claim that transcends human politics in permanently critical posture' (*WJ*, 218).[98]

O'Donovan then identifies the theological mistake underlying such global institutional mediation of justice: the unbearable hiddenness of Christ's rule, discernible only by faith:

> The temptation besets the church to make its hidden government visible by a representative icon of the ruling Christ. Charged to realise the premonarchical confidence of Israel that it had no king but Yhwh, the church compromises itself which it asserts from its midst a ruling entity to act on Christ's behalf, matching the claims of secular rulers with counterclaims. If Erastianism is an instance of the first mistake, papalism is a striking example of this one. (*DN*, 166)

In other words, a global institutional mediation of the rule of Christ alienates the church from its immediate subjection to Christ. But the representative moment in Christ cannot be duplicated. An immanent world state cannot represent humanity; the papal ministry cannot represent the church.

Leaving aside these idealisms, O'Donovan nonetheless also sees moments where they are positively integrated. First, the 'church as politeia' and moral agent embodies – and directs to worship God – the *society* that would otherwise atomize

---

[97] For a juxtaposition of Catholicism as abstract or concrete universality, see Slavoj Žižek, John Milbank and Creston Davis, *The Monstrosity of Christ: Paradox or Dialectic?* (Cambridge: MIT Press, 2009), p. 294.

[98] In this regard, he is as Protestant as Kant, whose ground of *Vernunft* was the mediate ground between church and state absolutism.

into pietist individual particulars. In that sense, O'Donovan fleshes out a political ecclesiology that neither Elshtain nor Ramsey explicitly formulated. For Christian realism, the church was either an institutional, administrative and hence political entity or a spiritual-individual horizon of subjective moral experience. Christians had to choose between church and state or assimilate the two. Both options drew the political sting out of it, hence the state was given the sole political burden. O'Donovan's ecclesial Other vis-à-vis government, in contrast, is *tri*-partite: a spiritual, a visible (in communion and Spirit) and an institutional entity.[99] Precisely this triadic understanding challenges the dual logical possibilities of separation or identity between church and state and merges the two into a continuous *calling*.[100] In that way, O'Donovan rechannels moral idealism into an actual alternative community:

> Of course, the mere imagination of a universal society, as an ideal or a project, will not suffice for such an *ascesis*; for it can provide no real social identity, but only entangle us in a contested cause. We must become actual members of a real community constituted by the real and present image of God as uniquely lord, and the real and present image of mankind as subject uniquely to God. Jesus Christ, very God and very man, is the double representative around whom such a community has come into being. (*COL*, 44)

Conceptually, the church as a political, spiritual and institutional factor preserves the continuous moral challenge to the state. But to avoid a merely general statement that there is a 'challenge', we need to look at how this works.

While the political act is the act of judgement, then the church heeds a 'Judge not, that you be not judged!' (Matt. 7.1). In that sense, the church can be a 'counter-political' source from which all reconciling 'evangelical counter-praxis' springs in its mediate position between antagonistic, sovereigntist realism and liberal-internationalist idealism and/or scepticism. If the paradox of contemporaneity between old and new Israel was the ground of the political act, there is now room for evangelical citizenship that transforms political citizenship. O'Donovan suggests a conceptually temporal opening, a 'door through which the political can re-enter the counter-political' (*WJ*, 235). This door, this transitional place, O'Donovan calls the 'moment of obedience' or the moment of 'transcendent criticism' (*DN*, 13). And here he thinks further the position of immediate connection to the universal, which Ramsey had related to his (Nietzschean) *agape*.

Beyond criticism, the 'Judge not!' and 'Judge for yourselves!' together remain paradox. It does not force an exclusivist or even abolitionist wedge of 'either-or' between church freedom and state obedience, moral reflection and practical deliberation (*DN*, 13) or an individual 'Judge not' against a political-representative 'Judge!' Instead, it holds the two together (*WJ*, 157). Crucially, O'Donovan is again reluctant to claim

---

[99] I find an interesting echo of this in Karl Popper, 'Three Worlds', Tanner Lecture on Human Values (1978), http://tannerlectures.utah.edu/lectures/documents/popper80.pdf (accessed 1 March 2012).
[100] This brings into political view the Pauline ministry and mission.

alliance with any political programme. In a key passage towards the end of *Ways of Judgment*, he articulates the paradoxical nature of freedom and obedience:

> When we judge for ourselves, we judge that the good that God by his own judgment has set before us to do is now open for us to do. When we persist in judging when judgment should have been given closure, we impose a division between evil and good that no longer corresponds to God's own division, and so fails to put before us the good that God has willed for us to do. (*WJ*, 236)

However, (dis)satisfying this may be for the reader searching for a statement on a particular conflict, here lies the source for O'Donovan's notion of 'sympathetic deliberation' on the just war. It is not 'freedom-as-defiance' (*WJ*, 67) but freedom within social structures. The free individual is not *ex ante* suppressed by 'the authorities that exist' but a communal being in solidarity. This must be 'the other side' of political obedience (*WJ*, 54). Judging for themselves, individuals are both asked to collaborate with authority but to do so quite while judging and acting independently. Effectively, the question, 'What is my role at this point and in this situation?' replaces the sentence 'If I was the president, I would…'.

O'Donovan's reference to Kierkegaard is no coincidence here. It was Kierkegaard who noted precisely this paradoxical freedom in obedience and obedience in freedom – despite himself in the spirit of Hegel and, after all, Luther. Bernd Wannenwetsch, stretching the positive, God-praising role of government more than O'Donovan is willing to, calls this 'soul citizenship'. We are neither completely free, spirited citizens nor mere subject bodies. In this sense, every person must consider her own role and responsibility (*JWR*, 16). This can be identified as the space for 'the possibility of informal [judicial] pronouncements which carry moral authority', perhaps not unrelated to what Ramsey in his transformist phase called a 'constitutional revolution'.[101] Hence, pace authors such as Rodin or Steinhoff (who had particular traditional authors in mind), just war thinking is *not* only for kings and queens, while subservient citizens quietly refer their judgement or disagreement to private religion, the family table or the digital swarms on Facebook[102] (*WJ*, 233). Liberal 'idealism' or scepticism is integrated after all but in both a more active ('responsible') and reduced (forgiving) nature.

In the same way, O'Donovan's dismissal of the United Nations' quasi-theological pretensions and institutional misconceptions does not altogether dismiss it. It is 'an international point of reference … to frame the decisions of national governments' and 'a framework of lawfulness within which action may be responsible and coordinated' (*WJ*, 218). In this role, as an admonitory, interpretative body, it corresponds to the international order described earlier. However, the unifying order of the world under Yhwh's ultimate mediating rule was always *law* – law as God's history and

---

[101] NB: O'Donovan drops Ramsey's constitutionalism on the grounds that it may become ideological; see *WJ*, 155–6.

[102] Certainly, Schmitt believed that a completely digitalized notion of democracy is the end of democracy. Norbert Campagna, *Le Droit, le Politique et la Guerre: Deux Chapitres sur la Doctrine de Carl Schmitt* (Saint-Nicolas: Les Presses de l'Université Laval, 2004), p. 58.

judgements – not a world government. Yhwh 'is present in a kind of concealed immediacy in the law' (*DN*, 50). Nonetheless, that doesn't amount to lega*lism*. International law, like any other institution, is 'concrete, limited, and therefore to some degree blind'. And although its development 'has been one of the most welcome achievements of the 20th century ... is certainly capable of its own deep blindness'. Yet, the 'pursuit of common good ... requires us to make sure that the search for a more competent and less blind institution goes on and responds to shifting international demands'.[103]

In short, O'Donovan relocates the political act in its ecclesial context. The church as a tripartite entity prevents it from becoming a merely spiritual dimension that acquiesces to sovereign, possibly dictatorial politics. Neither is it a fully political, institutional actor in the international sphere. Instead, the freedom and 'soul citizenship' of the individual within a peaceful, non-judging community can continuously challenge and redirect the 'secular' political act and institution.

Against sovereigntism, individual and global

O'Donovan's rejection of political realism focuses on private, sovereign, antagonistic authority. That also can take different forms.[104] If an idealistic, liberal internationalism treads upon the governance and freedom of Christ and church, 'realism' marks the retreat from these spheres for the sake of an ethical naturalism. That it can then again reclaim ecclesial and Christian freedom makes realism the matching opposite of idealism. As argued in Part One, they are two sides of the same coin – and potentially two forms of 'atheism', as Ramsey complained.

O'Donovan's critique of political realism is mainly a critique of voluntarism, the centrality of the individual will in connection with instrumental reason as the final arbitrator between humans and their surrounding world. This was already indicated in the analysis of 'political reality' above, but here the political subject is the focus. An ethic of successful imposition of will does not presume a peaceful interplay between agent and his surrounding environment, a vision of natural paradise. On the contrary, it presupposes a disjunction between individual will and an external reality, as O'Donovan points out repeatedly (*RMO*, 18, 131–7). And this is at odds with his 'reality principle' of a vindicated creation order in which humans freely participate.

Realist sovereigntism in an individualist mode explicates the largely self-defensive implications of human rights. The problematic collapse of ecclesial and political individualism in mind, O'Donovan's critique pits individual claim rights against

---

[103] Oliver O'Donovan, 'The Common Good: Does It Represent a Political Programme', 1 December 2017, Futures of Public Theology Conference, University of Edinburgh, https://www.youtube.com/watch?v=vuTx6Z2jkzU (accessed 13 August 2018). Here O'Donovan remarks, 'Those who developed Western institutionalism out of the twin legacies of Roman jurisprudence and Christian theology understood very well that the key to its success was not inventiveness of new institutions, but discovery of overlooked resources, [i.e.] ... the so-called *ius gentium*, half-rooted in nature, half in custom ... Within that tradition each nation could expect to find its own best practices and highest expectations reflected back to it by its international context.'

[104] Martin Luther, *Lecture on Romans*, ed. Wilhelm Pauck (Louisville, KY: Westminster John Knox Press, 2006), pp. 159–61.

justice-as-right order.[105] The possibility of the political act, 'the exercise of authority itself', is the question (*DN*, 249). The equation of individual rights and political judgement, he thinks, is incorrect. Private persons, who act on their own behalf, cannot 'establish a new public context'. Even if they serve the common good, private actions do not do it representatively 'on behalf' of the community (*WJ*, 23). Rights as 'primitive endowments of power' (*DN*, 262) lead to an 'acephalous society', which makes the political act impossible apart from technocratic forms of controlling and manipulating society. 'In championing the authority of the political act, however, we champion society itself.'

This is inseparable from questions of *common* goods and the common life, which is created sociality's *bene esse*. The fact that individuals are wronged is never *only* an infringement upon their rights but '[flows] from the concept of "a wrong" (the noun), which is an offence against the moral order governing relations among God's creatures'.[106] So, if individualist sovereigntism champions individual rights as *sui generis* authoritative, the common good gets lost (or becomes optional, potentially arbitrary, as we saw in Steinhoff). If the focus is on *individual* victims, the communal, social and indeed *cosmic* repercussions of injustice and suffering get lost. Combined with a utilitarian calculus that trumps the rights-as-trumps, such a loss can then become acceptable.

The common good or the welfare of human beings can hardly be reduced to the humanistic principle (explicitly at the heart of Rodin's proposal). So both O'Donovan and Joan Lockwood O'Donovan have suggested modifying this view.[107] The well-being of individuals is essential, but this can only take shape in a social and communal form, certainly also in view of a body like the church being a communal agent. If an ontological peace is the basic assumption of vindicated creation order, then a fundamental difference and contest between prior, subjective individual rights is untenable. Human nature and created order are different moments, but they are inseparable: 'Without "nature" around it in which it can take its place, "human nature" can be nothing but an insubstantial phantom, visible only through some ectoplasmic formula such as "radical freedom"' (*RMO*, 18).

Looking at the modern state as sovereign rights holder, the same problems arise. O'Donovan's challenge to statism has already been mentioned – the 'tidy regime of sovereign states as the sole legitimate authorities is untenable. But what about 'benevolent empire', which after all escapes the 'isolationism' of sovereign states? Two analytical approaches are possible. One could either see empire as the political institutionalization and enforcement of a universal ideal, the obverse of Rodin's liberal internationalism. Alternatively, it may be understood as the universal, even mythical

---

[105] For a critique, see e.g. Wolterstorff, *Justice: Rights and Wrongs*, pp. 68–75; responses in special issue of *Studies in Christian Ethics*, 23 (2010); in his response, O'Donovan notes that Wolterstorff's 'primary justice' of rights ironically is similar to the moral order O'Donovan suggests. 'The Language of Rights and Conceptual History', *Journal of Religious Ethics*, 37 (2009), 193–207, p. 199.

[106] Ibid.

[107] 'Faith and Globalization'; interview with Joan Lockwood O'Donovan, http://www.youtube.com/watch?v=5yV8Qg8wXuQ (accessed 7 October 2011).

extension of a defensive-expansive political agent.[108] When talking about *Christian imperialism*, O'Donovan discerns the former option and recognizes its theological root, not merely the power interests of *imperium*.[109] But he criticizes it as Christian moral idealism that praises in empire the *concordia* only God knows (*WJ*, 213). The heritage here is that of Rome and Eusebius's praise, which reoccurs in Dante's *De Monarchia*, with a world state reflecting Christ's rule.[110] That Dante (sometimes together with Aquinas) is read as a precursor of international 'idealism' should not obscure the fact that his world community under Christ's rule finds expression in a unified *political* rather than supra-political, papal structure. The influence of Aristotelianism explains this

> confidence in 'natural' political society with a solid and independent structure of its own, a society for which much more in the way of social virtue could be claimed than might be suggested by those who like to recall Augustine's aphorism about large-scale criminal gangs. Justice itself was a natural virtue. (*DN*, 207)[111]

O'Donovan himself has come under the suspicion of Constantinianism, but arguably his political conceptuality of Israel in the light of Christ's triumph explicitly sets it *against* such pretensions.[112] In O'Donovan's reading, Yhwh's rule safeguarded his people's welfare and the international order. The king of humanity may only be encountered in Christ now so that there is no space for humanity as a world community governed by a world state. The story of Babylon, the separation between peoples through language was 'Yhwh's safeguard against the titanism of imperial pretensions' (*DN*, 70). And even when God was acting through empires, it was to *reign in* and guide back on the righteous path his people (*DN*, 86). Again, a line is to be drawn between a (secular) neo-conservatism and what O'Donovan calls the 'idealist imperialism' (*WJ*, 259) in the wake of the Enlightenment that is the heir of papalism and canon law. As we saw in Part One, the *actual* agents are rather different, indeed opposed parties.[113] From a merely logical perspective, or a Christian witness to world peace, there is no difference (*WJ*, 16). To O'Donovan, Kant's 'imperial idealism' is as suspect as is 'imperial democratization' (*WJ*, 259), both pushed back by Christ and exposed as hubristic.[114] He reinforces this

---

[108] Henri Xavier Arquillière, *L'Augustinisme Politique: Essai sur la Formation des Théories Politiques du Moyen-Age* (Paris: J. Vrin, 1955), p. 54; Milbank, *Theology and Social Theory*, p. 425.

[109] O'Donovan's reading of Marsilius of Padua as an imperialist theologian (*DN*, 207) is matched by George Garnett's, *Marsilius of Padua and 'the Truth of History'* (Oxford: Oxford University Press, 2006).

[110] Dante Alighieri, *De Monarchia*, Bk. 1, Chapter iv–vi.

[111] O'Donovan here reads John of Paris, Dante and Marsilius closely together, see WJ, 60 n. 4.; *DN*, 207.

[112] *DN*, 72, 122, 130, 140, 147. See also Dorothea H. Bertschmann, *Bowing before Christ – Nodding to the State?: Reading Paul Politically with Oliver O'Donovan and John Howard Yoder* (London: Bloomsbury T&T Clark, 2014), pp. 50, 64.

[113] Mark Mazower, *Governing the World: The History of an Idea* (London: Allen Lane, 2012). See also Chapter 2.

[114] *Pace* Stephen H. Webb's astonishingly distorting *American Providence: A Nation with a Mission* (New York: Continuum, 2004), pp. 104–8. See William T. Cavanaugh, 'Messianic Nation', *University of St. Thomas Law Journal*, (2005), 261–80. For a new exploration of empire in the British context, though initially from a historical perspective, see Nigel Biggar's 'Ethics and Empire' project.

from an ecclesiological angle, especially the Hauerwasian demand for Israel to remain in Babylon: 'To treat the coexistence of Israel and Babylon as a permanent ordinance was, in effect, to accept the emperor's own assessment of himself, to bow down before his image of gold' (*DN*, 88).

Political action between (self-)love and law – faith performing reconciling judgement

So far it has become clear that for O'Donovan the political *act* constitutes and reinforces institutions, not vice versa. However, in terms of its theological understanding, how does this political act steer between moral idealism and realistic action?

First, the ruling God as the horizon of action elicits faith or 'recognition'. The *sola fide* sets faith-as-worship as the primary *point d'entrée* to evangelical counter-praxis, that is, just war action. Yet, this is no mere fideism. O'Donovan's Old Testament exegesis initially brings out the connection between worship and political authority:

> Yhwh's rule receives its answering recognition in the praises of his people. ... The link which ties the exercise of Yhwh's kingly rule to the praise of his people is that as the people congregate to perform their act of praise, the political reality of Israel is displayed. (*DN*, 47)

Subsequently, after the Christ-event, this political praise is replaced by faith. Israel, both old and new, is 'God's servant'. As judgement itself must be made in obedient faithfulness, it recognizes God's sovereignty.

This faithful obedience mends a fundamental disjunction, the Aristotelian dichotomy between theoretical insight and praxis. Following a Platonist-Augustinian instinct, O'Donovan mends them, not through a *tertium quid* but 'a union of the two, a *both-and*' as 'affective knowledge'.[115] 'We know only as we love', he quotes Augustine. Hence,

> Knowledge, which participates in the eternal Word of God, is consubstantial and coeternal with the Love that is God's eternal Spirit. All knowledge, then, has an affective aspect, just as all love has a cognitive aspect. Our experience of knowing is that of discerning good and welcoming it *as* good. (*COL*, 11)

Once I know what is right and just and true, O'Donovan says, there is even a '*sovereign uselessness* of moral reflection' (*COL*, 17). There is no 'theory' and separate 'praxis' of love. 'The object of love is not an act of our own, but simply – to use an

---

http://www.mcdonaldcentre.org.uk/ethics-and-empire (last accessed 9 August 2018). Biggar distinguishes between empire, imperialism and interventionism.

[115] Oliver O'Donovan, *Common Objects of Love: Moral Reflection and the Shaping of Community* (Grand Rapids, MI William B. Eerdmans, 2002), p. 9. Hereafter *COL*. Stephen Joel Garver, '"There Is Another King": Gospel as Politics – Notes towards a Theology of Community', in *Christian Body Politic*, ed. Christian Kim (Cheltenham: Hermit Kingdom Press, 2004), pp. 13–52, p. 19. See also 'The Trinity and the Moral Life: *In Memoriam John Webster*', see Introduction.

Augustinian phrase again – the "enjoyment" of its object, and "enjoyment" is not the name of something we do, but of a relation in which we stand' (*COL*, 16). The act of love, in other words, in O'Donovan's fusion is not the imposition of will (*pace* the voluntarist tradition) but peaceful relatedness-in-difference. Milbank, referenced in *JWR*, calls it the 'peaceful transmission of difference'. Harmony is the *telos* of difference and simultaneously requires difference in a non-violent form.

Yet O'Donovan's evangelical shortcut to political action is not merely a static or unprecedented love, especially in a social context of recollection and response to evildoing.[116] The union of theory and praxis or faith working through love also has a 'transitional duality' between law/judgement and love. The latter takes the divine, universal perspective. Yet, even though justified war means *facing* antagonistic praxis with a different praxis, that is not merely a form of universal, indiscriminate love. Specifically, the notion of discrimination brings this into focus:

> In the eyes of God the soul of a soldier is of no less value than the soul of a milkman: why hesitate, we may wonder, to kill the milkman, if we do not hesitate to kill the soldier? … We have a specific human duty laid upon us, which is to distinguish innocence and guilt as far as is given us in the conduct of human affairs, not in order to put in question the equality of all human persons before God, but in order to respect the limits which God sets upon our invasion of other people's lives. (*JWR*, 47)

Between a static ideal of love and potentially revengeful justice, O'Donovan's notion of 'the service of reconciliation' presents a 'third' derived from recognizing Christ's lordship. This residual duality or 'third', however, itself results from Christ's being and work, a not-yet fully complete reconciliation of God and humankind.

This brings to focus the relationship between the old and the new aeon, law and the gospel of love. Like Ramsey, O'Donovan draws attention to Jesus' saying, 'Do not suppose that I have come to destroy the law and the prophets. I have not come to destroy them but to fulfil them' (Mt. 5.17). He distinguishes two interpretations of 'fulfilment': either it means fulfilling all the requirements of law so that the law is no longer needed or love is an add-on to the law, an optional extra.[117] Both options, notably, sharply distinguish between love and law, both allowing either for the anti-legalism of a state's 'exceptionalism' or the moralizing of that state's politics.[118] Conversely, they allow for the dissolution of politics into an order of love.

O'Donovan again discerns a third possibility: '*expectation* is what Israel has inherited, *fulfilment* is the satisfaction of that expectation' (*DN*, 109). There is now a responsibility directly to God, the 'obedience within the hidden sphere of attitudes

---

[116] Oliver O'Donovan, 'Law, Moderation and Forgiveness', in *Church as Politeia – The Political Self-Understanding of Christianity*, ed. Christoph Stumpf and Holger Zaborowski (Berlin: Walter de Gruyter, 2004), pp. 1–12.

[117] The first version is closer to Milbank, the latter to liberal Christian realism.

[118] For O'Donovan's interaction with and parting from Lutheranism, though not necessarily Luther, see *RMO*, 144 f, 153–5; cf. also O'Donovan, 'Law, Moderation and Forgiveness', p. 1.

and actions that are open to God's eyes alone'.[119] The inner and the outer man are now public before God, requiring the same seriousness.

Elsewhere, O'Donovan relates reconciliation and judgement (i.e. hate the sin, love the sinner) to divine justification in God's act in Christ: 'God's decisive act of justice was a *constitutive* act, just by virtue of the justice it brought about, not solely by its response to obligation, and it took form as an act of forgiveness' (*WJ*, 93). Judgement, as indicated earlier, is only intelligible from a 'Judge not!', the 'point of transition between the political and the counter-political, the defining limit where closure is imposed upon the act of judgment'. In short, the moral dimension of judgement here is both more intense, because it includes the inner attitudes and motivations, and less intense, because it also includes the prospect of reconciliation.

Practically, this requires a perfection and generosity that does not stay 'within the limits which public rationality sets on its approval of benevolence'. It puts loving judgement in the realm of the heart and therefore makes intention morally relevant in the first place. To be content with a public legal framework is 'hypocrisy'. 'An extravagant, unmeasured goodness, corresponding to God's own providential care, defies the logic of public expectation' (*DN*, 109). A perfect synonym for generosity and the rejection of hypocrisy is 'performance' – active mediation, as one might understand it; meanwhile, the analogical act of judgement is limited by a reflective-critical self-transcendence, by 'judgment on judgment': 'Forgiveness corrects the established pattern of justice as the pattern of justice corrects itself by attending to itself and passing judgment on itself.' In view of Just War thinking, this thought turns out to be central, because it upholds the doctrine of double effect: discrimination has a focus on *intentions* and their objective, proportionate correlations. As Steinhoff (Chapter 3) had noted, it relies on an appeal to agents' hearts before a divine public court.

So although the biblical love command initially serves to understand Christian discipleship in war (Augustine) or the virtue of charity provided the starting point (Aquinas), love and justice do not collapse into each other (*JWR*, 9). Neither do they stand side by side, the political act being judgement, whereas love is non-judgement, suspended in a 'time of war' or relegated to a private forgiveness, the sphere of internal motive or a prospective 'after the war' (as for Elshtain). Instead, the dialectic between antinomian or private forward-looking forgiveness and a backward-looking Deist conception of mechanical justice here is replaced by an actually 'limited' judgement. Limited not by tragic failure ('Implementing democracy does not work') in view of an eschatological rift but limited because forgiveness – even in judgement – 'assumes a controlling immediacy' (*RMO*, 155). Love (or forgiveness) and justice stand in a paradoxical relationship when love 'can smite, and even slay' (*JWR*, 9). Faithful love and lethal judgement are kept distinct yet merge, flowing into analogous performance, the 'reconciling act of judgment' in 'the theatre of war'.

---

[119] Pace Steinhoff, God may be a 'spy' here, but this is certainly not accessible to others; and unlike a spy, God doesn't pretend to be someone else (as already Plato would let Socrates have it in the *Republic*).

O'Donovan's correction of the stark (Pauline) opposition between gospel love and the Mosaic Law also connects action to reality: in the light of the vindicated creation order, an ordered moral response is itself evangelical. First, the act of judgement is ordered by international law and corresponds to the ordered international sphere, a pluralistic set of nations.[120] Second, the law is there and already fulfilled from the point of view of God's generous love. This makes the analogical performance of judgement *possible* in the first place. O'Donovan's demand, with Vitoria, that in this vein a warring government must transcend its own interest and judge as between two claimants then entails the varied limitations of the act of judgement: not to aim for a destruction of the neighbour, to discriminate and to proportion one's action to a good. The median guilt of the soldier that leads to post-war immunity is equally included in this understanding, as is the notion of punishment, including between states. It is not merely reactive, authoritative retribution that presumes a hierarchy of states, even if just a temporary one. O'Donovan especially conceives the notion of punishment as having a *limiting* effect on the act of judgement, because it has both the wrongdoing of the other party as well as the horizon of settling a right with them in view.

Just War thinking as a prophetic task of the church

The fact that O'Donovan's approach is inextricably linked to a confession of Christian faith also changes what is meant by 'just war' thinking. Elshtain's Christian realism could see 'just war' as a 'theory' or 'account of statecraft', thus merely abstracting from 'the reality of the situation' and moralizing it in an attempt to edify. By contrast, Rodin set law against political praxis, an approach that – analogously to a frequent experience of the medieval church – is for the most part confined to 'tears and prayers', collapsed into tragedy or implied a (hypothetical) global war. While pushing humanistic principles to their conclusion, Steinhoff championed the defensive individual but above all offered a sharp critique of existing just war proposals. Similarly critical was Ramsey's agapeic scepticism of just war 'excuses'; via his 'just war as democracy', in later years he offered a 'mythopoetic' reading of political 'opposed systems'; he explicitly rejected the idea of just war thinking as some sort of 'prophecy' (particularly with theologians' left-liberal internationalism in mind).

O'Donovan's 'just-war theory' (he accepts the term only as a 'misnomer' [*JWR*, vii]) is first of all rooted in a consistent reluctance to separate 'ethics' from Christian theology in general and his hermeneutical theology specifically (*WJ*, ix–xii, *RMO*, *COL*). Ethics for him rather emerges as a condensed *extractum* of political theology which responds to 'ethical questions'. As he replaces the Kantian and Hegelian notions of divine–human dualism or immanent mediation with his own biblical-exegetical framework, both doing Christian theology and 'doing ethics' become a *prophetic* task. What does this mean?

---

[120] For an integration of O'Donovan into the field of international law and theory, see Antony Carty, 'The Moral Theologian, Oliver O'Donovan and International Law', *Political Theology*, 9 (2008), 339–62.

In *Desire of the Nations*, O'Donovan locates prophecy in between the divine and the actual situation, thus mediating a specific truth to contemporaries:

> To prophesy is to speak a word from God to the church as it is placed here and now; to declare that the present situation is this, and not that. It is not scriptural exposition: it brings forward something new and of the moment, something not wholly predictable. Yet it is not free and exploratory innovation, but is always predicated upon careful attention to the testimony of Israel's prophets and apostles to the Christ-event. In the light of that testimony, it discovers the present. (*DN*, 188)

The Christian witness cannot be sublated into philosophy: 'if God's word of judgment pronounced in Christ is the foundation for a new order of society, the witnesses who challenged the prevailing political order in the name of Christ were not acting anti-politically or purely negatively, but were preparing the way for a new foundation, one constituted by participation in the exercise of the Messiah's authority' (*BI*, 44). In this vein, Christian action responds to divine activity in history, in the faithful immediacy of Christ the mediator.

'Doing Christian ethics', however, is no different from acting ethically in any other vocation, since the paradigmatic umbrella of all the church's vocations is prophecy. 'Out of all its vocations the church prophesies: its administration, its charity, its music, its art, its theology, its politics, its religious ecstasy, its preaching. Prophecy is the archetypal charism, the paradigm of all the others. The church prophesies to the world, discovering the situation of the world and passing judgment on it' (*DN*, 188).

However, this is not merely a general statement about the church's mode of being. O'Donovan carves out the space from and to which the *Christian* political ethicist speaks, dynamically involving the political into the church:

> But the individual prophet, like all who exercise a charism, does not address the world immediately, but the church, and, by contributing to the church's prophetic identity, addresses the world through the church. There is no private Christian counsel to be delivered to the principalities and powers, bypassing their need to confront the social reality of the church. A theologian, for example, who is invited to participate in an exercise of secular deliberation about matters of social concern, has no independent standing to give advice. Such a one either speaks for and out of the church (not for its hierarchy or synods, of course, but for its faith and tradition) or is a false prophet. (*DN*, 188)

In short, not only do prophets make ethical statements, but doing Christian ethics is prophetic, as is the act of judgement. Both simultaneously point at the triune God revealed in Christ. Going beyond *mere* critique, they facilitate a *metanoia* in secular political authorities, a turning to God, through understanding of what they are at heart.

This has several implications. On the one hand, political theology is consciously 'limited' by the fact that it proclaims the truth as accepted by Christianity and emerges in the discourse of the church. As O'Donovan says in response to the Bishops of the Church of England writing on Iraq, '[The just war theory] makes assumptions about the political leaders it addresses, namely, that they are either part of the Christian community or interested in understanding it, and in either case they need to know how the community of the faithful is to conceive *its* obligations in relation to Iraq' (*JWR*, 129). Hence, the task is 'to communicate the *moral posture* of those who recognise their responsibilities for Iraq in Christ Jesus, rather than to dictate concrete policy conclusions, which, a month later, are already beginning to look out of date' (*JWR*, 129). Where 'religion' and 'politics' are seen as separate, or the state relies on its own mythological and/or ideological superstructure (whether liberal or otherwise), this approach will be regarded as 'sectarian'.

The specific purpose of *Just War Revisited*, however, is primarily explanatory: 'The task of political ethics at this point is to provide as full a general account of the reconciling praxis of judgment as may be possible' (*JWR*, 13). In that sense, political theology will be 'sectarian' and may well show its denominational colours. Yet, these limitations stand beside the universality of the gospel message, which presupposes no intrinsic limitation on its audience.[121] Theology as a discipline *of* the church is not exclusively done *for* the church and may speak *to* the state. Beginning with *Desire of the Nations*, O'Donovan in that sense set out to describe meaningful political action on the mediate borderline between the heavenly and the earthly city.

Does this mean he cannot render verdicts on concrete moral decisions? The answer has to be mixed. Just war theory does not take the 'judging for yourselves' (i.e. thinking for themselves) away from each person. It has a 'spirituality', 'by which is meant its capacity to make the reflecting subject conscious of his or her own responsible position before God in relation to other members of society who have their own differently responsible positions' (*JWR*, ix). Hence the just war theory refuses to render wholesale verdicts on whether this or that war is 'just'. '[It] is very often supposed that just-war theory undertakes *to validate or invalidate particular wars*. That would be an impossible undertaking. History knows of no just wars, as it knows of no just peoples' (*JWR*, 13). The reason is that '[major] historical events cannot be justified or criticised in one mouthful; they are concatenations and agglomerations of many separate actions and many varied results' (*JWR*, 13).

More positively, 'practical doctrine offers help ... for those who wish to learn *how to engage in* the praxis of judgment – to engage in it in *these* days and in *these* circumstances, where we actually find ourselves, here and now' (*JWR*, 13). So in between outright (pacifist or quasi-pacifist) critiques, as well as the legitimization of a particular war, both give way to introducing principles guiding each agent's decisions

---

[121] O'Donovan's dedicatory preface is addressed to Rowan Williams to '[put] a suitable edge on your thoughts for the service of the church and the political community' (*JWR*, ix). One may argue that there is a 'missionary frontier' to doing Christian ethics as much as there is a missionary frontier to government-as-judgement. It means that neither a congruency nor incongruence between church pronunciations and the political community can be presumed; it has to be tested. 'Simply as a manner of proceeding, the Bishops would have done better to address the question of Iraq on its own terms first, and only then, when they had proposed something, ask to what extent the policies of the US administration were in accord' (*JWR*, 130).

as they actually approach their specific concrete, historical situation. In some ways, this takes up Ramsey's saying that the Christian may not tell the politician *what* to think but *how* to think; just war theory is a 'tool' (*JWR*, 127).

O'Donovan quotes Ramsey there, yet his practical engagement is much more tentative than Ramsey's side-taking during the Vietnam War and support for the US national security strategy. The last chapter of *Just War Revisited* presents his own practical engagement with the crisis of 2002 that led to the Iraq War. It does – again without providing a concrete *verdict* – at least demonstrate how practical engagement according to O'Donovan's own understanding is possible. It is entitled 'without authority', he says, 'to mark the difference between outlining an principled approach, on which I certainly claim *some* authority, and interpreting actual events, in which I am as open to misjudgements as anyone' (*JWR*, vii). In this vein, he notes that 'practical reasoning towards decisions that others must take can only clear the way for them to understand their responsibilities before God and their neighbours' (*JWR*, 127). Drawing on the information and discourse presented to the public at the time, he supports the conclusions reached by the Bishops of the Church of England:

> That the policy of disarming Iraq of weapons of mass destruction is right; that the chief issue internationally is the authority of the UN; that this authority must be able to call upon military action in a last resort; but that 'a preventive war against Iraq' would be unacceptable 'at this juncture'; that the 'immense suffering' and 'unpredictable environmental, economic and political consequences' of war must be central to planning; and that the Middle East peace process must be revitalised. (*JWR*, 128)

At the same time, he criticizes the way the Bishops came to their conclusion, which was by way of *ex cathedra* recommendations. O'Donovan then argues that the penal, retributive and defensive aspects of the just cause may be employed in the deliberations between the United Nations and the United States in response to 'the question of Iraq' (*JWR*, 130). Nevertheless, neither predictions nor 'precise recommendations' are possible for any 'private' contributor to a political debate (*JWR*, 127). 'Useful recommendations will tend to be introduced by the useful word, "if". That is to say, they will address *hypothetical* practical situations, not basing themselves on a pretended knowledge about what is, or what will be, the case' (*JWR*, 127).

To the 'curiously entitled' section of the Episcopal document 'The Church of England and Iraq' organized 'even more curiously' under the headings 'Jus ad bellum' and 'Jus in bello' he cries out, 'What! Is the *Church of England* planning to make war on Iraq?' (*JWR*, 129). So, O'Donovan gives to others the conceptual tools for deliberation. The theologian outlines the theological grounds of authority, reality and the political act. Yet, he or she refrains from explicit political advocacy. The individual theologian may certainly address the church, and through it the world, but there is no distinct 'church discipline'. Echoing Ramsey, O'Donovan wants to avoid associating the church with a think tank, a political campaign or a party.

Conclusion

This chapter has been the culminating chapter of the present project for several reasons. First, I showed that O'Donovan presents a practical proposal that moves between just war sovereigntism and liberal-internationalist idealism, while also keeping open the freedom for the continuous practical doing of justice. O'Donovan's whole proposal centred on the 'political act': government-as-judgement and 'doing justice'. This, I argued in the analytical section, was the reflection of a fundamental theological shift. O'Donovan shifted from the post-Enlightenment duality of Jesus Christ that splits the 'ethic of Jesus' from a remote rule of Christ in a beyond or at the end of times. This dualism was essentially a philosophical, specifically sceptical precondition to which many modern theologies, and to a large extent ethics, remain allied. O'Donovan, however, began from the premise that the Kantian and Hegelian frameworks are theologically untenable, even though they had theological precedents and congruencies. He replaced them with a biblical-exegetical framework. This meant that the heart of the gospel, the mediation between God and humankind in Christ and the present rule of that mediator were taken as a paradoxical unity. It also meant that it could not allow for a theological dualism or immanent, historicist repetitions of that event. And it was the starting point to which political reality, authority and action were related. Notably, these aspects or analytical foci remain difficult to separate when looking at 'government-as-judgment'. The reason is that precisely when judgement was conceived as successful, their distinction is obsolete: in the practical reconciliation wrought through political judgement, the very separation of action from agent and both from 'reality' becomes questionable – mediating judgement reconciles agent and the acted-upon.

In taking the task of Christian theology seriously, O'Donovan's notion of the act of judgement was unequivocally evangelical. On the grounds of a *sola fide*, it remains noteworthy for being impossible to 'pin down' as a political philosophy. It is neither statist nor internationalist, neither individualist nor communitarian. Instead – from the perspective of solidarity, brought about by an ecclesial insight into a truthful community – it both recognizes and does not recognize institutional structures. After all, authority precedes institutions. In that regard, one of the implications is that the liberal revolutionary-democratic paradigm may be transcended (though not rejected), at least in so far as it oscillates between individualistic, ultimately private claim rights and an alienating, possibly unquestionable state structure.[122]

Equally, the theological and ecclesial equivalent of this paradigm resolved in the agency of Israel. Between subjectivist *agape* and love mediated by – and declared identical with politics – in a quasi-papal, collectivist structure, O'Donovan discerned the actual community of the faithful. The nature of the political act is then *primarily* grounded in faith. From here, the notion of love and justice – of non-violent, non-discriminate universal love and retributive, defensive justice can come into view as

---

[122] Whether tyranny is then understood as absolute subjectivism or absolute objectivism makes no difference, since tyranny is marked by the very fact that the two collapse into each other, resulting in nihilism.

two dimensions that must continuously be 'done' as justice must be done. In terms of the theo-logic, O'Donovan's approach is distinct from the previous ones as the dualism and dialectic of the politically real and the moral ideal here is replaced or rather sublated – integrated and transcended in the Christ narrative. While his approach may be *intelligible* through a philosophical-idealist comparative lens, it is nevertheless specifically Christian, tied to an ecclesial praxis of faith. Thus, O'Donovan's full reintegration of politics into an evangelical narrative makes it difficult to embrace active political engagement. But in order to allow for the ethics of war to be both Christian and practical-partisan, the transition of the political act from Ramsey's dualist–dialectical context into the theo-logic of the biblical narrative needs to be continuously reversed and revisited. This possibility will be examined in Chapter 6, which criticizes and further develops some aspects of O'Donovan's work.

6

Mediations: History, grace and combat

Introduction

The previous chapters have examined different approaches to just war thinking grounded in their underlying theo-logics of mediation: sovereign state *reaction* was contrasted with global law *enforcement*; the individual right to self-*defence* (Steinhoff) pointed towards Ramsey's movement from a sceptical and immediate *agape* to *charitable* national *defence*; finally, O'Donovan's act of judgement was examined before the backdrop of Christological *mediation*. O'Donovan's work represented a culmination: theologically as well as in terms of the practical possibilities of mediation. Following on from O'Donovan's work, this chapter will now examine three additional, albeit implicit *topoi* of mediation that will partly question and amend the previous chapter. First, in light of O'Donovan's theo-logic, I will examine in how far his rejection of philosophical idealism can be rigidly upheld. Second, if it cannot, then how can a transition be theologically conceptualized? Here, I will attempt to understand it in the context of *grace*. O'Donovan mentions grace only briefly in *The Just War Revisited*, yet arguably grace allows and encourages those who take on or hold political responsibility to risk the embarrassment of political engagement. This raises the question of the nature of practical engagement, more specifically, *combat*. How can such a confrontation be thought of as having anything to do with mediation? As we live in a supposedly post-heroic age, remote-controlled warfare apparently does away with confrontation, allowing militaries to 'remove' threats, while reducing the need for their own forces to risk injury or death. However, the inner logic of these weapons is troubling precisely *because* they remove confrontation and battle.

History: Possibilities of mediation

O'Donovan and Hegel – Christian ethics and idealism

The relationship between idealism and evangelical ethics has cropped up throughout the previous chapters. For many theological thinkers, particularly Hegel is a shibboleth for 'secular thought'; philosophical idealism is regarded as an enabler of twentieth-century totalitarianisms or even nihilism. Hegel appeared to initiate the possibility for the 'absolute spirit' to become incarnate, eventually as murderous, pharaonic regimes. This was the reading suggested by J. B. Elshtain. Alternatively, Hegel's seemingly anti-liberal project of a *sittlich* state seemed to engender a sense of moral suffocation and a lack of individual freedom that, within the ethics of war, impinges on the humanistic principle. As a form of anti-liberal collectivism, the Hegelian state appears to pave the way for soldiers to become both 'canon fodder' and excused for war crimes. This was the reading put forward by David Rodin.

However, not only does Hegel's thought provide the philosophical backdrop and language to much of theological ethics in the twentieth and still also in the twenty-first century. Besides that historical-traditional ground, and pace the post-Barthian narrativist focus on 'language', there is a sense of a permeability of *thought* and thus intelligibility that prevents Christian ethics from becoming insular and eventually obscure. Philosophical idealism significantly influenced early twentieth-century Christian ethics, notably Reinhold Niebuhr as well as Paul Ramsey. It allowed Ramsey to operationalize a Christian ethic: kenotic love had to be incarnate in historical, political and cultural forms of life. As shown in the previous chapter, in 'fixing' Ramsey's occasional theological dualism on a systematic and practical level, O'Donovan then decisively rejected Hegel and idealism's notion of (Christological) mediation. Indeed, already in *Resurrection and the Moral Order*, O'Donovan had voiced Tuttle's critique of Ramsey. Idealist incarnation '(without the definite article)' means that 'the meaning of the whole has been focused in a representative one'; so, eventually 'any concrete being may … be an "incarnation" of universal meaning in this sense'. In contrast, 'Christ's particularity belongs to his divine nature, his universality to his human nature. As the one whom God has sent he is irreplaceable; as the new man he is the pattern to which we may conform ourselves.'[1] Via this distinct theo-logic, O'Donovan averted a (post-)Niebuhrian incarnation of the Kingdom of Heaven taking immanent form in any concrete state (or conglomerate of states).[2] Just war and 'democracy' are not synonyms by default. Instead, '[w]hat is remarkable', O'Donovan says,

> and what only *the* incarnation can tell us of, is not the representation of universal order in any one being, but the coming within universal order of that which belongs outside it, the one divine Word which gave it its origin and which pronounces its judgment.[3]

This critique of idealism ran through O'Donovan's work, as an initial methodological point in *Desire of the Nations* and, less explicitly, as a critique of political ideologies jumping to historical conclusions in *The Just War Revisited*. But is it fully warranted?

---

[1]   Oliver O'Donovan, *Resurrection and Moral Order: An Outline for Evangelical Ethics*, 2nd ed. (Grand Rapids, MI: William B. Eerdmans, 1994), p. 143.
[2]   Earlier he had compared John of Patmos's reference to Nero with Hegel's remark that the universal and homogenous state would first come into being in America – Oliver O'Donovan, 'The Political Thought of the Book of Revelation', *Tyndale Bulletin* 37 (1986), pp. 61–94, p. 68.
[3]   O'Donovan, *Resurrection*, p. 144.

Both Hegel and O'Donovan have a central concern: reconciling dualities, overcoming the sceptical oscillation, the 'unhappy consciousness' of irreconcilable opposites spliced together. Whereas O'Donovan lifts reconciliation and mediation onto a biblical-exegetical plane, Hegel is concerned with its logical unfolding in history. Unification, writes O'Donovan quite reminiscent of Hegel, is not a *tertium quid* but 'a union of the two, a *both-and*' as 'affective knowledge'.[4] 'We know only as we love', he quotes Augustine.[5] Compare this with Hegel's notion of love encountered with Ramsey. For Hegel, love 'implies a distinguishing between two' who are actually 'not distinguished from one another'.[6] A person's self-consciousness is not in herself but in another; 'but this Other in whom alone I find satisfaction and am at peace with myself', 'just because it is outside of me, has its self-consciousness only in me'. Love *is* the medium between humans but equally between the dual choice of logical separation or identity. To love means to know and feel this duality-unity: 'Thus the two are represented simply by this consciousness of their being outside of themselves and of their identity, and of this perception, this feeling, this knowledge of the unity of love'.[7]

At the same time, once O'Donovan enters the nitty-gritty of jurisprudence, he incorporates a Hegelian mediating logic like a *fetus in fetu*.[8] In *Ways of Judgment*, for example, he explicates the notion of punishment, which is after all integral to judgement. With judgement, society pronounces the truth about the crime to the offender. It 'affords the occasion to acknowledge the social conditions of his own existence', what Hegel called 'the satisfaction of the offender's "explicit will"'.[9] The good of society is equally at stake – it is judgement itself, the basic condition of a common life.[10] Like in *Just War Revisited*, punishment here consists in the integration of subjective claim into an objective order of right. O'Donovan writes, 'Hegel's masterly discussion ... describes a convergence of the interests of offender and society upon the common need for a vindication of infringed right that will effectively express the moral and social "nullity" of the crime'.[11]

Does that mean O'Donovan is after all a dialectician? For his part, O'Donovan relies on an interpretation of Hegel similar to the post-theological interpreters,

---

[4] Stephen Joel Garver, '"There Is Another King": Gospel as Politics – Notes towards a Theology of Community', in *Christian Body Politic*, ed. Christian Kim (Cheltenham: Hermit Kingdom Press, 2004), pp. 13–52, p. 19. Similarly in *Desire of the Nations*, 'But as the hypostatic union in the Incarnation requires speaking of two natures, so with the Kingdom of God we cannot conceive the henosis of political and spiritual without the duality of the two terms held together in it'. And, 'The unity of the kingdoms, we may say, is the heart of the Gospel, their duality is the pericardium' (p. 82).

[5] Oliver O'Donovan, *Common Objects of Love: Moral Reflection and the Shaping of Community* (Grand Rapids, MI: William B. Eerdmans, 2002), p. 17.

[6] Cf. Ella Csikós, 'Zu Hegels Interpretation des Skeptizismus', in *Hegels Phänomenologie des Geistes: Ein kooperativer Kommentar zu einem Schlüsselwerk der Moderne*, ed. Klaus Vieweg and Wolfgang Welsch (Frankfurt am Main: Suhrkamp, 2008), pp. 270–85.

[7] Paul Ramsey, *Basic Christian Ethics* (London: SCM Press, 1953), p. 303; see also Hegel, *Phänomenologie*, IV B, 'Skeptizismus und das unglückliche Bewußtsein', pp. 163–4.

[8] Oliver O'Donovan, *The Ways of Judgment* (Grand Rapids, MI: William B. Eerdmans, 2005), p. 112.

[9] Ibid., p. 118.

[10] Ibid.

[11] Ibid., p. 117.

perhaps even more subjectivist. Although 'Hegel's account of punishment brings to theoretical completion the scattered insights of patristic Christianity', O'Donovan says, it 'remains abstractly suspended in the *psychological* context that is the matrix of so much of his thought, and so appears to be merely ingenious'.[12] Hegel lacks 'a way of relating penal practice to the wider range of practices that constitute political and social life'. So Hegel is fundamentally lacking. Nonetheless, Dorothea Bertschmann has pointed out the interplay between dialectic and eschatology in O'Donovan's own thought: 'It is not the case that "the eschatological language mysteriously drops out, to be replaced by a functional dialectical between institutional roles" ... *The dialectical or duality is precisely a consequence of eschatology*.' Indeed, there is even an interdependence: 'The dual institutions of church and state are precisely there to keep a basic eschatological tension alive, lest the state feels too complacent or the church gets corrupted.'[13]

As we heard, O'Donovan himself begins with a declaration of accomplished faith – whether as a friendly parting from non-believers, the *Te Deum*, or interpreting for the faithful their duties.[14] In the first volume of his final trilogy, he undertakes the 'architectural enterprise' of Christian ethics from within a house already built: 'those who will practice this discipline with me and after me ... must enter into the lived experience of practical deliberation for themselves, and inhabit it as residents, not as those visiting on occasional research trips.'[15]

In this sense, via Ramsey, and congruent with Hegel's jurisprudential logic, we might suggest that O'Donovan has consistently repatriated Christian ethics – and the logic of mediation – into its 'proper' home within the Christian narrative of divine mediation culminating in the unified rule of Christ. If Hegel sublated 'religion' into the concept, O'Donovan reversed this move: he sublates the Hegelian concept into the Christian life. The Barthian sublation of 'religion' into 'revelation' may well be read as a parallel here.

Does this mean that, once historicism and idealism have been partly absorbed and successfully rejected (i.e. *aufgehoben*), O'Donovan can safely preach to the converted? Certainly, he has invited suspicion also in this regard. Commentators such as Timothy Gorringe and Andrew Shanks shared the sense that O'Donovan, instead of doing political theology, does theology *in lieu* of politics. Today's protests and projects of civil society seem to impinge on the perfection of the biblical narrative of Israel rather than echo it.[16] It is at this point that O'Donovan's work may be opened up again, also from within his own work.

---

[12] Ibid., p. 119. Italics added.
[13] Dorothea H. Bertschmann, *Bowing before Christ – Nodding to the State?: Reading Paul Politically with Oliver O'Donovan and John Howard Yoder* (London: Bloomsbury T&T Clark, 2014), p. 20 n. 58, see also p. 20 n. 59.
[14] O'Donovan, *JWR*, p. 129.
[15] O'Donovan, *Self, World, and Time: Ethics as Theology*, vol. 1 (Grand Rapids, MI: Eerdmans, 2013), p. ix.
[16] Andrew Shanks, *God and Modernity: A New and Better Way to Do Theology* (London: Psychology Press, 2000), p. 105; Tim Gorringe, 'Authority, Plebs and Patricians', *Studies in Christian Ethics*, 11 (1998), 24–9.

Mediating justice in history: Apocalypse or *kairoi*?

Evidently the discussion about the relationship between philosophical idealism and Christian ethics is not merely a methodological one. It opens out to the much larger question of how Christian ethics and political history are connected. This is also, and not least, a question of mediation, the nature and mode of the relationship between human political history with God's life and salvation history. Is Christianity post- or a-political, as seems to be the case in much of contemporary continental Protestantism? If so, political conflict and *in extremis* the use of force are looked upon at best with liberal melancholia, at worst with indifferent moralism.[17] Or can historical events, institutions and even 'great men' embody or realize, even represent traces of the divine order of things? If so, 'Christian' ethics has to be an engaged ethics, 'risking the embarrassment of engagement'.

It is perhaps no coincidence that O'Donovan has addressed the question of history by looking at the book of Revelation. In an earlier article (1986, revised in 2005) on the book's political thought, he showed that – in contrast to the modern idea of the apocalypse as non-political – John of Patmos 'intends to say that the vindication of this-worldly justice and the fulfilment of this-worldly history are *included in the reign of God* in the new heaven and the new earth'.[18] Yet besides countering an altogether non-political reading of apocalypse, O'Donovan also steps out of the theological allegiances to different philosophies of history during the early part of the twentieth century. Instead, he aims to go *with* John of Patmos to push back the horizon of (the philosophy of) history altogether. This has the advantage that the question of theodicy, to which historical political forms are one answer,[19] is most sharply posed: What is the point of the horrors of history? *Ubi deus*? O'Donovan's answer is a hope in 'an alternative politics of worship',[20] a community of worship looking to the Alpha and Omega of history.

As he explains it, John's vision of the harlot Babylon-Rome, drawing on Jeremiah and Ezekiel, unmasks and depicts the final fate of empire, indeed all historical empires. Borrowing and parodying a divine 'unity',[21] empire amounts to a paradoxical contradiction of unity and rebellion that ends in catastrophic self-destruction.

---

[17] Tentatively one might define moralism as the direct adherence to, and re-endorsement of, a moral position whose context and agents are no longer given. For a critical approach from the perspective of Protestant ethics, albeit without a straightforward definion of moralism, see e.g. Ulrich H. Körtner, *Für die Vernunft: Wider Moralisierung und Emotionalisierung in Politik und Kirche* (Leipzig: Evangelische Verlagsanstalt, 2017).

[18] O'Donovan, 'Political Thought of the Book of Revelation', 70. Italics added.

[19] Cf. Richard Faber, *Political Demonology: On Modern Marcionism*, transl. Therese Feiler and Michael Mayo (Eugene, OR: Wipf & Stock, 2018), pp. 105–16, esp. p. 109 citing Hans Blumenberg's *Work on Myth*: 'Metaphysical dualism is not the threat that arises from the reduction of polytheism; rather, it results from the self-splitting of a monotheism that cannot cope with the problem of justifying its God in defense against the accusation of a world that is inadequate to the concept of him.'

[20] Oliver O'Donovan and Joan Lockwood O'Donovan, *Bonds of Imperfection: Christian Politics, Past and Present* (Grand Rapids, MI: Eerdmans, 2004) , p. 34.

[21] NB: The idealist project is frequently seen as the final attempt to create a philosophy of 'the whole'; cf. *Bonds of Imperfection*, p. 41.

The logic of the beast's end and the logic of the Whore's end are the same, predatory power collapsing in on itself. … The diabolical project of claiming sovereignty was a self-contradiction from the beginning. As the collapse of empire, then, reveals the operation of divine providence, so the collapse of this messianic empire will reveal the final rule of God's Messiah over history.[22]

With John of Patmos, O'Donovan here consistently puts the focus on the community of witnesses (but more often also isolated individuals) standing in 'irresoluble conflict with the organized community'.[23] With a view to Rev. 20.40,[24] he interprets,

The idea of an ordered social existence under the authority of divine *dikaiōma*, participating in the exercise of human *krima*, is not a paradoxical from. It conveys to us a hope that in the life which we are summoned to live with Christ we may experience as political reality that authority of truth and justice *which political society on earth has consistently failed to achieve*.[25]

John of Patmos's final words express the eschatological vision *coram Deo*, re-casting history vis-à-vis divine eternity (Rev. 21.6). 'History is summoned into being by God's ever-present declarative act, and there and then it is accomplished, reflecting back the glory of the one who summoned it, who can now be known as Alpha and Omega, its source and end.'[26] Such a God is not merely a 'self-subsisting' one but a self-communicating one. And, 'On that self-announcement mediated through prophetic writing the holy city is founded.'[27] Consequently, and in line with his subsequent political-theological project, O'Donovan locates 'true speech, divine speech' at the very 'heart of politics' that enters 'into conflict with the false orders of human society'.[28]

The difference between O'Donovan and modern philosophies of history may here be read analogously to the difference between Karl Barth and Paul Tillich, both of whom steered between two poles.[29] The Scylla Barth sought to circumnavigate were historical or present-day institutions and events being 'new sources of revelation', a danger he discerned in different ideologies (and at times perhaps too sweepingly, also in theologies) of the 1920s and 1930s. Congruently, O'Donovan noted that the Antichrist in different ages is always marked by 'the convergence in one subject claims to earthly political rule and heavenly soteriological mediation' (*DN*, 214). Yet, the Charybdis

---

[22] O'Donovan and Lockwood O'Donovan, *Bonds of Imperfection*, pp. 41–2.
[23] Ibid., p. 42; cf. 'standing against organised society' in 'The Political Thought of the Book of Revelation', p. 88.
[24] Rev. 20.4: 'And I saw thrones, and they sat upon them, and judgment was given unto them: and I saw the souls of them that were beheaded for the witness of Jesus, and for the word of God, and which had not worshipped the beast, neither his image, neither had received his mark upon their foreheads, or in their hands; and they lived and reigned with Christ a thousand years' (*KJV*).
[25] O'Donovan and O'Donovan, *Bonds of Imperfection*, p. 44.
[26] Ibid., pp. 46–7.
[27] Ibid., p. 47.
[28] Ibid.
[29] See Paul Tillich, 'History and the Kingdom of God', in *God, History, and Historians: An Anthology of Modern Christian Views of History*, ed. Carl Thomas McIntire (New York: Oxford University Press, 1977), pp. 157–75.

presents itself too: a *sceptical* relativism about political history, events and problems of the present age. Not least where theology is pitted against 'modernity' altogether, such a scepticism is a real possibility.[30] To counter such a possibility, Paul Tillich understood the *kairos* a 'decisive moment in history'[31] in which 'the unconditioned' breaks through. Tillich talks about 'bearers of revelation', who may become 'vessels of the unconditioned'. Where this is not *prophetic*, of course, it will once again be problematic. Hence, for Tillich, in a remarkable paradox the cross remains the final critical standard: 'what happens in the *Kairos* must be absolute and yet not absolute – it must stand under the judgment of the absolute.'[32] The early twentieth-century engagement of (Protestant) theology with the philosophy of history as a question of historical *mediation* of the divine sought to avert not least an apocalyptic Gnosticism.

How should the two approaches to Christian ethics and politics as a-temporal or historical practice – O'Donovan or Ramsey/Hegel but also Barth or Tillich – be related? Rather than picking and advocating or defending either of them, one might instead appreciate both as harbouring incisive critical possibilities (critical in the sense of *krinein*) and a liberating perspective. The idealists' and O'Donovan's are not necessarily two mutually exclusive projects but rather two legitimate moments.[33] O'Donovan's insistence on a transhistorical moment of obedience is as necessary as the ability to discern such moments within the political narratives and structures one encounters. This reflects also the eschatological tension Bertschmann mentioned earlier. In other words, we need to appreciate the *transition* from Hegel's own Christology to dialectics (including 'negative dialectics'[34]) as well as the *transition* from Ramsey's historically and practically engaged dualism to O'Donovan's Christological mediation.[35] An openness to the permeance between 'abstract psychology' (not least for the benefit of psychology) and Christological fulfilment, a transition constantly lost and *therapeutically* gained, allows also for a reconstructive, creative engagement with secular discourses, not least where they threaten to fizzle out into a nervous empiricism that fails to grasp its own morally laden concepts. In other words, while drawing on specific political-theological concepts at a particular moment in time can and will engender a political position,

---

[30] O'Donovan's insistence that the notion of the common good has not much to tell us about Brexit or the European migration crisis seems to render it curiously unproductive.

[31] Paul Tillich, Kairos I, in Tillich, *Der Widerstreit von Raum und Zeit. Schriften zur Geschichtsphilosophie*, ed. R. Albrecht (Gesammelte Werke, 6), 1963, 9–28, p. 13, 20; cited in Michael Beintker, 'Die Frage nach den Quellen der Offenbarung im Spiegel theologiegeschichtlicher Entwicklungen zwischen 1918 und 1934, in Beintker, *Krisis und Gnade*, ed. Stefan Holtmann and Peter Zocher (Tübingen: Mohr Siebeck, 2013), pp. 40–63, p. 56.

[32] Cited in Beintker, *Krisis und Gnade*, p. 57. Ibid.: 'Der Kairos, die geschichtliche Stunde, kann [...] nie von sich aus Offenbarung sein. Sie kann nur den Eintritt einer neuen Offenbarungskorrelation anzeigen.'

[33] When Nigel Biggar demands 'Less Hegel, more history', that may also be taken as a reminder that the *historical* task set by the Hegelian turn tends to be forgotten. Nigel Biggar, 'Less Hegel, More History! Christian Ethics & Political Realities', *Providence. A Journal of Christianity & American Foreign Policy*, Fall 2015, pp. 10–16, available at: https://providencemag.com/2016/05/less-hegel-history-christian-ethics-political-realities/ (accessed 17 December 2018).

[34] In the sense of an interdisciplinary epistemology that allows for a hermeneutic of phenomena e.g. in economics or art, as for example in the works of Karl Polanyi or Slavoj Žižek, respectively.

[35] Another attempt at this transition is e.g. the 'unsolvable' dispute between John Milbank and Slavoj Žižek, *The Monstrosity of Christ. Paradox or Dialectic?* (Cambridge: MIT Press, 2009).

that position itself is contingent and open to review in light of a refined understanding of – or initial drawing on – theological concepts.

Grace: The (im)possibility of political engagement

If we want to talk about such a continuous transition between an immanent, historical logic and the eschatological rooting and vision, then the notion of *grace* becomes highly relevant as a mediate term and a mediating movement. From the perspective of the Protestant Reformation, grace indicates three significant possibilities: first, the sharp difference between the historical-political and the life within the Christian *ecclesia*; this difference is established through crisis and graceful reconstitution. Second, the maintenance of this differentiation to varying extents, even as critical, potentially violent situations emerge. Conversely, grace then harbours also the very possibility of politics and *in extremis* the use of force to protect and defend the innocent.

Among other theological *topoi*, Karl Barth explored grace especially in his second edition of the *Letter to the Romans*. This work remains a highly relevant intervention in – as well as over against – the political, societal and even cultural crises of the early twentieth century. Barth here draws on Luther as well as Calvin with the differences between them not yet presenting a problem for him. With Kierkegaard (and Kohelet), Barth emphatically explored the 'absolute difference' between the human being and God in Paul's letter, whereby the 'divinization' of human endeavours, culture or institutions was flat-out contradicted by God's 'No!' The meaning of grace here is described as a 'fact' [*Tatsache*] of God's forgiveness of sins. Yet it is also as a divine *movement*, as a term of transition from the 'old', historical 'man' to the newly created human being. The death of Christ, with which one is identified in baptism, *is* grace. The reason: 'Because the shattering and undermining and disintegration which proceed from it are *the action of God*; because its negation is positive and its power is the primal authority; because the final word spoken over the man of this world is at once *hinge, and threshold, and bridge, and turning-point*, to the new man; because the baptized person – who must not be identified with the man who died – is identical with the new man who has been born.'[36] And on Rom. 6.9,[37] Barth comments, 'Grace is the truth of God about the individual and about the broad course of his whole life; and because grace is this, it brings him radically under crisis. Grace *cannot stand still and rest; it cannot silently abandon its claim; it cannot hand visible life over to sin in order that it may be satisfied with the righteousness of some "other" invisible and intangible life*.'[38] In this way, the 'old man' is readjusted and sublated into a reconciled relationship with God.

However, Barth repeatedly emphasizes the irreversibility of this movement and transition: a 'turn without a re-turn'.[39] Similarly, O'Donovan notes with St Paul's letter

---

[36] Karl Barth, *Epistle to the Romans*, trans. Edwyn C. Hoskyns (Oxford: Oxford University Press, 1968), p. 194; italics added.

[37] Rom. 6.19: 'Just as you used to offer yourselves as slaves to impurity and to ever-increasing wickedness, so now offer yourselves as slaves to righteousness leading to holiness.'

[38] Barth, *Epistle*, p. 221.

[39] Ibid., p. 188: 'the reverse process is impossible.'

to the Romans that 'the historical dialectic of grace overwhelming transgression' cannot be 'projected as a permanent law of the operation of grace in our moral experience' (*DN*, 128).[40] Barth's fundamental, existential crisis of, and judgement on, 'human logic' is echoed in O'Donovan's critical remarks on idealism and historicism. For Barth, it was the initial spark to subsequently develop a 'divine command ethics' for and within the church.[41] And although O'Donovan noted the problematic conjecture of BC and AD in Barth's later writings (which then made the work of the state an *opus alienum*), in effect both authors converge in an ethical non-judgement, especially on particular conflicts.

And yet, the biblical and post-biblical narrative enters a 'crisis' when it confronts a worldly reality that lacks its terms and conditions. It demands judgement on concrete situations. What is the task of the Christian ethicist here? If grace is understood as neither the action nor non-action of human beings but rather an attribute and way in which *God* acts – so the Reformation's classical *sola gratia* – then grace allows, enables and potentially even encourages risking the embarrassment of political engagement. The reason is precisely that grace or hope in salvation cannot be taken away; nor can anything be added to it.[42]

Dietrich Bonhoeffer has explicated a significant caveat here. When grace is a *premise* of all action, then one can safely go about one's political and social business, since the world has in principle been forgiven.[43] 'Cheap grace is the grace we give to ourselves.'[44] But in that case, 'the justification of the sinner in the world has become the justification of sin and the world. Expensive grace has become cheap grace without discipleship.' By contrast, expensive grace entails discipleship, which is far from good and easy: 'Luther knew that this grace had cost him a life and still cost him his life daily. For this grace had not suspended him from discipleship, but had actually pushed him into it.'[45] So when Luther says, *Pecca fortiter, sed fortius fide et gaude in Christo*, this is not a sudden reversal to 'cheap grace', that is, leaning back to do whatever 'the world' demands, since grace has been meted out abundantly already. Luther is not inviting a wilful commission of sin chanced upon grace. Rather, grace must be the 'result, the capstone, the final and conclusive word'. Bonhoeffer explains, 'For [Luther] the "sin courageously" is by no means a principled confirmation of his disobedient life, but the

---

[40] See *DN*, 129: 'Our moral experience is articulated biographically by the diremption of sin and grace, as decisive in our case as in Christ's. His death and resurrection were a representative act in which we participate – beginning at our baptism and culminating in the last resurrection of the dead (6. 2–8). Since in the representative's case the transaction from death to life was a final and decisive act of history (*ephapax*), we have to conceive our lives as radically transformed, free of the compelling authority, the "reign", of sin (6. 9–14).

[41] Karl Barth, *Ethics*, ed. Dietrich Braun, transl. Geoffrey W. Bromley (Eugene, OR: Wipf & Stock, 2013).

[42] So when Conor Cunningham sought to radicalize Radical Orthodoxy's 'move from "either/or" to "both/and" … to the degree that it becomes an approach of "both/and – either/or"', my suggestion is that it is precisely the *hyphen* that denotes the silent, transcendent move of grace. Conor Cunningham, *The Genealogy of Nihilism* (Abingdon: Routledge, 2005), p. xviii.

[43] This seems to be what Elshtain suggested, charging her humanist-idealist opponents with relying on 'cheap grace' or rather 'cheap guilt'.

[44] Bonhoeffer, 'Die teure Gnade', in Dietrich Bonhoeffer, *Nachfolge*, ed. Peter Zimmerling (Giessen: Brunnen, 2016), pp. 40–54, p. 41.

[45] Bonhoeffer, *Nachfolge*, p. 47.

gospel of the grace of God, before which we are always and in every estate sinners, and which finds and justifies us as sinners. Confess your sin courageously, do not try to escape it, but "believe even more courageously." [46]

This problematic of transition and engagement also underlies Nigel Biggar's disagreement with Oliver O'Donovan. Biggar (who has also written extensively on Barth) here advocates what I have called with Ella Csikós's commentary on Hegel, 'risking the embarrassment of involvement'.[47] Rather than refraining from offering precise recommendations to avoid 'damaging [one's] own moral authority' (so yet another possibility), Biggar argues that Christian ethicists *should* 'offer precise, albeit fallible judgments'.[48] Who else but the ethicist, Biggar asks, should be in a position to do so? Moreover, 'if judgements are to be made at all, then any judge will have to shoulder risks in making them, by entering territory where he is not entirely at home'. Biggar suggests, with St Augustine in mind, that it is a *pastoral* task to 'furnish "the burden-bearers of the world" ' – a phrase taken from Reinhold Niebuhr – 'with a model of moral reasoning against which to hone their own deliberation effectively in the light of the actual circumstances in which they find themselves'. Even if one turns out to be wrong (and Biggar's support of the 2003 Iraq War has hardly met universal agreement), then the ethicist's judgement 'will still have performed the good service of being a pebble in the shoe of public understanding, provoking reflection and refinement'. 'To adapt Luther, perhaps we should err boldly (though considerately) that truth may abound!'[49]

So one might say that just like the symmetrical beauty of classical art eventually becomes an ossified classicism, so a faithful declaration that 'God reigns' without its *acrimonious* unfolding in thought, life and history (and historical analysis) risks being the mere sound of words. It is because Hegel himself performs this transition – remember, 'the later dialectic is a working out of a Christological and philosophical principle' – that he allows for what one might call the *apostolicity* of history. With a growing, though never safely 'owned' backdrop of grace, ethicists of war (and anyone, really) may transform O'Donovan's remarkable inconclusiveness in *The Just War Revisited* into something concrete. In that sense, for all the difficulties with Ramsey's later realist just war ethics (and advocacy of the Vietnam War), he did risk the 'embarrassment of involvement'. Conversely, for all the dangers that come with throwing oneself into history in this way, there is the horizon of the accomplished human–divine mediation, the act and being of God O'Donovan describes. The transition between the two on the grounds of grace can initiate praxis (including sheer experience) and contemplation (including dogmatic exploration) as contributions to the demands for decisions as the need for them emerges. This cannot justify evil but puts it in a larger, eschatological context, intensifying what is at stake in a conflict.

---

[46] Ibid., p. 50.

[47] Nigel Biggar, 'Regime Change in Iraq: A Christian Reading of the Morals of the Story', in *The Authority of the Gospel: Explorations in Moral and Political Theology in Honor of Oliver O'Donovan*, ed. Robert Song and Brent Waters (Grand Rapids, MI: Wm. B. Eerdmans, 2015), pp. 52–71.

[48] Ibid., p. 53.

[49] Ibid., p. 55.

This approach may also help to address a significant problem with the (ab)uses of 'history' in contemporary ethics of war. The previous chapters have consciously reconnected different proposals to theo-logics of the past, emphasizing the recurrence of past confrontations and logics of war (e.g. the Investiture, the radical Reformation) under the auspices of modernity. Yet while there is an element of modified *recurrence* here, a church-historical awareness must refrain from *ex ante* demonizations on the grounds of seemingly obvious *repetitions*. At present, the seeming clarity of monstrous evils of past, particularly twentieth-century totalitarianisms, has resulted in an apparent proliferation of 'fascist' governments today.[50] They are fought with a hysterical vigour of *résistance* increasing proportionately to the temporal distance between us and previous generations. This has led to an impoverishment of concepts such as the state, the nation, political community or sacrifice to the point where basic intuitions are stifled by boundaries of thought that need a mere hinting-at to be effective. Significantly, though not surprisingly, it is from within analytical moral philosophy that a call for conceptual openness has been made. Seth Lazar, a frequent critic of David Rodin, has written,

> The thesis that nothing has value besides the constituents of individual well-being is both plausible in itself, and widely assumed in moral and political philosophy. Demonstrating that there are indeed other sources of moral reasons besides individual interests is difficult enough; showing that these are sufficiently weighty to justify killing innocent people is a further stretch still. However, if we want to retain our common-sense view of a political community's right to defend itself against purely political aggression, then I think we need to forge some argument along these lines. Moreover, we need to do so without proving too much: the view that collective or impersonal goods can justify overriding individual interests has been the normative opening for some of history's worst atrocities. Reclaiming these arguments from their history of heinous abuse is a profound challenge in itself.[51]

It would be naïve to believe that the ambiguity of political concepts can be overcome; corruption and betrayal are ever-present possibilities. Triumphs over evil may collapse into tragedy, be ironically subverted or again parodied (after all, Christ was betrayed by a kiss.) Yet moral-political conceptions cleansed of seemingly problematic terms will not only fail to grasp real suffering, they may politicize and eventually militarize greater swathes of society. Arguably, it is grace (the analogous good incarnate) that

---

[50] James Bryce's famous quote applies: 'As the chief practical use of history is to deliver us from plausible historical analogies, so a comprehension of the institutions of other nations enables us to expose sometimes the ill-grounded hopes, sometimes the idle fears, which loose reports about those nations generate.' Viscount James Bryce, *The American Commonwealth,* with an Introduction by Gary L. McDowell, 2 vols. (Indianapolis: Liberty Fund, 1995), vol. 1, p. 8.

[51] Seth Lazar, 'National Defence, Self-Defence, and the Problem of Political Aggression', in *The Morality of Defensive War,* ed. Cécile Fabre and Seth Lazar (Oxford: Oxford University Press, 2014), pp. 11–39 (online version), p. 36.

signifies both this ambiguity and the very possibility to reclaim concepts from histories of abuse in order to see how they illuminate the present.

Combat: Mediation and the heroic

This brings us to a closely related problem, frequently uncomfortable also for non-pacifist ethicists of war. The question sits at the borderline of the ethics of war and military chaplaincy. Granted that taking up arms in a particular situation is justified, how are we to understand the notion of combat within a theo-logic of mediation? For his part, O'Donovan does not elaborate the inner workings of combat or fighting, since he does not want to reintroduce the antagonistic term of *duellum*. In his view, 'judgment has only the same material means available to it as crime'. And, 'To take up *these* means, and to convert them to the service of that law-bound and obedient judgment, was the constructive work of Christian "poetics"' (*JWR*, 7). Yet by elaborating the moral practice of war in light of Christological mediation, O'Donovan's approach also implies the possibility to understand combat, including particular weapons systems, in light of such an essential logic of mediation – or lack thereof.

No dirty hands? Peace-building and drone warfare

Influenced by the 'just peace' movement or a residual pacifism, political ethics authors for several decades have tended to disguise violent combat. Preferred terms are 'peacebuilding',[52] 'conflict management', 'peace-keeping missions' and so on. Specifically, in a pastoral context, a pacifist, or at least anti-warist stance frequently subverts the task and mission of the soldier.[53] As an example, Ulrich von den Steinen, a former lead military dean for the Protestant Church in Germany, quotes a pastor addressing an audience of soldiers: 'You, the soldiers, do not want war. But we, we want peace.' With exasperation von den Steinen comments, 'What a semantic fraud! May nobody fall into that trap!'[54] Absorbing soldiering into a discourse of non-violence may defer political action to inaction or deny the potential need for military force in the first place (with e.g. juridification taking its place). Alternatively, such an understanding may dissolve military combat to a non-existent, pyrrhic victory. Yet, both are two sides of the same coin: they step over, or are oblivious of, the period of fighting as in itself a critical, transitional moment towards, *subsequently*, victory and the possibility of reconciliation.

---

[52] For example, Gerard F. Powers, 'From an Ethics of War to an Ethics of Peacebuilding', In *From Just War to Modern Peace Ethics*, ed. Heinz-Gerhard Justenhoven and William A. Barbieri, Jr (Berlin, NY: De Gruyter, 2012), pp. 275–312.

[53] On the problematic relationship between churches and their military chaplains, see e.g. Peter Howson, 'The British Churches and Their Chaplains: Standing Back to Back and Walking in Opposite Directions', in *Military Chaplaincy in Contention: Chaplains, Churches and the Morality of Conflict*, ed. Andrew Todd (Farnham: Ashgate, 2013), pp. 95–112.

[54] Ulrich von den Steinen, *Unzufrieden mit dem Frieden?: Militärseelsorge und Verantwortungsethik* (Göttingen: Vandenhoeck & Ruprecht, 2006), p. 186.

This is not to reintroduce a subtle militarism through the backdoor here but to argue that not only a lack of the language of combat but of combat as such is problematic. O'Donovan has to an extent cast light on the problem. He says that in countries where criminal law has replaced the death penalty (and war has not been declared, one should add) counter-insurgency forces are faced with a disequilibrium: the insurgents effectively have a monopoly on the power to kill. This disequilibrium may 'tempt security forces to resort to murder rather than entrust their adversaries to the over-tender care of the criminal justice system' (*JWR*, 74). Abroad we encounter this undesirable choice in counter-terrorism: in the absence of a viable international criminal system, targeted killing has become a preferred tactic.

If we follow a lead from Hegel, weapons are 'nothing but the essence of the combatants themselves, an essence which comes to light only for both of them reciprocally'.[55] Applied to drone warfare, we can see that here any potential logic of mediation is pre-empted by a logic of *eradication*. Indeed, it is the logical implication of the individual being the central concern and highest value in the ethics of war – the drone is its 'essence'. Implicitly, this reading runs through different analyses of drone warfare. In his 2015 *Drone Theory*, for example, Grégoire Chamayou argues that with drones the 'humanitarian' imperative comes to its final culmination. The 'drone-dream' combines the protection of one's own soldiers with the protection of enemy non-combatants through precision. The weapon is utterly separate from the soldier or combatant, indeed entirely disembodied. 'Nobody dies – except the enemy', Chamayou quotes a magazine advertisement from the early 1990s. As he puts it concisely,

> According to this view of military morality, to kill while exposing one's own life is bad; to take lives without ever endangering one's own is good. That first principle of drone necroethics is, paradoxically, vitalist. And it is in accordance with this logic that the drone can be said to be a 'humanitarian' weapon: the humanitarian imperative is to save *lives*. And the drone does indeed save *our* lives.[56]

Chamayou here rightly diagnoses an amalgamation of the humanitarian with the political and subsequently the military.[57] The resulting contradiction altogether perverts humanitarianism:

> What is emerging here, more fundamentally, is a regime of military violence that claims to be humanitarian but might equally be called *humilitarian*. It is a power that both kills and saves, wounds and heals, and it performs those double tasks in a single gesture, in an integrated manner: an immediate synthesis of a power of destruction and a power of caring, *murder* at the same time as *care*.[58]

---

[55] Georg Wilhelm Friedrich Hegel, *The Phenomenology of Spirit*, transl. and ed. Michael Inwood (Oxford: Oxford University Press, 2018), p. 153 (§ 383).
[56] Chamayou, *Theorie der Drohne*, p. 145; *Drone Theory*, transl. Janet Lloyd (London: Penguin, 2015), p. 136.
[57] NB: O'Donovan had also rejected a Clausewitzian vitalism (see *JWR*, 92; also see Chapter 5).
[58] Chamayou, *Theorie der Drohne*, p. 149; *Drone Theory*, p. 139.

With this, Chamayou describes the logical problem at the heart of precision weapons without combat: a lack of temporal distinction between, and amalgamation of, categories, which then allows for no mediating third. One is either 'fighting' in remote peace (i.e. not fighting at all) or being eradicated.

Remarkably, this *essential* logic of drones poses no fundamental problem for the Christian ethicist Kenneth R. Himes, although he voices concern along the lines of traditional just war criteria.[59] His sub-chapter 'The Nature of Drones' largely recapitulates the technical functionalities and, on the whole, usefulness of drone warfare. The moral permissibility of drones then hinges on whether counterterrorism counts as an 'armed conflict' under US and international law. If it does, 'targeted killings' are permitted in the same way as snipers. If not, drone killings count as 'extrajudicial killings', which are impermissible. In current US policy it remains difficult to define the situation, and arguably doing so is already a partisan move in any conflict. Either way, because Himes does not follow through on the essential (theo-)logic Chamayou identifies, he primarily wants to restrict the use of drones: 'For the sake of [the United States'] moral leadership the government should proclaim and abide by a code of behaviour for drone warfare. A major part of that code should reflect discrimination (e.g., genuine precision in targeting) and proportionality (e.g., not going after a low-level militant whenever collateral damage is likely).'[60] In that sense, Himes sees drones as a regular weapon for a morally superior nation, albeit with modifications and restrictions.

Closer to Chamayou is the German political scientist Herfried Münkler. Münkler has argued that drone warfare needs to be accepted as the best possible counterterrorist option for our Western 'post-heroic societies'. These societies are increasingly losing the theological notions of sacrifice essential for 'heroic' warfare, that is, giving one's limbs and life for the welfare of the larger community. Instead, they rely on sophisticated technology and mercenaries to maintain their security. 'Drones are the Zimmer frame of the post-heroic society.'[61] Avoiding the loss of (one's own) life or not risking it at all has the highest priority here. Arguably, the post-heroic is a symptom of a Christianity that has become (questionably) 'successful'. The *self*-mediation of the human being

---

[59] Kenneth R. Himes OFM, *Drones and the Ethics of Targeted Killing* (Lanham, MD: Rowman & Littlefield, 2016), p. 15; remarkably, Esther D. Reed also does not criticize Himes in that regard: 'Book Reviews: Kenneth R. Himes, OFM, Drones and the Ethics of Targeted Killing', *Studies in Christian Ethics*, 31.3 (2018), 336–9; *pace* Himes, a sustained legal analysis of targeted killing has been offered by Nils Melzer, *Targeted Killing in International Law* (Oxford: Oxford University Press, 2008).

[60] Himes, *Drones*, p. 154; cf. also Allen Buchanan and Robert O. Keohane, 'Toward a Drone Accountability Regime', *Ethics & International Affairs*, 29.1 (2015), 15–37. That the authors are unaware of the essential problem Chamayou identifies may be taken from the following point, for which, notably, they credit *David Rodin*: 'If usage changed, then the difference between drones and boots-on-the-ground occupation might diminish or even disappear. This would be the case if "clouds" of drones permanently patrolled airspace within a country and enforced embargoes at its borders. Such a use of drones would amount to occupation, morally and legally speaking' (p. 36, n. 3).

[61] 'Was bedeutet Krieg in unserer Zeit?', Interview with Herfried Münkler, Deutschlandradio, 19 October 2015, https://www.deutschlandfunk.de/kriegssplitter-von-herfried-muenkler-was-bedeutet-krieg-in.1310.de.html?dram:article_id=334482 (accessed 6 September 2018); Herfried Münkler, *Der Wandel des Krieges: Der Wandel des Krieges: Von der Symmetrie zur Asymmetrie* (Weilerswist: Velbrück Wissenschaft, 2006), pp. 323–38; *Kriegssplitter: Die Evolution der Gewalt im 20. und 21. Jahrhundert* (Berlin: Rowohlt, 2015).

ends up statically positing the *humanum*. Ironically, at the very moment of its triumph it turns out to be ubiquitously vulnerable.

Drone warfare has thrown the military ethos into a crisis, replacing virtues such as courage, endurance as well as technical skills. Both Chamayou and Münkler are well aware of the loss of the classic combatant. Chamayou observes that what used to be cowardice is now relabelled as courage; what used to be murder is now called combat. Nevertheless, although both authors admit that the heroic still plays *some* role, neither Chamayou nor Münkler regards a return to the classical paradigm of combat as a viable option. Chamayou thinks that 'the already questionable ideal of sacrificial heroism finds itself so openly proved false by the facts' that one should 'get rid of it' and 'seek to replace it with other notions of warriors' virtue'.[62] However, it is not clear what those notions should be. Although he offers a – also morally – highly constructive theoretical footnote on 'pragmatic co-presence',[63] in his main text Chamayou merely entices the echo chambers of the public to create a moral sentiment of disagreement and disavowal: 'Not in our name', the public is to protest. So after all a liberal-pacifist retreat? Münkler for his part insists that the situation should be accepted. Any critique of drone warfare 'merely expresses the ethics of a pre-bourgeois society with heroic-nostalgic ideals'. Such a critique, Münkler snubs, 'has not understood itself'. In the face of terrorist attacks, he recommends what he calls 'heroic calmness' – a stoic, passive deferral to the criminal justice system.

However acute their analyses, neither Chamayou's non-alternative nor Münkler's responses can be satisfactory. Waiting for the terrorist 'storm to be over' (Münkler) may be a preliminarily acceptable option for civilians. But where it is not a *reculer pour mieux sauter*, a government's phlegmatic inaction may well contribute to shaking civilians' trust, calmness and composure with every subsequent terrorist attack – something Münkler well foresees. Terrorists may feel encouraged. Worse, inaction amounts to tacit complicity, particularly when the legal maxim 'justice delayed is justice denied' is violated. And why should the 'defensive individual' (Steinhoff) not take justice into their own hands in such a situation? Notably, the fruits of Münkler's (not altogether new) recommendations may already be observed in the increasing political fragmentation and tension in European countries, particularly in the wake of terrorist attacks facilitated by open-border policies. 'Heroic calmness' is not only a contradiction in terms, it also fails as a political-military counterterrorism strategy. Governmental responsibility, particularly when engaged abroad, needs to be more prospective than the reactive criminal justice system can be, even if – as we learn from O'Donovan – the two are theologically closely linked.

On a more essential level, Chamayou, with Walter Benjamin, notes a structural, albeit *reversed* symmetry between remote technological warfare and today's kamikaze fighter, the suicide bomber.[64] The suicide bomber amalgamates the soldier and the weapon – death is certain. In contrast, the industrial remote weapon does not use

---

[62] Chamayou, *Drone Theory*, p. 100.
[63] Chamayou, *Drone Theory*, pp. 247–54, n. 8; NB: The fragmentation of the subject through drone tele-technology and hence the disturbance of intersubjectivity.
[64] Chamayou, *Drone Theory*, pp. 83–4.

the human being at all, fully separating weapon and soldier. Moreover, it allows for an industrial repetition of the act of killing. Death is excluded. 'The drone and the kamikaze stand in contrast as two opposed forms of moral sensibility, two kinds of ethos that mirror each other but are each other's antithesis and nightmare.'[65] But between both stands the classical soldier whose death is a possibility. Münkler insists on the asymmetric nature of present-day warfare but admits a certain level of 'resymmetrification' in terms of the available time frames and the unlimitedness of space, 'not the reinstalment of a duelling situation in the classical sense.'[66]

As a result, the possibility of victory (as a purely military term) gives way to a permanent stalemate that cannot even envision peace. The constellation drones-versus-suicide bombers turns out to be a form of *stasis*. Here, in so far as drone warfare is modified assassination, Kant's sixth preliminary article in the *Perpetual Peace* is instructive. Kant writes, 'No state shall, during war, permit such acts of hostility which would make mutual confidence in the subsequent peace impossible: such are the employment of assassins (*percussores*), poisoners (*venefici*), breach of capitulation, and incitement to treason (*perduellio*) in the opposing state.'[67] Kant sees that these are 'dishonourable stratagemes'; and because they throw the 'character of the enemy' into question, 'hostilities would degenerate into a war of extermination (*bellum internecinum*)'. From a slightly different angle, Kenneth R. Himes similarly notes the slippery slope towards continuous war. It seems therefore that the lack of combat or battle undermines the possibility of peace as a settled judgement. It excludes the recognition inherent in an act of judgement.

Confrontation – mediation

But this implies that classical combat and military virtue is not merely a present cultural reality within militaries, largely isolated from their surrounding societies. Rather, combat is a valid logical option: as an irreducibly antagonistic, non-mediating act it is – no longer paradoxically – a *mediate* term between eradication on the one hand and non-resistance to the point of complicity in crime on the other hand. The moment of fighting is aggressive, risk-laden, uncertain contention. It involves destruction, frequently and undeniably with disastrous non-combatant casualties. But as an operational concept and practice it can only be overlooked at the cost of creating the contradictions outlined above. A *moment* of enmity and combat has to be a real possibility, and in that sense Elshtain's sensibility (partly with Carl Schmitt) was right. Already during the Cold War, Paul Ramsey had recognized: just, and hence limited,

---

[65] Chamayou, *Theorie der Drohne*, p. 96; cf. *Drone Theory*, p. 86; translation slightly amended.

[66] Münker, *Kriegssplitter*, p. 197. NB: The question of symmetry can become highly political and has a sceptical element.

[67] He repeats this in *Metaphysics of Morals*, § 56 (6:348): 'A state against which war is being waged is permitted to use any means of defense except those that would make its subjects unfit to be citizens; for it would then also make itself unfit to qualify, in accordance with the rights of nations, as a person in the relation of states (as one who would enjoy the same rights as others).' Whether Kant is too idealistic here or not, he hints at the incompatibility of certain strategies with the very possibility of a 'just peace'. On the danger of stirring up and protracting conflict, see also Nils Melzer, *Targeted Killing*, pp. 428–9.

war had to be possible as a logical extension of the need to do justice. This would include combat. This task could not be dissolved into wholly irrational, ultimately fictional scenarios of nuclear destruction; neither could it be indefinitely deferred as a hypothetical possibility.

Enmity here is not necessarily (nor can it sustainably be) the permanent or even apocalyptic structure of political constitutionality suggested in some interpretations of Carl Schmitt. More adequately, we may talk about a transitional, operational enmity. This is an uncomfortable position for theological ethics but more palatable than pulling the trigger out of love for the enemy. As a mediate term, 'combat' and enmity imply a double possibility of a *transition*: from static injustice to effectively countering it, from unlimited symmetrical stasis of war to a temporary confrontation, victory and, subsequently, peace-building. It is of course difficult to give a prognosis what this may look like in practice today, since it depends on the political constellations that will emerge. But reconsidering the implications of O'Donovan's 'act of judgment' means one has to include the praxis of confrontative, hostile combat as a possible moment in the practice of mediating judgement.[68] Within a wider context, it means taking combatants serious as such. This would include, for example, not readmitting adult ISIS fighters into the country as if they were merely teenage delinquents. By fighting for the opposition, they have not only renounced but actively fought against the very states warranting the civil rights some of them now appeal to in order to return to Europe.[69]

Residues of heroicism and sacrifice

The possibility of combat also raises the question of whether sacrifice, particularly in the context of 'post-heroic' militaries, remains a defensible option.[70] It seems that even the 'post-heroic' era cannot altogether do without soldiers – or police officers, for that matter, who encounter heavier arms and increasingly insidious tactics. How

---

[68] Already on a political level, i.e. preceding the use of violent force, confrontations rather than 'dubious coalitions' may therefore be part of a strategy against *jihadi* strategies such as hyper-camouflage, dissimulation, the dissolution of self and the other, etc. For an artful analysis of these, see Reza Negarestani, 'The Militarization of Peace', in *Collapse I*, ed. Robin Mackay (Oxford: Urbanomic, 2007), pp. 53–92.

[69] As of 2018, arguments in favour of returning to the concept of treason are gaining more currency, at least in Britain; see e.g. Camilla Cavendish, 'Returning Isis Brides Expose a Woefully Inadequate Legal Armoury: Britain Must Face an Uncomfortable Reality: Some Acts That Should Be Illegal Are Not', *Financial Times*, 15 February 2019, https://www.ft.com/content/157c8e12-3053-11e9-8744-e7016697f225 (accessed 8 March 2019).

[70] In an earlier article, John Milbank explains well the flaws of suicidal self-sacrifice as suggested by e.g. E. Levinas or J. Derrida. Though he rightly anticipated the problems of formalistic, indiscriminate abstraction of 'the Other' and the subtle egotism and denial of convivial communion in such sacrifices, Milbank's relentless polemicizing against the liberal state leaves a huge practical gap between these critical insights and his disavowal of pacifism, including a possible 'war against war'. John Milbank, 'The Ethics of Self-Sacrifice', *First Things*, March 1999, available online at https://www.firstthings.com/article/1999/03/004-the-ethics-of-self-sacrifice (last accessed 24 October 2018); John Milbank, 'Radical Orthodoxy and Protestantism Today: John Milbank in Conversation', *Acta Theologica* (2017), Suppl 25, 43–72; briefly on 'prophylactic suicide' in Levinas, see also Cunningham, *Genealogy of Nihilism*, p. 249.

can their injuries and loss of life in service of individuals, the public, their country or neighbouring countries make sense?

Notably, with the question of sacrifice – which Münkler curiously mentions in one go with 'heroicism' – we are theologically at the heart of mediation. The Letter to the Hebrews describes Jesus Christ as the high priest and sacrifice and as such as the mediator of a new covenant. Sacrifice, as Veronika Hoffmann has noted, is the 'prime case [*Höchstfall*] of mediation' between God and humankind. Christ's death on the cross, and subsequently his resurrection, inaugurates the new creation in which the faithful participate.

In *The Desire of the Nations*, O'Donovan examines the different notions of warfare in the Old Testament. In the early *sacral war*, 'the military commander depends upon immediate divine direction (Num. 14.40—5; 2 Sam. 5.22—5 e.g.); the military array assumes a quasi-liturgical character; the sacred battle is paradoxically unexpected in its course and outcome; the forces of nature are involved in securing Yhwh's victory (Josh. 10.13; Judg. 5.20)' (*DN*, 54). Only in this context, *sacrifice* plays an explicit role for O'Donovan: 'the ban', the total, indiscriminate destruction of the enemy, is intelligible as 'a response to Yhwh's sovereign initiative'. However, sacral warfare was subsequently *challenged* by the ideal of the warrior-hero, embraced primarily in Israel's neighbouring cultures. That ideal also underlies the stories of the young David, and Jonathan, for example, in 1 Sam. 14. Here, king Saul is 'representative of an immobile priest-bound and altogether self-destructive approach to battle'. That proves incompatible with the 'heroic élan of his son, who is prepared to venture his life on the insecurity of a "perhaps" (1 Sam. 14:6)' (*DN*, 55).

O'Donovan's *The Just War Revisited* explicitly juxtaposes heroicism – its virtues, its instrumentality in building civilizations through periods of controlled, ritual bloodshed – with the evangelical ontological rejection of warfare. This is rooted in the uniqueness and irreversibility of Christ's triumph. As O'Donovan explained in *Desire of the Nations*, the writer to the Hebrews includes the moments of Christ on the cross, his death and resurrection into the description of Christ as 'pioneer', *archegos*. As such, the Christ-event also marks the end of sacrifice (both in the Old Testament's sense and the Hellenic world): 'That writer's famous *hapax*, "once only", by which he underlines the definitiveness of Christ's self-offering, extends from the moment of the cross to the moment of ascension (9.12), and defines the unrepeatable aspect of Christ's work, illuminating, purifying and judging the world, at every point (6.6; 10.2; 12.26)' (*DN*, 127–8). The resurrection is then *the* authoritative moment: it inaugurates a transformation predicated on the faithfuls' ascending with Christ to heaven: 'The new life lived under the sway of Christ's resurrection is a life commanded of us as a "service" to righteousness' (*DN*, 128). By emphasizing the uniqueness of Christ's sacrifice, O'Donovan repeats a central position of Reformed and Protestant theology, which is reluctant to embrace sacrificial thinking.[71] This reluctance has its roots in

---

[71] Veronika Hoffmann, *Skizzen zu einer Theologie der Gabe* (Freiburg i. Br.: Herder, 2013), esp. pp. 385–406, and *Christus – die Gabe* (Freiburg i. Br.: Herder, 2016); Ingolf U. Dalferth, *Umsonst: Eine Erinnerung an die kreative Passivität des Menschen* (Tübingen: Mohr Siebeck, 2011); Martin Wendte, *Die Gabe und das Gestell: Luthers Metaphysik des Abendmahls im technischen Zeitalter* (Tübingen: Mohr Siebeck, 2013).

the opposition to the late medieval ecclesial apparatus; it became defunct as Christ's sacrifice could no longer be re-instantiated through priestly mediation.[72]

Does that indicate a supersession of the hero-warrior by the prophetic task *post sacrificium Christi*? If Christ's sacrifice mediates a new covenant and allows for thinking mediation, then analogously, the service of justice mediates, indeed affects a transition, from conflict to peace. A potential loss of limbs and life *in extremis* may be a conduit towards a restored community – also with the enemy, who has not simply been turned into 'bug splat'. Such a sacrifice remains risk-laden and is hardly identical with a life of peaceful liturgy. Yet if we diagnose both late nineteenth-century militarism and the 'post-heroic' denial of combat as a logical amalgamation of sacred peace and war, the heroic-sacrificial is in fact the only option to alleviate this impasse; it is even *indicated* by Chamayou's avoidance and Münkler's abrasiveness.

Nuances in understanding such a sacrifice will arise in a comparative perspective. On the Reformed Protestant premise, the grace of God received in *gratitude* may facilitate a venturing in favour of the neighbour – both the unjustly attacked and the enemy neighbour, who is recognized in battle. This coheres not least with Luther's interpretation of Adam's *imago Dei*: 'not that [the human being] only knew God and believed that he was good, but that he also lived an altogether divine life, that is, that he was without fear of death and all dangers, grateful for the grace of God.'[73] Here receiving the gifts of grace and love and the subsequent, growing practice of receptivity desacralize worldly tasks, including soldiering. In recent Catholic thought, sacrifice has been examined as one potentially necessary element of a theological anthropology that grounds human beings in relationality, mutuality and communion.[74] Thus, with different emphases, contemporary thinkers from both traditions challenge a self-positing solipsism, whether political or cultural, but particularly under the guise of 'humanism'. There are no reasons why these considerations should not apply to warfare and combat. The heroic remains an imaginary for the soldier's task underlining the *worldly* task of judgement – a tacit, yet continuously effective *pre*-Christian underbelly that can prevent a Christian spiritualization of warfare while not being altogether alien to the Christian life.

This also seems to be an implication of the 'residual duality' between judgement and worship O'Donovan suggests. Indeed, *he* reminds us of the warrior-hero as well as the *miles Christianus* as historical cultural figures. With Thomas Aquinas, he speaks of an 'irascible contrariety'

---

[72] The later twentieth-century scepticism about sacrifice has its roots in the nineteenth century. During the revolutionary wars, sacrificial politics recurred as soldiers were to offer themselves on the militaristic altars of nations, empires or for political causes deemed sacred. This understanding permeated warfare until late in the twentieth century.

[73] Martin Luther, *WA*, 42, 47, 8–11, cited in Martin Wendte, *Die Gabe und das Gestell*, p. 416. NB: This can be in significant tension with more recent narrativist approaches in which theology is a form of literature; see e.g. Ralf Frisch, *Alles gut: Warum Karl Barths Theologie ihre beste Zeit noch vor sich hat* (Zurich: TVZ Verlag, 2018).

[74] See e.g. Ivan Strenski, *Contesting Sacrifice: Religion, Nationalism, and Social Thought in France* (Chicago, IL: University of Chicago Press, 2002); *Sacrifice and Modern Thought*, ed. Julia Meszaros and Johannes Zachhuber (Oxford: Oxford University Press, 2014), there esp. Julia Meszaros and Johannes Zachhuber, 'Introduction', pp. 1–11; see also above n. 52.

by which [Aquinas] meant that our passionate reactions to good and evil not only take the form of an instinctive attraction and repulsion, but also, as we see good and evil as presenting a challenge to our own capacities, of a reflective contrary movement, shrinking from or pressing towards action. So faced with an immediate threat to our lives, there is released within us a dialectical response, not only of extreme fear but of extreme boldness, on the basis of which a culture of the virtue of courage may be perfected. (*JWR*, 3)

O'Donovan here perhaps too quickly focuses on the immediate threat to one's own life, when practicing military virtue is to move beyond the instincts of fear and self-defence in the service of doing justice. He then goes on to say, 'The unbridled excess of war, the ritual mutilation of corpses, the slaughter of non-combatants, the rape of women, the destruction of property, every kind of violent display, in fact, are all indivisibly of a piece with its constructive, culture-building and virtue-perfecting aspects' (*JWR*, 3). Yet while it is surely the case that atrocities will happen, it is not clear why the constructive, culture-building and virtue-perfecting aspects should not be part of the 'act of judgment'. On the contrary, it is more likely to improve *in bello* restraint than the mere use of the means of crime.

This is still one step removed from Daniel M. Bell Jr's proposal, for whom just war itself is to be re-centred in the church *rather than* the state. While Bell targets the ideological use of formalistic 'Just War' checklists masquerading as moral content, just war as Christian discipleship 'focuses on the practices of the Christian life whereby God graciously forms the church into a community of disciples who love and seek justice for their neighbors (including their enemy neighbors) in war'.[75] It is a form of witness which 'rests on the truth of the claim that Jesus is Lord of history even now and not just in the future. Just War (CD) stands or falls on the truth of the claim that we are not alone, even now. God is with us.'[76] In this context, soldiers' sacrifice poses no problem: 'Christians can give even their lives in a just war for the sake of the common good of their neighbors because they know that though we and/or our loved ones die, in the end, like Job, we all will be restored and will have lost nothing.'[77] While Bell Jr., also with reference to Mt. 10.39, explains the meaningfulness of Christian soldiers' sacrifices, there is little in the way of a sacralization of the modern (US) military as long as it is not *overtly* utilitarian.[78]

For the Evangelical Lutheran military pastor Ulrich von den Steinen, by contrast, the difference between person and office remains structurally important. 'Paradoxically, the use of force is a *service of love* – namely, to protect the weak through violent means, risking one's own life. This contradiction, namely to use

---

[75] Bell Jr, *Just War as Christian Discipleship*, p. 81.

[76] Ibid., p. 242.

[77] Ibid., p. 149.

[78] Bell's more recent suggestion that 'Christ, and the life of fidelity to the truth-event that is Christ, is indifferent to crucifixion, suffering, and death' corroborates rather than challenges this interpretation. Daniel M. Bell Jr, *Divinations: Theopolitics in an Age of Terror* (Eugene, OR: Cascade, 2017), p. 3.

arms, leads the arms-bearer into a dilemma: as they serve, they become guilty, even though they let love for human beings be effective through emergency defence and emergency help.'[79] This 'paradox of the soldier's vocation' cannot be resolved. Instead of dreaming, inner piety [*Innerlichkeit*] or resignation in the face of injustice (and here one may well consider Münkler a target), acting 'responsibly on the border-line between life and death is always a venture [*Wagnis*] and never without risk'. In other words, the potential element of fighting in the mediating tasks of politics remains locked in the *paradox* of love and violent force, even if that paradox has a sharpness and clarity in light of the gospel. Nonetheless, the instrumentality of violent force for the sake of the neighbour, particularly with potentially lethal outcome for soldiers, sufficiently alleviates this paradox, albeit without entirely resolving it. It is neither an amalgamation in the sense we've observed in drone warfare nor does it militarize the church, which von den Steinen is additionally careful to not identify with the Word of God itself. The latter is then held out for consolation.

Conclusion

Oliver O'Donovan's just war proposal both critiqued and incorporated elements of those examined in Parts I and II. In this chapter, I have once again thrown into question what might have seemed a final culmination, going through permanent openings and possibilities of transition. The permeability between theology and philosophical idealism remains part of theology also in the decades to come. This has not merely intellectual-historical reasons, specifically Hegel's work and its formative impact on twentieth-century theology. It also prevents theology from aligning itself with fideism and – marking the defeat of ethics – moralism. In terms of the ethics of war, Paul Ramsey's and others' connection between Christian agape and idealism allowed for historical moments, persons and political entities to mediate justice. The notion of grace plays a central role in this, even if this could only be developed briefly here. In a Christ-analogous move, grace allows for a transition from a divine horizon of mediation to a practical 'embarrassment of engagement', albeit – if Bonhoeffer's distinction is heeded – without 'justifying sin'. This corresponds to the need for political practicability and actual political advocacy on the one hand but on the other hand equally readjusts political advocacy, that is, demands for it to be 'referred' to an order of reconciliation (St Augustine).[80] And it is here where the mere 'phenomenon' of history becomes the 'work' of the pilgrim.

From this perspective, then, the (theo-)logic of mediation also pertains to combat and, critically, the essence of contemporary weapons systems. Here I have mainly focused on drone warfare, which exemplifies the amalgamation of non-violence and warfare, the mutual collapse of (humanitarian) morality and politics, care and

---

[79] Ulrich von den Steinen, *Unzufrieden mit dem Frieden?*, p. 185.
[80] Cf. David Kim, 'The City of God', esp. pp. 126–34. Cf. Chapter 1.

murder. However, and far from being unenlightened, the notion of combat alleviates this contradiction. If this is accepted, the theology of sacrifice continues to illuminate, attenuate and differentiate the meaning of soldiers' service. Indeed, service and sacrifice may well be one of the concepts most thoroughly to be investigated by ethicists of war in the years to come.

Conclusions

The thesis of this book has been that the logics of war depend on and are indicative of the explicit or implicit theo-logics connecting God and the world. A critique of the former implies a critique of the latter and vice versa. Different authors in the Anglo-Saxon and continental traditions have been discussed as representatives of the various ways in which the mediation between God and world plays out in the field of ethics. A decisive shift underlay the narrative, a shift that occurred between the ontological mediation wrought in Christ and what I have called human self-mediation or the mediation of the *humanum*. In its wake, human beings themselves become 'princes of peace',[1] albeit repeating and echoing pre-modern theo-political constellations. In the last chapter on history, grace and combat, O'Donovan's evangelical theological proposal was extended and, in some respects, reopened. What remains to be done in these concluding remarks thus is to briefly recapitulate the argument, to indicate further theological paths ahead and to point out where problems of mediation may occur in the debates on conflicts to come.

Theo-logics – logics of authority – logics of war

Throughout the book, we have retraced a delicate connection between the metaphysical, political and ethical-practical logics at work. In Part One, political authority was conceived along the liberal-constitutional paradigm. If one follows Agamben, one might say it is an essentially juridical paradigm, divided between, on the one hand, the (potentially) anarchic rule of everyone in which defensive rights are foundational (the state of nature, at times polemically associated with the term 'populism') and, on the other hand, the rule of state law, a domestic(ated) legal system.[2] This dichotomy could also

---

[1] This seems significantly more convincing than a mere decentring or even loss of modern man, since that decentring coincides with an unprecedented expansion of activities, specifically warfare. An environmentalist extension of (post-)humanist anthropocentrism has recently put forward the notion of the 'anthropocene'; see e.g. John S. Dryzek and Jonathan Pickering, *The Politics of the Anthropocene* (Oxford: Oxford University Press, 2019).

[2] Contrary to certain kinds of romanticism, a revolutionary force within the liberal-constitutional paradigm is effectively disparaged. It may be a pre-political anarchy or effective foundational myth, but the point of juridical closure is precisely to make even a *morally* justified political overthrow of the constitutional system impossible. This conceptual gap between positive law and actual

be conceived globally, between the 'realism' of states' defensive rights and the 'idealism' of international law. Christianity in that constellation is the 'Old Testament of the declaration of the Rights of Man',[3] as Pierre Manent critically puts it and Kant seems to have been aware.

Coming from the realist side, Elshtain's approach was predicated on an ultimate Christological dualism that, practically, drew together Hobbesian, Schmittian, transcendentalist and Augustinian motifs. Elshtain then regarded the sovereign state as the sole moral-political authority and mediator, one which also accepted no decisive restrictions by international law. Claiming to embody and guarantee a panoply of religious options domestically, and a human rights order globally, the state would simultaneously extend its own national interest. Yet by absorbing the global humanitarian perspective, it turned into an agent of internationalist 'idealism' itself, in the form of 'benevolent empire'. The mediation and reconciliation between opposites was then either declared accomplished, through purporting 'enlightened self-interest', or impossible on the grounds of the nihilist irrationality of the opponent. In a war of national defence against terrorist aggressors, the sovereign nation-state clashed with its enemies as much as with its humanitarian-idealist and sectarian dissidents. But eventually it became both.

Particularly with a view to Michael Walzer, David Rodin began from the contrary perspective. He regarded international human rights law as the authoritative mediator between politics and morality. His legalism demanded that the 'idealist' *ius cosmopoliticum* be realized as a global state, governing a 'non-sovereign' political society. However, there was also a dialectical turn, indeed an irony: once the sheer normative power of the law runs out, Rodin's utopian impracticability collapses into legitimizing the powers that be. And once attempts are made to realize a global human rights order, they are bound to collapse into imperialism; this is by no means an 'unintended consequence', or entirely alien to liberalism, but rather its intrinsic logic, as, for example, the late Domenico Losurdo has argued. Even more ironically, Rodin paved the way for a return of *bellum iustum*. The place accorded to 'religion' here is syphoned off in a manner slightly different from Elshtain: it is deposited into the realm of 'inner convictions', or the sphere of 'intuitions', hence highly suggestive, yet ever so prone to deconstruction.

In contrast to Rodin, yet more of a variant of Elshtain's approach, Uwe Steinhoff emphasized individual Machiavellian authorities and mediators between Is and any feasible Ought of their desire. Not least in the wake of an unresolved theodicy after

---

revolution can already be observed in Kant's *Streit der Fakultäten*. An essential element of the Enlightened paradigm, that gap distributes moral energy to the developmental reason of humanity. But in actual history – the French Revolution in Kant's own time – it finds merely incidences before which humanity's tendency of moral evolution can prove itself. Hence, again, it is misleading to read Kant as suggesting 'instantiating' or 'realizing' the cosmopolitan ideal in history (or, for that matter, a revolution in that spirit). Cf. Immanuel Kant, *Der Streit der Fakultäten*, AA VII, pp. 88–9; Michel Foucault's enthusiasm about the Iranian Revolution in 1979 might be a parallel. Stathis Kouvelakis, *Philosophy and Revolution from Kant to Marx* (London, Verso: 2003), pp. 2–3.

3   Cited Pierre Manent in John Milbank, 'The End of Tolerance: On the Decline of Religious Freedom and the Return of Religious Influence', *ABC Religion & Ethics*, 24 August 2017, https://www.abc.net.au/religion/the-decline-of-religious-freedom-and-the-return-of-religious-inf/10095982 (accessed 26 February 2019).

Auschwitz, Steinhoff's rationalist, secularist liberalism also posited a radical separation of the political from substantial moral or indeed metaphysical content, leaving instead to the individual to decide which morality suits best. In doing so, Steinhoff encapsulated the political-theological heritage of the so-called radical Reformation, yet via John Locke also an element of the Calvinist theo-logic. Insisting on inalienable defensive rights, Steinhoff's work questioned the ideology of sovereign states, particularly US hegemony but equally cosmopolitanisms such as Habermas's and Rodin's. His liberalism could also absorb its opposite. It was consciously ideological and so a (negative) *Sittlichkeit* in itself, remarkably un-revolutionary, geared towards the sovereign state and liberal empire. Nonetheless, this theoretical consequence was outweighed by the practical implications of fundamental defensive rights within an overall pacific order of tolerance and individual freedom.

Paul Ramsey's remarkable intellectual journey partly resolved the modern oscillation between realism and idealism by travelling from one – the idealist – end to the realist other. As Stanley Hauerwas noted, the tensions between his theological interpretations were due to his search for a theology that suited his ethical intuitions. The most convincing, long-lasting, though also modified, contribution was his agapism, which insisted on everyone's duty to help the neighbour, no matter what. (In that sense, to put it anachronistically, Ramsey echoed Steinhoff's authority of everyone). The immediacy of divine *agape* here correlated with a duality between this aeon and the next. In his transformist period, however, Ramsey developed the logic of the political act. It was a dynamic search for a coincidence of the values of *ordo, lex* and *iustitia*, all before (or necessitated by) a sense of the gloom and shadow of this age, albeit a shadow thrown by the light of Christ. Ramsey's later realism may well be seen as a predecessor of Elshtain's statist realism. His insistence on acknowledging the reality of an 'opposed system' that is the international sphere was equidistant from utopianism and the 'good works' of internationalist legal institutions. Tied to a domino theory during the Vietnam War, however, Ramsey's extension of national interest to a global scale had imperialist implications. Yet, it remained significantly more reactive in nature than Elshtain's.

If Ramsey partly resolved the oscillation between idealism and realism, then O'Donovan went one step further, pushing back the horizon of the political to include the theological and metaphysical. The other authors may well have intimated this possibility, but either it remained outside the just war reflection or it was absorbed without residue by the political paradigm as morally self-sufficient. O'Donovan's ethical approach, in contrast, was derived from and responds to the universal history of Israel as narrated in Scripture. With this, he constructed a mediate and continuously mediating position of political authority vis-à-vis Christ's authority. This approach unmoors the idealist-realist paradigm from its immanence, locating political authority on the dividing line between humanity and an ultimately divine horizon of fulfilment.[4] That doesn't mean authority becomes a mediator that *replaces* the Christ mediator. The Christ-event radically strips political authority of its potential to act as such a mediator, even if it retains an 'angelic' character. Government, conceived as an act of judgement merely *analogous* to

---

[4] Cf. for similar conclusions from an Anglo-Catholic perspective, John Milbank, 'The Gift of Ruling: Secularization and Political Authority', *New Blackfriars*, 85.996 (2004), 212–38.

the mediating Christ-event, has to charitably divide innocent and guilty while offering (or at least intimating) the possibility of a reconciliation of belligerents in the future. It has to do so under the law, which is understood as an objective order of Right. In the international sphere, this order is a pluralism of nations and common goods connected by the *ius gentium*. Before this backdrop, law and judgement would remain potentially distinct, though not opposed (as Carl Schmitt at times seems to suggest).

Echoing and absorbing a Hegelian logic, O'Donovan's notion of judgement continuously both reintegrates and transforms individual subjective rights and an objective (and possibly positive) legal order. Judgement is and has the mediating task of representing individuals or belligerents, while objectivizing their claims and thus reconciling them. Political institutions are heeded, but they remain morally justified only by the task of judgement – not vice versa. The legitimating *grounds* of authorized judgement are objective, though not sacralized, forms of communal life given in creation. An 'anarchic' moment is equally reintegrated here; it is truly realized for the church, which knows no ruling authority except Christ; as such, the church is also a political society, not merely a spiritual entity or fiction. In O'Donovan's view, the (Christian) political society in and from which true, radical equality comes into view must also be heeded by political authorities. It is the dimension of 'soul citizenship' in the City of God through which citizens can conceive of and cooperate with authority in the first place rather than retreat in sceptical compliance. O'Donovan thus theologically incorporates a foundational sentiment of the modern liberal mind. If Steinhoff's radical individualist scepticism had been on the cusp of faith, even if he then turned away from it, Ramsey's agapeic freedom 'beyond good and evil' had opened a door. O'Donovan then walked through it with a biblically moored society of prophetic individuals.

Chapter 6 again problematized some of the implications of O'Donovan's proposal. In light of the eschatological vision, as much as the ultimate hope this will give, the chapter highlighted the need to discern the good and true in actual history. I argued here for a constant transition: between the eschatological narrative and endpoint (which the gospel of Mark associates with the Father[5]) and the engagement with theological structures, patterns and echoes in history, which one may well associate with the workings of Christ incarnate and the Spirit. The notion of grace was central here. But to prevent that from becoming a mere 'energy' for all sorts of political projects (Luther's *pecca fortiter* without the *fide fortius*), discipleship is indispensable. As O'Donovan in his critique of Hegel intimates, it requires a reconnection with liturgical life. Ultimately, this cannot be divorced from the eucharistic convergence of the temporal and the eternal and the questions of authority *that* raises.[6] But it also connects to the role of the Christian ethicist as a moral authority: how much should he or she take sides, risking the embarrassment of engagement? Again, a transition between both aspects is necessary, but also possible, signifying both freedom in concreteness and freedom from concreteness. Either way, theological reflection cannot confine itself to merely reporting back its observations of a plural or supposedly pluralistic status quo.

---

[5]   Mk 13.32.
[6]   Cf. *RMO*, 53–76.

Theological openings

Several strands of future enquiry emerge from the present project. One of them is the mediating dialectics throughout the Christian political tradition, and this indicates a continuation of O'Donovan's and others' projects of historical retrieval. In the present work, Augustine towered in the background, highly relevant for both contemporary theo-political liberalisms and anti-liberalisms seeking new groundings in the patristic heritage.[7] Another figure suggesting himself for future enquiry might be Gregory the Great, though not so much because he established papal supremacy in the sixth century. Gregory rather sees Scripture speak into a period of political and epistemological crisis, its words structuring a world and truth through its multiple layers of meaning.

In the previous chapters, I have also pointed at several historical and modern references to the papacy, the radical Reformation and figures such as Carl Schmitt.[8] The work of Habermas as a cosmopolitan has been orbiting the discussion, at least via Steinhoff's critique. Habermas represents an alternative normative-epistemological approach to cosmopolitanism in contrast to contemporary Anglo-American intuitionism.[9] Here one might wonder whether the alliance between theology and social theory, still prominent in German-speaking theology, should be revised, not least to reign in a frequent discourse-ethical approach petering out into common-sense generalities. Particularly in light of the Idealist inheritance, Reinhold Niebuhr would merit greater reception in continental theological ethics. Niebuhr continues to shape Christian politics in the United States, providing also a critical perspective on the realist-idealist expansionism since the early 2000s.[10]

In the present work, I also largely relegated Christian just war 'idealism' to footnotes. One reason is that today the place of such 'idealism', which goes back to Dante and even to Tertullian, has become virtually indistinguishable from cosmopolitanism. Looking at it through David Rodin, I indicated the ecclesiological overtones and problems one encounters here. One of the (admittedly controversial) inferences might be that in so far as Protestant churches endorse a certain form of human rights cosmopolitanism, they have successfully been 'Catholicized', albeit in an immanentist way many Catholic authors find increasingly unacceptable.[11] At times, I have also grouped Christian pacifism under the category of just war idealism. Yet even though

---

[7] For the role of mediation and ethics in Augustine, see e.g. Robert Dodaro, *Christ and the Just Society in the Thought of Augustine* (Cambridge: Cambridge University Press, 2004); also Theodor W. Adorno, *History and Freedom: Lectures 1964–1965*, ed. Rolf Tiedemann (Cambridge: Polity, 2006).

[8] Cf. e.g. Jens Meierhenrich and Oliver Simons (eds), *The Oxford Handbook of Carl Schmitt* (Oxford: Oxford University Press, 2017).

[9] See also Jürgen Habermas, *Glauben und Wissen* (Frankfurt: Suhrkamp, 2001).

[10] R. Ward Holder and Peter Josephson, *The Irony of Barack Obama: Barack Obama, Reinhold Niebuhr and the Problem of Christian Statecraft* (Farnham: Ashgate, 2012); Robin W. Lovin, *Reinhold Niebuhr and Christian Realism* (Cambridge: Cambridge University Press, 1995); Paul Rich, 'Reinhold Niebuhr and the Ethics of Realism in International Relations', *History of Political Thought*, 13 (1992), 281–98.

[11] An aphorism attributed to the polemicist Michael Klonovsky about Margot Käßmann, the former chair of the Council of the Evangelical Church in Germany, slightly overstated this point: 'If you put a Habermas speech into sugar water over night, you get a Käßmann sermon in the morning.'

they share a 'presumption against violence', this is a simplification of the nuances of the pacifist traditions as well as its 'conditional' iterations.

In the future, the 'ethics of war' of many nineteenth- and twentieth-century revolutionary political (anti-)theologies will also require further examination. If at least after Kant and Hegel anthropology sublates theology, then in some subsequent interpretations history itself becomes revelation, the revelation also *of* itself. Philosophy then becomes the mere exegesis of history. Yet once history's mode of advancement is revolution, such political action is hardly any kind of response to the singular revolution in Christ but its (parodic) re-enactment. As a quasi-revelatory event, such a revolution passes ultimate judgement between life and death, the only standard of discrimination being 'the revolution' itself or rather a person's allegiance or hindrance to it. In that regard, a deeper scrutiny of later Soviet as well as Maoist notions of mediation and dialectics could further the understanding of contemporary 'ethics of war', closely also connected to strategic studies.

Such an enquiry into (post-)Marxism then connects to postmodern ethics and critiques of ethics altogether, as for example in the work of Judith Butler or Alain Badiou. Postmodern interactions with theology, their specific deconstructions of the political, would make an analysis of those 'just war' ethics a worthwhile project of its own.[12] However, where anthropocentrism is a form of self-technique or self-creation (as suggested by Foucault), that is less a form of left-wing politics at the level of individual biographies but rather a form of liberalism (as Uwe Steinhoff has pointed out). One might even argue that here self-mediation of the humanum, inner-historical revolution and neo-liberalism merge in the most curious way. That may also explain why the old Left, when availing itself of postmodern theoretical figures, increasingly tends to be weak, frequently dissolving into Philistine identity politics, resorting to anarchist strategies – or simply self-destroying in ultimately meaningless acts of cultural and political self-sacrifice. One alternative to these tendencies might be to recover a more open-minded and socially aware conservatism.

Besides such ethically embedded (anti-)theologies, the task of theology *sui generis* will arguably become greater rather than diminish. Metaphysics and ontology are central here. With a view to the present work, Christology and the ontology of personhood as more than a substantivist individualism will require a greater reconnection with ethics. Where modern twentieth-century Protestant theology, influenced also by idealism, had looked to the work of the Son and the Spirit, it may have to once again enquire about the implications of divine Fatherhood, precisely to also counter 'radical monotheisms' and their different forms of *stasis*. This indicates a greater reconnection

---

[12] As regards the French historical background, the Résistance is a historical moment of significance here; see Alain Badiou, *Metapolitics* (London: Verso, 2005), esp. pp. 1–10 on Georges Canguilhem and the Résistance; Badiou (with Nicolas Truong), *In Praise of Love*, transl. Peter Bush (London: Serpent's Tail, 2012); Gilles Deleuze, *Spinoza: Practical Philosophy* (San Francisco, CA: City Lights, 1988); Judith Butler, *Giving an Account of Oneself* (New York: Fordham University Press, 2005), pp. 46–9; *Frames of War* (London: Verso, 2009); Slavoj Žižek, Eric L. Santner and Kenneth Reinhard, *The Neighbor: Three Inquiries in Political Theology* (Chicago, IL: University of Chicago Press, 2005), pp. 158–60.

to the Orthodox tradition, potentially also as a counterweight to liberal ennui and exhaustion.[13] Either way, for Protestants, it will no longer do to expound on central dogmatic topoi 'from the perspective of faith'. They will have to learn once again to argue about 'what there is'.

Most importantly, since the present work has been a study of contemporary theologies in the light of their practical proposals, the next step would be to extend that into deeper exegetical and biblical study. If systematic biblical hermeneutics are closely linked to the Christo-logics developed in systematics, then the historical-critical endeavour might require further expansion. Oliver O'Donovan's and Paul Ramsey's works in this respect have enjoyed the most sustained engagement.[14] The exchanges between Richard Hays and Nigel Biggar on pacifism and just war grounded in the New Testament were also directly to the point. A key question that is *also* hermeneutical is then how to interpret and integrate the Old Testament perspectives on warfare, particularly in conversation with Jewish political thinkers such as Michael Walzer. Either way, the turn to biblical interpretation has a monumental precedent in Augustine's *Confessions*: it was an entirely logical step, rather than a mere addendum, for him to turn from Christ the Mediator in the tenth book to an exegesis of Genesis – a transitional movement so characteristic of the pivotal minds in history.

Emerging conflicts

Besides the theological paths ahead, several emerging political developments may also require examination in light of the just war tradition. As the living memory of the early twentieth century has largely faded, the mere aim of preventing a repetition of its monstrosities tends to result in rhetoric grand-standing where theologically grounded, practical wisdom is required. Three developments are particularly worth mentioning.

First, the rise of algorithms and so-called artificial intelligence, whether as war machines or decision makers in domestic social administration, harbours conflict. These technologies' prestige may be a logical consequence of the waning of representative political authority, be that as a result of conceptual shifts or political-administrative mismanagement. The sense that responsible judgement can be outsourced to predictable calculation, and thus a depersonified form of *law*, in some places merges with transhumanist aspirations. It is of course banal to point out that algorithms have no 'moral agency' and to highlight the conditions of their use. Yet, to also parse the different 'values' embodied in algorithms (e.g. equity *or* equal outcome) is one aspect of the emerging field of 'algorithm ethics' or 'data ethics'. Robots partially embody and execute philosophical-theological convictions. These may well include a Spinozistic (re-)enchantment of nature and technology, one in which repetitive human

---

[13] Cf. Stephen Pax Leonard, *Travels in Cultural Nihilism: Some Essays* (London: Arktos, 2017).
[14] Craig G. Bartholomew (ed.), *A Royal Priesthood? The Use of the Bible Ethically and Politically: A Dialogue with Oliver O'Donovan* (Carlisle: Paternoster Press, 2002); Adam E. Hollowell, 'Just War and Statecraft in Paul Ramsey's Reading of Luke 14:28–33', *Journal of Scriptural Reasoning*, 11 (2012), https://dukespace.lib.duke.edu/dspace/handle/10161/17360 (accessed 15 July 2019).

agency is ultimately bereft of significance and transcendence. One delicate task for theologians in this field will be to put the aims programmed into algorithms into a wider context, to find historical, philosophical and theological analogies that allow us to see behind the façade created by the perpetual barrage of 'innovations'. Thus, the aim must be to distinguish the *usus* of machines from the *frui* of human fulfilment, quite in line with the priestly vocation of old: to distinguish the holy from the profane. Whether that entails a supposedly Luddite refusal or hearty endorsement: neither can be ruled out *ex ante* in favour of any readily available 'middle path'.[15]

Second, in Europe, the large influx of migrants beginning around 2010 and peaking around 2015 has been met by many church officials and theologians with a lack of awareness that precisely here the structures of ordered, mediating judgement are demanded. Endorsing open borders and suspended laws in a humanitarian, reverse Schmittian 'state of exception', Christian political ethics effectively failed. That moment of pseudo-revelatory enthusiasm has now subsided into widespread oblivion about the numerous victims, niggardly bafflement about the societal backlash or, worse, more or less soft forms of censorship. If mediating judgement was suspended then – almost as if to prove its need – societies are now divided within themselves. Where lacking executive means, such judgement takes the form of ubiquitous suspicion. Political moralism here merely descends into hysteria and double speak. By contrast, the just war tradition can practically uphold the demands of dignity, formulating consistent concerns for political responsibility, law, administrative form as well as territory in order to protect existing and emerging relations of peaceful practice.[16]

Third, and finally, as I am writing this, Britain is headed towards Brexit, a decision and political process that was also a reaction to mass migration on the European continent. For many, Brexit may seem like an abyss, with uncertainty and fear bereft of an object driving the commentariat. The coming months and years could indeed herald a period of greater division in Britain and political fissures across Europe, though perhaps more reminiscent of the seventeenth than the twentieth century. The situation may be exacerbated by the yet unclear rise of Chinese political-economic influence, Islamist metapolitics and the waning coherence of Anglo-American capitalism. At present, Western societies (still) oscillate between individualistic litigiousness and anonymous governance apparatuses. Yet, the new situation also harbours the possibility to recover a sense of political community from the silence beyond clamouring strife. In reflecting,

---

[15] Quite in line with an epigram by the seventeenth-century poet Friedrich von Logan, 'In highest dangers and distress, the middle way spells certain death.'

[16] Against moralism, see e.g. Ulrich H. Körtner, *Für die Vernunft: Wider Moralisierung und Emotionalisierung in Politik und Kirche* (Leipzig: Evangelische Verlagsanstalt, 2017); in the context of migration, Robert W. Heimburger mentions the just war only briefly, in *God and the Illegal Alien* (Cambridge: Cambridge University Press, 2018), p. 111; for a discussion of that book, see *Theology* (September 2019, special section), including contributions by Margaret Adam, Therese Feiler, and Rob Heimburger; remarkably, O'Donovan interprets mass migration as *only* a question of welcoming new neighbours, not a threat to the common good: 'The Common Good: Does it Represent a Political Programme?', lecture delivered at the Futures of Public Theology Conference, New College, University of Edinburgh, 1 December 2017, https://www.youtube.com/watch?v=vuT x6Z2jkzU&feature=youtu.be (accessed 4 March 2019).

and reflecting on, Christ's mediation, we may locate a point at which political action can be wrestled from irony, tragedy and oblivion. For the just war tradition was never merely about vitalist self-defence. It was a way of thinking for human beings, who, as they mature on a cosmic, corporate pilgrimage, would intimate orders of never-ending peace.

Bibliography

Abraham, David, *The Bush Regime from Elections to Detentions: A Moral Economy of Carl Schmitt and Human Rights* (2007), http://www.scribd.com/doc/52446194/A-Moral-Economy-of-Carl-Schmitt-and-Human-Rights (accessed 27 January 2013).

Adams, Nicholas, *The Eclipse of Grace: Divine and Human Action in Hegel* (Chichester: Wiley-Blackwell, 2013).

Adkins, Brent, *A Review of Jean Bethke Elshtain's Just War against Terror: The Burden of American Power in a Violent World*, https://www.elca.org/JLE/Articles/733 (accessed 2 July 2019).

Agamben, Giorgio, *Homo Sacer: Sovereign Power and Bare Life* (Stanford, CA: Stanford University Press, 1998).

Agamben, Giorgio, *State of Exception* (Chicago, IL: University of Chicago Press, 2005).

Allison, Henry E., *Kant's Transcendental Idealism*, rev. and enl. ed. (New Haven, CT: Yale University Press, 2004).

Althusser, Louis, *Lenin and Philosophy and Other Essays* (New York: Monthly Review Press, 2001).

Altwicker, Tilman, 'The International Legal Argument in Spinoza', in *System, Order, and International Law: The Early History of International Legal Thought from Machiavelli to Hegel*, edited by Stefan Kadelbach, Thomas Kleinlein and David Roth-Isigkeit (Oxford: Oxford University Press, 2017), pp. 183–98.

Anderson, Perry, *Spectrum. From Right to Left in the World of Ideas* (London: Verso, 2005).

Arquillière, Henri Xavier, *L'Augustinisme Politique: Essai sur la Formation des Théories Politiques du Moyen-Age* (Paris: J. Vrin, 1955).

Attwood, David, *Paul Ramsey's Political Ethics* (Lanham, MD: Rowman & Littlefield, 1992).

Audi, Robert, *Rationality and Religious Commitment* (Oxford: Oxford University Press, 2011).

Augustine of Hippo, *The City of God against the Pagans*, edited by Robert W. Dyson (Cambridge: Cambridge University Press, 1998).

Augustine of Hippo, 'From *On the Free Choice of the Will*, Bk. 1', in *From Irenaeus to Grotius: A Sourcebook in Christian Political Thought*, edited by Oliver O'Donovan and Joan Lockwood O'Donovan (Grand Rapids, MI: William B. Eerdmans, 1999), pp. 113–44.

Augustine of Hippo, *Answer to Faustus* (New York: New City Press, 2007).

Aus Gottes Frieden leben – für gerechten Frieden sorgen. Eine Denkschrift des Rates der Evangelischen Kirche in Deutschland, 2007, http://www.ekd.de/download/ekd_friedensdenkschrift.pdf (accessed 13 December 2018).

Babík, Milan, 'In Pursuit of Salvation: Woodrow Wilson and American Liberal Internationalism as Secularized Eschatology' (unpublished DPhil thesis, University of Oxford, 2009).

Babík, Milan, *Statecraft and Salvation: Wilsonian Liberal Internationalism as Secularized Eschatology* (Waco, TX: Baylor University Press, 2013).

Badiou, Alain, *Being and Event* (London: Continuum, 2005).

Badiou, Alain, *Metapolitics* (London: Verso, 2005).

Badiou, Alain, and Nicolas Truong, *In Praise of Love*, translated by Peter Bush (London: Serpent's Tail, 2012).

Baron, Marcia, 'Kantian Ethics and Supererogation', *Journal of Philosophy*, 84 (1987), 237–62.

Barth, Karl, *Epistle to the Romans*, trans. Edwyn C. Hoskyns (Oxford: Oxford University Press, 1968).

Barth, Karl, *Ethics*, Lectures at Münster (1928) and Bonn (1930), translated by Geoffrey W. Bromiley (Edinburgh: T&T Clark, 1981).

Bartholomew, Craig G. (ed.), *A Royal Priesthood? The Use of the Bible Ethically and Politically: A Dialogue with Oliver O'Donovan* (Carlisle: Paternoster Press, 2002).

Bayer, Oswald, 'Barmen zwischen Barth und Luther', in *Luther und Barth: Veröffentlichungen der Luther-Akademie e. V. Ratzeburg*, edited by Joachim Heubach (Erlangen: Martin-Luther-Verlag, 1989), pp. 21–36.

Beaney, Michael (ed.), *The Oxford Handbook of the History of Analytic Philosophy* (Oxford: Oxford University Press, 2013).

Beestermöller, Gerhard, 'Die humanitäre Intervention – Kreuzzug im neuen Gewand? Ein Blick auf die gegenwärtige Diskussion im Spiegel der thomanischen Lehre vom gerechten Krieg', in *Die humanitäre Intervention, Imperativ der Menschenrechtsidee? Rechtsethische Reflexionen am Beispiel des Kosovo-Krieges*, edited by Gerhard Beestermöller (Stuttgart: W. Kohlhammer, 2003), pp. 141–69.

Beestermöller, Gerhard, 'Thomas Aquinas and Humanitarian Intervention', in *From Just War to Modern Peace Ethics*, edited by Heinz-Gerhard Justenhoven/William A. Barbieri, Jr. (Berlin: De Gruyter, 2012), pp. 71–89.

Beintker, Michael, 'Die Frage nach den Quellen der Offenbarung im Spiegel theologiegeschichtlicher Entwicklungen zwischen 1918 und 1934', in *Krisis und Gnade*, edited by Stefan Holtmann and Peter Zocher (Tübingen: Mohr Siebeck, 2013), pp. 40–63.

Bell, Daniel M. Jr., *Just War as Christian Discipleship: Recentering the Tradition in the Church Rather Than the State* (Grand Rapids, MI: Brazos Press, 2009).

Bell, Daniel M. Jr., *Divinations: Theopolitics in an Age of Terror* (Eugene, OR: Cascade, 2017).

Benjamin, Walter, 'Critique of Violence', in *Continental Ethics Reader* (London: Routledge, 2003), pp. 113–26.

Bertschmann, Dorothea H., *Bowing before Christ – Nodding to the State?: Reading Paul Politically with Oliver O'Donovan and John Howard Yoder* (London: Bloomsbury T&T Clark, 2014).

Biagioni, Mario, *The Radical Reformation and the Making of Modern Europe: A Lasting Heritage* (Leiden: Brill, 2017).

Biggar, Nigel, *Aiming to kill: The Ethics of Suicide and Euthanasia* (London: Darton, Longman & Todd, 2004).

Biggar, Nigel, 'Review Article: The Just War Revisited', *Studies in Christian Ethics*, 19 (2006), 223–32.

Biggar, Nigel, 'The Value of Limited Loyalty: Christianity, the Nation, and Territorial Boundaries', in *Christian Political Ethics*, edited by John Coleman (Oxford: Princeton University Press, 2007), pp. 92–104.

Biggar, Nigel, 'On Defining Political Authority as an Act of Judgment: A Discussion of Oliver O'Donovan's Ways of Judgment (Part I)', *Political Theology*, 9 (2008), 273–93.

Biggar, Nigel, *In Defence of War* (Oxford: Oxford University Press, 2013).

Biggar, Nigel, 'Less Hegel, More History! Christian Ethics & Political Realities', *Providence. A Journal of Christianity & American Foreign Policy*, Fall 2015, pp. 10–16, available at https://providencemag.com/2016/05/less-hegel-history-christian-ethics-political-realities/ (accessed 17 December 2018).

Biggar, Nigel, 'Regime Change in Iraq: A Christian Reading of the Morals of the Story', in *The Authority of the Gospel: Explorations in Moral and Political Theology in Honor of Oliver O'Donovan*, edited by Robert Song and Brent Waters (Grand Rapids, MI: Wm. B. Eerdmans, 2015), pp. 52–71.

Blake William, 'The Human Abstract' [1794], in *Songs of Innocence and of Experience* (London: Penguin, 2017).

Blickle, Peter, *Der Bauernkrieg: Revolution des Gemeinen Mannes* (München: C. H. Beck, 2006).

Blum, Wilhelm, *Vermittlung und Politik: Untersuchungen zur politischen Philosophie und politischen Theologie in Antike und Gegenwart* (Waldsassen-Bayern: Stiftland-Verlag, 1982).

Blum, Wilhelm, *Wirklichkeit des Lebens: Vom Wesen der dialektischen Vermittlung in Politik und Religion* (Rheinfelden: Schäuble, 1985).

Blumenberg, Hans, *The Legitimacy of the Modern Age*, translated by Robert M. Wallace (Cambridge: MIT Press, 1985).

Bodin, Jean, *De la démonomanie des sorciers* [1580], edited by Virginia Krause et al. (Geneva: Librairie Droz S. A., 2016).

Bojanowski, Jochen, *Kants Theorie der Freiheit* (Berlin: Walter de Gruyter, 2006).

Bonhoeffer, Dietrich, *Ethik*, edited by Ilse Tödt and others (Munich: Kaiser, 1992).

Bonhoeffer, Dietrich, *Nachfolge*, edited by Peter Zimmerling (Giessen: Brunnen, 2016).

Bowker, Matthew H., *Rethinking the Politics of Absurdity: Albert Camus, Postmodernity, and the Survival of Innocence* (New York: Routledge, 2014).

Brian, Rustin E., *Covering Up Luther: How Barth's Christology Challenged the deus absconditus That Haunts Modernity* (Eugene, OR: Cascade, 2013).

Brock, Peter, *The Roots of War Resistance: Pacifism from the Early Church to Tolstoy* (Nyack, NY: Distributed by the Fellowship of Reconciliation, 1981).

Brunstetter, Daniel R., and Cian O'Driscoll (eds), *Just War Thinkers: From Cicero to the 21st Century* (London: Routledge, 2017).

Bull, Hedley, *The Anarchical Society: A Study of Order in World Politics* (London: Macmillan, 1977).

Bull, Hedley, Benedict Kingsbury and Adam Roberts (eds), *Hugo Grotius and International Relations* (Oxford: Clarendon Press, 1990).

Burke, Anthony, *Beyond Security, Ethics and Violence* (London: Routledge, 2007).

Campagna, Norbert, *Le Droit, le Politique et la Guerre: Deux Chapitres sur la Doctrine de Carl Schmitt* (Saint-Nicolas: Les Presses de l'Université Laval, 2004).

Carnahan, Kevin, *Reinhold Niebuhr and Paul Ramsey: Idealist and Pragmatic Christians on Politics, Philosophy, Religion, and War* (Lanham, MD: Lexington, 2010).

Casey, Shaun A., 'Eschatology and Statecraft in Paul Ramsey', *Studies in Christian Ethics*, 21 (2008), 73–193.

Castellio, Sebastian, *Das Manifest der Toleranz: Sebastian Castellio: Über Ketzer und ob man sie verfolgen soll: De haereticis an sint persequendi* [1554], edited by Wolfgang Stammler (Essen: Franz Steiner Verlag, alcorde Verlag, 2017).

Cavanaugh, William T., 'Beyond Secular Parodies', in *Radical Orthodoxy: A New Theology*, edited by John Milbank, Catherine Pickstock and Graham Ward (London: Routledge, 1999), pp. 182–201.

Cavendish, Camilla, 'Returning Isis Brides Expose a Woefully Inadequate Legal Armoury: Britain Must Face an Uncomfortable Reality: Some Acts That Should Be Illegal Are Not', *Financial Times*, 15 February 2019.

Chamayou, Grégoire, *Drone Theory*, transl. Janet Lloyd (London: Penguin, 2015).

Christie-Murray, David, *A History of Heresy* (Oxford: Oxford University Press, 1976).

Clark, Ian, *Waging War. A Philosophical Introduction* (Oxford: Clarendon Press, 1988).

Clausewitz, Carl von, *On War*, translated by J. J. Graham, 3 vols. (London: Kegan Paul, Trench, Trübner, 1908).

Coady, Tony (C. A. J.), *Morality and Political Violence* (Cambridge: Cambridge University Press, 2008).

Cohen, L. Jonathan, *The Dialogue of Reason: An Analysis of Analytical Philosophy* (Oxford: Clarendon Press, 1986).

Cole, Jonathan, 'Towards a Christian Ontology of Political Authority: The Relationship between Created Order and Providence in Oliver O'Donovan's Theology of Political Authority', *Studies in Christian Ethics*, first published online: May 6, 2018, 1–19. doi: 10.1177/0953946818775559.

Coujou, Jean-Paul, 'Political Thought and Legal Theory in Suárez', in *A Companion to Francisco Suárez*, edited by Victor Salas and Robert Fastiggi (Leiden: Brill, 2014), pp. 29–71.

Csikós, Ella, 'Zu Hegels Interpretation des Skeptizismus', in *Hegels Phänomenologie des Geistes: Ein kooperativer Kommentar zu einem Schlüsselwerk der Moderne*, edited by Klaus Vieweg and Wolfgang Welsch (Frankfurt am Main: Suhrkamp, 2008), pp. 270–85.

Curran, Charles E., *Politics, Medicine, and Christian Ethics: A Dialogue with Paul Ramsey* (Philadelphia, PA: Fortress Press, 1973).

Curtis, William, *Defending Rorty: Pragmatism and Liberal Virtue* (Cambridge: Cambridge University Press, 2015).

Dalferth, Ingolf U., *Umsonst: Eine Erinnerung an die kreative Passivität des Menschen* (Tübingen: Mohr Siebeck, 2011).

Davis, Creston, and Riches, Aaron, 'Metanoia: The Theological Praxis of Revolution', in *Theology and the Political*, edited by Creston Davis, John Milbank and Slavoj Žižek (Durham: Duke University Press, 2005), pp. 22–51.

Debray, Régis, *God: An Itinerary*, translated by Jeffrey Mehlman (London: Verso, 2004).

Dellavalle, Sergio, 'The Plurality of States and the World Order of Reason: On Hegel's Understanding of International Law and Relations', in *System, Order, and International Law: The Early History of International Legal Thought from Machiavelli to Hegel*, edited by Stefan Kadelbach, Thomas Kleinlein and David Roth-Isigkeit (Oxford: Oxford University Press, 2017), pp. 352–79.

Doerksen, Paul, *Beyond Suspicion: Post-Christendom Protestant Political Theology in John Howard Yoder and Oliver O'Donovan* (Bletchley: Paternoster, 2009).

Dombrowski, Daniel A., *Rawls and Religion: The Case for Political Liberalism* (Albany: State University of New York Press, 2001).

Dorrien, Gary J., *Social Ethics in the Making: Interpreting an American Tradition* (Malden, MA: Blackwell-Wiley, 2009).

Dorrien, Gary J., *Kantian Reason and Hegelian Spirit: The Idealistic Logic of Modern Theology* (Oxford: Wiley-Blackwell, 2012).

Draper, Kai, *War and Individual Rights: The Foundations of Just War Theory* (Oxford, NY: Oxford University Press, 2015).

Dryzek, John S., and Jonathan Pickering, *The Politics of the Anthropocene* (Oxford: Oxford University Press, 2019).

Dworkin, Ronald, *Law's Empire* (Oxford: Hart, 1998).

Ebach, Jürgen, 'Zeit als Frist. Zur Lektüre der Apokalypse-Abschnitte in der *Abendländischen Eschatologie*', in *Abendländische Eschatologie: ad Jacob Taubes*, edited by Richard Faber, Eveline Goodman-Thau and Thomas H. Macho (Würzburg: Königshausen & Neumann, 2001), pp. 75–92.

Edwards, Mark J., *Catholicity and Heresy in the Early Church* (Farnham: Ashgate, 2009).

Elert, Werner, *Der Christ und der völkische Wehrwille* (Leipzig: A. Deichertsche Verlagsbuchhandlung, 1937).

Elford, R. John, 'Christianity and War', in *Cambridge Companion to Christian Ethics*, edited by Robin Gill (Cambridge: Cambridge University Press, 2000).

Elshtain, Jean Bethke, *Augustine and the Limits of Politics* (Notre Dame, IN: University of Notre Dame Press, 1995).

Elshtain, Jean Bethke, 'The Bright Line: Liberalism and Religion', *New Criterion*, 17.7 (1 March 1999), http://www.newcriterion.com/articles.cfm/brightline-elshtain-2894 (accessed 12 July 2012).

Elshtain, Jean Bethke, 'Just War and Humanitarian Intervention', *Ideas*, 8 (2001), 2–21.

Elshtain, Jean Bethke, 'Don't Be Cruel: Reflections on Rortyian Liberalism', in *Richard Rorty*, edited by Charles B. Guignon and David R. Hiley (Cambridge: Cambridge University Press, 2003), pp. 139–57.

Elshtain, Jean Bethke, 'Augustine', in *The Blackwell Companion to Political Theology* (Oxford: Blackwell, 2004), pp. 35–47.

Elshtain, Jean Bethke, *Just War against Terror: The Burden of American Power in a Violent World* (New York: Basic, 2004).

Elshtain, Jean Bethke, 'The Just War Tradition and Natural Law', *Fordham International Law Journal*, 28 (2004), 742–55.

Elshtain, Jean Bethke, 'Reflection on the Problem of "Dirty Hands"', in *Torture: A Collection*, edited by Sanford Levinson (New York: Oxford University Press, 2004), pp. 77–89.

Elshtain, Jean Bethke, 'Against the New Utopianism', *Ethics and International Affairs*, 19. 2 (2006), 91–5.

Elshtain, Jean Bethke, 'On Never Reaching the Coast of Utopia', *International Relations*, 22 (2008), 147–72.

Elshtain, Jean Bethke, 'Response to Tom Farer's "Un-just War against Terrorism and the Struggle to Appropriate Human Rights"', *Human Rights Quarterly*, 30 (2008), 758–66.

Elshtain, Jean Bethke, *Sovereignty: God, State and Self* (New York: Basic, 2008).

Elshtain, Jean Bethke, 'Response to Reviews of Just War against Terror', https://www.elca.org/JLE/Articles/719?_ga=2.143439415.349152305.1562075516-1676087201.1562075516 (accessed 2 July 2019).

Elshtain, Jean Bethke, [Unedited] Jean Bethke Elshtain with Krista Tippett, On Being https://soundcloud.com/onbeing/unedited-jean-bethke-elshtain-with-krista-tippett (accessed 2 July 2019).

Elshtain, Jean Bethke, 'Religious Leaders Visit the White House', http://www.beliefnet.com/News/Politics/2001/10/Religious-Leaders-Visit-The-White-House.aspx?p=1 (accessed 4 March 2019).

Evans, Mark (ed.), *Just War Theory: A Reappraisal* (Edinburgh: Edinburgh University Press, 2005).

Faber, Richard, *Politische Dämonologie: Über modernen Marcionismus* (Würzburg: Königshausen und Neumann, 2007).

Faber, Richard, *Political Demonology: On Modern Marcionism*, translated and edited by Therese Feiler and Michael Mayo (Eugene, OR: Wipf & Stock, Cascade, 2018).

Fabio, Udo di, 'Recht ohne letzte Instanz? Das moderne Recht und sein Verhältnis zu Gott', in *Welt ohne Gott? Theoretischer und praktischer Atheismus*, edited by Axel Scheuzle (St Ottilien: EOS Verlag, 2000), pp. 247–63.

Fabre, Cécile, 'Killing in Humanitarian Intervention', seminar at the Oxford Institute for Ethics, Law and Armed Conflict, on 3 May 2011.

Fabre, Cécile, *Cosmopolitan War* (Oxford: Oxford University Press, 2012).

Feiler, Therese, 'From Dialectics to Theo-Logic: The Ethics of War from Paul Ramsey to Oliver O'Donovan', *Studies in Christian Ethics*, 28.3 (2015), 343–59.

Feiler, Therese, 'Book Review: Jonathan Chaplin and Gary Wilton (eds), *God and the EU: Faith in the European Project*', *Studies in Christian Ethics*, 31.2 (2018), 242–6.

Fiala, Andrew, *The Just War Myth* (Lanham, MD: Rowman & Littlefield, 2008).

Fiala, Andrew, 'The Democratic Peace Myth', in *Between Global Violence and the Ethics of Peace: Philosophical Perspectives*, edited by Edward Demenchonok (Chichester: Wiley-Blackwell, 2009), pp. 77–100.

Fichte, Johann Gottlieb, *Beitrag zur Berichtigung der Urteile des Publikums über die französische Revolution* [1793] (Hamburg: Felix Meiner Verlag, 1973).

Finnis, John, *Human Rights and the Common Good: Collected Essays* (Oxford: Oxford University Press 2011).

Firestone, Chris L., *Kant and Theology at the Boundaries of Reason* (Farnham: Ashgate, 2009).

Francis, Diana, *Rethinking War and Peace* (London: Pluto Press, 2004).

Freeden, Michael, *Ideologies and Political Theory* (Oxford: Oxford University Press, 1998).

Freeden, Michael, *Ideology: A Very Short Introduction* (Oxford: Oxford University Press, 2003).

Freedland, Jonathan, 'A Black and Disgraceful Site', *New York Review of Books*, 56.9 (28 May 2009), http://www.nybooks.com/articles/22691 (accessed 15 October 2009).

Galli, Carlo, *Genealogia della Politica: Carl Schmitt e la Crisi del Pensiero Politico Moderno* (Bologna: Il Mulino, 1996).

Garnett, George, *Marsilius of Padua and 'the Truth of History'* (Oxford: Oxford University Press, 2006).

Gierke, Otto Friedrich von, *Political Theories of the Middle Age* (Cambridge: Cambridge University Press, 1900).

Gierke, Otto Friedrich von, *Natural Law and the Theory of Society*, 2 vols., translated by Ernest Barker (Cambridge: Cambridge University Press, 1934).

Goodchild, Peter, *J. Robert Oppenheimer: Shatterer of Worlds* (London: British Broadcasting Corp, 1980).

Goodman, Ryan, 'The Power to Kill or Capture Enemy Combatants', *European Journal of International Law*, 24.3 (2013), 819–53. doi:10.1093/ejil/cht048.

Gorringe, Tim, 'Authority, Plebs and Patricians', *Studies in Christian Ethics*, 11 (1998), 24–9.

Graf, Friedrich W., *Der heilige Zeitgeist. Studien zur Ideengeschichte der protestantischen Theologie in der Weimarer Republik* (Tübingen: Mohr Siebeck, 2011).

Gregory, Eric, *Politics and the Order of Love. An Augustinian Ethic of Democratic Citizenship* (Chicago, IL: University of Chicago Press, 2008).

Gregory, Eric, 'The Spirit and the Letter: Protestant Thomism and Nigel Biggar's "Karl Barth's Ethics Revisited"', in *Commanding Grace: Studies in Karl Barth's Ethics*, edited by Daniel L. Migliore (Grand Rapids, MI: William B. Eerdmans, 2010), pp. 50–9.

Grotius, Hugo, *De Jure Belli Ac Pacis Libri Tres*, translated by Francis W. Kelsey, 2 vols. (Oxford: Clarendon Press, 1925).

Habermas, Jürgen, *Glauben und Wissen* (Frankfurt am Main: Suhrkamp, 2001).

Habermas, Jürgen, *Europa am Scheideweg, Handelsblatt*, 18 June 2011, http://www.handelsblatt.com/politik/international/essay-europa-am-scheideweg/4298474.html (accessed 4 March 2019).

Habermas, Jürgen, and Josph Ratzinger, *Dialectics of Secularization: On Reason and Religion* (San Francisco, CA: Ignatius Press, 2006).

Hamacher, Werner, 'The Right Not to Use Rights. Human Rights and the Structure of Judgments', in *Political Theologies: Public Religions in a Post-Secular World*, edited by Hent de Vries and Lawrence Eugene Sullivan (New York: Fordham University Press, 2006), pp. 671–90.

Hare, John E., *The Moral Gap: Kantian Ethics, Human Limits, and God's Assistance* (Oxford: Clarendon Press, 1996).

Harnack, Adolf von, *Marcion: Das Evangelium vom Fremden Gott: Eine Monographie zur Geschichte der Grundlegung der katholischen Kirche* (Leipzig: J. C. Hinrichs, 1924).

Harnack, Adolf von, *Marcion, Der Moderne Gläubige des 2. Jahrhunderts, der erste Reformator: Die Dorpater Preisschrift (1870)*, edited by Friedemann Steck (Berlin: Walter de Gruyter, 2003).

Harris, Charles E., 'Love as the Basic Moral Principle in Paul Ramsey's Ethics', *Journal of Religious Ethics*, 4 (1976), 239–58.

Haspel, Michael, *Friedensethik und Humanitäre Intervention: Der Kosovo-Krieg als Herausforderung evangelischer Friedensethik* (Neukirchen-Vluyn: Neukirchener, 2002).

Haspel, Michael, 'Justification of Force in the Trans-Atlantic Debate: Towards a Moderate Institutionalist Cosmopolitanism', *Studies in Christian Ethics*, 20 (2007), 102–17.

Hauerwas, Stanley, and Griffiths, Paul, 'On doctrine and ethics', in *The Cambridge Companion to Christian Ethics*, edited by Colin E. Gunton (Cambridge: Cambridge University Press, 1997), pp. 21–40.

Hauerwas, Stanley, and Griffiths, Paul, *The Peaceable Kingdom: A Primer in Christian Ethics* (London: SCM Press, 2003).

Hauerwas, Stanley, and Griffiths, Paul, 'War, Peace & Jean Bethke Elshtain', *First Things*, October 2003, http://www.firstthings.com/article.php3?id_article=534 (accessed 24 November 2008).

Hauerwas, Stanley, and James Fodor, 'Remaining in Babylon: Oliver O'Donovan's Defense of Christendom', *Studies in Christian Ethics*, 11 (1998), 30–55.

Hays, Richard B., *The Moral Vision of the New Testament: Community, Cross, New Creation: A Contemporary Introduction to New Testament Ethics* (Edinburgh: T&T Clark, 1997).

Hegel, Georg Wilhelm Friedrich, *Phenomenology of Spirit*, translated by A. V. Miller (Oxford: Clarendon Press, 1979).

Hegel, Georg Wilhelm Friedrich, *Phänomenologie des Geistes* (Frankfurt am Main: Suhrkamp, 1986).

Hegel, Georg Wilhelm Friedrich, *Wissenschaft der Logik II* (Frankfurt: Suhrkamp, 1986).

Helmholz, Richard H., *Kanonisches Recht und europäische Rechtskultur*, translated by Jörg Müller (Tübingen: Mohr Siebeck, 2013).

Hillerbrand, Hans J., *The Division of Christendom: Christianity in the Sixteenth Century* (Louisville, KT: Westminster John Knox, 2007).

Hilpert, Konrad, *Menschenrechte und Theologie: Forschungsbeiträge zur ethischen Dimension der Menschenrechte* (Freiburg, Switzerland: Universitätsverlag, 2001).

Himes, Kenneth R., OFM, *Drones and the Ethics of Targeted Killing* (Lanham, MD: Rowman & Littlefield, 2016).

Hirschl, Ran, *Towards Juristocracy: The Origins and Consequences of the New Constitutionalism* (Cambridge, MA: Harvard University Press, 2004).

Hitchens, Christopher, 'In Defense of Endless War', *Slate Magazine*, 19 September 2011, https://slate.com/news-and-politics/2011/09/endless-war-a-decade-after-9-11-civilization-must-still-defend-itself.html (accessed 4 December 2018).

Hobbes, Thomas, *Leviathan*, edited by Richard Tuck (Cambridge: Cambridge University Press, 2010).

Hobsbawm, Eric, 'The Myth of the Cowboy', *Guardian*, 20 March 2013, http://www.guardian.co.uk/books/2013/mar/20/myth-of-the-cowboy (accessed 30 April 2018).

Höffe, Otfried, *Kant's Cosmopolitan Theory of Law and Peace* (Cambridge: Cambridge University Press, 2006).

Hoffmann, Veronika, *Skizzen zu einer Theologie der Gabe* (Freiburg i. Br.: Herder, 2013).

Hoffmann, Veronika, *Christus – die Gabe* (Freiburg i. Br.: Herder, 2016).

Hollenbach, David, *The Common Good and Christian Ethics* (Cambridge: Cambridge University Press, 2002).

Hollowell, Adam E., *This Side of the Ploughshares: Concepts of Covenant and Repentance in Paul Ramsey's Political Theology* (PhD thesis, University of Edinburgh, 2009).

Hollowell, Adam E., 'Revising Basic Christian Ethics: Rethinking Paul Ramsey's Early Contributions to Moral Theology', *Studies in Christian Ethics*, 23.3 (2010), 267–83.

Hollowell, Adam E., *Power and Purpose: Paul Ramsey and Contemporary Christian Political Theology* (Grand Rapids, MI: William. B. Eerdmans, 2015).

Hollowell, Adam E. and James F. Cubie, ' "Where Have We Been? Where Are We Going?" – Paul Ramsey, Paul Lehmann, and Karl Barth's Doctrine of God', in *Explorations in Christian Theology and Christian Ethics: Essays in Conversation with Paul L. Lehmann*, edited by Philip G. Ziegler and Michelle J. Bartel (Farnham: Ashgate, 2009), pp. 79–101.

Horton, Michael, 'In Praise of Profanity: A Theological Defense of the Secular', in *Evangelicals and Empire: Christian Alternatives to the Political Status Quo*, edited by Bruce Ellis Benson and Peter Goodwin Heltzel (Grand Rapids, MI: Brazos Press), pp. 252–66.

Howson, Peter, 'The British Churches and Their Chaplains: Standing Back to Back and Walking in Opposite Directions', in *Military Chaplaincy in Contention: Chaplains, Churches and the Morality of Conflict*, edited by Andrew Todd (Farnham: Ashgate, 2013), pp. 95–112.

Hudson, Winthrop S., 'John Locke, Heir of Puritan political theorists', in *Calvinism and the Political Order*, edited by George L. Hunt and John T. McNeill (Philadelphia, PA: Westminster, 1965), pp. 108–29.

Ignatieff, Michael, 'Human Rights as Idolatry', in *Human Rights as Politics and Idolatry*, edited by Amy Gutmann (Princeton, NJ: Princeton University Press, 2001).

Janssen, Dieter, 'Bellum iustum und Völkerrecht im Werk des Hugo Grotius', in *Krieg und Kultur: Die Rezeption von Krieg und Frieden in der Niederländischen Republik und im Deutschen Reich 1568–1648*, edited by Horst Lademacher and Simon Groenveld (Münster: Waxmann Verlag, 1998), pp. 129–56.

Joas, Hans, *Die Sakralität der Person: Eine neue Genealogie der Menschenrechte* (Berlin: Suhrkamp, 2011).

Johnson, James Turner, *Just War Tradition and the Restraint of War: A Moral and Historical Inquiry* (Princeton, NJ: Princeton University Press, 1981).

Judt, Tony, 'Bush's Useful Idiots', *London Review of Books*, 28.18 (2006), 3–5.

Jüngel, Eberhard, *Gott als Geheimnis der Welt: zur Begründung der Theologie des Gekreuzigten im Streit zwischen Theismus u. Atheismus*, 3rd ed. (Tübingen: Mohr, 1978).

Kahn, Paul W., 'On Political Theology', *The Art of Theory*, http://www.artoftheory.com/on-political-theology-paul-kahn/ (accessed 12 May 2012).

Kahn, Paul W., *Political Theology: Four New Chapters on the Concept of Sovereignty* (New York: Columbia University Press, 2012).

Kahn, Paul W., 'Sacrificial Nation', *Utopian*, 29 March 2010, http://www.the-utopian.org/tagged/Paul_W._Kahn (accessed 5 December 2018).

Kant, Immanuel, 'Der Streit der Fakultäten', in *Kant's Gesammelte Schriften*, edited by the Königlich Preußische Akademie der Wissenschaften, vol. vii [AA 7] (Berlin: Georg Reimer, 1917), pp. 38–44.

Kant, Immanuel, *The Moral Law, or, Kant's Groundwork of the Metaphysic of Morals*, edited by Herbert James Paton (London: Hutchinson, 1948), pp. 96–7.

Kant, Immanuel, *Die Religion*, edited by Hermann Noack and Karl Vorländer (Hamburg: F. Meiner, 1956).

Kant, Immanuel, *Metaphysik der Sitten*, 2 vols (Hamburg: Meiner, 1986–90).

Kant, Immanuel, *Kritik der reinen Vernunft* (Hamburg: Felix Meiner Verlag, 1998).

Kant, Immanuel, *Die Religion innerhalb der Grenzen der bloßen Vernunft* (Stuttgart: Philipp Reclam Jr, 2007).

Kant, Immanuel, *Zum ewigen Frieden* (Stuttgart: Philipp Reclam Jr, 2008).

Katongole, Emmanuel, *Beyond Universal Reason: The Relation between Religion and Ethics in the Work of Stanley Hauerwas* (Notre Dame, IN: University of Notre Dame Press, 2000).

Keefer, Angie, 'The Sky Is Not the Limit', *Dot Dot Dot*, 18 (2009), 58–67.

Kennedy, Caroline and Rengger, Nicholas, 'The New Assassination Bureau: On the "Robotic Turn" in Contemporary War', 6 November 2012, http://www.carnegiecouncil.org/publications/ethics_online/0075.html (accessed 15 January 2013).

Kirk, Michael, and Michael Wiser, *The Secret History of ISIS* (PBS Frontline documentary, 2016).

Kirkpatrick, Matthew D., *Bonhoeffer's Ethics: Between Pacifism and Assassination* (Cambridge: Grove, 2011).

Kleist, Heinrich von, *Michael Kohlhaas* (1811), http://kleist.org/phocadownload/michaelkohlhaas.pdf (accessed 2 July 2019).

Körtner, Ulrich H. J., *Evangelische Sozialethik. Grundlagen und Themenfelder* (Göttingen: Vandenhoeck & Ruprecht, 1999).

Körtner, Ulrich H. J., *Für die Vernunft: Wider Moralisierung und Emotionalisierung in Politik und Kirche* (Leipzig: Evangelische Verlagsanstalt, 2017).

Koskenniemi, Martti, *From Apology to Utopia. The Structure of International Legal Argument* (Cambridge: Cambridge University Press, 2005).

Kraus, Herbert, *Von ehrlicher Kriegsführung und gerechtem Friedensschluss. Eine Studie über Immanuel Kant* (Tübingen: J. C. B. Mohr <Paul Siebeck>, 1950).

Kroeker, P. Travis, *Messianic Political Theology and Diaspora Ethics: Essays in Exile* (Eugene, OR: Wipf & Stock, Cascade, 2017).

Küng, Hans, *Menschwerdung Gottes; Eine Einführung in Hegels theologisches Denken als Prolegomena zu einer künftigen Christologie* (Freiburg i. Br.: Herder, 1970).

Lackey, Douglas, 'Book Review: The Morality of Defensive War, Cécile Fabre & Seth Lazar (eds) 2014 Oxford, Oxford University Press', *Journal of Applied Philosophy*, 32.1 (2015), 111–13.

Lazar, Seth, 'War and Associative Duties' (unpublished doctoral thesis, University of Oxford, 2009).

Lazar, Seth, 'Evaluating the Revisionist Critique of Just War Theory', *Daedalus*, 146.1 (2017), 113–24.

Lazreg, Marnia, *Torture and the Twilight of Empire* (Princeton, NJ: Princeton University Press, 2008).

Lee, Peter, *Blair's Just War: Iraq and the Illusion of Morality* (Basingstoke: Palgrave Macmillan, 2012).

Leonard, Stephen Pax, *Travels in Cultural Nihilism: Some Essays*, (London: Arktos, 2017).

Lepore, Jill, 'The Dark Ages. Guanatanamo and Legal History', in *New Yorker*, 18 March 2013, pp. 28–33.

Llanque, Marcus, *Politische Ideengeschichte – ein Gewebe politischer Diskurse* (Munich: Oldenbourg, 2008).

Locke, John, *Two Treatises of Government*, edited by Peter Laslett (Cambridge: Cambridge University Press, 1988).

Lockwood O'Donovan, Joan, 'Subsidiarity and Political Rule in Theological Perspective', in Oliver O'Donovan and Joan Lockwood O'Donovan, *Bonds of Imperfection: Christian Politics, Past and Present* (Grand Rapids, MI: William B. Eerdmans, 2004), pp. 225–45.

Long, D. Stephen, *Tragedy, Tradition, Transformism. The Ethics of Paul Ramsey* (Eugene, OR: Wipf & Stock, 2007).

Losurdo, Domenico, *Nietzsche, il ribelle aristocratico: Biografia intellettuale e bilancio critic* (Turin: Bollati Boringhieri, 2002).

Löwith, Karl, *Meaning in History: The Theological Implications of the Philosophy of History* (Chicago, IL: University of Chicago Press, 1957).

Löwith, Karl, *Weltgeschehen und Heilsgeschehen: Die theologischen Voraussetzungen der Geschichtsphilosophie* (Stuttgart: J. B. Metzler, 2004).

Luban, David, 'War as Punishment' (2011). *Georgetown Law Faculty Working Papers*. Paper 145. http://scholarship.law.georgetown.edu/fwps_papers/145 (accessed 25 August 2011).

Luther, Martin, *Lecture on Romans*, edited by Wilhelm Pauck (Louisville, KY: Westminster John Knox Press, 2006).

Manuel, Frank E., and Fritzie P. Manuel, *Utopian Thought in the Western World* (Oxford: Blackwell, 1979).

Marcuse, Herbert, *Reason and Revolution. Hegel and the Rise of Social Theory* (London: Routledge & Kegan, 1955).

Maritain, Jacques, *Man and State* (Chicago, IL: University of Chicago Press, 1951).

Markham, Ian, 'Distinguishing Hope from Utopian Aspiration: Revisiting Reinhold Niebuhr', in *Reinhold Niebuhr and Contemporary Politics: God and Power*, edited by Richard Harries and Stephen Platten (Oxford: Oxford University Press, 2010), pp. 129–40.

Mattox, John Mark, *Saint Augustine and the Theory of Just War* (London: Continuum, 2006).

McCarraher, Eugene, 'The Enchanted City of Man', in *Augustine and Politics*, edited by John Doody, Kevin L. Hughes and Kim Pfaffenroth (Oxford: Lexington, 2005).

McCready, Douglas, 'When Is Torture Right?', *Studies in Christian Ethics*, 20 (2007), 383–98.

McGrath, Alistair, *Reformation Thought: An Introduction* (Oxford: Basil Blackwell, 1988).

McIlroy, David H. 'The Right Reason for Caesar to Confess Christ as Lord' (2008), http://klice.co.uk/uploads/EST08McIlroy.pdf (accessed 15 January 2013).

McKenzie, Michael C., *Paul Ramsey's Ethics. The Power of 'Agape' in a Postmodern World* (Westport, CT: Praeger, 2001).

McMahan, Jeff, *Killing in War* (Oxford: Clarendon Press, 2009).

Meeks, Wayne A., *The Origins of Christian Morality. The First Two Centuries* (New Haven, CT: Yale University Press, 1993).

Meillassoux, Quentin, *After Finitude: An Essay on the Necessity of Contingency* (London: Continuum, 2008).

Melzer, Nils, *Targeted Killing in International Law* (Oxford: Oxford University Press, 2008).

Meszaros, Julia, and Johannes Zachhuber (eds), *Sacrifice and Modern Thought* (Oxford: Oxford University Press, 2014).

Mieth, Dietmar, *Die Spannungseinheit von Theorie und Praxis. Theologische Profile* (Freiburg/Switzerland: Universitätsverlag; Freiburg im Breisgau: Herder, 1986).

Milbank, John, *The Word Made Strange* (Oxford: Blackwell, 1997).

Milbank, John, 'The Ethics of Self-Sacrifice', *First Things*, March 1999, available online at https://www.firstthings.com/article/1999/03/004-the-ethics-of-self-sacrifice (accessed 24 October 2018).

Milbank, John, *Theology and Social Theory: Beyond Secular Reason*, 2nd ed. (Oxford: Blackwell, 2006).

Milbank, John, *The Future of Love: Essays in Political Theology* (Eugene, OR: Cascade, 2009).

Milbank, John, 'Paul against Biopolitics', in *Paul's New Moment*, edited by John Milbank, Slavoj Žižek and Creston Davis (Grand Rapids, MI: Brazos Press, 2010).

Milbank, John, 'Against Human Rights', http://theologyphilosophycentre.co.uk/papers/Milbank_AgainstHumanRights.pdf (accessed 17 June 2010); 'Against Human Rights: Liberty in the Western Tradition', *Oxford Journal of Law and Religion*, 1.1 (2012), 1–32.

Milbank, John, 'Theologizing Brexit I: Europe, Sovereignty and Nation, ABC Religion and Ethics, 20 July 2016, http://www.abc.net.au/religion/articles/2016/07/20/4503780.htm (accessed 28 March 2018).

Milbank, John, 'Nothing Is Ever Over Until the end: On Religion, Power and Order', Opening Lecture of the academic year 2016–17, 2 September 2016, Protestantse Theologische Universiteit Utrecht, https://www.pthu.nl/actueel/nieuws/Nieuwspdf/oajtekstrede.pdf (accessed 02 July 2019).

Milbank, John, 'The End of Tolerance: On the Decline of Religious Freedom and the Return of Religious Influence', *ABC Religion & Ethics*, 24 August 2017, https://www.abc.net.au/religion/the-decline-of-religious-freedom-and-the-return-of-religious-inf/10095982 (accessed 26 February 2019).

Milbank, John, 'Radical Orthodoxy and Protestantism Today: John Milbank in Conversation', *Acta Theologica*, Suppl 25 (2017), 43–72.

Mill, John Stuart, *On Liberty and Other Essays* (Oxford: Oxford University Press, 1998).

Miller, Richard B., 'Love, Intention and Proportion: Paul Ramsey on the Morality of Nuclear Deterrence', *Journal of Religious Ethics*, 16 (1988), 201–21.

Moll, Sebastian, *The Arch-Heretic Marcion* (Tübingen: Mohr Siebeck, 2010).

Monod, Jean-Claude, 'Heaven on Earth? The Löwith-Blumenberg Debate', in *Radical Secularization? An Inquiry into the Religious Roots of Secular Culture*, edited by Stijn Latré, Walter Van Herck and Guido Vanheeswijck (London: Bloomsbury Academic, 2014), pp. 7–16.

Moore, G. E., *Principia Ethica*, rev. ed. (Cambridge: Cambridge University Press, 1993).

Müller, Jan, 'Carl Schmitt's Method: Between Ideology, Demonology and Myth', *Journal of Political Ideologies*, 4 (1999), 61–85.

Münkler, Herfried, *Kriegssplitter: Die Evolution der Gewalt im 20. und 21. Jahrhundert* (Berlin: Rowohlt, 2015).

Münkler, Herfried, *Der Wandel des Krieges: Der Wandel des Krieges: Von der Symmetrie zur Asymmetrie* (Weilerswist: Velbrück Wissenschaft, 2006).

Murphy, Jeffrie G., *Kant: The Philosophy of Right* (London: Macmillan, 1970).

Negarestani, Reza, 'The Militarization of Peace', in *Collapse I*, edited by Robin Mackay (Oxford: Urbanomic, 2007), pp. 53–92.

Niebuhr, Reinhold, *Faith and History: A Comparison of Christian and Modern Views of History* (New York: Charles Scribner's, 1949).

Niebuhr, Reinhold, *Moral Man and Immoral Society* (New York: Charles Scribner's, 1932).

Nietzsche, Friedrich, *Ecce Homo*, edited by Giorgio Colli and Mazzino Montinari (Berlin: De Gruyter, 1988).

Niebuhr, Reinhold, *Twilight of the Idols* (Oxford: Oxford University Press, 1998).

Niebuhr, Reinhold, *The Irony of American History* (Chicago, IL: University of Chicago Press, 2008 [1952]).

Nietzsche, Friedrich, *The Antichrist*, translated by Anthony M. Ludovici (Amherst, NY: Prometheus, 2000).

Northcott, Michael S., *An Angel Directs the Storm: Apocalyptic Religion and American Empire* (London: I. B. Tauris, 2004).

Ockham, William of, *Texte zur Theorie der Erkenntnis und der Wissenschaft: Lateinisch/ Deutsch*, edited by Ruedi Imbach (Stuttgart: P. Reclam, 1984).

O'Donovan, Joan Lockwood, 'Political Authority and European Community: The Challenge of the Christian Political Tradition', *Scottish Journal of Theology*, 47 (1994), 1–18.

O'Donovan, Joan Lockwood, 'Faith and Globalization', Interview with Joan Lockwood O'Donovan, http://www.youtube.com/watch?v=5yV8Qg8wXuQ (accessed 7 October 2011).

O'Donovan, Oliver, 'How Can Theology Be Moral?', *Journal of Religious Ethics*, 17 (1989), 81–94.

O'Donovan, Oliver, 'Karl Barth and Ramsey's "Uses of Power"', *Journal of Religious Ethics*, 19 (1991), 1–30.

O'Donovan, Oliver, *Resurrection and Moral Order: An Outline for Evangelical Ethics*, 2nd ed. (Grand Rapids, MI: William B. Eerdmans, 1994).

O'Donovan, Oliver, *The Desire of the Nations: Rediscovering the Roots of Political Theology* (Cambridge: Cambridge University Press, 1996).

O'Donovan, Oliver, *Common Objects of Love: Moral Reflection and the Shaping of Community* (Grand Rapids, MI: William B. Eerdmans, 2002).

O'Donovan, Oliver, *The Just War Revisited* (Cambridge: Cambridge University Press, 2003).

O'Donovan, Oliver, *The Ways of Judgment* (Grand Rapids, MI: William B. Eerdmans, 2005).

O'Donovan, Oliver, 'Judgment, Tradition and Reason: A Response', *Political Theology*, 9 (2008), 395–414.

O'Donovan, Oliver, 'The Language of Rights and Conceptual History', *Journal of Religious Ethics*, 37 (2009), 193–207.

O'Donovan, Oliver, 'The Future of Theological Ethics', *Studies in Christian Ethics*, 25.2 (2012), 186–98.

O'Donovan, Oliver, 'Good without God? A Christian Philosopher probes the foundation for Ethics', https://www.youtube.com/watch?v=F3VEMI9cnyY (accessed 15 August 2012).

O'Donovan, Oliver, 'The Common Good: Does It Represent a Political Programme?', 1 December 2017, Futures of Public Theology Conference, University of Edinburgh, https://www.youtube.com/watch?v=vuTx6Z2jkzU (accessed 13 August 2018).

O'Donovan, Oliver, and Joan Lockwood O'Donovan (eds), *From Irenaeus to Grotius: A Sourcebook in Christian Political Thought* (Grand Rapids, MI: William B. Eerdmans, 1999).

O'Donovan, Oliver, and Joan Lockwood O'Donovan, *Bonds of Imperfection: Christian Politics, Past and Present* (Grand Rapids, MI: Eerdmans, 2004).

O'Driscoll, Cian, 'Jean Bethke Elshtain's Just War against Terror: A Tale of Two Cities', *International Relations*, 21 (2007), 485–92.

O'Keefe, Derrick, *Michael Ignatieff – The Lesser Evil?* (London: Verso, 2011).

Orentlicher, Diane F., 'Relativism and Religion', in *Human Rights as Politics and Idolatry*, edited by Amy Gutmann (Princeton, NJ: Princeton University Press, 2001), pp. 141–58.

Ormerod, David, QC, and Karl Laird, *Smith and Hogan's Criminal Law*, 14th ed. (Oxford: Oxford University Press, 2015).

Owens, Patricia, 'Beyond Strauss, Lies, and the War in Iraq: Hannah Arendt's Critique of Neoconservatism', *Review of International Studies*, 33 (2007), 265–83.

Pabst, Adrian, 'Commonwealth or Market-State? Europe's Christian Heritage and the Future of the European Polity', in *God and the EU: Faith in the European Project*, edited by Gary Wilton and Jonathan Chaplin (London: Bloomsbury, 2016), pp. 109–28.

Padget, Alan G., 'Practical Objectivity', in *Blackwell Companion to Science and Christianity* (Oxford: Wiley-Blackwell, 2012), pp. 93–102.

Papageorgiou, Konstantinos A., 'Kant, ein Rechtsmoralist? Ein Blick auf seine angewandte Ethik', in *Rechtssystem Und Praktische Vernunft / Legal System and Practical Reason: Verhandlungen des 15. Weltkongresses für Rechts- und Sozialphilosophie*, edited by Ralf Dreier (Stuttgart: Franz Steiner Verlag, 1993).

Paul Ramsey 100th Birthday Celebration, Millsaps College, 2 December 2013, available at https://www.youtube.com/watch?v=XdH1AAmWQps (accessed 13 July 2018).

'Paul Elie, Jean Bethke Elshtain, and Robin Lovin: Moral Man and Immoral Society: Rediscovering Reinhold Niebuhr', *On Being with Krista Tippett*, https://onbeing.org/programs/paul-elie-jean-bethke-elshtain-and-robin-lovin-moral-man-and-immoral-society-rediscovering-reinhold-niebuhr/ (accessed 2 July 2019).

Perloff, Marjorie, '"To Become a Different Person"': Wittgenstein, Christianity, and the Modernist Ethos', in *Wittgenstein and Modernism*, edited by Michael LeMahieu and Karen Zumhagen-Yekplé (Chicago, IL: University of Chicago Press, 2017), pp. 41–56.

Perreau-Saussine, Emile, 'Heaven as a Political Theme in Augustine's City of God', in *Paradise in Antiquity: Jewish and Christian Views*, edited by Markus Bockmuehl and Guy G. Stroumsa (Leiden: Cambridge University Press, 2009), pp. 179–91.

Perry, John, *The Pretenses of Loyalty: Locke, Liberal Theory, and American Political Theology* (Oxford: Oxford University Press, 2011).

Popper, Karl, 'Three Worlds', Tanner Lecture on Human Values (1978), http://tannerlectures.utah.edu/_documents/a-to-z/p/popper80.pdf (accessed 2 July 2019).

Powers, Gerard F., 'From an Ethics of War to an Ethics of Peacebuilding', in *From Just War to Modern Peace Ethics*, edited by Justenhoven, Heinz-Gerhard and William A. Barbieri, Jr (Berlin: De Gruyter, 2012), pp. 275–312.

Quash, Ben, 'Radical Orthodoxy's Critique of Niebuhr', in *Reinhold Niebuhr and Contemporary Politics: God and Power*, edited by Richard Harries and Stephen Platten (Oxford: Oxford University Press, 2010), pp. 59–70.

Ramsey, Paul, 'The Theory of Democracy: Idealistic or Christian?', *Ethics*, 56 (1946), 251–66.

Ramsey, Paul, *Basic Christian Ethics* (London: SCM Press, 1953).

Ramsey, Paul, *Nine Modern Moralists* (New York: University Press of America, 1961).

Ramsey, Paul, *War and the Christian Conscience: How Shall Modern War Be Conducted Justly?* (Durham, NC: Duke University Press, 1961).

Ramsey, Paul, *The Just War: Force and Political Responsibility* (Lanham, MD: Rowman & Littlefield, 2002).

Ramsey, Paul, and Stanley Hauerwas, *Speak Up for Just War or Pacifism: A Critique of the United Methodist Bishops' Pastoral Letter "In Defense of Creation"* (University Park, PA: Pennsylvania State University Press, 1988).

Rawls, John, *Justice as Fairness. A Restatement*, edited by Erin Kelly (Cambridge, MA: Harvard University Press, 2001).

Raz, Joseph, *The Morality of Freedom* (Oxford: Clarendon Press, 1986).

Reader, Soran. 'Cosmopolitan Pacifism', *Journal of Global Ethics*, 3 (2007), 87–103.

Reed, Esther D., *The Ethics of Human Rights. Contested Doctrinal and Moral Issues* (Waco, TX: Baylor University Press, 2007).

Reed, Esther D., 'In Defence of the Laws of War', *Studies in Christian Ethics*, 28.3 (2015), 298–304. https://doi.org/10.1177/0953946814565314.

Reed, Esther D., 'Book Reviews: Kenneth R. Himes, OFM, Drones and the Ethics of Targeted Killing'. *Studies in Christian Ethics*, 31.3 (2018), 336–9.

Rengger, Nicholas, 'Just a War against Terror? Jean Bethke Elshtain's Burden and American Power', *International Affairs*, 80 (2004), 107–16.

Rengger, Nicholas, 'Jean Bethke Elshtain (1941—2013), in *Just War Thinkers: From Cicero to the 21st Century*, edited by Daniel R. Brunstetter and Cian O'Driscoll (London: Routledge, 2017), pp. 216–26.

Reuter, Hans-Richard, 'Ethik und Politik der Versöhnung. Prinzipielles zu einem aktuellen Thema', in *Politik der Versöhnung*, edited by Gerhard Beestermöller and Hans-Richard Reuter (Stuttgart: Kohlhammer, 2002), pp. 15–36.

Rist, John M., *Augustine: Ancient Thought Baptized* (Cambridge: Cambridge University Press, 1996).

Rist, Jonathan, 'Judgment, Reaction and the Common Good', *Political Theology*, 9 (2008), 363–72.

Robertson, Jon M., *Christ as Mediator: A Study of the Theologies of Eusebius of Caesarea, Marcellus of Ancrya, and Athanasius of Alexandria* (Oxford: Oxford University Press, 2007).

Röcker, Fritz W., *Belial und Katechon: Eine Untersuchung zu 2Thess 2,1-12 und 1Thess 4,13-5,11* (Tübingen: Mohr Siebeck, 2009).

Rodin, David, *War and Self-Defense* (Oxford: Oxford University Press, 2004).

Rodin, David, 'The Moral Inequality of Soldiers: Why Jus in Bello Asymmetry Is Half Right,' in *Just and Unjust Warriors*, edited by David Rodin and Henry Shue (Oxford: Oxford University Press, 2008), pp. 44-68.

Rodin, David, 'Torture, Rights, and Values: Why the Prohibition of Torture Is Absolute.' Inaugural Lecture of the Carnegie-Uehiro Fellowship, 2008, http://www.youtube.com/watch?v=3ijki1J19eo&feature=relmfu (accessed 25 June 2010).

Rodin, David, 'How We Can Effectively Reduce or Even Eliminate Armed Conflict,' Royal Society Showcase 2010, http://www.youtube.com/watch?v=tdOtR54dn5c (accessed 26 November 2012).

Rodin, David, 'Should We Be Free to Criticize Serving Soldiers?', BBC Magazine, 14 January 2010, http://news.bbc.co.uk/1/hi/magazine/8457885.stm (accessed 24 October 2012).

Rodin, David, 'The Myth of National Self-Defense', in *The Morality of Defensive War*, edited by Cécile Fabre and Seth Lazar (Oxford: Oxford University Press, 2014), pp. 69-89.

Rodin, David, 'Personenrechte und die Kriegsrechtsbestimmungen', in *Den Gegner schützen?: Zu einer aktuellen Kontroverse in der Ethik des bewaffneten Konflikts*, edited by Bernhard Koch (Baden-Baden: Nomos; Münstern: Aschendorff, 2014), pp. 165-94.

Rodin, David, 'The War Trap: Dilemmas of *jus terminatio*', *Ethics*, 125 (April 2015), 674-95.

Rosebury, Brian, 'Private Revenge and Its Relation to Punishment', *Utilitas*, 21 (2009), 1-21.

Roterberg, Sönke, *Hegels Begriffslogik und die Embryologie* (Würzburg: Königshausen & Neumann, 2015).

Russell, Frederick H., *The Just War in the Middle Ages* (Cambridge: Cambridge University Press, 1975).

Ryan, Cheney, 'Moral Equality, Victimhood, and the Sovereignty Symmetry Problem', in *Just and Unjust Warriors: The Moral and Legal Status of Soldiers*, edited by David Rodin and Henry Shue (Oxford: Oxford University Press, 2008), pp. 131-52.

Safferling, Christoph Johannes Maria, *Vorsatz und Schuld: Subjektive Täterelemente im deutschen und englischen Strafrecht* (Tübingen: Mohr-Siebeck: 2008).

Schilbrack, Kevin, 'Review: Just War on Terror. By Jean Bethke Elshtain,' *Journal of the American Academy of Religion*, 74 (2006), 539-43.

Schmitt, Carl, *Gesetz und Urteil: Eine Untersuchung zum Problem der Rechtspraxis* (Berlin: Duncker und Humblot, 1912).

Schmitt, Carl, *Politische Theologie: Vier Kapitel zur Lehre von der Souveränität*, 2nd ed. (Munich: Duncker und Humblot, 1934).

Schmitt, Carl, 'Die vollendete Reformation: Bemerkungen und Hinweise zu neuen Leviathan-Interpretationen', *Der Staat*, 4 (1965), 51-69.

Schmitt, Carl, *Politische Theologie II* (Berlin: Duncker und Humblot, 1984).

Schmitt, Carl, *Die Diktatur* (Berlin: Duncker und Humblot, 1994).

Schmitt, Carl, *The Nomos of the Earth*, translated by Gary L. Ulmen (New York: Telos Press, 2003).

Schmitt, Michael N., 'Wound, Capture, or Kill: A Reply to Ryan Goodman's "The Power to Kill or Capture Enemy Combatants"', *European Journal of International Law*, 24.3 (2013), 855-61.

Schwab, Dieter, 'Der Staat im Naturrecht der Scholastik', in *Naturrecht und Staat: Politische Funktionen des europäischen Naturrechts*, edited by Diethelm Klippel (Munich: Oldenbourg, 2006), pp. 1–18.

Schweiker, William, 'Freedom and Authority', *Scottish Journal of Theology*, 54 (2001), 110–26.

Schwöbel, Christoph, *Gott in Beziehung* (Tübingen: Mohr Siebeck, 2002).

Seglow, Jonathan, 'Associative Duties and Global Justice', *Journal of Moral Philosophy*, 7 (2010), 54–73.

Shanks, Andrew, *A Neo-Hegelian Theology: The God of Greatest Hospitality* (London: Routledge, 2016)

Shanks, Andrew, *Theodicy Beyond the Death of 'God': The Persisting Problem of Evil* (London: Routledge, 2018)

Shue, Henry, 'Do We Need a Morality of War?', in *Just and Unjust Warriors: The Moral and Legal Status of Soldiers*, edited by David Rodin and Henry Shue (Oxford: Oxford University Press, 2008), pp. 87–111.

Shue, Henry, *Fighting Hurt: Rule and Exception in Torture and War* (Oxford: Oxford University Press, 2016).

Sieber-Lehmann, Claudius, *Papst und Kaiser als Zwillinge?: Ein anderer Blick auf die Universalgewalten im Investiturstreit* (Köln: Böhlau Verlag, 2015).

Simmonds, Nigel E., *Law as a Moral Idea* (Oxford: Oxford University Press, 2007).

Skinner, Quentin, *Machiavelli* (Oxford: Oxford University Press, 1981).

Skinner, Quentin, 'Hobbes and the Person of the State', Agnes Cuming Lecture, University College Dublin, 18 November 2015, https://www.youtube.com/watch?v=NKD7uYnCubg (accessed 4 December 2018).

Skinner, Quentin, *Thomas Hobbes und die Person des Staates*, translated by Christian Neumeier (Berlin: Duncker & Humblot, 2017).

Smith, David H., 'Paul Ramsey, Love and Killing', in *Love and Society: Essays in the Ethics of Paul Ramsey*, edited by James Johnson and David Smith (Missoula: Scholars Press, 1974).

Song, Robert, *Christianity and Liberal Society* (Oxford: Oxford University Press, 2006).

Sowle Cahill, Lisa, *Global Justice, Christology and Christian Ethics* (Cambridge: Cambridge University Press, 2013).

Spariosu, Mihai, *God of Many Names: Play, Poetry, and Power in Hellenic Thought from Homer to Aristotle* (Durham, NC: Duke University Press, 1991).

Steinhoff, Uwe, *Effiziente Ethik* (Paderborn: mentis Verlag, 2006).

Steinhoff, Uwe, *Kritik der kommunikativen Rationalität: Eine Darstellung und Kritik der kommunikationstheoretischen Philosophie von Jürgen Habermas und Karl-Otto* (Paderborn: Mentis, 2006).

Steinhoff, Uwe, 'Why There Is No Barbarization but a Lot of Barbarity in Warfare', in *Warrior's Dishonour: Barbarity, Morality and Torture in Modern Warfare*, edited by George Kassimeris (Aldershot: Ashgate, 2006), pp. 101–11.

Steinhoff, Uwe, 'Yet Another Revised DDE? A Note on David K. Chan's DDED', *Ethical Theory and Moral Practice*, 9 (2006), 231–6.

Steinhoff, Uwe, *The Philosophy of Jürgen Habermas – A Critical Introduction* (Oxford: Oxford University Press, 2009).

Steinhoff, Uwe, 'What Is War – And Can a Lone Individual Wage One?', *International Journal of Applied Philosophy*, 23 (2009), 133–50.

Steinhoff, Uwe, 'Ethics and Mercenaries', in *New Wars and New Soldiers: Military Ethics in the Contemporary World*, edited by Jessica Wolfendale and Paolo G. Tripodi (Farnham: Ashgate, 2011), pp. 137–51.

Steinhoff, Uwe, 'Rights, Liability, and the Moral Equality of Combatants', unpublished manuscript, 2011.

Steinhoff, Uwe, *Zur Ethik des Krieges und des Terrorismus* (Stuttgart: Kohlhammer, 2011).

Steinhoff, Uwe, 'Legalizing Defensive Torture', *Public Affairs Quarterly*, 26 (2012), 19–32.

Steinhoff, Uwe, 'Review: Cécile Fabre, Cosmopolitan War, Oxford University Press, 2012', *Notre Dame Philosophical Reviews*, 30 March 2013, https://ndpr.nd.edu/news/cosmopolitan-war/ (accessed 7 December 2018).

Steinhoff, Uwe, 'Rodin on Self-Defense and the 'Myth' of National Self-Defense: A Refutation', *Philosophia*, 41 (2013), 1017–36.

Steinhoff, Uwe, 'Is There a Duty to Militarily Intervene to Stop a Genocide?', in *Military Interventions: Considerations from Philosophy and Political Science*, edited by Christian Neuhäuser and Christoph Schuck (Baden-Baden, Germany: Nomos, 2017), pp. 59–80.

Stevenson Jr., William R., *Christian Love and Just War: Moral Paradox and Political Life in St. Augustine and His Modern Interpreters* (Macon, GA: Mercer University Press, 1987).

Strenski, Ivan, *Contesting Sacrifice: Religion, Nationalism, and Social Thought in France* (Chicago, IL: University of Chicago Press, 2002).

Stümke, Volker, *Das Friedensverständnis Martin Luthers: Grundlagen und Anwendungsbereiche seiner politischen Ethik* (Stuttgart: W. Kohlhammer, 2007).

Stumpf, Christoph A., *The Grotian Theology of International Law* (Berlin: Walter de Gruyter, 2006).

Sullivan, Roger J., *Immanuel Kant's Moral Theory* (Cambridge: Cambridge University Press, 1989).

Tillich, Paul, 'History and the Kingdom of God', in *God, History, and Historians: An Anthology of Modern Christian Views of History*, edited by Carl Thomas McIntire (New York: Oxford University Press, 1977), pp. 157–75.

Tully, James, *Rethinking Human Rights and Enlightenment. A View from the Twenty-First Century*, Oxford Amnesty Lecture on 10 February 2010, http://web.uvic.ca/polisci/people/faculty/Tully/publications/Oxford%20Amnesty%20lecture.pdf (retrieved 28 August 2010).

Tuttle, Robert W., 'All You Need Is Love: Paul Ramsey's "Basic Christian Ethics" and the Dilemma of Protestant Antilegalism', *Journal of Law and Religion*, 18 (2002–3), 427–57.

Ullmann, Walter, *A Short History of the Papacy in the Middle Ages* (London: Methuen, 1972).

University of Chicago, Divinity School, Faculty staff website, http://divinity.uchicago.edu/faculty/elshtain.shtml (accessed 10 July 2012).

Vincent, R. J., 'Grotius, Human Rights, and Intervention', in *Hugo Grotius and International Relations*, edited by Hedley Bull, Benedict Kingsbury and Adam Roberts (Oxford: Clarendon Press, 1992), pp. 241–56.

Vischer, Benedict, 'Systematicity to Excess: Kant's Conception of the International Legal Order', in *System, Order, and International Law: The Early History of International Legal Thought from Machiavelli to Hegel*, edited by Stefan Kadelbach, Thomas Kleinlein and David Roth-Isigkeit (Oxford: Oxford University Press, 2017), pp. 302–28.

Voltaire (François-Marie Arouet), 'Essai sur les mœurs et l'esprit des nations', *Œuvres complètes de Voltaire*, edited by Louis Moland, vol. 12 (Paris: Garnier, 1878).

von den Steinen, Ulrich, *Unzufrieden mit dem Frieden?: Militärseelsorge und Verantwortungsethik* (Göttingen: Vandenhoeck & Ruprecht, 2006).

Wagner, Markus, 'The Battlefield from Afar: Independently Operating Weapons Systems and Their Compatibility with the Laws of Armed Conflict', ELAC/CCW Seminar Series, 15 February 2011, http://podcasts.ox.ac.uk/battlefield-afar-independently-operating-systems-and-their-compatibility-laws-armed (accessed 2 July 2019).

Waldron, Jeremy, 'Kant's Legal Positivism', *Harvard Law Review*, 109 (1996), 1535–66.

Walsh, Lynda, *Scientists as Prophets: A Rhetorical Genealogy* (New York: Oxford University Press, 2013).

Walz, Gustav Adolf, *Die Kantische Staatsphilosophie* (Berlin-Grunewald: Dr Walther Rothschild Verlag, 1928).

Walzer, Michael, *Just and Unjust Wars* (New York: Basic, 1977).

Walzer, Michael, *Arguing about War* (New Haven, CT: Yale University Press, 2006).

Walzer, Michael, 'Response to McMahan's Paper', *Philosophia*, 34 (2006), 43–5.

Wannenwetsch, Bernd, 'Luther's Moral Theology', in *Cambridge Companion to Martin Luther*, edited by Donald K. McKim (Cambridge: Cambridge University Press, 2003), pp. 120–35.

Wannenwetsch, Bernd, 'Soul Citizens: How Christians Understand Their Political Role', *Political Theology*, 9 (2008), 373–94.

Wannenwetsch, Bernd, *Political Worship* (Oxford: Oxford University Press, 2009).

Wannenwetsch, Bernd, 'Just War', in *Cambridge Dictionary of Christian Theology*, edited by Ian A. McFarland, et al. (Cambridge: Cambridge University Press, 2011), pp. 255–7.

Ward, Bruce, *Redeeming the Enlightenment: Christianity and the Liberal Virtues* (Grand Rapids, MI: William B. Eerdmans, 2010).

Ward, Graham, 'How Hegel Became a Philosopher: Logos and the Economy of Logic', *Critical Research on Religion*, 1 (2013), 270–92.

Ward, Graham, *How the Light Gets In: Ethical Life I* (Oxford: Oxford University Press, 2016).

Weber, Max, *Politik als Beruf* (München: Duncker & Humblot, 1919).

Weber, Max, *Wirtschaft und Gesellschaft* (Tübingen: J. C. B. Mohr [P. Siebeck], 1947).

Weigel, George, *Tranquillitas Ordinis: The Present Failure and Future Promise of American Catholic Thought on War and Peace* (Oxford: Oxford University Press, 1987).

Weissbach, Jürgen, *Christologie und Ethik bei Dietrich Bonhoeffer* (München: Chr. Kaiser Verlag, 1966).

Welsh, Jennifer, 'How Iraq Changed How We Think about Human Rights', 19 March 2013, https://www.opencanada.org/features/how-iraq-changed-how-we-think-about-human-rights/ (accessed 9 July 2019).

Welz, Claudia, *Love's Transcendence and the Problem of Theodicy* (Tübingen: Mohr Siebeck, 2008).

Wendte, Martin, *Gottmenschliche Einheit bei Hegel: eine logische und theologische Untersuchung* (Berlin: Walter de Gruyter, 2007).

Werpehowski, William, 'Karl Barth and Just War: A Conversation with Roman Catholicism', in *Commanding Grace: Studies in Karl Barth's Ethics*, edited by Daniel L. Migliore (Grand Rapids, MI: William B. Eerdmans, 2010), pp. 60–82.

Wessels, Ulla, *Die gute Samariterin* (Berlin: De Gruyter, 2002).

What We're Fighting For: A Letter from America, February 2002, Institute for American Values, http://www.americanvalues.org/html/wwff.html (accessed 10 July 2012).

Wight, Martin, 'Christian Pacifism', *Theology*, 33 (1936), 12–21.

Williams, Bernard, *Morality: An Introduction to Ethics* (Cambridge: Cambridge University Press, 1972).

Williams, Bernard, *Shame and Necessity* (Berkeley, CA: University of California Press, 1993).

Williams, Howard, *Kant and the End of War: A Critique of Just War Theory* (London: Palgrave Macmillan, 2012).

Williams, Huntston, *The Radical Reformation*, 3rd ed. (Kirksville, MO: Sixteenth Century Journal, 1992).

Williams, Rowan, 'Introducing the Debate: Theology and the Political', in *Theology and the Political: The New Debate*, edited by Creston Davis, John Milbank and Slavoj Žižek (Durham: Duke University Press, 2005), pp. 1–3.

Wolterstorff, Nicholas, *Justice: Rights and Wrongs* (Princeton, NJ: Princeton University Press, 2008).

Woodard, Christopher, 'War and Self-Defense' (Review), *Mind*, 114 (2005), 455–7.

Yoder, John Howard, *The Original Revolution* (Scottdale, PA: Herald Press, 1977).

Zehfuss, Maja, 'The Tragedy of Violent Justice: The Danger of Elshtain's Just War against Terror', *International Relations*, 21 (2007), 493–501.

Žižek, Slavoj, John Milbank and Creston Davis, Creston, *The Monstrosity of Christ: Paradox or Dialectic?* (Cambridge: MIT Press, 2009).

Zupan, Dan, 'A Presumption of the Moral Equality of Combatants: A Citizen-Soldier's Perspective', in *Just and Unjust Warriors*, edited by David Rodin and Henry Shue (Oxford: Oxford University Press, 2008).

Index

Lightning Source UK Ltd.
Milton Keynes UK
UKHW020936180621
385731UK00003B/72